W9-CPC-814

CONTEMPORARY COLLECTIVE BARGAINING IN SEVEN COUNTRIES

CORNELL INTERNATIONAL INDUSTRIAL AND LABOR RELATIONS REPORTS—*NO. 4*

PUBLISHED BY

The Institute of International Industrial and Labor Relations

The New York State School of Industrial and Labor Relations
A Unit of the State University of New York
at Cornell University

IN THIS SERIES

Labor Unions and National Politics in Italian Industrial Plants, by Maurice F. Neufeld. 160 pp. $2.00, paper

American Labor and the International Labor Movement, 1940 to 1953, by John P. Windmuller. 260 pp. $3.00, paper

Jobs and Workers in India, by Oscar A. Ornati. 236 pp. $3.00, paper; $4.00, cloth

Contemporary Collective Bargaining in Seven Countries, Adolf Sturmthal, Editor. 392 pp. $4.50, cloth

Contemporary Collective Bargaining in Seven Countries

ADOLF STURMTHAL

Editor

THE INSTITUTE OF INTERNATIONAL
INDUSTRIAL AND LABOR RELATIONS
CORNELL UNIVERSITY, ITHACA, NEW YORK

Library of Congress Catalog Card Number: 56-63539

PRINTED IN THE UNITED STATES OF AMERICA BY
W. F. HUMPHREY PRESS INC., GENEVA, NEW YORK

Contents

Preface

COLLECTIVE bargaining had its first systematic application in Great Britain in the early nineteenth century, although sporadic examples of such bargains, just as examples of strikes, can be found long before the last century. Gradually progressing throughout British industry, the principle of setting wage rates and determining working conditions by agreements between unions and employers spread also to other industrial countries. There, however, it received decisive impetus on the whole only after World War I. The great depression and the establishment of totalitarian régimes during the thirties reduced the field of application of collective bargaining throughout Europe, just at the time when the New Deal legislation and the progress of trade unionism in the United States caused large parts of American industry to accept collective agreements. Even in Europe the setback proved to a large extent to have been temporary; after World War II the system resumed its expansion with renewed vigor.

The Webbs have shown in their *History of Trade Unionism* how mediaeval protection gradually broke down in the course of the eighteenth century in England. "The struggle over (the) Woolen Cloth Weavers' Act of 1756 marks the passage from the old ideas to the new," the Webbs report.[1] The victory of laissez-

[1]Sidney and Beatrice Webb, *The History of Trade Unionism,* edition of 1920 (London: Longmans, Green, 1950), p. 51. See also the interesting "Notes on the Begin-

faire, however, was limited in both time and space. Collective bargaining and factory legislation, "expedients...discovered in the nineteenth century," were introduced after a painful interval and in the twentieth century minimum wage laws marked a further departure from laissez-faire. Outside of England, on the Continent, many of the protective devices of earlier periods survived and collective bargaining when it was introduced was fitted into the existing framework rather than established in the void left by the disappearance of earlier arrangements. Not only that: being added to and integrated with elements of a different nature, collective bargaining on the Continent took on some of the characteristics of the institutions with which it was now to join in regulating wages and working conditions. Many examples of this kind of mixture will be found in the pages that follow. An expression in a recent source of this alliance between what were elsewhere regarded as disparate elements is a statement to the effect that in Sweden "it is not uncommon for legislation to be based word for word on labor-management agreements."[2] In England and the United States, on the other hand, the progress of labor legislation and of administrative decisions in the field of industrial relations considerably modified the free contract nature of labor-management agreements.

This evolution leading to different mixtures of contract, law, and elements combining some features of both law and contract makes international comparative studies of collective bargaining particularly interesting and fruitful. This applies even more to the most recent phases of the development, namely, the reconstitution of collective bargaining after World War II.

This book provides information on the development of collective bargaining after World War II in a number of Western countries. Such a presentation, I believe, serves several purposes. It combines in a convenient form information which otherwise exists only in dispersed fashion and in sources not always and every-

---

nings of Collective Bargaining" by Vernon H. Jensen, *Industrial and Labor Relations Review*, Vol. 9, No. 2, January 1956.

[2]Oliver A. Peterson, "Industrial Conflict—Sweden," in Arthur Kornhauser, *et al.*, eds., *Industrial Conflict*, (New York: McGraw-Hill, 1954), p. 488.

where readily available. To the student of collective bargaining this volume may, therefore, be of some technical assistance. In the second place, this collection may draw the reader's attention to similarities and differences between collective bargaining in the United States and in a number of other countries sufficiently foreign to offer contrasts, but still within the range of what is commonly called Western civilization so as to make comparison meaningful. Comparison, it is said, when used intelligently opens insights into one's own institutions and their functioning that are not easily obtained in any other way.

There is, thirdly, a growing interest in labor movements and labor relations abroad. Partly this results from the involvement of the United States in foreign economies by investments, trade, and other connections. Finally, this growing interest corresponds to a realization of the vital significance of organized labor in the great struggles of our time.

For these and other reasons this volume will, I hope, meet a real need, not only in college instruction, but also in management, union, and government offices concerned with labor abroad.

The choice of the countries studied was determined either by their intrinsic significance or by some interesting aspects which their collective bargaining system presented. Some of the articles contained in this volume are revised and up-to-date versions of essays previously published. This is true for the reports on France, Germany, Holland, Norway, and Professor Vannutelli's article on the Italian wage structure. The remaining essays—those dealing with the United States, England, and Professor Sanseverino's report on collective bargaining in Italy—were added because it was felt that in this way a fairly well-rounded picture of contemporary collective bargaining in the Western world could be obtained. Professor Chamberlain's essay is slightly different in content from the others. Since he deals with the United States in a volume addressed to American readers, he combined his presentation of the facts with a survey and analysis of some of the main issues of collective bargaining dealt with in the recent literature. This, I trust, will give the volume particular interest for American readers without detracting in the slightest from its value as a source of information on American collective bargaining.

The last chapter represents an attempt to examine a few problems of collective bargaining in the light of international experience. The selection of these topics was partly determined by the available material and—within the limits set by the material—by the editor's judgment of relevance and interest. Other editors, with equal justification, would perhaps have made a different selection. Whatever the shortcomings of this particular essay, I hope that this study will encourage others to continue work in this field, using the methods of comparative research.

Earlier versions of the essay were read by Professors Neil Chamberlain of Columbia University and Al Rees of the University of Chicago. I have greatly profited from their criticism and suggestions. My special thanks go to the New York State School of Industrial and Labor Relations at Cornell University. The plan for this volume was drawn up when I was serving as Visiting Professor at the School. I have benefited from the advice and assistance of the School, of Dean M. P. Catherwood, and Professor Leonard P. Adams in carrying out the plan. The School has furthermore shouldered the financial burdens involved in preparing and publishing this volume and provided excellent editorial assistance through Miss Frances Eagan. For permission to use in modified form material previously published as stated above, the editor expresses his thanks to the *Bulletin of the Oxford University Institute of Statistics*, the *Industrial and Labor Relations Review*, and the *Review of Economic Conditions in Italy*.

ADOLF STURMTHAL

Roosevelt University
Chicago, Illinois
September 1956

I

Great Britain

ALLAN FLANDERS

GREAT BRITAIN is said to be the "home of collective bargaining," but the metaphor is not entirely apt. For a long time this child of industrialism remained unwanted and unloved. Many attempts were made to smother it before it gained sufficient acclaim to be encouraged. Thus it grew up haphazardly, in rebellion against the parental authority of the state until the mellowing influence of experience brought about a reconciliation. The consequences can still be seen today. Institutions, like individuals, are the product of their history. Some of the most characteristic features of the institution of collective bargaining in Great Britain—the great diversity of organization and practice, or the relative absence of legal regulation—are obviously a heritage from the past. If we wish, then, to understand recent developments and the problems arising out of full employment, or nationalization, or the struggle for national solvency, we cannot examine them only against the contemporary background. The prevailing patterns of organization and the traditional attitudes of the bargaining partners must be explained by reference to the influence of history.

The Influence of History

Generally it can be said of Great Britain, as of most other industrial countries, that trade union organization and industrial conflict brought collective bargaining into being. The growth of trade unions led to counter organization among employers—at first to resist what they regarded as external interference in the conduct of their businesses. Later, usually in times of good trade, the employers found it convenient to come to terms with the unions and regulate wages by joint agreement. Yet, if this is taken to be the general theme, it had many important variations.

By the end of the nineteenth century the practice had been established mainly among two substantial groups of manual workers: the skilled craftsmen, employed largely but not wholly in the engineering, shipbuilding, building, woodworking, and printing industries; and the less-skilled and predominantly piecework workers in coal mining, iron and steel production, cotton textiles, boot and shoe manufacture, together with a few smaller industries. This division is significant when we look at the origins of collective bargaining.

In the skilled trades collective bargaining grew out of the enforcement of trade union "working rules." Before employers were prepared to negotiate with them the craft unions stipulated the conditions to be observed by their members before accepting employment. This they were able to do with some success for two reasons: through apprenticeship they could exercise some control over entry into their trades; and the provision of various trade and friendly benefits provided them with the sanctions to uphold their internal discipline. The latter was undoubtedly the more important factor; the observation of union rules was secured both by the imposition of penalties on transgressors and by the support of members during hard times. As the Webbs remarked in *Industrial Democracy,* "the application of mutual insurance may be made the method of enforcing any Common Rule whatsoever; and a very effective instrument it is."[1]

Where employers had come tacitly to accept union "working rules" their embodiment in the terms of a written collective agreement was an obvious next step bringing advantages to both sides. Not that the transition was always smooth or complete. For reasons

[1]Sidney and Beatrice Webb, *Industrial Democracy* (London and New York: Longmans, Green & Co., 1920), p. 171.

which cannot here be analyzed, the building and engineering industries provided the greatest contrast in this respect. In the former, by the end of the century, an elaborate code of mutually agreed "working rules," covering all the more important terms and conditions of employment, was arranged at local conferences between master builders and union officials throughout the country. In the latter, the men were twice defeated after lockouts (in 1852 and 1897) and the employers upheld their "prerogatives" in such matters as the numbers of apprentices, the manning of machines, the working of overtime and piecework; only on wages and hours did collective bargaining develop on a district basis.

The need to regulate piecework prices on the basis of mutual agreement appears to have been the other important origin of collective bargaining practice. This can be seen in some of the skilled trades, notably in shipbuilding and printing, where payment by results was traditional and accepted by the unions. The "London Scale of Prices for Compositors' Work" has probably to be regarded as the first collective agreement; it is known to have been in operation as far back as 1785 and was altered by mutual consent of employers and workmen nine times between then and the end of the nineteenth century. Among the factory and extractive industries, however, collective bargaining had its genesis solely in the regulation of piecework prices. Employers and workers had a common interest in bringing this most acute form of wage competition under control.

The principles and methods adopted to regulate piecework prices varied from industry to industry. In cotton textiles collective agreements in the form of standard price lists, covering all the firms in a particular district, made an early appearance. The Bolton spinners and the Blackburn weavers negotiated such agreements with their employers in 1853. For weaving a "Uniform List" for the whole of North and North-East Lancashire was adopted in 1892, while spinning retained two major lists, the Bolton and Oldham lists, and a number of minor ones. Collectively agreed district price lists were accepted in several other industries: tailoring (Scotland) in 1867; boot and shoemaking and coopering in 1872; tinplate making in 1874; carpet weaving in 1882; shipbuilding (Tyne and Wear) in 1884; hosiery making in 1886; and lace making (Nottingham) in 1889.[2]

The employers took the initiative in some industries in introducing local boards of conciliation and arbitration to minimize friction over wage fixing, without, at first, recognizing the trade unions as their bargaining partner. Mr. A. J. Mundella pioneered such an experiment for the hosiery trade of Nottingham in the 'sixties. As the operatives chose their union leaders to represent them, he "saw the wisdom of making trade unions an active partner in the machinery" and of abandoning his role as an arbitrator in favor of mutually agreed decisions.[3] The North of England iron trade also set up a Board of Conciliation and Arbitration in 1869, but three years later the permanent arbitrator was dropped. Instead, his proposal was accepted for regulating wages by a selling price sliding scale—an arrangement which subsequently became the most characteristic feature of collective bargaining in the greater part of iron and steel production.[4] Collective bargaining in coal mining was first established in the 'seventies mainly on the basis of agreed selling price sliding scales, but the agitation for a minimum wage and for an eight-hour day enforced by law—the two issues responsible for the creation of the Miners' Federation of Great Britain—led to the termination of these agreements by the men in one county after another; the sliding scale had its longest run in South Wales where it disappeared in 1902.

These few references to the origins of collective bargaining in the piecework industries may at least serve to illustrate the variety of the devices employed to bring piecework prices under control: uniform lists, selling price sliding scales, minimum time rates of wages, and the use of arbitration. But, whatever the device, an impulse was given to the growth of organization on both sides and to the acceptance of defined procedures for settling their differences. For a time collective bargaining in most of these industries was concerned with little more than wages. In contrast to the

[2]Ministry of Labour, *Report on Collective Agreements between Employers and Workpeople,* Vol. 1, 1934, p. ii.

[3]I. G. Sharp, *Industrial Conciliation and Arbitration in Great Britain* (London: Allen and Unwin, 1950), p. 3.

[4]Until 1940, when it was stabilized at a stated percentage and replaced by a cost-of-living sliding scale.

skilled craftsmen, the workers here had to turn to the method of legal enactment for protection in regard to their working hours and other conditions of employment. The cotton operatives and coal miners, for example, were in the forefront of a political agitation aimed at supplementing their bargaining activities by legal regulation.

The more collective bargaining became an accepted practice, however, the less important became the original contrast between its origins in the skilled trades and the piecework industries. Among the former, mutual insurance lost its early significance as an aid to the enforcement of trade union regulations when these were replaced by collective agreements. Among the latter, legal enactment became increasingly subservient to negotiations with employers as the subject matter of their agreements was extended. Contrary to the Webbs' prediction,[5] as the trade unions became strong enough to regulate wages and working conditions by direct negotiation they preferred to dispense with government assistance. Collective bargaining became not one among their several activities but the foundation of them all.

The Trade Union Act of 1871 (amended in 1876) and the Conspiracy and Protection of Property Act of 1875 were intended to establish the legality of collective bargaining, but it was only after the passing of the Trade Disputes Act of 1906 that all legal obstacles hampering the industrial activities of trade unions were swept away. And it was not until 1910 that the "New Unionism," heralded by the successful strikes of the match girls in 1888 and the dockers in 1889, came fully into its stride. This can be seen in the figures for total trade union membership, which stood at roughly two million in 1900, two and one-half millions in 1910, and over four millions in 1913; the Transport and General Labor groups of unions increased their membership from 338,000 in 1910 to 1,052,000 in 1913.

The part played by legislation and government action in bringing about the extension of trade unionism and collective bargaining to those workers who were unable to establish permanent

[5] "The Trade Unionists, having obtained the vote, now wish to make use of it to enforce, by Legal Enactment, such of their Common Rules as they see a chance of getting public opinion to support." *Industrial Democracy,* 1920 ed., p. 538.

organizations on their own account throughout the nineteenth century is not always appreciated. The passing of the Conciliation Act in 1896 was an unambiguous sign of approval of the practice of collective bargaining. Repealing earlier measures, which had attempted to prevent industrial conflict by compulsory arbitration, it assigned to the Government only the role of a conciliator, helping employers and trade unions to reach agreement with a minimum of friction. The formation of conciliation boards and the voluntary use of arbitration were now energetically encouraged. Direct government intervention led to the establishment of conciliation schemes on the railways, through which the unions were able to bargain collectively although they were not fully recognized by the companies until 1919. The Trade Boards Act of 1909 and the reformulation of the "Fair Wages Clause" in government contracts in the same year were designed to strengthen the voluntary system as well as to raise the wages of the lower-paid workers. New protective labor legislation, such as the Coal Mines Eight Hours Act, 1908, and the Coal Mines (Minimum Wage) Act, 1912, added political gains to the industrial achievements of the trade unions. It is true, of course, that governments were spurred to action by public agitation (the activities of the Anti-Sweating League which preceded the Trade Boards Act), by political competition (the rise of the new Labour party), and by industrial conflict (the 1912 Act was introduced to settle a costly national stoppage in the mining industry). The fact remains that state power was used for the first time during this period both to promote the growth of collective bargaining and to make good some of its inadequacies.

The *Report on Collective Agreements between Employers and Workpeople in the United Kingdom,* 1910 (Cmd. 5366) showed that there were in all some 1,696 trade or district agreements, which were estimated to cover directly 2.4 million workpeople, or less than a quarter of the total number of "industrial workers."[6] Of these agreements, 30 were sliding scales (nearly all in iron and steel manufacture), 563 were piecework price lists[7] (mainly in ship-

[6]Most agreements embodying terms agreed upon by a single firm and its employees were not included.

[7]They usually included provisions relating to working conditions as well as wages.

building, minor metal trades, textiles, boot and shoe, tailoring, printing, dock and waterside labor), and 1,103 were working agreements of various kinds (of which 801 were in the building trades). The greater part of collective bargaining still took place locally on a district or, in some trades, on a single establishment basis. For the settlement of disputes, however, provision had been made by agreement in a number of industries for ultimate reference to national bodies or national conferences. This was the case in building, engineering, shipbuilding, and in cotton textiles.

If the view is accepted that, as regards collective bargaining, the 1914–1918 war "warped the normal evolutionary process to a surprisingly small extent; what it did was to quicken it,"[8] then it must be recognized that the speed of change was greatly accelerated. The most important permanent results were a further enlargement of the area of collective bargaining and a shift of emphasis from local to national agreements. Military and industrial mobilization led inevitably to a greater degree of government intervention, including the use of compulsory arbitration to prevent stoppages of work. These conditions, together with the labor shortage and the unprecedented rise in the cost of living, forced the growth of trade unions and employers' associations, of joint national bodies for industry-wide negotiations or, alternatively, of national agreements for the periodic revision of wages by flat rate increases. Shipping was a sector of employment in which collective bargaining was first established during the war. The National Maritime Board was set up in 1917, with the Government providing the chairman and secretary, and with its decisions binding upon all shipowners since the whole of the mercantile marine was under state control. In 1919, although retaining its original name, it became a voluntary negotiating body. Engineering may be taken as an illustration of the shift to national bargaining. In 1917 a national wage agreement was negotiated for this industry by the chairman of the Committee on Production—the leading arbitration tribunal—which authorized that body to determine general wage changes at its four-monthly regular hearings. After the war the practice was continued of changing the wage rates of all male manual workers in the indus-

[8]J. W. Rowe, *Wages in Practice and Theory* (London: Routledge, 1928), p. 144.

try by altering the amount of "war bonus" (later called "national bonus") to be added to various district rates.

Out of the war there came, too, the five reports of the government-appointed Whitley Committee on Relations between Employers and Employees.[9] The principles underlying the main proposals of the Committee had already been accepted in practice, but they were made explicit by it, and subsequently became the norms of government policy regardless of its political complexion. It was recognized that "an essential condition of securing a permanent improvement in the relations between employers and employed is that there should be adequate organization on the part of both"; and "a continuance, as far as possible, of the present system whereby industries make their own agreements and settle their differences themselves" was accepted as advisable. To the economic sanctions of mutual insurance and strike action, on which the trade unions largely depended to uphold their bargaining rights during the nineteenth century, had been added a powerful social sanction—the force of public opinion.

Some of the Whitley proposals passed into new legislation: the Trade Boards Act, 1918, and the Industrial Courts Act, 1919. The first of these measures served to enlarge the scope of statutory wage regulation. Under it the Minister of Labour could make an order to set up a Trade Board if he was "of the opinion that no adequate machinery exists for the effective regulation of wages throughout the trade." The emphasis was shifted from unduly low wages—the criterion of the 1909 Act—to the absence of voluntary organization; and thirty-seven new Trade Boards were formed in the years 1919 to 1921 in addition to the eight already existing in Great Britain. All of these Boards continued to function during the inter-war years. They withstood the challenge which came first from the employers in 1920, leading to the Cave Committee's Report in 1922, and later from within the trade union movement in 1931, leading to an inquiry by the TUC's Trade Boards Advisory Council. But very few new Trade Boards were established and these mainly after 1937. In other industries, however, statutory wage regulation gained ground under separate legislation. In agriculture

[9]Cmd. 8606, 9001–2, 9099, 9153.

a legal minimum wage had been introduced during World War I and, after having been allowed to lapse, was reintroduced on a county basis for England and Wales in 1924 and for Scotland in 1937. In 1938 the Road Haulage Wages Act substituted statutory regulation of wages by joint boards for a voluntary system which had broken down owing to lack of organization on both sides, and the Holidays with Pay Act empowered Trade Boards (and other statutory wage boards) to give directions providing for holidays with pay up to one week in the year.

The emergence of a separate Ministry of Labour, with a staff of conciliation officers, together with the provisions of the Industrial Courts Act, 1919, helped to extend the facilities for public intervention to promote industrial peace by voluntary methods. The Act established the Industrial Court as a permanent institution for voluntary arbitration and also permitted the Minister of Labour to appoint single arbitrators or special ad hoc Boards of Arbitration if this course was more acceptable to the disputing parties. Despite its name the Industrial Court is no part of our judicial system and its awards are not legally binding. But since a dispute can only be submitted to it for an award with the consent of both parties, only on rare occasions have its findings not been accepted. The Industrial Courts Act further provided for the appointment of special Courts of Inquiry to investigate and report on the facts and underlying causes of serious disputes not likely to be settled in other ways. This device was added to the less formal Committee of Investigation permitted under the Conciliation Act, 1896. The recommendations of a Court of Inquiry cannot be enforced but they usually provide a basis for further negotiations and a settlement. In practice the Ministry of Labour observes a clear order of priority in the use of these various methods of public intervention, an order which follows from the preference for voluntary agreements. It does not intervene at all as long as there is a likelihood of the parties settling their differences for themselves and until their own voluntarily agreed procedure has been exhausted. The next step is mediation, then arbitration, and in the last resort, public inquiry.

The other main recommendation of the Whitley Committee

was that in all reasonably well-organized industries Joint Industrial Councils should be formed. The conception was essentially a theoretical one. On paper it seemed obvious enough that a standard type of joint organization, with a written constitution and defined functions, with a network of national, district, and works councils, and with consultative as well as bargaining activities, was the logical and desirable outcome of the existing trends. But employers and trade unions made of this proposal, which was no more than a suggestion to them, what they severally preferred and jointly could agree upon. In most of the industries which had already developed their own firm arrangements for collective bargaining, they disregarded it. Two exceptions were boot and shoe manufacture and printing, but the JIC's formed for these industries did not fix rates of wages, although the one in printing adopted a conciliation procedure. Altogether 73 JIC's and 33 Interim Industrial Reconstruction Committees (a less formal type of organization which it was hoped would pave the way for the setting up of a JIC) were formed in the years 1918 to 1921. Many of these bodies failed to withstand the effects of the postwar slump, and the majority of those which survived became little more than national negotiating bodies. In the early 'thirties some fifty of them remained in existence, and only twenty of these had district or local joint bodies associated with the national council. Practically all the works committees set up in the first flush of postwar enthusiasm were, by then, defunct.

What happened to the arrangements for collective bargaining during the interwar years, either in the industries with their own separate and distinct procedures or in those which had accepted Joint Industrial Councils, seems to have depended more than anything else upon whether they were relatively sheltered or exposed to foreign competition. Certainly in the export industries, which had flourished when Britain was *the* "workshop of the world," in coal mining and cotton and wool textiles for example, there were severe setbacks. The miners were compelled to return to district negotiations after their defeat in 1926. The cotton weavers only saved their long-standing agreements from disintegration with the Cotton Manufacturing Industry (Temporary Provisions) Act,

1934, which provided for their legal enforcement. The Joint Industrial Council for Wool and Allied Textile Industry, formed in 1919, collapsed in 1927 and for a decade no contact was established between the two sides.

On the other hand, the trend toward a highly centralized and complete system of national joint regulation of wages and working conditions continued unbroken in such employments as building and railways. The National Joint Council for the Building Industry graded towns and districts to facilitate national regulation and established uniform rates for all craftsmen in each grade, with the laborers' rate settled as a fixed proportion of that of the craftsmen. In 1924 and again in 1930 the trade unions, dissatisfied with the wage position and the slowness of the constitutional procedure, gave notice to secede from the Council, but each time—although in 1924 only after a national stoppage and the appointment of a Court of Inquiry—agreement was eventually reached and the powers of the Council were extended.

The range of employments in which collective bargaining was successfully developed during the interwar years through the agency of Joint Industrial Councils was equally significant. They included, in the first place, public administration, the public utilities, and transport (apart from road haulage). In all these consumer services, public influence was strong and selling competition was largely, if not entirely, absent. In addition, the industries where JIC's flourished were those, like flour milling, bricks, cement, and chemicals, where the main employers were a few, prosperous combines, susceptible to public opinion and with sufficient price control and expanding markets to make it relatively easy and advantageous for them to come to terms with the unions. "Whitleyism" had its greatest success in the Civil Service. Here it not only introduced—one might almost say overnight—a complete system of collective bargaining, but eventually led to cooperation between the official and staff sides to improve the efficiency of the public administration.

Home conditions during World War II gave the same impetus to extend the area of collective bargaining and to promote the national regulation of wages and working conditions as they did during World War I. Only this time the change took place principally through an increase in the number of Joint Industrial Councils. Altogether, fifty-six JIC's or similar bodies were revived or newly established in the years 1939 to 1946.[10] One field of employment which they entered for the first time was retail distribution. Coal mining can be taken as an example of the further shift to national bargaining facilitated by wartime government intervention. When the newly created Ministry of Fuel and Power took over operation control of mines in 1942, it was recognized in a White Paper "that a system should be developed by which wages and conditions in the mining industry would be dealt with on a national basis and by a properly constituted national body."[11] The scheme prepared by a government-appointed Board of Investigation provided for the setting up of a National Negotiating Committee, representative of both sides of industry, and a National Reference Tribunal, composed of three members not engaged in the industry, empowered to make a binding arbitration award on any question referred to it by the Committee. It left district questions to be dealt with as before by the existing district conciliation arrangements.

The wartime expedient which left the greatest imprint on our voluntary system was the Conditions of Employment and National Arbitration Order, 1940, familiarly known as Order 1305. To meet the wartime need "of preventing work being interrupted by trade disputes," Order 1305 superimposed a general system of compulsory arbitration on the various voluntary provisions for the settlement of disputes. Strikes and lockouts in connection with trade disputes were prohibited with the one proviso that they were legal if the Minister of Labour, having had the dispute reported to him, failed to take action to secure a settlement within three weeks. The Order also established, as a final authority for the settlement of disputes, a National Arbitration Tribunal, normally consisting for the purposes of a particular case, of three appointed members (including the chairman) and two representative members, one each from the trade unions' and employers' panels. The

[10]Ministry of Labour and National Service, *Report for the Years 1939–1946* (Cmd. 7225), 1947, p. 276.

[11]Cmd. 6364.

Tribunal was not intended to displace or weaken the accepted practices of collective bargaining or voluntary arbitration. Under the Order the Minister was obliged to see that any existing joint machinery suitable for settling the dispute was used before a case was referred to the Tribunal. Any awards or agreements made as a result of a reference by the Minister of Labour under the Order became legally binding as an implied term in the individual contract of employment of the employees to whom the awards or agreements applied.

Order 1305 also helped to enlarge the application of already existing collective agreements, and, in doing so, to strengthen employer and union organization. The question whether representative collective agreements should be legally enforced had been debated for thirty years without practical result.[12] Part III of this Order made it obligatory for all employers to observe terms and conditions of employment not less favorable than those which had been settled by agreements made "between organizations of employers and trade unions. . .representative respectively of substantial proportions of the employers and workers in the trade in the district in which the employer is engaged," or by the decisions of Joint Industrial Councils and similar bodies, or by arbitration awards. This meant that nonfederated, as well as federated employers, were compelled to comply with the terms of collective agreements. If they failed to do so, they could be reported by a trade union or employers' association operating in the industry to the Minister of Labour, who must then refer the case to the National Arbitration Tribunal for an award, which was enforceable in a court of law by each worker and against each employer to whom it applied. This arrangement proved of great value to the trade unions in forcing those employers to bargain who had previously refused to do so; and since the initiative for enforcement lay in practice with the trade unions, it helped them in their organizing activities.

In sharp contrast to the experiment with compulsory arbitration

[12]The short-lived Industrial Council created in 1911 recommended in its 1913 Report (Cmd. 6952) a conditional legal enforcement of agreements after inquiry. Bills were introduced into the House of Commons in 1924 and on five occasions in 1930–1935, all designed in various ways to achieve this end.

during the First World War, the general working of Order 1305 was sufficiently smooth and acceptable both to employers and trade unions for the central organizations on both sides to favor its continued operation for six years after the ending of hostilities. All the same the general prohibition of strikes and lockouts which it contained could not be indefinitely maintained when the nation was no longer at war. The issue was brought to a head by the prosecution of strikers to enforce this prohibition in 1950. This led to an overwhelming trade union demand for the repeal of Order 1305, and from August 1951 it was replaced by a new Industrial Disputes Order (No. 1376) after its terms had been agreed by the British Employers' Confederation, representatives of the nationalized industries, and the TUC General Council.

The penal prohibition of strikes and lockouts was abolished, but limited provisions for compulsory arbitration were retained. The Industrial Disputes Tribunal, which has taken the place of the National Arbitration Tribunal—though similarly constituted—considers "disputes" and "issues" referred to it by the Minister of Labour, and its awards become an implied term of contract between the employer and the workers to whom an award applies. The definition of a "dispute" given in Order 1376 is narrower than that given to a "trade dispute" in its predecessor and excludes the Tribunal from considering disputes concerned with the employment or nonemployment of any person or the obligation of a worker to belong to a trade union. The new term "issue" is used for a dispute as to whether a particular employer should observe "recognized terms and conditions of employment" in the district. Employers are no longer placed under a general and absolute obligation in this respect, as they were when Order 1305 was in operation, but since this obligation could then only be enforced by an award of the National Arbitration Tribunal, the trade unions have retained the substance of this support to their voluntary efforts.

The other provisions of Order 1376 have been designed "to strengthen the authority of existing voluntary systems of negotiations and arbitration and to uphold the sanctity of agreements and awards." Disputes can only be reported to the Minister for action by representative trade unions and employers' associations or by individual employers, and not as previously "by or on behalf of either party to the dispute." The Minister has discretion to stay arbitration proceedings or to refuse access to the Tribunal in the event of a stoppage of work or a substantial breach of a procedural agreement.

The wartime experience with arbitration encouraged an increasing acceptance of its use in the last resort under the terms of voluntary agreements. In all the nationalized industries, with the exception of the railways,[13] there is a binding commitment to this effect. Another illustration of the change in attitude is provided by the building industry. Up to 1940, if there was a disagreement on the National Joint Council, either a special joint committee could be appointed to work out a settlement, or the dispute could be referred to arbitration, but only if both sides agreed. Under the new constitution adopted in 1941 there is still the first alternative, but if it fails, as a second alternative "it shall be the duty of the Council to refer the matter to arbitration," the method to be determined in each case "by a majority of the Council present and voting."

The completion of the system of statutory wage regulation was a further achievement of the past decade. The main legislation passed to achieve this objective was: the Catering Wages Act, 1943; the Wages Council Act, 1945 (amended in some particulars in 1948); and the Agricultural Wages (Regulation) Act, 1947.[14] Today the number of workers for whom minimum national wage rates are enforced by law must be in the neighborhood of three and a half millions. Catering and retail distribution, the two large fields of employment in which wages were not previously regulated, account for some one and a half million employees. It must be realized, however, that some of these workers are also covered by collective agreements. Compared with the old Trade Boards, which

[13]Under the new agreement which came into force on July 1, 1956, any party may refer a dispute for arbitration to the Railway Staff National Tribunal, provided the opposing party is notified. Previously the terms of reference to the tribunal had to be agreed.

[14]This Act made permanent the wartime arrangements which had introduced a national *minimum* wage into agriculture. It was subsequently consolidated with earlier legislation in the Agricultural Wages Act, 1948 and the Agricultural Wages (Scotland) Act, 1949.

they replaced, the Wages Councils and the other statutory boards have considerably wider powers. They can make provisions for a guaranteed week; they can give directions for holidays with pay (for more than one week in the year—the limited power granted to the Trade Boards by the Holidays with Pay Act, 1938); and they can advise the Minister of Labour on such matters as training, recruitment, and working conditions.

Some of the wartime regulations had a permanent influence on the subject matter as well as the form of collective bargaining. The Essential Work Orders, since they severely limited the freedom of employees in scheduled undertakings to quit their jobs, guaranteed, under certain qualifications, a minimum weekly wage to timeworkers and a daily minimum to pieceworkers. Before the Orders were withdrawn three months' notice was given by the Minister of Labour to enable affected industries to negotiate voluntary agreements for a guaranteed week. A large number of industries did so, including engineering, iron and steel manufacture, cotton spinning and weaving, wool textiles, hosiery, boot and shoe, rubber, government establishments, and in a modified form, building.[15] For dock workers the guaranteed weekly wage and the greater regularity of employment, which they achieved during the war, were made permanent by the Dock Workers' (Regulation of Employment) Act, 1946.

The nationalization of the fuel and power and transport groups of industries has led to relatively few changes in their collective bargaining procedure, since most of them already had firmly established arrangements. The main exception was civil aviation, where a National Joint Council for Civil Air Transport was formed for the first time in 1946. In road haulage, where previously wages had been subject to statutory regulation under the Road Haulage Wages Act, 1938, nationalization led to the setting up of a National Staff Council for the publicly owned sector of the industry, with separate national negotiating committees for the three main groups of employees. The Road Haulage Central Wages Board was converted into a Wages Council in 1948 and covers the privately

[15]For an account of the negotiations in some industries, see J. B. Jefferys "The Guaranteed Weekly Wage in the British Metal Trades," *International Labour Review,* March 1949.

owned sector. A Pit Conciliation Scheme was adopted by national agreement in the coal-mining industry at the beginning of 1947 "to provide for the speedy settlement of disputes arising in individual collieries." Such disputes, if they cannot be settled by negotiation in the colliery concerned, are referred to a joint District Disputes Committee, which if unable to agree, refers them to an umpire, selected from an agreed panel, for a binding decision.

One significant consequence of nationalization has been to extend the area of collective bargaining to all nonmanual workers in the industries and services concerned. Some of them, like the railway clerks and the electrical power engineers, already had collective agreements and were on the whole as well organized as the manual workers. But the Nationalization Acts made it necessary for the new employing authorities to "maintain machinery for the settlement by negotiation of the terms and conditions of employment" for all their employees. As a result colliery managers and undermanagers, represented by the British Association of Colliery Management, have their separate arrangements for negotiation and conciliation with the National Coal Board. Or—to take another example, from electricity supply—here, in addition to the Joint Industrial Council which has been retained for negotiating with the manual workers' unions, there are separate national joint negotiating bodies for the clerical and administrative workers, for the technical engineering staff, and for the managerial grades.

A final reference to the growth of collective bargaining among the professions provides a fitting conclusion to this brief historical survey, for this shows as clearly as anything how great has been the change in British public opinion during the twentieth century. In their introduction to the 1902 edition of *Industrial Democracy* the Webbs asserted that the opinion of the professional as well as the propertied classes was then "even more hostile to trade unionism and strikes than it was a generation ago."[16] Not only has this hostility largely disappeared, but professional workers have increasingly followed the example of manual workers and claimed for themselves the advantages of independent organization and negotiation. The authors of the most authoritative study of the

[16]1920 ed., p. xxvi.

professions in Great Britain have suggested that the medical profession was particularly responsible for this change in attitude toward collective bargaining. "The fact that this ancient and dignified profession adopted the method and used it with success gave it a measure of respectability and accounts for its wide use."[17] The National Insurance Act of 1911, by leaving the question of the doctors' remuneration unsettled and a subject of negotiation between the Government and the British Medical Association, set the ball rolling. Afterward a proper collective bargaining procedure was elaborated, with the Insurance Act Committee of the BMA "recognized" by the Ministry of Health for this purpose. Several professional associations, notably those of teachers and local government servants, have followed a similar course of development adding to their original functions this, the most characteristic, function of a trade union. It should be noted, however, that collective bargaining among the professions has flourished mainly in the sphere of public employment. Generally what resistance still remains alive today to acceptance of the practice, both on the part of employers and, to some extent, on the part of the employees themselves, is concentrated among the salaried staffs in private industry. By the end of 1950 about four fifths of the total employee population of Great Britain had their wages and working conditions regulated either by voluntary agreements or by Wages Councils and the like.[18] Since then the proportion has certainly not declined.

Trade Unions and Employers' Organizations

In tracing the historical development of the arrangements for collective bargaining in Great Britain we have had to neglect a very relevant part of the subject, the organization of the bargaining partners. Now that we turn to a closer examination of the present system we cannot proceed without some reference to the structure of employee and employer organization. Here also allegiance to the voluntary principle is the reason for the complex pattern of

[17] A. M. Carr-Saunders and P. A. Wilson, *The Professions* (Oxford: The Clarendon Press, 1933), p. 458.

[18] *Annual Report of the Ministry of Labour and National Service for 1950* (Cmd. 8338), p. 116.

overlapping and interlocking bodies which exist on both sides.

At the end of 1954 there were still 674 separate trade unions in the United Kingdom; 372 of them had less than a thousand members. The fact that any group of workers can, if they wish, maintain their separate organization has resulted in the continued existence of a large number of small unions. On the other hand, the most significant trend in the structural development of British trade unionism during the twentieth century has been the growth of large unions through a process of voluntary amalgamation. The total number of trade unionists in 1954 was about nine and a half millions or more than two fifths of all employees. Two thirds of them belonged to seventeen trade unions with more than a hundred thousand members, and nearly 92 percent to ninety unions with more than ten thousand members.[19]

Amalgamations have not taken place according to any one pattern of union organization. Some, but by no means all of the various craft unions, which still formed the bulk of the movement at the beginning of the century, have become merged into large, national, multicraft unions (e.g., the Amalgamated Society of Woodworkers). A few of these in turn (e.g., the Amalgamated Engineering Union) have admitted the less-skilled workers employed in close connection with their trades. Yet there are still plenty of single craft unions confining their membership to one locality (e.g., the London Typographical Society). The emergence of the two great general unions, the Transport and General Workers' Union and the National Union of General and Municipal Workers, which together cast more than a quarter of the votes at the annual Trades Union Congress, is another result of unplanned development. One reason for their success has been their flexibility in organizing; the fact that they acknowledge no theoretical limits to their domain enabled them to enter those fields of employment which other unions were prepared or compelled to ignore. The development of industrial unions in this country has also been one, but only one, of the results of the general process of amalgamation. Some of them (e.g., the National Union of Railwaymen) were created with the conception of industrial unionism as the ideal

[19]*Ministry of Labour Gazette,* October 1955.

form of organization, while others (e.g., the National Union of Boot and Shoe Operatives) developed without preconceived theories, as the most suitable type of organization for the workers concerned. None of the industrial unions has been entirely successful in occupying the whole of its chosen sphere.

Compared with that of most other countries the general picture of trade union organization in Britain is still a very untidy one. More than a dozen separate trade unions may well be represented in one establishment. But in the midst of all this diversity there has undoubtedly been a steady trend toward the closer integration of the industrial policy of trade unions and the lessening of inter-union conflict. This has been helped forward by the strengthening of industrial federations of unions (e.g., the Printing and Kindred Trades Federation, the National Federation of Building Trade Operatives, and the Confederation of Shipbuilding and Engineering Unions) and by the formation of Joint Industrial Councils. The Disputes Committee of the Trades Union Congress has also contributed greatly to diminishing friction among unions competing for membership by arbitrating in disputed cases in accordance with principles agreed by Congress.

The existence of one central body, the Trades Union Congress, which can fairly claim to speak in the name of the trade union movement as a whole, has been a further simplifying factor in this complex structure. It is true that in 1955 only 183 trade unions were affiliated to the TUC, but some of them were, in fact, federations of unions,[20] and their aggregate membership exceeded eight millions. There are only two large unions (with more than a hundred thousand members) which are not affiliated, the National Association of Local Government Officers and the National Union of Teachers, but both of them are on good terms with the TUC. Most of the other unaffiliated unions of any size organize employees in national or local government service.

When the Trades Union Congress was reorganized in the early twenties the main idea was that the new General Council (which replaced the previous Parliamentary Committee) should act as a

[20]The constituent unions of these federations are counted separately in the figures for the total number of unions already given.

kind of "general staff, which would be capable of guiding and solidifying the movement on national issues."[21] The present constitution of the TUC, which has not been altered fundamentally since 1924, still reflects the prevailing concerns and composition of the trade union movement at that time. The very limited powers granted to the General Council, for example, were defined mainly with an eye to mobilizing mutual support in times of industrial conflict. In practice the General Council succeeded in strengthening its moral authority largely on account of the increasing participation of the Government in economic affairs. This shifted the emphasis from industrial to political action, and the representation of the workers' interests in regard to impending legislation or administrative action could best be undertaken by a central body.

The Trades Union Congress has no control over the collective bargaining activities of its affiliated unions. Under one of the rules in its constitution they are pledged to keep the General Council informed of any major disputes in which they may become engaged, either with employers or among themselves. If a peaceful settlement seems likely, the General Council cannot intervene unless requested to do so, but in the event of a breakdown in negotiations it may give advice to the unions involved. If this advice is accepted and a strike or lockout results, the TUC is then under an obligation to organize material and moral support. This rule was the basis of the General Council's action in the 1926 General Strike.[22] It represents the full extent of the formal powers of the TUC. What influence the General Council exercises otherwise, for example by declarations of policy, is due to its prestige and representative character. The limits of such a moral authority have been sharply revealed, as we shall see, in the postwar attempts to give leadership on wage policy.

Employers' organizations fall broadly into two main classes. There are the trade associations, which often regulate competition among employers and generally provide them with joint services

[21]Walter M. Citrine, *The Trade Union Movement of Great Britain* (Amsterdam: International Federation of Trade Unions, 1926), p. 67.

[22]An amendment was carried at the 1955 Trades Union Congress which will allow the General Council to interest themselves in an industrial dispute before a deadlock is reached.

in their trading activities. There are also the employers' federations which were formed largely as a response to the growth of trade unions and act as their counterpart in collective bargaining. Some bodies undertake both functions, but the existence of two central organizations—the Federation of British Industries for economic and commercial questions and the British Employers' Confederation for labor questions—reflects the prevalence of a division of function.

In November 1952, according to the Ministry of Labour's *Industrial Relations Handbook,* 1953,[23] there were some eighteen hundred employers' organizations active in the field of industrial relations, but less than one sixth of them were national federations and the remainder were, for the most part, local or regional branches of these federations. The great majority of organized employers are concentrated in relatively few associations or federations, but as they do not publish information on their membership the degree of concentration cannot be measured. It is significant, however, that only some 63 of them are affiliated with the British Employers' Confederation, although firms represented by this body certainly cover the majority of the workers employed in private industries. For obvious reasons employers are usually organized on an industrial basis, although some independent organizations are local in character or cover only a section of an industry. An earlier edition of the *Industrial Relations Handbook* in 1944 gave details of the organizations represented on 188 "Standing Joint Industrial Councils, Committees etc. established by voluntary agreement" outside government and local authority services. On 138 of these a single organization represented the employers, as compared with 90 in which the workers' side was one union or a federation of unions.[24]

The formal relationship of the British Employers' Confederation to its affiliates is much the same as that of the Trades Union Congress; in both cases the constituent organizations yield up no part of their autonomy to the central bodies. In practice, however, the

[23]P. 13.

[24]A detailed analysis of comparative representation can be found in K. G. J. C. Knowles, *Strikes—A Study in Industrial Conflict* (Oxford: B. Blackwell, 1952), pp. 71–72.

influence of the BEC over the collective bargaining policies of its members is less than that of the TUC. It has never taken part in negotiations or disputes. After the war it set up a committee to inquire into wage movements, but only for the purpose of collecting and distributing information.

Outside the ranks of the federated employers there are now relatively few firms which refuse to negotiate with trade unions. A large number of small firms, although they observe agreements, do not think it worth while to join a federation. There are also some large nonfederated firms which prefer, for a variety of reasons, to sign their own separate agreements with the trade unions. Both the local authorities and the cooperative societies undertake collective bargaining through organizations with a somewhat analagous position to the private employers' federations. The Association of Municipal Corporations and the County Councils' Association represent the former and the Co-operative Union, Ltd., the latter. Finally we have the Civil Service and the nationalized industries, which together account for about one sixth of the total number of employees. Here no special, external organization is required for collective bargaining.

Bargaining Procedure and Agreements

The arrangements for collective bargaining in Great Britain vary from industry to industry; there is no standard pattern. Some of the reasons for this have already been made apparent. Their evolutionary development and the structural diversity of organization among employers and employees, as well as many factors peculiar to each industry—its geographical distribution, the size of undertakings, the form of wage payment—are all responsible for variations in bargaining procedure. It is not an easy task, then, to describe it; there are always so many exceptions and qualifications to add to every summarizing statement attempted.

It might seem convenient, for example, to begin by classifying the various industries and services into three groups: those which have evolved their own special arrangements, those with Joint Industrial (or Whitley) Councils, and those subject to statutory regulation by Wages Councils or their equivalent. But even this division can easily mislead the reader.

The difference in law between voluntary and statutory bodies is clear enough, but there are no industrial demarcation lines separating the voluntary and statutory parts of the system. Some of the industries with Wages Councils also have Joint Industrial Councils (as in retail distribution) or are covered in part by voluntary agreements providing terms and conditions more favorable than the statutory minima. These agreements may relate only to particular firms but they may also be concluded on a broader basis. In the clothing industry there have been national agreements between certain sections of the trade and the National Union of Tailors and Garment Workers for many years. The union usually tries to negotiate a wage increase with the employers' organizations on a voluntary basis and afterward apply it to the whole of the industry through the medium of the Wages Councils.

Moreover, the original contrast between voluntary and statutory regulation has been narrowed considerably since the first Trade Boards were introduced. The Wages Councils, like the Trade Boards, consist of an equal number of employers' and workers' representatives with not more than three independent members, including the chairman. All members are appointed by the Minister of Labour at his discretion, but in practice the great majority of the representative members are now nominated by trade unions and employers' associations. Although the proposals of the Wages Councils only become effective when confirmed by the Minister after time has been given for objections to be lodged, he cannot himself fix wages. The most he can do is refer back the recommendations for further consideration, but even this right has been exercised only on rare occasions. Consequently, there is a strong element of collective bargaining in this form of statutory regulation. Even the presence of independent members does little more than provide for the constant use of mediation and arbitration where there is some degree of organization on both sides; voluntary conciliation boards with an independent chairman empowered to make a binding award are not so dissimilar in their working.

Once confirmed by the Minister, the minimum wages and

conditions agreed by Wages Councils become legally binding on all employers concerned and a special staff of inspectors is employed to see that they are observed. Employers violating the Orders are liable to fine and imprisonment as well as to the payment of any arrears of wages due to the workers. The powers of legal enforcement are strict, and necessarily so in employments where voluntary organization is too weak for effective policing. All the same, the voluntary bodies for collective bargaining are now able to obtain a fair degree of state support for their agreements. The special case of cotton manufacturing has been mentioned.[25] But generally, with the help of Fair Wages Clauses in government contracts[26] and the provisions of Order 1376[27] trade unions are not compelled to rely entirely on their own sanctions for extending the influence of their agreements.

If it is difficult to know where statutory regulation ends and voluntary regulation begins, it is still more difficult to discover any practical significance in the distinction between industries with Joint Industrial Councils and those with some other arrangements for collective bargaining. What are called the "decisions" of the JIC's "are as much collective agreements as the agreements reached by the two sides meeting for the purpose of *ad hoc* negotiations."[28] The fact that they are permanent bodies with a

[25]See above pp. 10–11.

[26]The "Fair Wages Clause," first introduced into government contracts in 1891, has become an increasingly important form of governmental support of voluntary agreements. It was reformulated by a House of Commons resolution in 1909 to provide that contractors "shall under a penalty of a fine or otherwise, pay rates of wages and observe hours of labour no less favorable than those commonly recognised by employers and trade societies...in the trade in the district where the work is carried out." During the interwar years, in a series of acts providing financial assistance to industries from the Public Exchequer, beginning with the British Sugar (Subsidy) Act, 1925, a "Fair Wages Clause" was included, and strengthened as compared with the 1909 resolution. For example, the principle of compulsory arbitration was introduced to enforce the observance of the clause and to settle disputes of interpretation. In 1946 the House of Commons substantially amended the 1909 resolution to bring it in line with the changed circumstances resulting from the growth of the voluntary system. The main standard of fair wages became that established by representative collective agreements and by arbitration awards. Government contractors were compelled to observe "fair" conditions of labor (not only wages and hours as before), to recognize the freedom of their workpeople to be members of trade unions, and to see that their subcontractors also complied with the same conditions. Local authorities have similar fair wages clauses in their contracts.

[27]See above p. 14.

[28]*Report on Collective Agreements,* 1934, p. v.

written constitution in no way distinguishes them, say, from the National Joint Council for the Building Industry. They can all be said to have a common origin in the recommendations of the Whitley Committee, but since employers' associations and trade unions have been left to adapt the model scheme to their own preferences they are, as we have seen, by no means uniform in their structure or their functions. That the Ministry of Labour has taken a hand in their formation, by bringing the various unions and employers' associations together for this purpose, suggests a distinction which loses its force when it is remembered that in a number of other industries, such as railways and coal mining, public intervention has had no less a formative influence on their existing arrangement for collective bargaining.

Admittedly, in the industries which had evolved their own arrangements for collective bargaining during the nineteenth century, and which subsequently have not been influenced greatly by any form of public intervention, we can still find more diversity of arrangement and practice than elsewhere. Engineering and shipbuilding, iron and steel, boot and shoe, and printing are examples. Engineering and shipbuilding are among the few well-organized industries without any permanent joint councils for conducting national negotiations; they take place at special conferences called on the initiative of either side. Iron and steel is remarkable both for its bewildering tangle of national, district, and works agreements and for the extent to which customs and decisions have never been expressed in written collective agreements. There are a dozen or so joint bodies operating in this industry, but they apply only to certain regions or sections of the industry. Boot and shoe has its own unique arrangements, which include a national conference meeting every second year. Printing undertakes part of its collective bargaining through the agency of a Joint Industrial Council, but there are many separate wage and apprenticeship agreements—some national and some local—between the various unions and employers' organizations.

Negotiations are usually undertaken by a standing joint body with a written constitution, but they may take place at joint conferences held at regular intervals or at special meetings called when a fresh claim is raised by either side. The one generalization which can safely be made is that the main changes in wages and working conditions result from negotiations conducted between the headquarters of trade unions (or their industrial federations) on the one hand, and employers' associations or public authorities on the other. Does this imply that collective bargaining is predominantly "industry-wide"? Only in a limited sense. It never means that a collective bargain covers all the employees in a particular industry; for there are invariably separate agreements for manual and nonmanual workers. There are also the cases where the main occupations of one industry are carried on within what are usually taken to be the frontiers of another. The building and engineering workers employed in iron and steel manufacture or in the railways workshops, for instance, have their own distinct bargaining procedures and agreements within these industries. Again, even the existence of an industry-wide joint negotiating body does not necessarily prevent the trade unions represented on it from bargaining separately with the employers on occasions, as happens in printing, or on the railways, or with the Civil Service. Negotiations on hours and holidays are sometimes conducted on a wider scale than negotiations on wages. Both the Printing and Kindred Trades Federation and the United Textile Factory Workers' Association have agreements with the employers on hours and holidays which cover the whole of the manual workers employed in the printing and cotton textile industries, although they have not yet been entrusted by their affiliated unions with the negotiation of general wage agreements with a similar coverage.

Apart from the scale of negotiations their degree of regulation over the individual terms of employment varies. We have at the one extreme spheres of employment, like the railways, in which wages and working conditions are wholly determined in central negotiations. In others, of which the building industry is probably the best example, regional and local deviations are permitted but only with the approval of the national body; this does not prevent employers paying more than standard rates. There are again industries, such as coal mining, where certain basic minimum rates of wages are settled nationally, but district and, in this example, pit bargaining continues on its own volition unless it leads to a dispute with national implications. Finally, at the other extreme, we have the examples of engineering and shipbuilding, in which only general wage changes are negotiated nationally, while a veritable chaos of local rates and practices, inherited from the past, remains outside national control.

Apart from tradition, probably the most important single factor which influences the extent of centralization and national control in collective bargaining is the method of wage payment. The regulation of time rates of wages throughout the whole of an industry by one collective agreement presents no technical difficulties providing the necessary grading of employees is undertaken to reduce the number of different rates to reasonable proportions. But when we have any form of payment by results, even straight piecework, it is impossible to settle the payment completely in national negotiations. There are broadly three ways of regulating by national agreement the earnings of workers paid by results: a standard piecework price list can be negotiated for the industry as a whole (or a segment of it)—this is only possible where the product and the work operations are not too varied; a level of earnings can be settled by agreement, bearing a specified relationship to time rates, which will be taken as the norm in determining actual piecework prices; or a minimum time rate is nationally agreed and the extra earnings gained from payment by results are settled entirely by individual or works bargaining. All of these methods have been adopted in various British industries, but none of them entirely eliminates wage bargaining below the national level. This is obvious with the second and the third methods, but even a standard list also raises complicated questions of interpretation (or disputes over conditions of work) which can only be settled locally by compromise.

The great majority of collective agreements in Great Britain do not run for any stated term; they remain in force until one of the parties gives notice to terminate or revise them. This means that fresh negotiations can be started at any time. There are a few notable exceptions. National agreements in boot and shoe manufacture last for two years, during which period neither side can open up wage questions, and six months' notice of intention to revise wages has to be given prior to the terminable date of the agreement. The agreements in the printing trades, which were concluded on the pattern of the agreement reached between the London Master Printers' Association and the London Society of Compositors after the dispute in 1950, provided that they should remain in force for a period of five years, while recent agreements in the industry have been made for three years. In both of these cases, it must be noted, there are cost-of-living sliding scales.

Most voluntary agreements regulating bargaining procedure include provisions for the settlement of disputes between the parties without resort to aggressive action. Frequently, a distinction is drawn between national and local disputes, and they are dealt with in different ways. Before we look at the variations in procedure, some explanation is required of the significance of this distinction in British practice.

In other European countries, where collective agreements are legally enforceable, the more familiar distinction is between "economic" and "legal" disputes. A publication of the International Labour Office defines the former as disputes "regarding interests," where the two parties "while mutually recognizing each other, cannot agree as to the terms of a collective agreement," and the latter as any individual or collective disputes which result "from differences of opinions regarding the interpretation or application of regulations already laid down or of rights already acquired, whatever their basis may be—individual contract of employment, collective agreement, legislation or custom."[29] In Great Britain, while most national disputes are disputes over the terms of a new agreement in view of the predominance of national negotiations, it would be misleading to identify local disputes with "legal" disputes as defined by the ILO. They may, of course, be disputes over the interpretation of agreements. If they are, they are more likely to be settled by an acceptable compromise

[29]International Labor Office, *Labour Courts in Latin America* (Studies and Reports, No. 13), 1949, p. 3.

than by anything remotely resembling a "legal" decision, depending on the meaning given to the words in a formal text. More often than not, however, they are disputes arising out of issues which are not specifically regulated by agreement: the withdrawal of existing privileges; changes in production methods, coupled perhaps with a failure on the part of management to consult the workers affected; the employment of nonunionists; alleged victimization; even the use of insulting words on the part of a foreman. Whether these are conflicts of interest or conflicts over established rights might be taken as a problem for philosophical speculation, but it has no bearing at all on the course of collective bargaining. Local disputes are, in fact, any disputes, whatever their cause, which start below the level of national negotiation, although most of them arise in one establishment.

With national disputes, if the parties reach a deadlock in negotiations, the final alternative to direct action is some form of arbitration. And many industries have provided for its use within the terms of their agreements or in the constitution of their joint bodies. Engineering and shipbuilding are probably the most important examples of industries which have no provisions of their own for the use either of conciliation or arbitration in national disputes. They have, however, made use of the National Arbitration Tribunal and of its successor, the Industrial Disputes Tribunal. Printing is an industry in which the traditional aversion to an outside third-party decision is strongly maintained—the London Society of Compositors refused to give evidence before the Court of Inquiry in 1950 on the grounds that direct negotiations with the master printers were the only satisfactory way of settling the dispute. But the constitution of the Printing JIC provides a conciliation procedure for the settlement of national as well as local disputes; they are first considered by its small Conciliation Committee and, failing settlement there, by a full meeting of the JIC.

The voluntarily agreed provisions for the use of arbitration to settle national disputes take various forms. There are industries with their own arbitration tribunals; they include coal mining, Civil Service, and railways. Some national negotiating bodies have an independent chairman who may be called upon to act as an arbitrator; the National Conference of the boot and shoe industry and the Joint Conciliation Committee in the manufacturing section of cotton textiles are examples. More frequently the constitution of a joint body provides for a final reference to arbitration, mentioning, perhaps, the Industrial Court or an individual arbitrator appointed by the Minister of Labour, or leaving the authority open for mutual agreement, as in the building industry. Sometimes mutual consent may be required before a dispute can be referred to arbitration, but more often than not a binding commitment has been accepted to resort to and abide by an arbitration award if a deadlock is reached.[30]

In stressing the extent to which arbitration has come to be accepted as preferable to aggressive action we have, however, to guard against a possible misunderstanding, namely, that it is replacing direct negotiation. The order of preference—it must be emphasized once more—is very clearly established throughout the voluntary system and is the basis of all labor legislation since 1896 as well as the daily practice of the Ministry of Labour: direct negotiation is better than mediation, and mediation is better than arbitration. We cannot make an exact estimate of the relative importance of these different methods of settling disputes. There are no figures for the number of disputes resolved by direct negotiation and, though there is a record of the number of arbitration awards and conciliation settlements made under the auspices of the Ministry of Labour, we cannot assess their individual significance—they may cover less than a hundred or more than a million workers. The most telling comparison we have is that, during the period 1945 to 1951, three quarters of the total amount secured in weekly wage increases was attributable to negotiated agreements; of the remaining one quarter, two parts resulted from the decisions of statutory bodies and only one part from arbitration awards (or 8 percent of the total). Throughout these years

[30]According to a statement made by the Minister of Labour in 1954, the procedural agreements of 75 industries, out of a total of 152, included provisions for the use of arbitration. In 51 of these the parties had agreed in advance to refer unresolved disputes to arbitration, while in 24 it was only provided that disputes might be referred. *Trades Union Congress Report 1954,* p. 239.

(apart from the last five months), compulsory arbitration under Order 1305 was in force.

Nearly every industry with voluntary arrangements for collective bargaining has some kind of agreed procedure for dealing with local disputes. The procedure may be defined in the constitution of a joint body (as in the case of the JIC's) or by normal collective agreements (as in coal mining, railways, boot and shoe manufacture, cotton textiles, engineering, and shipbuilding) or largely by custom (as in iron and steel). But in nearly all cases it is accompanied by a provision that there shall be no stoppage of work until the procedure has been exhausted.

There is probably more variety in the procedure adopted for the settlement of local disputes than in any other aspect of collective bargaining in Great Britain. In the first place the arrangements for dealing with grievances within individual establishments differ greatly. They are seldom determined by national agreement and, until recent years, many trade unions have paid little attention to their organization in the workplace. Even where shop stewards are elected there may be no proper works committee; trade unions which are acting together in national negotiations may not display the same degree of cooperation at this level. The attitudes of management are equally diverse. Some of the more progressive firms go to great lengths to develop suitable joint arrangements both for negotiation and consultation to make sure that, as far as possible, all grievances are settled speedily within the establishment. Others may at the most concede the right of the workers to appoint a delegation to meet them, with the local trade union official being called in if a grievance cannot otherwise be settled.

In the agreed procedure for dealing with disputes which have passed beyond the individual establishment and involve the trade unions and the employers' associations there are also all kinds of combinations of the use of conciliation and arbitration. There may be provision for the reference of the dispute upwards through a whole chain of joint meetings before the procedure is exhausted. This is the case in engineering, although the meetings can hardly be described as "joint." Here under the 1922 agreement, if a works conference has failed to dispose of the dispute it goes on to a local conference, or, if necessary, to a national conference, but at both levels the trade union representatives appear before the assembled representatives of the employers' federation and then retire while the latter reach a decision; there is no provision for arbitration at any stage. Another device, with a more successful history, is the so-called "neutral committee" employed in the iron and steel industry. Disputes arising in one establishment, if they cannot be settled by those directly concerned, are referred for a decision to a local committee composed equally of employers' and union representatives, who are not themselves involved in the disputes under consideration. Failing a settlement here, the "neutral committee" refers the question back to the employers' association and trade union to deal with by negotiation, or submits the dispute to arbitration. The Port Consultants appointed by and from among the District Panels of the National Maritime Board are a sort of neutral committee to settle any dispute which might otherwise hold up "the prompt manning of vessels" but they have "no power to alter, vary or amend any rules, rates, scale, principles or procedure formulated by the National Maritime Board."[31] The local Boards of Conciliation and Arbitration in boot and shoe manufacture and the Pit Conciliation Scheme in coal mining both provide for the use of umpires, whose decisions are final and binding, if an agreement cannot otherwise be reached by conciliation. On the whole the use of a third-party decision *from outside the industry* is not favored for the settlement of local disputes.

There is then a marked contrast in attitude toward the use of arbitration in the settlement of industrial disputes as between the United States and Great Britain. While in the United States arbitration is generally rejected as a method of settling a deadlock over the terms of a new agreement and generally accepted for resolving conflicts arising out of the interpretation of existing agreements, the opposite is broadly true of Great Britain. At least there is a far greater readiness to resort to arbitration in national than in local disputes.

We have been looking at the process of collective bargaining in

[31]The National Maritime Board: *Year Book 1952,* p. 140.

Great Britain as it appears in the various procedures adopted for negotiation and the settlement of disputes. It can also be viewed from its outcome, the collective agreement. The scope of collective agreements can be said to vary in two dimensions: according to the employees to whom they apply (their coverage); and according to the subjects with which they deal (their contents). In Britain, as in most other democratic countries with increasingly powerful trade unions, the trend in the evolution of collective bargaining has been toward the progressive enlargening of its scope in both dimensions.

As regards their coverage collective agreements are usually considered to fall into three classes: (1) works agreements, made between a single employer and the whole or some of his employees; (2) district or local agreements, applying to particular towns or geographical areas variously defined; (3) national agreements, relating to the whole or the greater part of an industry wherever it may be carried on. This classification, though useful, oversimplifies the picture. The coverage of agreements varies occupationally as well as geographically. They may relate to a single trade, or to several, or to all manual workers in a particular industry at each of the three levels already mentioned. National agreements may cover both sections of an industry (e.g., railway workshops) and groups of industries (e.g., engineering). Moreover, their application may extend over England and Wales, or Scotland, or Great Britain, or the United Kingdom.

The situation is made the more complicated by the fact that the same employees may well have their wages and working conditions regulated by the combined effect of works, district, and national agreements, as well as by such protective labor legislation as the Factories Acts. This is still true even of the nationalized coal-mining industry, although in 1955 a national wage structure was introduced for the day wage men—more than half the total labor force. In the metal industries (iron and steel, engineering, and shipbuilding, etc.), the tangle of agreements which in one way or another have a regulative influence on wages is so complicated as to defy description. With the exception of a few industries, however, the general trend has been toward simplification.

The contents of collective agreements in Great Britain vary from industry to industry in the same way as bargaining procedure, which is itself one subject of agreement. Apart from other procedural aspects of the joint relations between employers and employees, such as the setting up of joint consultative committees or joint arrangements for the selection and training of apprentices, their subject matter can broadly be classified with the aid of the legal definition of a trade dispute given in the Trade Disputes Act, 1906. This definition was intentionally made wide enough to cover all disputes with an industrial connection, as distinct from those serving political purposes. The wording of the definition is "any dispute between employers and workmen, or between workmen and workmen, which is connected with the employment or non-employment, or the terms of employment, or with the conditions of labor of any person." Since a dispute is the starting point of collective bargaining and an agreement its outcome, the *possible* subject matter of the one is the same as the other.

There is one important proviso, however. The regulative influence of collective bargaining is not fully reflected in the contents of formal agreements. In certain British industries there are many uncodified practices accepted by employers and trade unions alike, often but not exclusively confined to particular establishments, which are virtually the subject of unwritten agreements. Moreover, anything appertaining to the working life of any employee may become the subject of a dispute, and therefore of negotiation, so that there is no ascertainable limit to the subjects which may on occasion be regulated by a joint agreement or understanding.

As far as written agreements are concerned, terms of employment are undoubtedly the most important and, in many industries, the only subject. Under this heading are to be included provisions relating to: payment by results as well as minimum or, in some cases, standard rates of pay; shift working, overtime, and holidays as well as the length of the normal working week; arrangements for a guaranteed week; all kinds of extra allowances and emoluments; and such auxiliary matters as the grading of employees (occupationally or geographically) and the definition of work duties.

Conditions of labor, that is, the external physical conditions under which people work, have been regulated more by law than by collective agreement. The Factories Acts impose legal minimum standards of safety, health, and welfare and regulate the hours and times of work of women and young persons, although they do not apply to all fields of employment. The need to protect the physical well-being of employees against the worst hazards of industrialism has been recognized for a long time, and government intervention for this purpose was regarded as legitimate even during the first half of the nineteenth century. But it is noticeable that conditions of labor, in advance of any legal minima, are increasingly becoming the subject of negotiation and sometimes of formal collective agreement. An interesting example is the code of welfare conditions adopted in 1948 by the National Joint Council for the Building Industry which covers shelter from inclement weather, accommodation for clothing, accommodation and provisions for meals, provision of drinking water, sanitary conveniences, washing facilities, first-aid and site conditions; the council declared that "it shall apply to building sites with the same authority as a National Working Rule."

Clauses in collective agreements relating to the employment or nonemployment of any person are certainly not as frequent in Great Britain as in the United States. By and large, union security and job security are not protected by formal agreements. It would be a great mistake, however, to conclude from this that they are not protected at all. This is the province of collective bargaining in which unwritten practices and customs are most important. The Webbs described the compulsion on a skilled craftsman to belong to his union during the nineteenth century as "silent and unseen." Today a union card is still the key to employment in many of the skilled trades, and the employers turn to the unions in the first place to help them to fill their vacancies. Similarly, the seniority rule, "last in, first out," is accepted practice in many large industrial establishments when employees have to be dismissed, although it has rarely been made the subject of a written agreement between employers and trade unions. One reason for the contrast with the United States has been the emphasis on national agreements in collective bargaining, instead of the plant contract; and these are matters which cannot easily be regulated on a uniform basis for

the whole of an industry. All the same, the subjects which are dealt with by collective agreements in some industries include: union membership, demarcation between men's and women's work, the number of apprentices or young people who may be employed, redundancy, disciplinary procedure, and promotion.

Consequences of Postwar Full Employment

So far, this essay has dealt mainly with the institutional framework of collective bargaining in Great Britain. We have seen how in the course of a century this has evolved continuously—apart from some setbacks during the interwar years. From various spontaneous origins it has grown into a fairly complete system for regulating the wages and working conditions of the vast majority of employees, upheld by an intricate combination of economic, social, and legal sanctions. To anyone with a passion for uniformity it is a system which must appear most unsystematic. Nevertheless, it has the qualities of its defects. An organic mode of development has given collective bargaining deep and strong roots in the social structure. Supported by tradition, by consent, by practical experience, and—one must add—by entrenched interests, the prevailing forms of organization are knitted together, if not by any consistent theory, at least by certain common assumptions. Of these assumptions, one stands out almost as a supreme article of faith: that good industrial relations are best created by voluntary action. Any proposals which it is thought might tamper with the freedom of employers and trade unions to conclude agreements on whatever terms they find acceptable are instinctively distrusted, not only by the employers and the trade unions but by most of the general public. In no aspect of economic organization has laissez faire so many champions.

When we come now to examine the impact on collective bargaining of the changed economic environment of the postwar years, this climate of opinion is particularly relevant in interpreting the course of events. New and difficult problems have appeared on the scene, but the attempt has always been made to solve them within the limits imposed by strict adherence to the voluntary principle.

Before we proceed to elaborate this theme, however, more of the background must be provided.

Clearly it is impossible within the scope of this essay to trace all the internal and external changes in the British economy since 1945[32] or to attempt an assessment of their influence on collective bargaining. It must be advanced largely as a personal opinion that the maintenance of full employment can be singled out as the condition which has had the most decisive influence on industrial relations. The reasons for turning the spotlight on full employment will become apparent as we proceed, but they can be summed up in one proposition: it is not only a desirable end in itself, but a dynamic condition—one that continually promotes the achievement of other equally desirable ends by transforming the power relations between employers and employees and their attitudes toward each other.

Here we are concerned not with all aspects of industrial relations but with collective bargaining. The way in which full employment has, for example, encouraged the growth of joint consultation and personnel management has to be ignored. We will confine our attention to its impact on some of the more generally measurable results of collective bargaining. Its consequences in upholding a high level of trade union organization and the wartime achievements in extending the arrangements for collective bargaining have already been described.

First let us take what may, perhaps, be regarded as the negative results of collective bargaining, its economic cost as expressed in terms of working days lost through strikes. The contrast between the total number of working days lost through industrial disputes in the United Kingdom after the two world wars is familiar but impressive: in the years 1946–1950 about 9½ million days were lost as compared with 178 million in the years 1919–1923. Since 1933 the highest figure reached in any one year was 3.7 million days in 1944, and this spread over the whole of the working population was equivalent to no more than an annual loss of 1½ working hours on the part of every worker. A small price to pay for freedom!

[32]For such a survey, see *The British Economy 1945–1950*, G. D. N. Worswick and P. H. Ady, eds. (Oxford and Toronto, 1952).

The absence of costly large-scale stoppages, involving the whole or a substantial part of an industry goes back to the early 'thirties in Great Britain. The strengthening of the arrangements for collective bargaining and the increasing readiness to accept arbitration, when it remained the only alternative to direct action, have tended to eliminate the strike as a weapon in union strategy, used on a national scale to advance union claims. On the other hand, during this period economic conditions have not compelled them to resort to it to defend ground previously won. Throughout the past two decades the trade unions have been able to gain concessions for their members in their bargaining activities by peaceful means, and their membership and financial resources have steadily improved.

The most significant contrast in the situation before and after World War II lies in the increase in the *number* of strikes. This is brought out in Table 1, which also covers the war years.

Most of these strikes are local in character, often confined to one establishment, and of short duration. The great majority are also "unofficial," that is, not sanctioned or recognized officially by union headquarters. In view of the many conciliation agreements which bind the unions not to resort to aggressive action in local disputes until the agreed procedure has been fully exhausted, this is not surprising. Indeed with the maturing of national bargaining relationships the whole significance of strike action has changed. Increasingly it has become a form of spontaneous protest on the part of organized employees in a particular establishment either against the actions of management on matters not regulated by agreement or against the agreements and decisions accepted by their own union headquarters. Naturally their increased bargaining power under full employment has favored such an assertion of their independence on the part of workers with militant traditions and strong organization at their place of work. During the postwar years the Communist party has undoubtedly exploited the situation whenever it could, but this is an effect rather than a cause.

The problem, why unofficial strikes occur, has led to a great deal of speculation in postwar Britain. Most of the universal explanations advanced—communist agitation or the remoteness of the

Table 1. NUMBER OF STRIKES, ETC., 1933–1954.

Year	*Number of Strikes**	*Number of Workers Involved† 000's*	*Working Days Lost† 000's*
1933	357	138	1,072
1934	471	134	959
1935	553	279	1,955
1936	818	322	1,829
1937	1,129	610	3,413
1938	875	275	1,334
1939	940	337	1,356
1940	922	299	940
1941	1,251	361	1,079
1942	1,303	457	1,527
1943	1,785	559	1,808
1944	2,194	826	3,714
1945	2,293	532	2,835
1946	2,205	529	2,158
1947	1,721	623	2,433
1948	1,759	426	1,944
1949	1,426	434	1,807
1950	1,339	303	1,389
1951	1,719	379	1,694
1952	1,714	416	1,792
1953	1,746	1,374	2,184
1954	1,989	450	2,457

Source: Ministry of Labour Gazette, May 1955.
*Beginning during the year.
†In stoppages in progress during the year.

leadership from the rank and file in large unions—only serve to grind the political axe of their exponents. To some extent, unofficial strikes are an inevitable consequence of the trend toward national regulation. When large organizations are involved in the making of collective bargains, as is frequently the case today, serious grievances affecting a small minority of their members may be overlooked or dealt with too tardily. In such circumstances, an outburst of protest, though contrary to the rules, may be far less costly in the long run—if measured only in economic terms—than smoldering resentment, which can impede production in many less obvious ways.

Any systematic investigation of the problem would have to start

Table 2. Industrial Concentration of Strikes, 1934–1951.

	Mining and Quarrying	*Metal, Engineering and Shipbuilding*	*Transport*	*All Other Industries*
Number of strikes				
1934–1939........	1,934	841	266	1,745
1940–1945........	4,879	2,990	451	1,428
1946–1951........	6,336	2,002	579	1,252
Working days lost (1,000)				
1934–1939........	5,541	1,812	1,056	2,437
1940–1945........	5,736	3,456	1,859	852
1946–1951........	3,349	3,562	2,459	2,055
Percentage of total labor force employed in each group of industries (May 1950)..	4	18	7	71

Source: Ministry of Labour Gazette, May issues throughout the period, and February 1951, for distribution of employees. The adoption of the Standard Industrial Classification in 1949 does not materially affect the table.

from the fact that some industries are far more "strike prone" than others, and consistently so, as can be seen from Table 2.

The industrial breakdown is not a very detailed one. From 1949 onward the Ministry of Labour adopted the new Standard Industrial Classification for strike statistics and more information is now provided. It may be added, however, that throughout the whole period the vast majority of the strikes under mining and quarrying were in coal mining; while under the metal group, iron and steel and, under transport, railways were relatively strike free. The big increase in the number of working days lost in transport during the postwar years was due to the unofficial dock strikes, which led on two occasions to the Government making use of its Emergency Powers and employing troops to deal with perishable cargoes. Coal mining, engineering and shipbuilding, docks and road transport appear to have been the main centers of unofficial strike activity. Why this is so can, in the present state of our knowledge, only be a subject for conjecture.

If strikes are taken to be negative results of collective bargaining, then wage changes must be regarded as among its main positive

Table 3. MOVEMENT OF WAGES, ETC., 1933–1954.

	Wage Rates	Earnings	Cost of Living		Unemployment
	(Bowley index)	(Weekly)	Old index	Improved index	% insured industrial population (U.K.)
1933.........	90	—	90	—	19.9
1934.........	90	—	90	—	16.7
1935.........	91	—	92	—	15.5
1936.........	93	—	94	—	13.1
1937.........	97	—	99	—	10.8
1938.........	100	100(Oct.)	100	100	12.9
1939.........	101	—	101	103	16.6
1940.........	112	130(July)	118	117	9.7
1941.........	122	142(July)	127	129	6.6
1942.........	131	160(July)	128	137	2.4
1943.........	137	176(July)	127	142	0.8
1944.........	144	182(July)	129	145	0.7
1945.........	151	180(July)	130	148	1.2
1946.........	163	190(Oct.)	—	154	2.5
1947.........	169	203(Oct.)	—	163	3.1
1948.........	177	220(Oct.)	—	175	1.8
1949.........	182	229(Oct.)	—	180	1.6
1950.........	186	240(Oct.)	—	185	1.5
1951.........	201	265(Oct.)	—	203	1.2
1952.........	218	285(Oct.)	—	221	2.1
1953.........	228	301(Oct.)	—	228	1.8
1954.........	238	323(Oct.)	—	232	1.5

Source: London and Cambridge Bulletin, The Times Review of Industry, September 1955, 1. xiv; and *Ministry of Labour Gazette,* March 1955 and earlier issues.

results. The general movement of wages since 1933, compared with changes in the cost of living and the proportion of working population registered as unemployed, is shown in Table 3.

Throughout the period wage rates have been rising steadily and actual earnings, for various reasons, more rapidly than rates. At the same time the cost of living has been going up as fast as rates, so that the increase in the average level of real wages has not been substantial.

During the early years of the war the rise in the cost of living was one of the main arguments advanced by the trade unions in claiming increased wage rates, but in the average wages were soon rising more rapidly than the old index, that is, than the extent provided for under cost-of-living, sliding-scale agreements at that time, although they fell slightly behind the actual rise in retail prices as measured by an improved index. In the postwar years the movement of the wage-rate index for a time forged ahead of that of the cost-of-living index. In 1945 the loss in earnings, resulting from decreased overtime and other factors, developed a strong and effective trade union pressure for compensatory increases in wage rates. Thus the upward movement of wages in the full employment years, especially in the period 1945–1948, cannot be explained solely as a result of the rising cost of living.

The general movement of wages, as reflected in the indices quoted, does not represent an even increase in wage incomes all round. On the contrary, in the full employment period wage movements have varied a great deal in the different occupations and industries; it would be no exaggeration to speak of a gradual revolution in the national wage structure. This will be seen from Table 4.

We also know that in the same period the wage rates of unskilled workers have risen more than those of skilled workers; that the earnings of women have risen more than those of men, and of juveniles more than adults; that salaries have risen less than wages, and least of all in higher ranges.[33]

A possible explanation for this levelling shift in wage structure is suggested by a priori reasoning. In the days of mass unemployment most wage earners were compelled to stay in whatever jobs they had for fear of losing a job altogether. In these conditions it was possible for some of the more arduous and less pleasant occupations to remain among the worst paid. Wages varied according to ease of entry into the occupation, the prosperity of the industry, and the degree of organization among the workers. The greater freedom which full employment has given wage earners in their choice of a job has changed this state of affairs. Over the years it has become increasingly necessary to compensate for the dissatisfactions attached to a particular occupation by a correspondingly

[33]See K. G. J. C. Knowles and D. J. Robertson, "Differences between the Wages of Skilled and Unskilled Workers," *Bulletin of the Oxford University Institute of Statistics,* April 1951, and Dudley Seers "The Leveling of Incomes," *ibid.,* October 1950.

Table 4. AVERAGE HOURLY EARNINGS IN THE UNITED KINGDOM, 1938–1950.
(All classes of workers)

	% Increases Oct. 1938– April 1948	*% Increases Oct. 1948– Oct. 1950*
Pottery (p)	153	10
Chemicals and Allied Trades	120	8
Pig-iron (Blast Furnaces) (p)	85	7
Iron and Steel Melting, Rolling, etc. (p)	97	7
Tinplate (p)	74	8
Iron and Steel Tubes (p)	113	8
Wire and Wire Manufactures (p)	126	9
Motor Vehicles and Aircraft (including Components and Repairs)	108	6
Bolts, Nuts, Screws, etc.	164	6
Shipbuilding and Ship Repairing	123	1
Textiles (average)	150	13
Cotton (p)	177	12
Wool (p)	143	12
Rayon, Nylon, etc. (p)	116	15
Linen, etc. (p)	140	14
Hemp, Rope, etc.	167	12
Jute (p)	131	16
Textile Finishing (p)	123	12
Lace (p)	105	12
Leather, Leather Goods, and Fur	141	7
Clothing	130	8
Food, Drink, and Tobacco	123	8
Manufactures of Wood	127	10
Printing, Publishing, etc. (p)	90	8
Rubber	152	6
Building, Contracting, etc.	96	10
Electricity, Gas, and Water	100	6
Local Authorities (Nonindustrial)	85	4
Average for Industries Covered by Ministry of Labour Inquiry	120	6
Coal (Average for all Workers per Manshift Worked)	179	7
Agriculture (Male Workers: Weekly)	165	11

Source: The British Economy 1945–1950, pp. 242–243.

Notes: The estimates of changes in hourly earnings are based on half-yearly data collected by the Ministry of Labour, but not all the industries covered by these inquiries are represented separately in the table. In 1948 the basis of the statistics

greater remuneration. The existence of undermanned industries in postwar Britain, notably coal mining and agriculture, has been part of the visible evidence of the change.

It has been argued that what Lord Beveridge in his *Full Employment in a Free Society* called the "competitive sectional" character of collective bargaining tends to obstruct these necessary adjustments. Unions have lived by securing wage advances and the prestige of union officials still depends, at least in part, on their capacity to obtain greater or earlier advances than their competitors. Where any one union is in a strong position, for whatever reasons, to force up the wages of its members, its example is likely to be followed by other unions seeking to maintain the customary wage relationship. This makes a wage increase given at any one point in the system spread throughout until it becomes general, thus discouraging the movement of workers into those industries or occupations where they are most needed and intensifying the danger of the vicious spiral of wages and prices.

The shifts in wage structure under full employment in Great Britain appear to invalidate this argument. Certainly they are evidence that trade unions do not bring as complete a rigidity into wage relationships and the labor market as has frequently been suggested. But the effect of maintaining compulsory arbitration throughout the period, after its introduction in 1940, must be taken into account. The trade unions have been restrained, with their collective consent, from using their bargaining power to the full. They have of necessity resorted to arbitration to a far greater extent than in any previous period, and the various arbitration tribunals, although not subject to government direction, have

---

was modified and the New Series, starting with October 1948, is not strictly comparable with the old. Coal and agriculture were never covered by the inquiry. The postwar figures for agriculture are legal minimum weekly wages; in view of the new regulations about hours, overtime, and holidays, these figures understate the improvement.

Within the group of manufacturing industries, those followed by (p) had first preference for additional manpower in 1948.

The figures are averages for all workers (except in agriculture) and may therefore be affected by changes in the proportion of skilled to unskilled workers, by changes in the respective rates of pay of skilled and unskilled, and by changes in the proportions in which men, women, and juveniles are employed and in their respective rates of pay.

L1 Nw

naturally given more weight to the national consequences of their awards than any particular group of employers and trade unions would be likely to do in arriving at a wage settlement.

Whatever theoretical conclusions can be drawn from British postwar experience on the working of collective bargaining under full employment, there can be no doubt that by 1948 the Labour Government was convinced that it had an obligation to restrain wage increases if its economic policy for restoring national solvency was to succeed. The method it adopted and the results must now be described.

The White Paper and Wage Restraint

During the war the Coalition Government, strongly influenced by Mr. Bevin, as Minister of Labour, had eschewed any policy of direct control of wages.[34] Instead it relied on the introduction of compulsory arbitration, the pegging of the old and very imperfect wage earners' cost-of-living index by food subsidies, and the good sense and moderation of the trade unions. In June 1941 it issued a *White Paper on Price Stabilization and Industrial Policy (Cmd. 6294)* which emphasized the need for minimizing wage increases, but on the insistence of the TUC General Council amendments had been made to an original draft so that it would not appear to be a plea for a "wage freeze." Wages, as we have seen, continued to rise but not at a rate which seriously disrupted the war economy.

By the latter half of 1947 the wartime policy appeared to be breaking down. The new interim index of retail prices adopted in June of that year was providing a truer reflection of the changes in the cost of living. Wage increases which were considered essential in the undermanned industries—and had been encouraged by the Government—were stimulating fresh claims elsewhere. Trade unions were inclined to take the view that now that the war was over restraint was no longer necessary, and many employers were willing

[34] "Freedom of opportunity to make claims and to have them discussed, said Mr. Bevin, was essential to industrial peace; it would, moreover, be a dangerous thing if the Government made the independence of statutory wage-fixing and arbitration bodies suspect by offering them 'guidance.'" W. K. Hancock and M. M. Gowing, *British War Economy. History of Second World War* (London: H.M. Stationery Off., 1949), p. 338.

to increase wages in order to hold or attract labor. This was the situation which led the Labour Government to publish its statement on *Personal Incomes, Costs and Prices (Cmd. 7321)* in February 1948. It was a bold move, a radical departure from tradition, even from the more recent tradition of previous consultation in these matters with the TUC.

The White Paper recognized that it was not desirable for the Government "to interfere directly with the income of individuals otherwise than by taxation," but it put forward certain principles with the request that "all those engaged in negotiations or decisions which might result in an increase in wages or other personal incomes" adhere to them. There was, it said, "no justification for any *general* increase of individual money incomes" which would "merely raise costs of production, without making more goods available." It did not follow from this, however, that:

> it would be right to stabilise all incomes as they stand today. There may well be cases in which increases in wages or salaries would be justified from a national point of view, for example where it is essential in the national interest to man up a particular undermanned industry and it is clear that only an increase in wages will attract the necessary labor. It does, however, follow that each claim for an increase in wages or salaries must be considered on its national merits and not on the basis of maintaining a former relativity between different occupations and industries.

It is further conceded that "if at some future time there should be a marked rise in the cost of living the level of those personal incomes which as a result became inadequate would need reconsideration." The Government pledged itself to follow these principles in its own negotiations, hoping this would serve as an example to others, and beyond this proposed no sanctions to enforce its policy other than the threat to use its powers of price control to prevent the passing on to the consumer of wage changes which could not be justified in terms of the White Paper.

The Trades Union Congress lodged an immediate protest with the Prime Minister "against this departure from the established practice of prior consultation.[35] Within a week the Prime Minister

[35] Trades Union Congress, *A Policy for Real Wages,* p. 11.

and four other interested Ministers met with a subcommittee of the General Council. Out of this meeting a compromise emerged whereby the General Council agreed to support the Government providing it was allowed to make substantial modifications in the proposed policy. In addition they were granted the concession of a dividend limitation policy. At the conference of trade union executives, called by the TUC to consider the White Paper, the resolution passed by a substantial majority formulated five conditions on which the principles of the document could be regarded as acceptable to the trade union movement. Three of them did not differ greatly from the terms or spirit of the White Paper, but the other two, admitting the need for wage increases for "workers whose incomes are below a reasonable standard of subsistence" or "to safeguard those wage differentials which are an essential element in the wages structure of many important industries," provided big enough loopholes to justify any claims as being in the national interest.

Although the White Paper may be regarded as an extremely tentative and ambiguous statement of a positive and flexible wage policy, this effort foundered on the rock of trade union opposition and was abandoned. What it achieved in practice by its "shock tactic" was to persuade a large part of the trade union leadership of the necessity for voluntary restraint. They had collectively only pledged themselves to restrict wage claims to those which were compatible with the terms of their own declaration. In fact many of them went a good deal further and tried—for a time successfully—to hold back all claims.

The policy of "wage restraint" had some interesting results, worth recalling for the light they throw on the difficulties inherent in such an experiment. The White Paper had advanced the view that "it is essential that there should be the strictest adherence to the terms of collective agreements" on the grounds that one of the main advantages of collective bargaining was that "it tends to ensure that wage and salary movements take place in an orderly manner and with due regard to the general as distinct from the individual interest." One consequence of "wage restraint" was to encourage wage increases outside of the terms of national agreements. In the printing trades they took the form of "merit money," which in some districts became so universal as to lose anything of its original significance. In engineering, to take another example, production bonuses and other increases in payment by results became "veiled" wage increases to attract labor, rather than to provide an incentive to increase output.

If "wage restraint" tended to undermine national agreements it became no less of a threat to the internal authority of trade union executives. The restraint was largely imposed from above and met with relatively little understanding on the part of rank-and-file trade unionists. This came out most clearly when, after the devaluation of the currency and in response to appeals from the Chancellor of the Exchequer, Sir Stafford Cripps, the TUC General Council recommended what amounted to a wage standstill until the end of 1950. The conference of trade union executives in January 1950 called to consider this recommendation approved it by so small a majority that it clearly could not be put into effect. Prior to the conference the miners had held a ballot which, by 518,000 votes to 147,000, reversed the decisions of their union executive to support the General Council's recommendation. When the season of union annual conferences began at Easter, the distributive workers rejected the advice of the executive to support the policy, and a number of others followed suit.

The fear that government leadership might influence the awards made by arbitration tribunals—although there is no conclusive evidence to show that it did—also led some unions into devious tactics to circumvent compulsory arbitration. The Typographical Association, for example, gave notice to terminate its 30-year-old national agreement with the British Federation of Master Printers and the Newspaper Society, declaring in the accompanying statement that it was withdrawing its wage claim at national level and advising its local chapels and branches to seek corresponding wage advances from individual employers. The Confederation of Shipbuilding and Engineering Unions decided to ballot the members of its affiliated unions on the question whether to resort to strike action to enforce their claim for a £1 a week increase in wages (at a time when such action would, of course, have been illegal) or submit it to the National Arbitration Tribunal. Strike action was in fact rejected by a large majority; even in the case of the Amalgamated Engineering Union, with its traditional antagonism to arbitration, only a quarter of the members who voted were in favor of a strike.

Another outcome of the Government's efforts to curb wage increases was the apprehension among the unions of its own employees that they were being singled out for discriminatory treatment. In March 1950 the Staff Side of the Civil Service National Whitley Council addressed a letter to the Prime Minister complaining against a statement by the Official Side, speaking on government instructions, "that they were not prepared to allow any claims to be discussed which had been made after the end of September (1949)." The letter was moderately worded and offered no challenge to the principles set out in the White Paper, but protested "against the singling out of Civil Servants for a more ruthless standstill on wages than the White Paper demands" and against the "mockery of arbitration" when the Government "enjoins the Tribunal not to exercise their functions impartially on the merits of the case before them, but to reject them all automatically."[36]

This is not the whole of the story of voluntary restraint and its consequences, but it is, perhaps, enough to explain the breakdown of the experiment. After the conference of union executives the TUC General Council had to recognize that they could not face Congress with the "wage freeze" proposal unrevised. In June 1950 they sent out a statement to affiliated unions admitting "that there must be greater flexibility of wage movements in future" and adding that they were "firmly convinced that there is no formula which can be devised as to how this flexibility can operate." Even then they were subsequently defeated at Congress by a narrow majority.

With the return of a Conservative Government after the 1951 General Election, the likelihood of the trade unions returning to a policy of "wage restraint" was slight. And they were still less likely to favor any growth of government influence over wage determina-

[36]*Whitley Bulletin,* April 1950, pp. 52 ff.

tion. A Court of Inquiry into disputes in the engineering and shipbuilding industries, which reported in 1954,[37] made an unusual recommendation. Having pointed out that some of the issues raised by the wage claims before it were part of much wider problems affecting the national economy as a whole, it went on to suggest the appointment of an "authoritative and impartial body" to consider such problems. What precisely was to be the purpose of such a body, even whether it would be permanent or temporary, the Court did not explain. That it should concern itself with more than investigating economic facts and argument was, however, implied by the remark that it could "give advice and guidance as to broad policy and possible action." The Minister of Labour put the recommendation to his National Joint Advisory Council, on which the trade unions and employers are represented, but the TUC emphatically rejected it.

The TUC General Council in their periodic statements on the economic situation have, it is true, continued to call attention to the dangers of the wage-price spiral. Congress, too, has rejected Communist-inspired resolutions calling for the abandonment of all restraint and support for every wage demand. Now, even this cautious policy is fading after the Autumn Budget of the Conservative Government in 1955. Support for it had come particularly from the two general unions. The attitude of the larger, the Transport and General Workers' Union, was made plain by its acting General Secretary in January 1956: "To re-state our position as a union in a single sentence—we are not prepared that our members should stand still while the Government continually hand out largesse to those who are more favourably placed."[38]

The recent history of collective bargaining in postwar Britain is, perhaps, most remarkable for its lack of innovations. The traditional pattern has been extended— although this took place mainly during and immediately after the war—but it remains substantially the same in form and content. The experiment in voluntary restraint initiated by the 1948 White Paper, although a bold departure from tradition, had no permanent effects and, certainly,

[37]Cmd. 9084.
[38]*Times,* Jan. 5, 1956.

provided no satisfactory solution to the problems for which it was designed. The American observer is always impressed by the maturity of collective bargaining relations in Great Britain, and this is undoubtedly rooted in a strict adherence to the "voluntary principle." Yet maturity is not an unmixed blessing. To those who see it close at hand it sometimes looks very much like stagnation. A less pessimistic view—and one that the writer holds—is that change itself takes longer to mature.

II

Trade Unionism and Wage Policy in Norway since the War[1]

J. INMAN

EXPERIENCE in recent years has made it increasingly clear that the determination of wages is greatly affected by the framework of institutions through which industrial relations are carried on, as well as by the extent to which the various individuals and organizations concerned have clearly defined and well worked-out lines of policy. This is certainly true of Norway, where deliberate planning has played a large part in the structure of employers' and workers' organizations alike, as well as in their recent policy and that of the Government.

Machinery for collective bargaining and wage negotiation is highly centralized in Norway. The main historical reason for this appears to be that in the early days of the trade union movement, at the beginning of this century, leadership devolved largely upon the Federation of Trade Unions (the equivalent of the TUC), since only in this way could the scattered individual trade union organizations of that period bring their influence to bear. The Federation thus gained an ascendancy which it has never lost, and its authority

[1]The author is indebted to the editor of the *Bulletin of the Oxford University Institute of Statistics* for permission to reprint parts of this chapter which have already appeared in Vol. 12, 1950, of the Bulletin.

over the unions affiliated with it has since grown rather than diminished. As a counterweight to the Federation of Trade Unions, the employers also set up a central organization which has if anything greater authority over its affiliated associations for individual industries than has the Federation over its affiliated unions.

At the end of 1949 the Federation had thirty-nine affiliated unions with a total membership of 473,000; at the end of 1955 there were forty-three affiliated unions with a total membership of 540,000. The number of potential union members in Norway at the latter date was about seven hundred thousand, so the percentage of union organization is very high. It approaches 100 percent in many important industries.[2]

The trade unions are by far the strongest nonofficial organization in the country, and through their close cooperation with the Government, their widely spread membership, and their effective organization, they have a very great influence on policy. In 1923 the Federation decided that its general form of organization should be industrial unionism. This has gradually been extended, so that today between 85 and 90 percent of trade union members are organized by industry. Only a small number of craft unions remain. The prevalence of organization by industry makes membership demarcation lines clear, and interunion disputes comparatively rare; in the settlement of such disputes, the Federation has power to make binding decisions. Of the affiliated unions, three—the Iron and Metal Workers, the Building Workers, and the Municipal Workers—have over fifty-thousand members; one—the Seamen's Union—between forty- and fifty-thousand; six between twenty- and forty-thousand; and the rest less than twenty-thousand. Thus no one union, or small group of unions, is powerful enough to dominate the movement.

The growth of trade unionism was especially rapid in the thirties, when it came to include many office workers and civil servants, who had not been previously organized; and organization extended rapidly among workers in seasonal occupations, such as agriculture, forestry, and road maintenance. The membership of

[2]The population of Norway was approximately 3,400,000 at the end of 1954.

unions affiliated with the Federation grew from 114,000 in 1929 to 356,000 in 1939.

Politically, there is a close association between the trade unions and the Labor party, which has carried the responsibilities of government since 1935. All of the leading members of the trade unions are members of the Labor party, and there is a permanent joint committee (which includes the chairmen of both organizations) for cooperation between the Labor party and the Federation.[3] Communist influence in the unions has been rapidly diminishing and is now slight.

The Secretariat of the Federation is elected by its Congress every fourth year; it consists of fifteen persons, of whom four—the chairman, vice-chairman, secretary, and treasurer—are full-time officials, and the remainder normally chairmen of individual unions who hold both posts. They are divided as far as possible among the principal trades, and it is a rule that not more than two of them are to come from any one union.[4] There is also a Representative Council of 124 members which meets as required between Congresses and serves as an important link between the Federation and the membership. The Council is the supreme authority of the Federation between Congresses, and the Secretariat's policy in regard to wages and working conditions must receive its sanction.

The Federation is thus organized as a body, with a large measure of independence, which can provide leadership for the trade union movement as a whole, and its wide powers and authority in relation to the individual unions have enabled it to determine common policies for the movement on most important issues. It is usual for the individual unions to consult with the Secretariat on policy regarding wages, working conditions, the steps to be taken in disputes, and other important matters, and for the Secretariat to give them advice as to their line of action. If a dispute with employers is likely to involve more than one union, or if any union wants economic support from the Federation, it must obtain prior approval from the Secretariat before the dispute is entered on, and

[3]The Federation is not affiliated with the Labor party, but trade union branches can affiliate with local Labor party branches and such affiliation is common, though by no means universal.

[4]The chairman is the chief executive officer of the union.

the Secretariat can take over the leadership of the dispute in co-operation with the unions concerned. Individual unions may not engage in stoppages of work before negotiation has been tried, nor in conflict with current agreements. The Federation has considerable funds at its disposal, derived from the affiliation fees paid by the individual unions, which can be used for strike benefits, though individual unions have their own strike funds as well.

The Employers' Association includes firms employing about half the workers in the most important industries—generally speaking, the larger firms. Certain important groups of employers, such as those in the paper industry, the forest owners, and the tramp shipping owners, have independent associations. The Employers' Association comprises eighteen national industrial groups which have their own executive organs. Members of the Association must not negotiate agreements with union representatives directly, but only through the Central Executive of the Association or their national groups, and in the latter case local negotiations regarding existing or new agreements must not take place without the consent of the Central Executive. All dealings with the Federation of Trade Unions must take place through the Central Executive. Members undertake to observe the Central Executive's decisions or decisions of a national group, approved by the Central Executive, which has a predominant voice in deciding whether agreements are to be entered into or terminated and what procedure is to be followed by members of the Association in case of strikes. Fines can be levied on members who do not keep to the decisions of the Central Executive. The Association gives members financial support in case of strikes or lockouts approved by the Central Executive, to an amount sufficient to cover factory maintenance expenses.

For many years the Federation of Trade Unions and the Employers' Association have taken a leading part in regard to disputes and negotiations in the major industries, though they have left more secondary matters to be settled between the representatives of the industries concerned. As agreements concluded with firms in the Employers' Association have often been extended to firms outside it, its influence has been wider than its membership. Norway's industrial history was stormy until about 1935, but since then relations have steadily improved and can now be described as good. Disputes regarding trade union recognition are virtually unknown, while the trade unions are prepared to accept the contention of the employers that managerial and administrative decisions must, in the last resort, be made solely by them, even though there may be prior consultation with employees.

There is in Norway no special trade union law, and there have never been any restrictions on freedom of association, so long as the objects of the association concerned are legal. Similarly, strikes have been legal, though of course they must not be accompanied by illegal actions, for example, violence. There is a statutory Labor Court which can give binding decisions on the interpretation of industrial agreements, so that strikes on this issue are illegal. There is also compulsory mediation—a State Mediator must intervene and make a recommendation before a strike can take place. Under normal circumstances both employers and trade unions are opposed to compulsory arbitration, but by an agreement made in Stockholm in 1944 between the Employers' Association and the Federation of Trade Unions, and subsequently given legal force, it was decided that, in the disturbed circumstances which were expected to follow the war, there should be a Wages Board (with representatives of the employers, the trade unions, and the State, the last-named having a majority),[5] which should have power to make binding decisions regarding wages if agreed settlements could not be reached. Thus no authorized strikes or lockouts could take place, though direct government control of wages has been avoided. The authority of the Wages Board was subsequently extended to cover working conditions as well as wages. Under the same agreement, affiliated organizations were to submit all requests for changes in wages (and subsequently working conditions as well) to the Employers' Association or the Federation of Trade Unions, which, together with the affiliated organizations interested, was to negotiate regarding them.

Complete control over all wage negotiations was thus given to the two central organizations; the more so as, after such negotia-

[5]The Board had seven members: three State representatives, all with separate votes; two employers' and two workers' representatives, with only one vote between two.

tions had resulted in a collective agreement, its terms were to be legally binding not only on their affiliated organizations but also on nonmembers. This last provision was removed in June 1946 because the trade unions, especially in the building trades, objected to the attempts of the Employers' Association to prevent unorganized employers granting terms more favorable to the workers than those in the recognized agreements. The Federation tried to persuade unions not to conclude such agreements but met with limited success. In September 1947 a wage stop law was introduced, though it was found politically impracticable to extend it beyond the end of the year. At the end of 1947 the 1944 agreement was modified by legislation so as to prevent employers' associations or trade unions not affiliated with the central organizations from terminating agreements without permission of the Ministry of Labour, and also to give legal backing to the authority in this respect of the central organizations over their own affiliates. Thus strong central control over the making of agreements was maintained in a slightly different form.[6]

In February 1949 the powers of the Wages Board were considerably reduced; compulsory arbitration was in future only to be applied to claims for changes in wages and working conditions not approved, or only partly approved, by the Federation of Trade Unions or the principal employers' associations. There has therefore been a partial return to free negotiation. The trade unions felt that to restore greater reality to collective bargaining would help them to maintain their authority over their members, and the increased stability of economic conditions appeared to justify the step which was also favored by the employers. Under the new arrangements official strikes have of course been legal in certain circumstances, and a few small stoppages have taken place.

In June 1949 changes were made in the rules of the Trade Union Federation, giving it greater authority over its affiliated organizations. The new rules appear to give a constitutional expression to what has in fact been the practice since 1945: no union can put forward claims for a new agreement, terminate an existing

[6]See Walter Galenson, *Labor in Norway* (Cambridge: Harvard University Press, 1949), pp. 277–288, for a full account of the legislation regarding the Wages Board in the period up to 1949.

agreement, or enter upon a strike, without the prior approval of the Secretariat, and if negotiations which are being carried on by the union concerned do not lead to a settlement, the Secretariat can take over their conduct. Under the revised system, therefore, the central organizations continue to have practically complete control over policy in regard to wages and working conditions and only if there is a breakdown in their discipline over their affiliates, or in the case of unresolved claims by unaffiliated organizations, is compulsory arbitration used.

These arrangements appear to have worked satisfactorily, on the whole, and agreements have generally been modified without a breakdown in negotiations, but special Wages Boards with compulsory powers had to be appointed by the Government in 1949 to avoid a conflict in one of the chief export industries (fish canning), and in December 1950 when the Trade Union Federation and the Employers' Association could not reach agreement regarding a general cost-of-living bonus. In 1949 an important decision by the Labor Court confirmed the powers of the Wages Board to require agreements with unorganized employers (specifically in the building trades) not to grant better terms than are contained in agreements with employers who belong to the Employers' Association. As from the beginning of 1953 a further change has been made; there is now to be voluntary recourse to the Wages Board, at the request of the parties, if conciliation has proved unsuccessful.

Through the Trade Union Federation and the Employers' Association, therefore, with the assistance of state mediation and arbitration, a fairly extensive degree of control has been exercised over wage movements, though general economic conditions have of course continued to have a great deal of influence. The Norwegian economic system as a whole has also been subject to a large measure of planning during the postwar period. There has been rigorous control over prices, both wholesale and retail, with the object, up to the early part of 1950, of keeping them stable and subsequently of checking their increase as far as possible; not until and only in 1954 was this control somewhat relaxed. Dividends have been limited to 5 percent per annum, except in special circumstances and with the permission of the price control administration, and export levies have checked undue profits from high export prices. Until 1955 interest rates were kept down to 2½ percent. There has also been licensing of imports and rationing of scarce raw materials, though since 1950 these controls have been gradually relinquished. Until the spring of 1950 the main foodstuffs were heavily subsidized, but since that date subsidies have been reduced by stages. Economic policy has been directed to the carrying out of a large program of reconstruction to replace the 25 percent of the national wealth estimated to have been lost during the war and to expand industry so as to make possible a satisfactory international trade position and an improvement in the standard of life. Capital investment has therefore been extremely heavy, amounting to between 20 and 25 percent of the net national income in each postwar year. In these circumstances there has been a great demand for labor; registered unemployment has been about 1 percent most of the time, rarely as much as 2 percent. There has not, however, been any government control of the movement of labor, except for a law of 1947 which requires that official permission be obtained for the employment of more than three building workers. The law also states that they must not be paid more than the rates specified in the recognized agreements. The object of this law has been to check the excessive demand for building labor and unduly high rates of wages in building.

Wage Policy until 1949

In Norway, as in other countries, movements of the cost of living have always played a very important part in negotiations regarding wage levels, and since the beginning of the war in Europe in September 1939 the trade unions have sought to have the movements of all wages linked in one way or another to the cost-of-living index. The other main endeavour in Norwegian wage policy has been to raise the standards of the less well-off sections of the community. This also has its origins in the years before the war and has been the concern not only of the trade unions, but of the labor movement as a whole, which, from the beginning of the Labor party's period in office in 1935, has sought to bring the depressed sections—farmers, fishermen, and workers in the older export trades, such as fish canning and the paper and pulp industry, where the standard of equipment is not high—up to the average level. On the trade union side, this has found expression in the form of a unified wage policy to be pursued by the movement as a whole, the unions to concentrate on securing better conditions for under-paid groups of workers, rather than on supporting the claims of the better-paid groups for further improvements. Since the war this policy has come to be fully accepted by the trade union movement, the Government, and persons connected with industrial life generally.

In January 1940 an agreement was reached between the Federation and the Employers' Association that there should be a flat increase in all wage rates, equivalent to an increase in the average wage for adult men proportionate to the increase in the cost of living from September to December 1939; that subsequently wage rates should be adjusted at quarterly intervals; but that increases proportionate to only three quarters of the increase in the cost of living should be given, in order that wage earners should bear some of the burdens of the conditions brought about by the war. In fact, only one of these latter increases came into effect, in April 1940, and the Germans subsequently introduced a wage stop. During the occupation some wages were increased, particularly in occupations such as engineering and public works to which the Germans wanted to attract labor, but these increases were never recognized by the legitimate Norwegian authorities, or by the trade unions, which in any case lost their freedom of action after the first year of the German occupation.

Under an agreement made in Stockholm in 1944, an increase of 30 öre[7] an hour for men and 20 öre for women was given on all wage rates from the date of the liberation, May 8th, 1945, and a further increase of 20 öre an hour for men and 14 öre for women was awarded by the Wages Board in September 1945. It was estimated that, together with the wage increase which had taken place

[7]100 öre = 1 krone = 1 English shilling. The exchange value of the krone was approximately 24½ U. S. cents in 1938 and 20 cents from 1945 to September 1949. Since September 1949 it has been 14 cents.

unofficially during the war years, this would mean that three quarters of the increase in the cost of living was covered. In other respects agreements existing at the time of the German attack in April 1940 were to be regarded as valid, except that it was not provided that wage rates should rise automatically if the cost of living increased, though if the cost-of-living index rose by 5 points negotiations on wages were to take place between the employers and trade unions. The index did not, in fact, rise to this extent until 1950.

The tendency of these flat-rate increases was to improve the position of the lower paid workers, relatively both to those in better paying industries and to better paid groups within industries; and this tendency was strengthened by a further award by the Wages Board in the autumn of 1945, giving moderate increases to workers receiving less than 1.50 kr. an hour. When a comprehensive revision of agreements in individual industries took place in 1946, the lower wage rates were raised and proportionately larger wage increases were made in low-paying industries—though these increases were not as a rule sufficient to cause workers in them to achieve full parity with the better paying industries. The higher rates of pay were not directly affected by these agreements.

In 1946 also the Federation of Trade Unions made a claim that full, instead of three quarters, compensation should be given for the increase in the cost of living. The Employers' Association strongly resisted on the ground that full compensation could not be afforded at the existing rate of industrial production, and statements by leading members of the Government indicated that they did not believe that at that period the full prewar standard of living could be restored.[8] In June, however, the Wages Board decided that the increase sought by the Federation should be granted, but in three installments of 5 öre an hour each on all wages in September 1946, March and September 1947, respectively. The principle of full compensation for increases in the cost of living was also approved for the future; for each five points by which the cost-of-living index rose or fell, for the months of February and August in any year, above or below the figure of 155.8 (1938–100) at which

[8]See Galenson, *op. cit.*, pp. 291–292.

it stood in July 1945, there should be an automatic increase or decrease in all wages of 1.5 öre an hour for each point. (The cost of living did not, in fact, rise so as to bring this arrangement into effect during the period 1945–1949).

Since 1946 the Federation of Trade Unions, while it has been concerned to gain benefits for its members as far as possible, has had continually to bear in mind the need to avoid such wage pressure as would be incompatible with the Government's policy of stabilization and would thus tend to bring about an inflationary price-wage spiral. The agreements made in 1946 were to run for two years, and only a few changes in industrial tariffs took place in 1947. In 1948, in order to maintain the policy of stabilization, the Federation decided that agreements should be prolonged for another year, except for those in industries with very low wage rates (for example, the paper industry, whose workers all received a 10 öre an hour increase under a new agreement). It was also agreed with the Employers' Association that an increase of not more than 10 öre an hour should be given to male workers receiving less than 2.50 kr. an hour (2.60 kr. in Oslo) and to female workers receiving less than 1.60 kr. an hour (1.70 kr. in Oslo) up to these amounts. The increase was only to be given where piecework amounted to less than 25 percent of total earnings.

In 1949 the same trend continued. In two of the low-paid industries, paper and canning, the Wages Board awarded general increases in hourly rates for both men and women: 5 öre for all workers, in the former; 10 öre for ordinary and 15 öre for skilled workers, in the latter. In certain other industries moderate increases were given, and the process begun in 1948, of improving the pay of civil servants according to a new scale, was continued. Most of the new agreements were to run for two years. Finally, by agreement between the Employers' Association and the Trade Union Federation, all male workers with average hourly earnings of less than 2.65 kr. (2.75 kr. in Oslo) and all female workers with less than 1.70 kr. (1.80 kr. in Oslo) received up to 10 öre an hour, and at least 5 öre an hour, to reach these earnings. This did not apply to pieceworkers.

In addition, in the years from 1945 to 1952, the Wages Board made several awards substantially raising wages in forestry and agriculture, which before the war were the occupations in which workers' standards were lowest. They were included in the national unemployment insurance scheme for the first time in 1948. The Wages Board also made awards shortening weekly summer hours in agriculture from 55 to 51 in 1947, and in 1948 (effective 1949) to 48; winter hours have been 48 weekly throughout. In 1946 the Government introduced allowances of 4 kr. weekly for all children other than the first. Since 1947 there has been a statutory three weeks' annual paid holiday period.

The great majority of agreements on wages and working conditions since the war have been reached by negotiation between unions and employers—often with the participation of the Federation of Trade Unions and the Employers' Association in the case of the more important agreements, and in a fair number of instances with the assistance of the State Mediator. Only in a small proportion of cases has it been necessary to have recourse to compulsory arbitration by the Wages Board, but these have included many of the crucial decisions involving substantial rises in the standard of living—for instance, the general increases granted in 1945 and 1946,[9] and the raising of wages which took place step by step especially in the early postwar years in such low-paying industries as paper, canning, agriculture, forestry, and a number of other less important trades, in all of which there was strenuous opposition from the employers.[10]

The Wages Board has generally awarded a wage somewhere between what the employers offered and the unions claimed, though it has if anything been sympathetic toward the workers and has taken into account the Government's policy of raising unduly low standards and the need to maintain the labor force in low-paying occupations as well as the economic position of the employers, and of the country generally, at the time. It has thus played an extremely important part in bringing about equalization of wages among occupations, a main objective of postwar wage policy.

[9]And subsequently, by a special Wages Board appointed by the Government in 1951.

[10]Norway has never had statutory regulation of wages in low-paying or unorganized industries.

Though it may be said that economic forces—in particular, the shortage of labor—would have brought this about in any case, the intervention of the Wages Board speeded up the process and helped to prevent an interruption of production through failure to recruit young workers. In agriculture, however, where most of the employers and workers are unorganized, the shortage of workers has been such that the wages actually paid have tended to be above the rates laid down by the Wages Board.

While the Board has had power to make decisions on any matter concerning wages or working conditions and has, in fact, had to do so on a large number of not very important questions, it cannot be said to have been the instrument of any large change in the wage system or the structure of wages within industries. For the most part, these do not seem to have been altered in any fundamental way, and such changes as have taken place have been achieved by negotiation between both sides of the industry concerned. Piece rates, and rates based on individual skill—which are prevalent, for example, in engineering—have moved up with basic minima, though the relationship between them has not necessarily remained the same. Where, as in a fair number of industries, the wage structure has consisted of a series of recognized rates for different jobs, the flat-rate additions made in the postwar settlements have tended to bring these rates nearer together, but (as will be shown later) this tendency has often been counteracted by changes, largely outside the recognized terms of agreements, made within individual firms.[11]

The Government, the trade unions, and the employers have all been anxious to avoid stoppages. The system of compulsory arbitration was established largely with this end in view. In fact, compulsory arbitration awards have been accepted without much complaint; almost no official strikes have occurred and few unofficial ones, so that the number of working days lost has been much smaller than in prewar years. Except for the Communists, there has not been much opposition within the unions to the policies introduced by the trade union leadership. It would seem that the

[11]Cf. Galenson, *op. cit.,* Chs. 9 and 12, for a lengthy discussion of the wage systems current in Norwegian industry and the awards of the Wages Board.

function of the Wages Board has been, in the main, to bring about results that, in its absence, would probably have been achieved by the strength of the trade unions acting in economic and social circumstances favorable to them, but not without at least some stoppages and a consequent worsening of the industrial atmosphere. The Board has also, to some extent, sheltered the trade union leadership from openly bearing the responsibility for agreements that have not granted all the workers' claims.

Results of Wage Policy until 1949

We may now review the available evidence as to how far Norwegian wage policy succeeded in the period up to 1949 in bringing about a more even distribution of earnings among different categories of workers and in helping to stabilize prices.

In 1949 the total number of employed persons was approximately 860,000. Of these about 300,000 were employed in manufacturing industry, about 110,000 in building and construction, 75,000 in transport and communications, and 100,000 in agriculture and forestry (this figure refers to employees, not to the considerably larger number of small proprietors). The main industrial groups (with their approximate numbers of employees) were: engineering and shipbuilding, 70,000; timber and woodworking, 29,000; food industries, other than canning, 25,000; clothing, including boot and shoe manufacture, 24,000; paper and pulp, 20,000; textiles, 19,000; chemical and electrochemical, 11,000; printing and bookbinding, 10,000; canning, 8,000. The field of women's industrial employment is rather restricted, women workers being found mainly in clothing, 18,000; textiles, 12,000; food, other than canning, 6,500; printing and bookbinding, 4,000; and canning, 4,000. Between 1946 and 1949 the total number of employed persons increased by about 10 percent and the numbers employed in manufacturing by about 25 percent. Expansion in the different industrial groups has taken place at fairly similar rates. Norway has had no substantial problem of industrial readjustment to face, and the policy of raising wages in the lower-paying occupations has been a social rather than an economic one, though it has in fact helped to keep up the supply of labor in these occupations.

Official statistics are available regarding average earnings for adult men and women, respectively, in the principal industrial groups and in certain other occupations. Timework, piecework, and overtime earnings are included; the latter are stated to be of relatively small importance, and to account for not more than 3 percent of total earnings. As already mentioned, except in agriculture, there has been no appreciable reduction of weekly hours worked as compared with before the war. In industry the 48-hour week has remained standard, though with the introduction in 1947 of the three weeks' annual holiday the average number of hours worked per year has been reduced by about 2 percent. Geographical differences in wages are fairly marked, rates in all occupations tending to be relatively higher in the towns and Eastern Norway, and lower in the west, northwest, and country districts generally, but there is no evidence that they have changed substantially since before the war.

Tables 1 and 2 show the movements of average earnings for men and women, respectively.[12] The movements of wages shown in these tables suggest the following conclusions. In regard to men's earnings, with one exception (textiles) the groups whose average earnings were below the level of industry as a whole in 1938 were in 1949 less far below it, and one group (boots and shoes) was above it. Most of the groups above the average level in 1938 retained a roughly similar relationship; two (chemical and unskilled building workers) considerably improved their position; skilled building workers stayed a good deal less above the average than previously, and food workers had fallen below it.

[12](a) Statistics of earnings are based on returns from enterprises which are members of the Employers' Association, employing about 44 percent of all industrial workers, and are regarded by the statistical authorities as adequate to indicate the movement of earnings in the larger industrial groups.

(b) Boot and shoe manufacture is an important subdivision of the clothing industry; canning, though it does not employ a large number of workers, is extremely significant from the point of view of wage policy, since it is almost wholly an export industry in which the wage level has been extremely low. Wage statistics for these industries have therefore been given separately in Tables 1 and 2, although they are also included in larger groups.

Table 1. AVERAGE HOURLY EARNINGS (KRONER): ADULT MEN.

		1938 (3rd quarter)	*1940*	*1945*	*1946*	*1947*	*1948*	*1949 (2nd quarter)*
Building Trades		2.25*	2.32	2.43	2.86	3.20	3.46	3.73
(skilled workers)	%	100.0	103.1	108.0	127.2	142.2	153.8	165.8
(unskilled workers)		1.82*	1.87	2.17	2.72	2.99	3.22	3.73
	%	100.0	102.8	119.2	149.5	164.3	176.9	204.9
Printing and Bookbinding		2.06*	2.18	2.64	3.14	3.36	3.51	3.74
(skilled workers)	%	100.0	105.8	128.1	152.4	163.1	170.4	181.6
(unskilled workers)		1.58*	1.67	2.03	2.31	2.53	2.66	2.87
	%	100.0	105.7	128.4	146.2	160.1	168.4	181.7
Chemical and Electro-		1.70	1.84	2.30	2.72	3.03	3.16	3.54
chemical	%	100.0	108.2	135.3	160.0	178.2	185.9	208.3
Clothing (including		1.65*	1.80	2.28	2.51	2.79	3.01	3.17
Boots and Shoes)	%	100.0	109.1	138.1	152.2	169.0	182.1	192.2
Engineering		1.64	1.77	2.28	2.64	2.86	3.02	3.16
	%	100.0	107.9	139.0	161.0	174.4	184.1	192.7
Food (including Canning)		1.69*	1.79	2.10	2.40	2.57	2.70	2.85
	%	100.0	105.9	124.3	142.0	152.1	159.8	168.6
Industry as a whole		1.63	1.72	2.17	2.52	2.78	2.94	3.11
	%	100.0	105.5	133.1	154.6	170.6	180.4	190.8
Boot and Shoe†		1.58	1.82	2.31	2.52	2.82	3.09	3.27
	%	100.0	115.2	146.2	159.5	176.5	195.6	205.5
Textiles		1.49*	1.56	1.86	2.24	2.53	2.68	2.76
	%	100.0	107.2	124.8	150.3	169.7	179.9	185.2
Paper		1.42	1.54	1.85	2.30	2.59	2.77	2.93
	%	100.0	108.4	130.3	162.0	182.4	195.1	206.4
Canning†		1.30	1.39	1.73	2.09	2.30	2.45	2.55
	%	100.0	106.9	133.1	160.8	176.9	188.5	196.5
Agriculture (daily		5.68	6.70	12.84	15.06	17.08	18.44	——
summer earnings)	%	100.0	118.0	226.1	265.2	300.7	324.6	——
Forestry (daily earnings)		5.41	6.70	13.81	15.63	17.60	19.10	——
	%	100.0	124.1	293.6	288.9	324.3	353.0	——

*1938 figures estimated.

†See note 12(b), p. 67.

Table 2. AVERAGE HOURLY EARNINGS (KRONER): ADULT WOMEN.

		1938 (3rd quarter)	1940	1945	1946	1947	1948	1949 (2nd quarter)
Clothing (including Boots and Shoes)		1.04*	1.09	1.40	1.55	1.74	1.87	2.00
	%	100.0	104.8	134.6	149.0	167.3	179.8	192.3
Food (including Canning)		1.01*	1.07	1.35	1.52	1.75	1.87	1.93
	%	100.0	105.9	133.7	150.3	173.3	185.1	191.1
Industry as a whole		0.97	1.03	1.32	1.53	1.76	1.89	1.98
	%	100.0	106.2	136.1	157.7	181.4	194.8	204.1
Boot and Shoe†		0.94	0.95	1.36	1.52	1.73	1.91	2.06
	%	100.0	101.0	144.9	161.7	184.0	203.2	219.2
Paper		0.91*	0.97	1.29	1.55	1.78	1.96	2.04
	%	100.0	106.6	141.8	170.3	196.7	215.4	224.2
Textiles		0.86	0.91	1.19	1.47	1.71	1.84	1.90
	%	100.0	105.8	138.4	170.4	198.8	212.8	221.0
Canning†		0.80	0.86	1.23	1.42	1.61	1.75	1.76
	%	100.0	107.5	153.8	177.5	201.3	218.8	220.0
Agriculture (daily summer earnings)		3.65	4.33	8.40	9.79	11.02	12.01	—
	%	100.0	118.7	230.8	268.9	302.8	329.9	—

*1938 figures estimated.
†See note 12(b), p. 67.

The level of women's earnings over industry as a whole rose relatively to that of men's, from 59.5 percent to 63.6 percent. Of the groups which were below the level of industry as a whole in 1938, two (boots and shoes, and paper) had risen above it, and the remainder had bettered their relative position. Of the groups above the average level in 1938, one was barely above in 1949, and the other was below it. Altogether, therefore, divergences from the average had become proportionately less than they were before the war.

Table 3 summarizes the relative changes in average hourly earnings in the various groups.

Table 3. AVERAGE HOURLY EARNINGS (SUMMARY).

Adult Men	*Industry (as a Whole)*	*Engineering*	*Clothing*	*Food*	*Chemical and Electro-chemical*	*Building (unskilled)*
1938 (3rd qtr.)	100.0	100.6	101.3*	103.7*	104.2	111.6*
1949 (2nd qtr.)	100.0	101.6	102.0	91.6	113.9	119.9

Adult Women	*Industry (as a Whole)*	*Clothing*	*Food*	*Boot and Shoe*	*Paper*	*Textiles*
1938 (3rd qtr.)	100.0	107.2*	104.1*	96.9	93.8*	88.6
1949 (2nd qtr.)	100.0	101.0	97.5	104.0	103.0	96.0

*1938 figures estimated.

Differences in average earnings in various industries depend largely on the extent to which piecework is used. A writer in the *Monthly Bulletin* of the Central Bureau of Statistics[13] has given the following statistics regarding the proportion of total work performed at piece rates in various industries, together with estimates of the increased earnings due to more work at piece rates. (Piece

Table 4. HOURS ON PIECEWORK AS PERCENTAGE OF TOTAL HOURS WORKED.

	Industry (as a Whole)	*Engi-neering*	*Boot and Shoe*	*Textiles*	*Paper*	*Canning*	*Chemical and Electro-chemical*
Adult Men							
1945 (1st half)	36.6	47.7	47.5	22.3	23.1	4.3	45.7
1949 (2nd qtr.)	59.4	88.2	66.1	42.3	22.7	3.4	73.8
Increase in hourly earnings due to increased piecework (öre)	15	19	21	10	—	—	23
Adult Women							
1945 (1st half)	43.0	44.7	38.6	61.4	59.6	42.3	—
1949 (2nd qtr.)	55.0	83.7	53.7	62.2	54.2	36.2	—
Increase in hourly earnings due to increased piecework (öre)	6	19	13	—	—	—	—

[13]Kjönstad, "Lönnsutvikling," *Statistiske Meldinger,* No. 3, 1950, pp. 52–58.

rates generally yield earnings 25 to 30 percent above those of workers on time rates; it is probable that this differential has not changed markedly since before the war, though there is no wholly reliable statistical evidence on this point.)

Piecework has in fact become increasingly popular in Norway, many of the former objections to it having been broken down. As might be expected the industries which have not extensively adopted piecework are prominent among those whose earnings are below the average, and vice versa. The chemical and electrochemical industry, which had the largest increase in piecework, also had the largest increase in earnings; but in the total of industrial employment it is a small group, and, as Norway's most modern and efficient industry, with labor costs small in relation to capital equipment, it is in rather a special position.

Table 5 shows how, if the amount of piecework had not increased, earnings would have been considerably more equal.

Table 5. Actual Average Hourly Earnings (A), and Earnings with Piecework as in 1945 (B) (Figures in Kroner, 2nd Quarter 1949).

	Canning	*Textiles*	*Paper*	*Industry (as a Whole)*	*Engineering*	*Boot and Shoes*	*Chemical and Electrochemical*
Adult Men							
A.	2.55	2.76	2.93	3.11	3.06	3.25	3.54
B.	2.55	2.66	2.93	2.96	2.97	3.04	3.31
Adult Women							
A.	1.75	1.84	1.96	1.98	—	2.06	—
B.	1.75	1.84	1.96	1.92	—	1.93	—

The writer in the *Monthly Bulletin* also discusses ways in which increases in earnings have come about in different industries. He points out that, as well as the cost-of-living bonus which was awarded to all workers, and the special increases which were granted to lower paid workers (by agreements in both cases), there were also various wage increases in individual firms (for example, individual or group bonuses, and production bonuses—often associated with increased piecework—or unusually quick promotion to better paid grades). These increases were encouraged by the general shortage of labor. Table 6 estimates the amounts per head of the various increases, over industry as a whole, from the end of the occupation in May 1945 to the 2nd quarter of 1949.

Table 6. INCREASES IN AVERAGE HOURLY EARNINGS FROM MAY 1945 TO SECOND QUARTER OF 1949.

	Men	*Women*
General cost-of-living bonus	65 öre	49 öre
Agreement revisions and bonus to low-paid workers	20 öre	25 öre
Increases within firms	36 öre	8 öre
Total	121 öre	82 öre

There was a tendency for workers in the better-paying industries, who were not extensively affected by awards other than the general cost-of-living bonus, to receive "unofficial" increases which were more or less equivalent to what workers in the lower-paying industries had received officially.

There are no statistics regarding the numbers of skilled and unskilled workers in industry, and it is not possible to say how the proportions in various industries have changed. On the whole they have probably not changed very much. Norwegian industry has not experienced really far-reaching technical developments since the war, though there has been a good deal of renewal of plant. Until 1950 no comprehensive statistics were obtained regarding variations in wages within industries, but from those published since that date, covering certain industries, it appears that they are considerable.[14] There is reason to believe that the earnings of young workers increased relatively to those of adults, which is to be expected in a period of rapid industrial expansion when it is necessary to maintain recruitment at a high level.

Evidence on the relation between the wages of skilled and unskilled workers is limited and inconclusive. Table 7 shows the position in regard to those occupations for which official statistics are available.

[14]Cf. Kjönstad, *loc. cit.*, p. 55; *Lönnstatistikk 1950* (Statistisk Sentralbyrå).

Table 7. AVERAGE HOURLY EARNINGS (UNSKILLED AS PERCENTAGE OF SKILLED).

	1938 (3rd quarter)	*1940*	*1945*	*1946*	*1947*	*1948*	*1949 (2nd quarter)*
Engineering.......	85.7	85.9	91.4	90.7	90.7	92.9	91.1
Building..........	80.9*	80.6	89.3	95.1	93.5	93.0	100.0
Printing Trades....	76.7*	76.6	76.9	73.6	75.3	75.8	76.7

*1938 figures estimated.

Thus, in both engineering and building, unskilled rates rose relatively to skilled rates, as compared with before the war; in building, indeed, the differential disappeared in the second quarter of 1949.[15] Hourly earnings in this group are notoriously high, though over a longer period earnings are liable to be affected by interruptions of work from weather and other causes. There is a great deal of piecework, and output in the Norwegian building industry is high as compared, for example, with the British. In printing, on the other hand, a comparatively large differential remained practically unchanged.

Average earnings in agriculture and forestry, of course, rose sharply, and by 1949 were about 80 percent of industrial earnings as compared with about 40 percent in 1938. No official statistics are available regarding the earnings of transport workers; permanent railway personnel are state employees and shared in the improvements brought about under the new scales introduced since 1948.

Measured against the cost-of-living index, which has remained at about 157 during the period from 1946–1949, real earnings for all workers increased. But the burden of taxation on wage earners has been considerably heavier than before the war, although in 1948 and 1949 about one third of the total proceeds of taxation was spent on food subsidies. The share of the national income going to wages increased from approximately 50 percent in 1938 to 53–54 percent in the postwar years up to 1949.

[15]It reappeared again in the 3rd quarter, when unskilled earnings were 97.6 percent of skilled. There are also a considerable number of unorganized building enterprises, not covered by the official returns, which have paid wages above the recognized rates.

Over industry as a whole there was an increase in both total production and output per head, as Table 8 shows.

Table 8. Industrial Production and Output per Head.
(1938 — 100)

	Production	*Average Output per Head**
1946	97.2	94.2
1947	114.9	98.8
1948	128.3	103.3
1949	137.4	107.8

*This is a revised index, which represents the most accurate measurement of productivity as yet made. It does not, however, include either the metal trades or printing. Cf. *Statistiske Meldinger,* No. 7, 1952, pp. 208–209.

As compared with before the war, there was a decrease in output per head in most industries in the immediate postwar period; it was regarded as being due, in varying degrees, to uneven supplies of raw materials, worn-out plant (the lack of replacement during the war years was only gradually made good), increased absenteeism, and reduced effort at work. Subsequently, however, the position showed a gradual improvement in all industries. In particular industries there has been no clear relationship between the rate of increase in output per head and the rate of increase in earnings since the war, but by 1949 the prewar output per head had been exceeded in nearly all the important industrial groups, the chemical industry being a notable exception. The increase in productivity was above the average in paper, textiles, and clothing. In paper, there had been a great deal of re-equipment; in textiles and in clothing, raw material supplies only became adequate after a long period of shortage. Of these industries, only clothing has very much piecework, and in general increased piecework does not appear to have been associated with a marked rise in individual output. Lack of incentive has undoubtedly been a problem during the postwar period, and there have been complaints by the employers that unduly high piece rates, introduced during the war to evade the wage stop, have been allowed to remain unmodified.

We may now consider the relation between wages and the price level. The Norwegian wholesale index, which is so constructed as to give a fair indication of the changes in the general internal price level, moved as follows in the period up to 1949: 1938, 100; 1946, 169; 1947, 175; 1948, 181; 1949, 184.

Since 1946, the lowest postwar year, there was thus a rise of less than 10 percent—one of the smallest rises in Europe. In the period from 1946 to January–August 1949, import prices rose approximately 17 percent,[16] and since the value of imports amounted to nearly 30 percent of the national income in 1946 and about 40 percent in each of the remaining postwar years, this rise in import prices would seem to be sufficient to account for the wholesale price increase. As has been said, the cost-of-living index remained practically stable from 1945 to 1949 at the level of approximately 157. Substantial rises in both wholesale and retail indices were avoided by subsidies on the main foodstuffs, such as milk, butter, bread, and meat, and on imported feeding stuffs (which kept down farmers' costs of production), and, to a limited extent, on a few other imports.[17] Expenditure on subsidies increased from 238 million kroner in 1945 to a maximum of 750 million kroner in 1949. The growth was brought about partly by increased payments to farmers to keep their incomes on a parity with those of other sections of the community and to cover the increased wages of farm labor.[18] It was estimated that in 1948 a removal of subsidies would have brought about a rise of 38 points—about 24 percent—in the cost-of-living index.

The increase in the wages of agricultural workers together with that in the incomes of agricultural proprietors, would, therefore, have brought about a considerable rise in the price level if it had not been counterbalanced by subsidies; but these rises were in-

[16]*Statistiske Meddelelser,* No. 12, 1949, p. 647. A corrected index has been used; the regular published index showed a rise of 21 percent. The devaluation of the krone, in September 1949, did not cause any appreciable rise in wholesale prices in 1949.

[17]The proportions in which these subsidies were given to both imports and home-produced goods do not diverge sufficiently from the proportion between the total respective values of these materially to affect the part played by import prices in bringing about a rise in wholesale prices generally.

[18]The prices of agricultural products are fixed by negotiation between the Government and the farmers' organizations.

tended and allowed for, and the wages of nonagricultural workers were not supported by subsidies. Otherwise it seems correct to say that the achievement of a stable price level was not disturbed by upward pressure from wages and salaries, and that these just about kept pace with economic expansion generally. Norway has been fortunate in that a large proportion of her primary production (for example, canned fish and wood products) other than agricultural output, is exported. It was mainly in the industries responsible for this production that wages were abnormally low, and the much higher relative prices of primary products since the war have made it easier to raise the wages of the workers producing them than would otherwise have been the case. Insofar as there were rises in the domestic costs of these products, they were sufficiently balanced by reductions in other prices to maintain the stability of the general level.

Wage Policy from 1950 to 1955

During the years 1950–1952 international developments, beginning in September 1949 with the devaluation of sterling in terms of the dollar—and with it, the Norwegian krone—brought about a continuously rising level of prices in Norway as in other countries, and the policy of maintaining a stable cost of living had necessarily to be abandoned. In fact, the rising tendency of the cost-of-living index was enhanced through the abolition by the Government, in successive stages in April and August 1950 and September 1952, of most of the subsidies on the principal foodstuffs and other important articles of consumption, the maintenance of which, with the steady increase in prices, would have meant an unduly heavy burden on the State budget; and in addition the rate of purchase tax levied on the great majority of articles was increased from 6.25 percent to 10 percent in April 1951. The giving up of the stabilization policy by the Government naturally entailed a new approach to wage questions on the part of the trade unions. Broadly speaking the trade union policy has been to seek to secure compensation—though not necessarily full compensation—for the increased cost of living, but to mitigate as far as possible the tendency of increased wages to make prices rise still further. The general lines on which wage negotiations have been conducted continued as in the previous period, with the Trade Union Federation either negotiating directly with the Employers' Association on behalf of all wage earners or playing a large part in determining the policy to be followed by individual unions in their negotiations with the employers in their respective industries.

The new conditions had already been foreshadowed in the arrangement made between the Trade Union Federation and Employers' Association in the summer of 1949, by which the automatic adjustment of wages to movements in the cost-of-living index was replaced by an agreement that if the index were to rise or fall more than 7 points from the level of May 1949 (158.6) either side could demand negotiations for an adjustment of wages, and if an understanding was not reached a month's notice could be given to terminate existing wage agreements. The index did not in fact move so as to bring this arrangement into effect, and in March 1950 its operation was extended to September 15. By this date the index had reached 179.5, and negotiations which took place in the following month resulted in an agreement between the two central organizations, without the intervention of the Government, that there should be an increase of 18 öre an hour for all adult workers from the middle of October. (It has been estimated that this increase gave compensation for the increased cost of living resulting from the reduction in food subsidies, which amounted to approximately 64 percent of the total increase since May 1949.)[19] Also, it was agreed that if by March 15, 1951 there was a rise or fall of 5 points or more in the cost-of-living index from the level at which it stood on September 15, 1950 (108.3 on the new basis, 1949 = 100) there should automatically be an increase or decrease in wages of 2.6 öre per point for adult workers, and that in the event of a subsequent rise or fall of 5 points or more six months later there should be further negotiations, at the request of the Trade Union Federation in the case of a rise, or at the request of the Employers' Association in the case of a fall; and that all agreements for particular industries which were due to expire in 1951 should be prolonged

[19]Cf. *Økonomisk utsyn over året 1950* (Statistisk Sentralbyrå), p. 140.

until 1952. In particular industries there were a few revisions of agreements in the earlier part of 1950, most of which provided for some increases in wages, the most important being that for agricultural workers, who were awarded a substantial advance by the Wages Board. Forest workers received an increase from September 15 in accordance with the rise in the cost-of-living index.

Since by March 1951 the cost-of-living index had risen to 115.0, wages were increased from April 15 by 17 öre an hour for all adult workers, in accordance with the agreement of October 1950. By September 15 there had been a further rise in the cost-of-living index to 125.8. Negotiations were opened between the Employers' Association and the Trade Union Federation, but no agreement was reached, and the trade unions gave notice for the termination of agreements. Mediation having also proved unsuccessful, the Government set up a special Wages Board, which awarded an increase of 21 öre an hour for all adult workers, effective from October 15. Since agreements generally were not terminated in 1951, there were few other changes in the terms of employment, but in January all workers in the paper industry were given an increase of 5 öre per hour at the beginning of the year, with a further 25 öre per hour to shift-workers on night shifts (in addition to the general increases affecting all workers), and forest workers received a further increase in September. The Government increased allowances for children (after the second child) and reduced rates of national and municipal income tax on the smaller incomes during the year.

In 1952 there was no new general agreement between the Trade Union Federation and the Employers' Association covering industry as a whole, but practically all agreements in individual industries expired and they underwent a very comprehensive and thoroughgoing revision. Before this revision took place the Trade Union Federation, in consultation with the individual unions, laid down certain general lines of policy to be followed in the negotiations for new agreements. Attention was directed to a statement by the Government that prices would probably not continue to rise as a result of external developments, and that a moderate wage policy should be followed in order to prevent their rising from internal causes. It was pointed out that, although the National Budget stated that an increase in consumption of about 4 percent as compared with 1951 would be possible if there was no stoppage of work, there were many elements of uncertainty which might prevent this forecast from being realized. Further, circumstances were not favorable for an attempt to increase the share of the national income going to labor, and this should be postponed. In the meantime the object must be to stabilize prices and, if possible, to bring them down. Only claims by individual unions in accordance with this policy would be approved by the Federation, and in revising agreements, the unions should also try to make sure that piece rates should not be increased proportionately more than time rates; that the use of piece rates and other systems of payment linked to output should be encouraged; that the differential for skilled workers should be increased; that bonuses for long service should be extended, to encourage stability in the labor force and the acquisition of better qualifications; that the difference between men's and women's wages should be lessened, and the principle of equal pay for equal effort be put into operation as far as possible. Finally, insofar as wage increases were possible, they should go to the less well-off groups who were without opportunities for piecework or bonuses, and in the case of the better-paid groups, though anomalies should be removed, there should be no general increases.

The changes in the agreements show common characteristics, both because of the policy directives of the Trade Union Federation, and also because one of the most important agreements (which was among the earliest to be negotiated), that covering engineering workers, was the subject of an award by the Wages Board in April 1952; this award largely determined the changes to be incorporated in agreements negotiated subsequently. Awards were also made by the Wages Board in some other important cases—for example, agriculture and the paper industry—but in most cases the terms of revision were agreed by negotiation. Generally speaking, the revised agreements granted increases of from 10 öre to 20 öre per hour for adult men and women; piece rates were raised by about 5 percent. Women received on the whole larger percentage increases than men in the same trade, but smaller absolute increases. The tendency to equalization of wages between industries, which was one of the features of the policy of flat-rate over-all increases followed previously, continued, since on the whole the lowest-paid industrial groups received the largest relative—and in some cases absolute—increases, but there was a change in policy in that skilled workers were generally given greater increases than unskilled, in order to bring about a needed increase in the supply of skilled labor. This policy was also followed in regard to workers employed by local authorities, and increases given to civil servants were larger for the higher-paid categories, to restore the relationship which existed in 1948, prior to increases which had given greater benefits to lower grades.[20] The revision as a whole was thus affected by a combination of factors—government policy, the control and policy-making influence of the Trade Union Federation, the particular aims of the individual unions, and the sanction of the Wages Board.

The cost of living continued to rise during the greater part of 1952, but from 1953 to 1955 there was a period of much greater stability, with the cost of living remaining at about the same level during 1953 and only showing a moderate rise thereafter. In January 1953 the Trade Union Federation decided to recommend that agreements due to expire in 1953 should not be terminated, and they were in general extended for a further year. Among the reasons for this decision—which was approved by nearly all the individual unions, only a few unions with a small minority of the total membership dissenting—were that production had not risen during 1952, and that Norway's international competitive position would be worsened and full employment endangered by a further rise in wages. Agricultural workers, however, were given an increase by negotiated agreement. The Government for its part increased the subsidy on milk and abolished the import duties on sugar and coffee to reduce the cost of living and also gave certain tax reliefs. Similar considerations regarding Norway's international economic position continued to apply in 1954, and as early as November 1953 the Trade Union Federation warned against any all-round wage increase in the forthcoming revision of agreements.

[20]A full account of the 1952 changes is given in *Økonomisk utsyn over året 1952* (Statistisk Sentralbyrå), pp. 91–92.

General improvements in 1954 were therefore confined to the introduction of payment for certain week-day holidays, and for absence due to factory accidents (by agreement between the Employers' Association and the Trade Union Federation), which together were estimated as equivalent to a wage increase of about 1½ percent per annum, though there were various increases for timeworkers (but not pieceworkers) in individual industries or groups with low wage levels, most of which were also granted by agreement. Agricultural wages were increased by voluntary arbitration. All agreements made for two years were to be subject to the condition that if the cost-of-living index rose or fell by 7 points by the middle of March or September 1955, the Trade Union Federation or the Employers' Association should be able to demand negotiations for a wage adjustment not exceeding the change in the cost of living. The cost-of-living index did not rise to this extent in 1955, and as most of the agreements made in 1954 were for two years there were few further revisions in the following year.

Results of Wage Policy from 1950 to 1955

Let us now consider the outcome of the wage policy followed in the period since 1949. The general economic background during 1950–1952 was, apart from rising prices, very similar to that in the years 1946–1949. There was no change in basic economic policies such as price control, heavy investment programs, and the maintenance of full employment, and unemployment was throughout at the very low levels characteristic of the earlier period. The expansion of industrial employment was, however, much less—about 5 percent in the latter period; most industrial groups had some increase in the numbers employed and only a few had decreases. The increase in the number of women employed in industry was about 8 percent. In agriculture and forestry, on the other hand, there was a steady fall in employment, and in 1952 the total number employed was about 15 percent below the 1949 level.

The following tables show the movement of average earnings for adult men and women in a number of the principal occupations and in industry as a whole.

Table 9. AVERAGE HOURLY EARNINGS (KRONER): ADULT MEN.

		1949 (year)	*1950 (2nd qtr.)*	*1950 (4th qtr.)*	*1951 (2nd qtr.)*	*1951 (4th qtr.)*	*1952 (2nd qtr.)*
Building Trades (skilled workers)		3.73	3.81	4.05	4.18	4.58	4.66
	%	100.0	102.1	108.6	112.1	122.8	124.9
Building Trades (unskilled workers)		3.63	3.74	4.09	4.10	4.63	4.54
	%	100.0	103.0	112.7	112.9	127.5	125.1
Printing and Bookbinding (skilled workers)		3.72	3.94	4.12	4.43	4.57	4.97
	%	100.0	105.9	110.8	119.1	122.8	133.6
Printing and Bookbinding (unskilled workers)		2.86	3.06	3.23	3.61	3.68	3.94
	%	100.0	107.0	112.9	126.2	128.7	138.7
Chemical and Electrochemical		3.49	3.64	3.75	4.09	4.26	4.49
	%	100.0	104.3	107.4	117.2	122.1	128.7
Boots and Shoes		3.20	3.38	3.54	3.85	3.90	4.03
	%	100.0	105.6	110.6	120.3	121.9	125.9
Clothing (including Boots and Shoes)		3.13	3.30	3.44	3.75	3.84	4.00
	%	100.0	105.4	110.0	119.8	122.7	127.8
Engineering		3.13	3.27	3.44	3.72	3.94	4.24
	%	100.0	104.5	110.0	118.8	125.9	135.5
Industry as a whole		3.09	3.26	3.45	3.75	3.97	4.18
	%	100.0	105.5	111.7	121.4	128.5	135.3
Cost-of-living Index	%	100.0	104.4	110.5	122.2	126.3	130.8
Paper		2.94	3.10	3.50	3.79	4.06	4.12
	%	100.0	105.4	119.0	128.9	138.1	140.1
Food (including Canning)		2.83	3.03	3.09	3.45	3.58	3.95
	%	100.0	107.1	109.2	121.9	126.5	139.6
Textiles		2.79	3.00	3.14	3.43	3.59	3.78
	%	100.0	107.5	112.5	122.9	128.7	135.5
Canning		2.58	2.72	2.82	3.10	3.22	3.49
	%	100.0	105.4	109.3	120.2	124.8	135.3
Agriculture (daily summer earnings) *			19.25	20.59		22.98	
	%		100.0	107.0		119.4	
Forestry (daily earnings) †			19.63	21.39		24.80	
	%		100.0	109.0		126.3	

Table 10. AVERAGE HOURLY EARNINGS (KRONER): ADULT WOMEN.

		1949 (year)	1950 (2nd qtr.)	1950 (4th qtr.)	1951 (2nd qtr.)	1951 (4th qtr.)	1952 (2nd qtr.)
Boots and Shoes		2.05	2.22	2.33	2.61	2.75	2.84
	%	100.0	108.3	113.7	127.3	134.1	138.5
Paper		2.04	2.12	2.43	2.70	2.87	2.91
	%	100.0	103.9	119.1	132.4	140.7	142.6
Clothing (including Boots and Shoes)		2.00	2.16	2.29	2.55	2.69	2.85
	%	100.0	108.0	114.5	127.5	134.5	142.5
Industry as a whole		1.98	2.11	2.24	2.52	2.68	2.84
	%	100.0	106.6	113.1	127.3	135.4	143.4
Cost-of-living Index	%	100.0	104.4	110.5	122.2	126.3	130.8
Food (including Canning)		1.93	2.06	2.16	2.43	2.60	2.82
	%	100.0	106.7	111.9	125.9	134.7	146.1
Textiles		1.92	2.04	2.17	2.44	2.58	2.74
	%	100.0	106.2	113.0	127.1	134.4	142.7
Canning		1.81	1.86	2.01	2.24	2.37	2.57
	%	100.0	102.8	111.0	123.8	130.9	142.0
Agriculture (daily summer earnings)*		12.80	13.77		15.53		
	%	100.0	107.6		121.3		

*Average earnings in the hay-making season in each of the years concerned.

So far as men are concerned, average earnings in industry as a whole had risen slightly more than the cost of living by the second quarter of 1952 as compared with 1949, but throughout 1950 and 1951 the correspondence between earnings and the cost of living was very close. There appears to have been a tendency for earnings in different industries to become more equal. In none of the industries where earnings in 1949 were below the average for industry as a whole had there been by the second quarter of 1952 a percentage increase less than the percentage increase for industry as a whole,

Notes to Table 9:

*Average earnings in the hay-making season in each of the years concerned.

†Average earnings in winter seasons 1949–1950, 1950–1951, and 1951–1952 respectively.

and in most of them the increase had been greater, while for all the higher-paid groups, except printing and bookbinding, the percentage increase had been considerably less than that for industry as a whole. Since by the last quarter of 1952 only a proportion of the revisions of agreements in that year had taken place the statistics for the 4th quarter of 1951 probably give a better indication of the relative position of different industries, and it is noticeable how comparatively similar the percentage increases for the various industries were at that date. The most striking change is perhaps that in the position of the paper industry, which from being one of the lowest-paying industries before the war, and paying only moderately well by 1949, had become one of the best paying by the end of 1951 (the industry did not receive its 1952 increases until August, so that they do not appear in the figures for the second quarter of 1952). In agriculture, however, there was a tendency to fall behind the average in 1951.

Both on the average and in all the principal groups the percentage increase in women's earnings was considerably greater than that in the cost-of-living index, and they rose from about 64 percent of men's earnings in 1949 to about 68 percent in the second quarter of 1952. Here again the percentage increases in different industries were very similar, and except that the paper industry rose to being the best paying instead of the second best paying their relative positions were practically unaltered. In agriculture there was again a failure to keep up with the increased cost of living in 1951.

As in the earlier period, as well as the increases given through the general cost-of-living bonuses covering all workers, and those resulting from the revision of agreements in particular industries, there were also increases within firms, not provided for in the agreements. The following table from the annual review for 1952 issued by the Central Bureau of Statistics[21] gives particulars regarding the amounts of increases arising from agreements and within firms respectively.

These figures indicate that increases within firms outside the terms of agreements were a steadily diminishing proportion of the total. There are no statistics available regarding changes in the

[21] *Ibid.*, p. 90.

Table 11. Wage Increases, 1950–1952.

	1949 (1st qtr.) –1950 (1st qtr.) %	*1950 (1st qtr.) –1951 (1st qtr.)* %	*1951 (1st qtr.) –1952 (1st qtr.)* %
Men:			
Increase from cost-of-living bonus and agreement revisions	2.3	6.3	11.0
Increases within firms	2.7	3.5	4.1
Total Increase	5.0	9.8	15.1
Women:			
Increase from cost-of-living bonus and agreement revisions	3.1	8.8	16.7
Increases within firms	3.7	3.4	2.2
Total Increase	6.8	12.2	18.9
Increase in cost-of-living index	1.3	12.8	14.7

proportion of workers on piecework, but it seems likely that piecework did not continue to increase as in the earlier period. The effect of the equal cost-of-living bonuses granted to men and women in bringing about a relative increase in women's earnings is clearly brought out in this table. There was a definite policy both of endeavoring to secure equal pay for equal work, and also of improving women's earnings in order to attract more women into industry.

The statistics of earnings of skilled and unskilled workers, in the three occupations for which they are available—engineering, building, and the printing trades—do not suggest any clear trend during the period 1950–1952.

Table 12. Earnings of Skilled and Unskilled Workers. 1950–1952

Average hourly earnings (unskilled as % of skilled)	*1950 (2nd qtr.)*	*1951 (2nd qtr.)*	*1952 (2nd qtr.)*
Engineering	93.8	94.8	94.1
Building	98.2	98.1	97.4
Printing Trades	77.7	81.5	79.3

In 1950 and 1951 total industrial production was considerably higher than in 1949, but the rise did not continue to the same extent in 1952. The movements in the index were as follows:

	1949	*1950*	*1951*	*1952*
1938 = 100	137.4	148.5	157.0	157.0

As the labor force in industry increased by about 5 percent, this represents a decided increase in productivity. The increase in production was particularly marked in the chemical industry, in which output was about 36 percent higher in 1952 than in 1949, and did not show any falling off as compared with 1951; the number of persons employed increased by about 5 percent, so that there was a large increase in productivity—in contrast to the period up to 1949, when output per head remained considerably below the prewar level. Up to 1951 the textile industry also showed an increase in production above the average, but there was some falling off in 1952. In other main groups, production moved similarly to the average, but there was a sharp falling off in the boot and shoe industry in 1952 and a smaller reduction in the paper and pulp industry.

In general, therefore, the wage policy followed in the period 1949–1952 can be described as an extremely moderate one. Though wages rose on the whole rather more than the cost of living, they did not rise in accordance with the increased productivity of industry, and there does not appear to be reason for believing that wage increases brought about domestic inflation over and above the increase in domestic costs which naturally accompanies any adjustment to a higher international price level.[22] The other noticeable feature of wage movements during this period is the high degree of stability which was shown in the relations of wages in different industrial occupations. Equalizing tendencies were at work to a greater degree than in the period 1946–1949, and in most industries average money earnings increased in roughly the same proportion, so that the relative level of earnings in different industries (and between skilled and unskilled workers) did not change very much.

[22]This is borne out by the fact that the share of the national income going to wages fell from 54.7 percent in 1949 to 50.9 percent in 1951 and 52.8 percent in 1952, in spite of the increase of about 5 percent in the total number of persons employed. Cf. *ibid.*, p. 94 and *Statistisk Årbok for Norge, 1952,* p. 312.

The conclusion may, perhaps, be tentatively drawn that some degree of stability in Norway's industrial structure prevailed during those years, so that the relative importance of various industries and occupations remained much the same; the adjustment to a higher price level could thus take place without great changes in real wages, and the equalizing characteristics of the unified wage policy could operate without strong countervailing forces.

The period 1953–1955 was, by contrast, one of still greater stability, and what rise in the cost of living there was—amounting to about 5 percent—took place mainly during 1954. Price controls on most articles were done away with in January 1954, though they were retained on certain foodstuffs, especially those in receipt of subsidies. The foreign balance, on which there was a small surplus in 1952, showed a considerable deficit in each of the three following years, and thus presented a continuing problem. Reductions in the investment program were made in 1954, and at the beginning of 1955 more drastic steps were taken to reduce the volume of investment and lessen the demand for imports. These included the raising of the central bank rate from 2½ percent to 3½ percent, some reductions in government expenditure, and measures to reduce building (other than dwelling houses and agricultural building), and to restrict bank loans. At the same time the control of retail prices was made stricter again, with the object of reducing the cost of living. These restrictive measures were, however, only beginning to take effect toward the end of 1955, and investment continued to be very high—over 35 percent of the gross national product—in all three years, and unemployment showed no signs of increase from its very low level. The numbers employed in industry grew by about 5 percent, but employment in agriculture and forestry fell by about 16 percent and averaged only 68,000 in 1955. Most industrial groups had moderate increases in employment, but the increase in building was very large—about 20 percent from 1952 to 1954 and 1955.

The following tables show the movement of average earnings for adult men and women in a number of the principal occupations and in industry as a whole.

Table 13. AVERAGE HOURLY EARNINGS (KRONER): ADULT MEN.
(*Indices 1949 = 100*)

		1952 (4th qtr.)	*1953 (2nd qtr.)*	*1953 (4th qtr.)*	*1954 (2nd qtr.)*	*1954 (4th qtr.)*	*1955 (2nd qtr.)*
Building (all occupations)		5.14	5.05	5.36	5.42	5.79	5.79
	%	135.3	132.9	141.0	142.7	152.4	152.4
Printing Trades (all		4.86	5.21	5.16	5.43	5.30	5.80
occupations) *	%	134.3	143.9	142.5	150.0	146.4	160.3
Chemical and Electro-		4.33	4.56	4.49	4.76	4.75	5.04
chemical	%	124.1	130.7	128.7	136.4	136.1	144.4
Engineering		4.28	4.35	4.43	4.67	4.67	5.02
	%	134.4	139.8	142.4	150.2	150.2	161.4
Paper		4.22	4.35	4.40	4.53	4.71	5.08
	%	143.5	148.0	149.7	154.1	160.3	172.8
Industry as a whole		4.22	4.32	4.37	4.57	4.61	4.91
	%	136.6	139.8	141.4	147.9	149.2	158.9
Cost-of-living Index	%	136.0	135.0	137.0	140.0	143.0	143.0
Boots and Shoes		4.03	4.16	4.21	4.43	4.45	4.77
	%	125.9	130.0	131.6	138.4	139.1	149.0
Clothing (including Boots		4.01	4.04	4.07	4.23	4.25	4.54
and Shoes)	%	128.1	129.1	130.0	135.1	135.8	145.1
Textiles		3.90	3.93	3.97	4.16	4.27	4.42
	%	139.8	140.9	142.3	149.1	153.0	158.4
Food (including Canning)		3.86	3.94	3.90	4.12	4.16	4.40
	%	136.4	139.2	137.8	145.6	147.0	155.5
Canning		3.49	3.50	3.50	3.61	3.69	3.86
	%	135.3	135.7	135.7	139.9	143.0	149.6
Agriculture (daily		25.11		26.09		27.52	
summer earnings) †	%	130.4		135.5		143.0	
Forestry (daily earnings) ‡			26.66		27.77		24.11
	%		135.8		141.5		148.3

*Statistics of the earnings of skilled and unskilled workers, comparable with those for earlier years, are not available.

†Average earnings in the hay-making season in each of the years concerned.

‡Average earnings in winter seasons 1952–1953, 1953–1954, and 1954–1955 respectively.

Table 14. AVERAGE HOURLY EARNINGS (KRONER): ADULT WOMEN.

(Indices 1949 = 100)

		1952 (4th qtr.)	*1953 (2nd qtr.)*	*1953 (4th qtr.)*	*1954 (2nd qtr.)*	*1954 (4th qtr.)*	*1955 (2nd qtr.)*
Paper		3.04	3.13	3.12	3.24	3.38	3.57
	%	149.0	152.9	155.4	155.9	162.3	175.0
Clothing (including Boots		2.98	3.07	3.06	3.22	3.20	3.41
and Shoes)	%	149.0	153.5	153.0	161.0	160.0	170.5
Industry as a whole		2.89	2.97	2.96	3.11	3.11	3.32
	%	146.0	150.0	149.5	157.1	157.1	167.7
Cost-of-living Index	%	136.0	135.0	137.0	140.0	143.0	143.0
Boots and Shoes		2.84	2.88	2.93	3.03	3.05	3.28
	%	138.5	140.5	142.9	147.8	148.8	160.0
Textiles		2.78	2.84	2.83	2.97	2.99	3.20
	%	144.8	147.9	147.4	154.7	155.7	166.9
Food (including Canning)		2.70	2.72	2.74	2.85	2.88	3.01
	%	139.9	140.9	142.0	147.7	149.2	156.0
Canning		2.64	2.62	2.63	2.70	2.75	2.83
	%	145.9	144.8	145.3	149.2	151.9	156.3
Agriculture (daily		16.85		17.82		18.93	
summer earnings)*	%	131.6		139.2		147.9	

*Average earnings in the hay-making season in each of the years concerned.

It can be seen that the earnings of both men and women rose more rapidly than the cost of living during this period. In the second quarter of 1955 women's earnings in industry as a whole were about the same proportion of men's earnings (approximately 68 percent) as they had been three years earlier, and in both cases the increase in real earnings was about 11 percent as compared with the fourth quarter of 1952. This increase corresponded to the rise in productivity between 1952 and 1955, as industrial production rose by 16 percent, and the numbers employed in industry by 5 percent. The share of the national income going to wages rose from 53 percent in 1952 to an estimated 55–56 percent in each of the years

1953–1955. This actual rise in earnings was considerably greater than was provided for in the revisions of agreements which took place in this period, and though there is no detailed information on the question it seems clear that for such a rise to have occurred there must, as on other occasions, have been increases on a considerable scale outside the terms of agreements. The rise in the cost of living which took place in 1954 was mainly due to increases in the prices of foodstuffs, and in the latter part of the year to an easing of rent restriction, and it does not appear that the increase in industrial wages was to any important extent responsible for it. (Wholesale prices rose about 1½ percent from 1953 to 1954, but the rise did not continue into 1955.) The increases in earnings in the second quarter of 1955, as compared with 1954, are largely due to the arrangements for holiday pay made in 1954, which did not show their full effect until the following year.

There were practically no changes, in the case of men's or women's earnings, in the position of the various industrial groups relative to each other, and except in the paper industry—which was enjoying unusual prosperity—earnings in the groups receiving more than the average for industry as a whole did not show any increase markedly greater than the increase in this average, and some of them had smaller increases. On the other hand, earnings in groups receiving less than the average for industry as a whole tended to rise less than the increase in this average and the spread of earnings between the higher- and lower-paid groups had thus become greater in 1955 than it was in 1952. (The average itself is, however, very much affected by the earnings in the larger groups, since, for example, engineering employs over one third, and engineering and building together one half, of all industrial workers.) The canning industry in particular lagged very much behind other groups. Earnings for men in agriculture and forestry remained about the same relative to the average for industry, but women's earnings in agriculture showed a moderate relative increase. The movement of earnings in the various industrial groups appears to have been closely associated with their degree of prosperity. The demand for the products of the capital-goods industries—notably building and engineering—was especially strong during this period, and the same applies to the paper industry, while demand in industries producing for the home market was more moderate. The canning industry was not particularly prosperous in any of the three years, 1953–1955. The general conclusion seems to be, therefore, that the investment boom and the increasing productivity of industry were in these years the determining influences on the pattern of wages, and that they largely frustrated the policy of the Trade Union Federation, which was to keep general wage increases at a moderate level so as to lessen domestic demand and costs and improve the foreign balance, while bettering the relative position of the lower-paid workers. On the other hand, it can be argued that in view of the rise in the productivity of industry the policy of the Trade Union Federation in regard to wages was unduly cautious, and also that only when financial and administrative action had been taken by the Government to restore economic stability and correct the foreign balance could the Federation's object of furthering equality in earnings be achieved.

General Conclusions

The available evidence, then, suggests that Norwegian wage policy has had considerable, if not complete, success in achieving its objects. Over a considerable number of years it helped to improve the living standard of the less well-off groups, even if there was not a full measure of restraint on the earnings of the better-off; during the period up to 1950 it helped to maintain a stable price level; and subsequently contributed to preventing the rise in prices from getting out of hand. What have been the main elements in its success?

An extremely important part has undoubtedly been played by the Norwegian price control system, which up to 1954 was unusually comprehensive and has been very strictly administered. The knowledge that official policy was strongly against price increases except for virtually unavoidable causes, checked the willingness of industrialists to grant increases in wages which could only be met by passing them on to the consumer; and during the period of stabilization it was thus one of the principal factors, very likely the principal, in preventing a wage-price race. It is significant that the greatest difficulty in holding wages in check was in building and construction, where for various reasons it is difficult to fix prices for the finished product, and the final price is based on the labor costs actually incurred. By and large the effectiveness of price control has helped to quell an important element in inflation, namely the belief that prices are going to rise and that it is safe to incur commitments which can only be profitably met if they do. The system of export levies in effect extends price limitation to export sales even if export prices rise.

The policy of linking the wage level as a whole to the movement of the cost of living has two important consquences. It helps to focus the attention of the trade union membership on real wages rather than, as has been traditionally more common, on money wages. Also it brings about a widespread awareness of the dangers of inflation and the uselessness of increases in money wages which will soon be absorbed by rising prices. From a practical point of view, both these consequences would seem to be very much what are required in a controlled economy under conditions of full employment. The Norwegian community has, perhaps, tended for some time to be more conscious than most of the consequences of monetary manipulation. The deflationary policy which was followed for a considerable period between the wars was especially ruinous to the agricultural community and was the subject of widespread controversy, and since the war the leaders of the Government and especially the labor and trade union press have continually stressed the evils of inflation and pointed to its consequences in other countries. In these circumstances the Government's policy of monetary stabilization during the 1946–1949 period had the support of all sections of the community. Inflation was undoubtedly a constant danger in that period, particularly up to 1948. After that date increased production, budget surpluses, and a more cautious investment program probably checked excess monetary demand though national resources continued to be utilized to the maximum. In the period from 1950–1952, though because of the international economic situation it was impossible to maintain a stable price level, both the trade unions and public opinion generally were in favor of limiting the rise in prices and regaining stability at the earliest opportunity.

The leadership which the Federation of Trade Unions has been able to provide as a result of its predominance in relation to its affiliated unions has been of great value in the formulation of a clear policy on wage questions. The individual unions are expected to concentrate on establishing what amounts to a national minimum and are discouraged from using their full strength to raise the general standard of their own members irrespective of the position of other groups of workers. The authority of the Federation has tended to grow, and it now possesses far-reaching constitutional powers to prevent the individual unions from pushing sectional claims, together with a strong sanction in that it can withhold financial support from a union which becomes involved in an unauthorized dispute. The power of the Employers' Association to prevent departures from a unified policy is more restricted since its membership is not so comprehensive, but here legislation requiring general adherence to the terms of centrally established agreements has to some extent filled the gap.

It can be said that the Federation has succeeded in stopping the kind of uncoordinated, interunion competition in putting forward successive wage claims which is common in countries without a unified wage policy, and it has also brought about another very important development. It has succeeded to a great extent in causing the justice of wage claims to be judged by the absolute standard reached by the group of workers in question, rather than by the standard which they have enjoyed in the past in relation to other workers. Even so, it must be remembered that the structure of Norwegian trade unionism continues to represent a compromise between the powers of the Federation to promote the interests of the workers generally and the freedom of indivdual unions to further the interests of their own members independently. As has been shown, the movements of wage rates other than basic minima remain very largely outside the scope of the central wage policy and to some extent outside the control of the individual unions. In many cases the determination of these higher wage rates is left to individual bargaining, in which competition between both firms and workers—along with, of course, traditional differentials for effort and skill—plays a considerable part. In industries with standard rates, while the unions concerned have been willing to accept some degree of relative increase in the lower rates in industrial agreements, in many cases arrangements within firms have preserved the advantages of the higher-paid groups. In both instances there has been reduced pressure to get the higher rates raised, as compared with what would have been the case if the full bargaining strength of the individual unions had been used; but it would clearly be asking a great deal to expect their members to forego completely the advantages offered by the shortage of labor, and the experience of the years 1953–1955 seems to show that in times of great prosperity and rising productivity central control becomes very much weakened. An extension of control—whether by the Federation of Trade Unions or the Government— over the higher wage rates in individual industries would obviously be a matter of considerable delicacy and difficulty. It would mean a further limitation on the autonomy of the unions, as well as an interference with numerous traditions and practices which it would be hard for persons unacquainted with the special conditions of each industry to judge correctly. Certain steps of this sort have, however, been taken, such as the checks placed on payment of excessive wage rates by unorganized employers in the building trades, and the wage stop introduced for a short period in 1947. The maintenance of the jurisdiction of the Wages Board over claims unsupported by either of the central organizations also means that some restraint could be brought to bear on the more unreasonable demands by either side, which were unlikely to receive backing from the Federation of Trade Unions or the Employers' Association.

On the whole, however, it can be said that the movement of wages upward or downward—which under an uncoordinated wage system is determined mainly by the profitability of different sectors of industry and the relative strength of employers and workers —is, under the Norwegian system, very much determined by the effect of wage changes on the general price level, and by the claims of social justice. In the case of working conditions other than wages, it is generally recognized that the interests of all groups of workers must be considered. For example, one of the principal claims made by chemical shift-workers who engaged in a lengthy illegal strike in the autumn of 1948 was for shorter hours on account of the trying nature of their work.[23] The attitude taken by the Government—and supported by the Federation of Trade Unions—was that while nothing could be done unless there was an immediate return to work, a claim for shorter hours, which would require legislation, must be considered in the light of similar claims from other groups of workers and of the national need for as high production as possible. Subsequently, in 1949, an Act was passed providing for shorter hours for workers engaged in continuous shift-work—which went some way toward meeting the demands of the chemical workers—and also for certain workers in mining whose claims were held to be equally strong.

It is of great importance not only that there is agreement on a definite wage policy in the trade union movement, but also that this policy is in accordance with the general social and economic policy of the Government. Indeed it is hardly too much to say that a wage policy cannot exist independently, but only within a wider framework of defined social and economic aims of which it forms a part. The strength of the Norwegian system is that this framework does exist. The Government's social and economic policy is understood and accepted by all sections of the labor movement, and by much opinion outside labor ranks, insofar as it includes a levelling-up of the conditions of the poorer sections of the community. There has thus been a harmony of outlook among the various organizations and institutions dealing with industrial relations, and they have been able to work together in the knowledge that differences of opinion which might arise would be of degree rather than kind. Moreover, the general limitation of profits has played a large part in bringing about the willingness of the trade unions to restrain their claims.

Finally, it has been realized that in matters which closely affect the living standards of many thousands of persons it is not enough

[23]The organization of the strike was largely in Communist hands, and it was timed with a view to inflicting damage on the Marshall Plan. But, as often in stoppages of this sort, a real grievance was exploited.

to have a policy the merits of which can be defended, but it is necessary actively to defend these merits. A very large amount of educational work is done within the trade unions, through the Workers' Educational Association (which in Norway is run jointly by the Labor party and the unions) and the trade union and Labor party press, to explain both the Government's economic and social policy in general and, in particular, the policy being followed by the trade unions in regard to wages. It has been an advantage that the basic ideas of this policy can be easily grasped and their justice appreciated. All the workers' representatives in industry—who as has been shown have an accepted and important status—and other trade union officials attend courses organized by the Workers' Educational Association and are expected to pass on to their members the knowledge of government and trade union policy thus gained. A good understanding of Norway's economic problems has thus been brought about, and it has generally been appreciated that a very rapid advance in living standards cannot be secured while a large proportion of national energies and resources must be devoted to recovery from war damage, to further economic development so that Norway may be able to face the changed international economic circumstances of the postwar world, and to defence. There is also an Economic Coordination Council, consisting of leading representatives of industry, trade, agriculture, and labor organizations, to which the Government can make its policy and the national economic position clear, and from which it can receive advice on the practical aspects of economic matters. This Council plays an important part in securing an understanding of government policy.

In many respects Norway has been unusually fortunate. The structure of the trade union movement and its tradition of unified action, the small population of the country and the comparative simplicity of its economic life, the determination of the Government to prevent inflation arising from domestic policies and to check as far as possible increased prices resulting from international conditions, the extent of confidence and mutual understanding between it and the trade unions, and the fact that economic trends have worked in favor of, rather than against, many of the Government's social policies—all these have helped to achieve satisfactory results. Norwegian experience would appear to have shown that, given freedom from large international disturbances, it is possible for full employment to be maintained without continually rising price levels and an accompanying race between prices and wages.

III

The Development of Collective Employment Agreements in the Netherlands

P. S. PELS

A PUBLICATION on the development of collective agreements in the Netherlands could, theoretically speaking, be divided into two distinct sections: one giving a description of the organizational aspect—relations between contracting parties, growth of organized consultations, drawing up of the collective employment agreement, and the like—the other dealing with the main provisions of the collective agreement itself. However, when these are set forth in detail, various parts are seen to be closely related. For instance, in dealing with the main provision of a collective agreement—that of wages—it will be evident that the postwar wage policy has, to a very great extent, been conducted along the lines of organizational deliberations between employers' and employees' associations, and between industry and government. This implies equality of rights of the contracting parties and means that certain forces within society are operative in the determination of social policy, as a result of which certain changes are brought about in the structure of society.

At first this method of operation of the employers' and employees' associations was limited to social matters, but in course of time the scope of operation was widened to include economic problems as well. As a result the initial task of the associations has been modified and greatly enlarged.

The whole process, which is here treated in detail, is further characterized by increasing cooperation in industry. In this connection one has to concentrate in practice upon the things that tend to bring the parties together, rather than upon those that tend to make cooperation impossible. In addition there is the fact that by reason of its origin and nature, the structure of the Netherlands is strongly democratic—which, along with other psychological characteristics, has exerted an accelerated catalytic effect upon the whole process of social development. It is against this background that the various sections of this essay should be viewed.

Development of the Collective Agreement

Up to the end of the nineteenth century, a high degree of arbitrary action and of indifference to principles of justice governed the position of the worker in the production process and his remuneration, and other social provisions. Labor was merchandise. Its rate of remuneration was decided mainly by the economic position of the undertakings concerned. As no element of bargaining power existed, such as is now afforded by associations of employees, these matters were more often than not dealt with in a one-sided and prejudiced manner. The result was social uncertainty and undesirable social conditions. These symptoms, which in principle were international, are set forth in the copious literature dealing with conditions of the working classes in the nineteenth century.

Once he gained political liberty, however, the worker in the Netherlands as elsewhere became a citizen instead of a subject. With this liberty the working classes were able to develop into a political and economic force. It was, in fact, through political rights that the first legal relationships between workers and employers came about. At first, especially at the beginning of the nineteenth century, these legal relationships were of an individual nature; later, particularly in the twentieth century, they took on increasingly the form of collective agreements, due mainly to the fact that during this period of growth individual employees combined into trade unions, which entered into collective employment agreements for and on behalf of their individual members.

The trade unions made it their business to approach individual employers in regard to individual employment agreements; this often involved a struggle. However, by their efforts over the years to better conditions of employment, trade unions finally became recognized institutions; then, more and more, in cases where the labor unions took action to draw up an employment agreement, such action was conducted in the form of negotiations. These negotiations were collective and led to agreements about the rights and obligations of the employers and employees concerned: the collective agreement.

As may well be expected, employment agreements arising from the legal relationship mentioned above—which regulated not only the all-round social standing of the worker but also his rate of pay—were at first arbitrary in form and content. Moreover, they showed very little, if any, connection with each other. Only at a later date, and then largely by way of the influence exerted by the Government upon these agreements and following the growth of the workers' associations, was a bond of collective organization established. This affected not alone the members of the organizations concerned, but also workers who did not join an organization. The organized group thus acted also on behalf of the unorganized (or nonunion) workers.

An important result of these developments was that the regulation of collective agreements became a matter that was legalized by the Government. The (Netherlands) Act of December 24, 1927 provided for the regulation of collective employment agreements. The institution of collective employment agreements proved to be of benefit to employer and employee alike in regulation of the conditions of employment of labor, as it created an atmosphere of greater stability and security in industry. In times of a slump in trade, however, it was felt to be a drawback that the competition of unorganized employers became more keen, while unorganized workers were either unable to benefit by the collective agreement or were in a position to act in contravention to it. It was, therefore, considered necessary to do away with these obstructions. This led to the (Netherlands) Act of May 25, 1937, whereby the provisions of collective employment agreements could be declared by the Minister of Labor to be universally applicable and enforceable, or not ("extension").[1] After World War II the duties of the Minister in this respect were assigned to a Government Mediation Board by virtue of the (Netherlands) Extraordinary Decree on Labor Relations of 1945.

Collective agreements often contain clauses regulating the manner of settling any disputes that may arise. Courts of arbitration are usually assigned for this purpose, or a committee is appointed to pronounce an arbitral decision. In the Act of 1937 such provisions are excluded from "extension" by the Minister, as the Act would otherwise clash with constitutional law. In the explanatory memorandum to this Act it is pointed out by the Government that, from the point of view of legal security, it would be open to objection for employers and workers outside the scope of the collective agreement to be subject to decisions or advisory reports of committees which had been established by parties to the collective employment agreement. Prior to 1940, by virtue of this Act, the provisions in regard to wages of four collective employment agreements were declared to be universally binding. This applied to the shoe industry, the printing and copperplate engraving industry, the painting industry, and the brick industry in the area bordering upon the big rivers.

In this way the will of the group (that is, the joint decision of the employers' and employees' associations and, hence, that of their members) was made decisive for establishing the conditions of employment of unorganized workers. This means that, through the medium of government intervention, an agreement entered into voluntarily—as is characteristic of a collective agreement—can be declared to be applicable to other persons who are not parties to the contract.

This growth of the scope of collectivity, the development of the

[1]Extension is based on the condition that the agreement applies to a large majority of the persons employed in the industry concerned, taking into account the particular conditions ruling in that industry.

power of the associations concerned, their cooperation on a higher level—accompanied and upheld by a certain degree of government intervention—was interrupted by the war in 1940. Immediately after 1945, however, all this was continued under new conditions, as a result of which the area of contacts among employers, workers, and government was greatly extended.

The development of the collective agreement can be further illustrated statistically:

Table 1. NUMBER OF WORKERS COMING WITHIN THE SCOPE OF A COLLECTIVE AGREEMENT.

Jan. 1911	*Jan. 1920*	*June 1930*	*June 1940*	*Jan. 1951*	*Jan. 1955*
23,000	273,600	385,800	351,800	950,000	1,330,000

Source: (Netherlands) Central Bureau of Statistics.

The following table should be considered in conjunction with the above statistics.

Table 2. NUMBER OF COLLECTIVE AGREEMENTS.

Dec. 31, 1949:	296
Dec. 31, 1950:	364 of which 45 are operative throughout the country.
Dec. 31, 1951:	388 of which 47 are operative throughout the country.
Dec. 31, 1954:	469 of which 71 are operative throughout the country.

Source: (Netherlands) Central Bureau of Statistics.

According to a statement of the Central Statistical Bureau it may be assumed that, in 1940, about 15 percent of the employed persons came within the scope of a collective agreement or a universalized collective agreement. At present there are about one million employees who come within the scope of a collective agreement or a universalized collective agreement, representing about 34 percent of the total number of wage earners. Since 1945 various regulations of wages and conditions of employment have also been established which were in many respects comparable to a collective agreement but which for a number of reasons (often of a technical nature) could not for the time being be established in that form. These adjustments, which were bindingly established by the Government, were usually made after the employers' and employees' associations concerned had submitted a corresponding proposal to the Government and the matter had been worked out with these associations.

Table 3. NUMBER OF WAGE ADJUSTMENTS APPROVED AS BINDING AGREEMENTS.

Jan. 1947	*Jan. 1948*	*Jan. 1949*	*Dec. 31, 1950*	*Dec. 31, 1952*
150	180	200	215	234

Source: (Netherlands) Central Statistical Bureau, "Regelingen van lonen en andere arbeidsvoorwaarden in Nederland" (Regulations of Wages and Other Conditions of Employment), Dec. 31, 1950.

It may be concluded that, while 34 percent of the total number of employed persons come within the scope of a universalized or nonuniversalized collective agreement, another 48 percent are covered by other regulations of working conditions which have been established in a binding form. This means that the legal position of about 82 percent of the total number of wage earners has been laid down in agreements declared by government to be universally binding. These statistics give a picture of the trend and rate of progress of the development of collective agreements in the Netherlands.

Relations between Employers' and Employees' Associations

In the early stages of union development, negotiations with employers or their associations were in many cases impossible, since the workers were usually not regarded as full partners in social matters. The demands of the unions in this period were often accompanied by threats of strikes or actual strikes. With the growth of unions and employees' associations, a new stage was reached. During the decade following World War I, the unions demanded that they be given the right to negotiate on social matters and to be heard on economic problems.

About 1920 the first notions in regard to an industrial organization made their entry into the political life of the Netherlands. From 1920 to 1940 a certain growth in this direction became noticeable, which was at first limited to the inclusion of representatives of labor unions in certain advisory committees dealing with social affairs. Furthermore, various forms of organized cooperation between employers and workers came into being in the field of social insurance, especially as regards its administration. These early signs of more complete cooperation between employers' and employees' associations were to a large extent consolidated and extended after World War II.

During the German occupation of the Netherlands, in the years 1940–1945, it was realized more and more in the central associations of employers and employees that the country would not be able to perform its future task of restoration and reconstruction unless it could be assured of peaceful labor conditions and social justice. This conviction and the desire to transform the incidental prewar cooperation between employers and employees into cooperation at a higher, broader, and more permanent level between the central organizations of employers and employees, and between organizations in the various industries and enterprises, were expressed in secret meetings during the war. Yet, at the same time, plans were made to decide in what manner the extensive field of social affairs could, after liberation of the country, be controlled jointly by the employers' and employees' organizations on a basis of equality of status and rights. In this way the Labor Foundation—the foremost instrument of labor-management cooperation—came into being in May 1945. The Foundation, which operates under civil law, is an institution in which the large, bona fide central organizations of employers and employees can cooperate on a basis of equality of status and rights. It is, therefore, a two-party, top-level institution, originating from and based upon voluntary agreement and free negotiation by the central organizations of employers and employees.

In the Netherlands, employers and employees are organized into associations along ideological and denominational lines. There are three main trade union centers: a socialist organization (the Netherlands Federation of Trade Unions, known as the NVV), a Roman Catholic organization (the Catholic Workers' Movement, known as the KAB), and a Protestant organization (the Christian National Federation of Trade Unions in the Netherlands, known as the CNV). Each of these central trade union organizations comprises, for instance, trade unions of workers in the metal industry, the building industry, food establishments, transport undertakings, miscellaneous branches of industry, as well as unions of government servants, office staff, and the like. A similar structure exists on the side of the employers: the Central Social Employers' associations, the General Catholic Association of Employers' trade unions, and an association of Protestant Christian Employers.

During the war these organizations were, in semblance, disbanded as a result of drastic measures taken by the enemy in occupation, but their leading figures kept contact with each other, with the result that immediately after the war—in May 1945—these organizations came to life again and the Labor Foundation was established. The Foundation issued a manifesto announcing to the Dutch people that, as a result of organized cooperation of employers and employees, good social relationships of a permanent nature should be achieved in the economic system of the Netherlands. The following statement was made in the manifesto:

> Provision has been made for joint consultation in the sphere of social affairs, both individually on behalf of each industry and within the framework of national and central organizations. The Foundation furthermore places itself at the Government's disposal for the fulfilment of assignments entrusted to it on behalf of community interests.

The manifesto also contained a particularly important declaration to which later reference will be made—regarding the necessity for the establishment of lower institutional organs operating in the domain of public law. The method of putting this into effect and the question as to how further cooperation in the economic field could be stimulated would be studied without delay by government, by management, and by the employees. The Labor Foundation was thus intended to confine its activities to *social* matters, on the understanding that soon suitable forms of procedure would be arrived at whereby the workers' trade union movement could be included in the regulation of *economic* problems.

In the field of social activity, the Foundation did not interpret the term "social matters" in the vague, conventional sense which had been common in the past, to denote the abolition of certain bad social conditions. On the contrary, the existence and structure of the Foundation were a recognition in the Netherlands that social conditions had now come within the province of labor in its legal aspect; in other words, a new code of law for labor had been created. In this way, the subject of labor relationships—man and his role in life—had become the pivotal problem of labor law.

The principle of joint negotiation in social matters, as manifested within the Labor Foundation in the form of joint deliberations of the central organizations, led also to the encouragement of similar two-party negotiations in the industries themselves. The Foundation in this way accorded recognition to bipartite committees in various branches of industry—in the metal industry, the textile industry, the shoe industry, and others. These are called "Trade Councils."

Shortly after its establishment, the Foundation was recognized by the Government as the official advisory organ on social problems with which it was expected to deal. The Foundation was also to issue from time to time advisory reports to the Government without being expressly requested to do so. Yet the Foundation is free and independent of the Government. Based entirely on the free operation of cooperative forces in industry, it is thus an institution for and on behalf of industry—a channel through which the opinions of industry[2] can reach the Government, and vice versa. This, too, was a further link in an evolutionary process and the expression of a desire for further cooperation—cooperation between industry and government.

The advisory task of the Foundation with regard to the Government was legalized in the Extraordinary Decree on Labor Relations of 1945, which provided for the appointment by the Minister of Labor of a "Board of Government Mediators." This Board

> may, at the request of employers' and employees' associations or by virtue of its office, make regulations of or in connection with wages and other employment conditions of employees in a binding manner. Such regulations have the same force as provisions

[2]Throughout this essay, the term "industry" means management and labor.

which have been declared binding by virtue of the Act for declaring the provisions of collective employment agreements to be universally binding or non-binding.

Furthermore, the Board must approve all collective agreements and acts in general for the Minister with regard to the "extension" of collective agreements. In all of these matters the Board "will obtain advice from the Labor Foundation" (Art. 19). In fact, therefore, the setting of wages is no longer abandoned to the "free play of social forces."

Development of Wage Policy

Before World War II, the rate of pay in the Netherlands, as elsewhere, was dependent upon widely varying factors: the relation between demand and supply, the situation of the labor market, the economic position of industrial undertakings—particularly the difference between protected and unprotected industries—the mutual relationship between employers and employees, the influence of trade unions. The wage structure was, therefore, usually built up in a chaotic manner, and there was little consistency in wage relationships within different enterprises or industries.

Prior to 1940 wage rates for comparable occupations, with few exceptions, varied considerably within one and the same industry, or even within one and the same district. The growth of the trade unions created power differentials which caused the rates of pay in large towns to be considerably higher than those in smaller places. Methods of wage computation for different skills differed from industry to industry. For factory workers, for instance, the guaranteed minimum wage of unskilled workers was used as base pay from which the rates of semiskilled and skilled workers were computed. In the so-called "craftsmen's industries," on the other hand—such as the metal industry, the building trades—the rates of the skilled workers were the base of the wage structure.

Even the progress of collective agreements did not produce uniformity. In many medium-sized and small districts the local wage standard was usually determined by the wages of one big enterprise. In other cases, differential wage rates were related to wage zones, with the size of the population in a community usually the determining factor.

Before 1940 the influence exerted by government upon wages was of a more indirect nature, consisting of but occasional interference with the free operation of social forces. Government influence thus took the form of supervision to ensure the payment of wage rates stipulated by contract. By virtue of the Home Employment Act of 1933 the Government was empowered to set wages in certain sections of industry. During the years of economic depression after 1930, laws were enacted enabling collective agreements in the agricultural sector to be declared binding through the machinery of compulsory arbitration. Finally, before 1940 an act "extending" collective agreements made it possible for the Government to take certain forms of action—including the setting of wages in a binding manner—in certain sectors, on behalf of which an application to this effect had been made by the organized section of an industry. This represented a certain degree of wage control, but only in those parts of industry in which powerful associations of employers and employees existed. This trend was interrupted by the war in 1940 but was continued in an intensified form after 1945 with very much more contact and consultation among employers, workers, and government in regard to the wage structure.[3] During the war period, 1940–1945, no activity in the field of wage policy was, of course, possible. No trade unions formed and operating democratically existed.

The disastrous position of the country as a result of the war gave rise to special problems—among them, the development of a suitable wage structure. With liberation in May 1945, measures were at once taken for general "restoration and reconstruction," to use the terms of the government program for that year. It was necessary to ensure that the work of reconstruction would not be jeopardized by inflationist tendencies. Special attention had to be paid to the country's precarious monetary situation. Wage and price controls were adopted.

[3]See Dr. P. S. Pels, *De ontwikkeling van de loonvorming (The Development of the Wage Structure)*, Rijn: Samson, 1952.

The war resulted in a most acute shortage of all the means of production—stocks, basic materials, workers. There had been ruinous devastation, not only of material but also of human lives. Moreover, there are but few raw materials in the Netherlands. The country was therefore largely dependent upon supplies from foreign sources. The need for imports also entailed the necessity for exporting. There were difficulties in Indonesia and that country separated itself from the Netherlands. Rationing was continued during the first few years after the war; serious shortages existed in the supplies of textiles and other consumer commodities, of housing, etc.

These and many other factors made it necessary to adopt a planned social and economic policy. Confronted with a difficult task, the unions did their share in carrying out the policy and supported it, out of devotion to the national interest. Without this cooperation and without the collaboration of the Labor Foundation, the task of bringing about the gradual recovery of the country could not have been successfully accomplished.

Some idea of the development of the country since 1945 may be gained from the following recent statistics, which afford sufficient evidence of the rate at which the country has recovered, thanks to the policy pursued. As a result of the principle of consultation which was applied within the Labor Foundation and between industry (that is, labor and management) and government, the number of strikes has been exceedingly small, a factor which has assisted materially in the country's rapid recovery. Last but not least, the great increase in population has created its own particular problems.

The trend of the general situation since 1945 is shown by the following tables, which have been compiled from statistical data furnished by the (Netherlands) Central Bureau of Statistics.

Table 4. IMPORTS AND EXPORTS.
(% COVERAGE OF IMPORTS BY EXPORTS)

Year	%
1938	73.5
1946	33.0
1947	44.0
1948	54.9
1949	71.9
1950	68.3
1951	76.7
1952	94.0
1953	90.0
1954	84.0

Table 5. PRODUCTION PER WORKER IN INDUSTRY.
(EXCL. BUILDING)

	Production Index		*Production per Worker*	
Year	1938 = 100	1949 = 100	1938 = 100	1949 = 100
1945 2nd half	31	—	—	—
1946	74	—	70	—
1947	94	—	77	—
1948	113	—	83	—
1949	126	100	88	100
1950	139	112	93	108
1951	145	116	95	109
1952	—	116	—	112
1953	—	127	—	120
1954	—	140	—	128

Table 6. POPULATION.

Date	*Number*
1945 (Jan.)	9,220,294
1946	9,304,301
1947	9,542,659
1948	9,715,890
1949	9,884,415
1950	10,026,773
1951	10,200,280
1952	10,435,631
1953	10,550,737
1955 (1 Sept.)	10,775,960

Table 7. Strikes and Lockouts.

Year	*Number of Disputes*	*Maximum Number of Employees Concerned*	*Number of Workdays Lost*
1938	139	about 9,000	124,800
1945	118	36,500	161,200
1946	266	71,700	681,600
1947	272	64,440	203,400
1948	183	19,030	131,400
1949	116	15,402	289,400
1950	79	20,944	162,500
1951	85	15,324	66,700
1952	40	3,852	31,237
1953	58	11,383	29,852

Table 8. Unemployment.

Year	*Number in Thousands*
1946	93.0
1947	46.9
1948	43.3
1949	63.1
1950	80.2
1951	93.4
1952 Jan.	174.9
Dec.	175.8
1953 Jan.	150.8
Dec.	99.8
1954 Jan.	109.8
Dec.	72.9
1955 Jan.	82.6
July	30.1
Sept.	26.8

Wage Policy since 1945

Almost immediately after the liberation of the country, it became necessary to formulate a controlled wage policy. Government and organized industry, as embodied in the Labor Foundation, were of the opinion that wage control should be based on efforts to secure "social justice" and that the wage structure would be founded on the principle of a "social minimum wage." For this a concrete standard had to be found, which involved several months' work. To stabilize the trend of wages, permission was given for wages to be fixed at a level of 125 percent of May 1940. The Extraordinary Decree on Labor Relations of 1945 provided that any wages above this limit would be subject to approval by the Mediation Board, which in turn would obtain advice on the matter from the Labor Foundation. The first limitation of wages was described as the "first wage round." It was followed by several other wage rounds, which are described below.

The social minimum wage was established in September 1945 on the basis of the minimum budget necessary for the family of an unskilled worker (man, wife, and two children) in the big cities. In the absence of a better classification of workers, a rough division into unskilled, semiskilled, and skilled was at first adopted. Furthermore, the difference in pay between unskilled and skilled workers was, for the time being, maintained at about 20 percent.

The differences in cost of living (including house rents, etc.) in different areas rendered it necessary to divide the various municipal districts into five classes. After consultation between government and industry a wage differential between town and country of f.4.– per week was established.

In this way it became possible to draw up a scheme of wages for hourly and weekly rates of pay of workers. Its observance and the drawing up of the various collective agreements on the basis of this plan were entrusted to the Mediation Board, with the cooperation of the Labor Foundation.

In view of the rising trend of prices and hence of the cost of living, it was considered necessary on several occasions after 1945 to raise the level of the first wage plan. Furthermore, at the end of 1946 it was decided by the Government that at that moment wages should only be increased if the increase was accompanied by increased productivity. Hence a new element was added to the wage structure involving the problem of incentive wages: rate setting, merit rating, special allowances, and the like. In addition, there was the element of special need, which was met by granting, for instance, children's allowances.

Summarizing, it may be stated that during the period 1945–1947 wage standards were built mainly out of the following elements: basic wages based on the consumers' price index; a functional classification; a classification according to wage zones; income standards relating to incentives; and the factor of need. Brief comment follows on the development of each of these aspects during subsequent years.

Relation between Wages and Prices

The rise of world prices, especially those of basic materials, found its repercussion in a rise of the price indices of family consumption, often wrongly designated as the cost of living. From the point of view of employment opportunities, position of the balance of payments, exports, and the like, it was of course unwarranted to accelerate the upward movement of prices by constantly increasing wages to the same extent. The dangers of such a vicious circle were acknowledged by the trade unions. The Government endeavored in various ways to put a brake on the rise of prices, e.g., by granting considerable subsidies for commodities that were of essential importance to family budgets and by manipulating the machinery of price control. The latter was particularly necessary and was possible during the years immediately following the war, when many commodities were still rationed. It was of course impossible to "freeze" prices altogether, because of the considerable rise in the price level of other countries—the result often of international political events and tensions, as the devaluation of September 1949, the Korean crisis, etc. The wage and price level was, therefore, constantly watched and was made the subject of frequent consultations between government and industry, with the result that new measures were enacted in regard to both wages and prices.

In this way many changes were made in the basic scheme of wages during the period that has elapsed since 1945, each change of this kind being described as a "wage round." The trend of the standards adopted for hourly pay is illustrated in Table 9.

The wage policy also made it possible—especially at moments when increases in wages were out of the question—to carry out various social measures which were of value to the workers in terms

Table 9. STANDARDS OF HOURLY PAY.
(In Cents)

Wage Zone	Unskilled Workers End of 1947	Jan. 1950	Jan. 1951	Mar. 1951	Oct. 1954	Skilled Workers End of 1947	Jan. 1950	Jan. 1951	Mar. 1951	Oct. 1954
I	78	84	88	92	103	94	101	106	111	126
II	75	81	85	89	100½	91	98	103	108	123½
III	72	78	82	86	98	88	95	100	105	121
IV	69	75	79	83	95½	85	92	97	102	118½
V	66	72	76	80	93	82	89	94	99	116

of real income. This was done by using the machinery of collective negotiation to set up compulsory Works Pension Funds (e.g., in the metal industry, building trade, agriculture, textile industry, cigar industry, butchers' establishments). The premium payable to these pension funds, which varies from 2 to 3 guilders weekly, is borne equally by the employer and the employee. The employee's contribution was made possible by increasing the wages of employees by an amount equal to that of the premium due from them. Similar measures were put into effect regarding rules governing loss of work time (in consequence of frost, rain, etc.), part pay or unemployment insurance, and the like.

The machinery of collective bargaining has, after several years, also provided for the inclusion in collective agreements of a compulsory vacation allowance amounting to 2 percent of annual earnings (in 1956, 4 percent). Concurrently with the establishment of this obligation under the terms of collective agreements, permission was given to employers outside the scope of such agreements to grant a similar allowance to their employees. In this way, practically all workers are now assured of an allowance for their vacations.

Functional Classification

The initial classification of employees in the three functional groups of skilled, semiskilled, unskilled entailed difficulties both for industry (especially the workers) and for the Government. This classification could not very well be based on impartial standards, and its institution often gave rise to tension in industrial establishments. One of the most serious drawbacks of such a summary method of classification undoubtedly lies in the fact that it only allows for limited possibilities of wage rate differentials. The drawback for the Government was that this classification and its often incorrect application constituted a danger to the general wage level. In view of this, negotiations were conducted between government and industry regarding a finer functional classification based on previous studies of job classification. Although there were many difficulties to be overcome at the start, an increasing number of wage regulations were drafted on the basis of a system of job classification. Within a short time, for instance, a fully planned system of functional classification based on job classification will be included in the collective agreement for the entire metal industry. The increasing use of job classification has rendered it necessary to arrive at a greater unification of the systems employed. After years of preparatory work, a Standardized Method of Job Classification was established in 1952. While this refers particularly to the technique of establishing wage rates, it was considered desirable to pay some attention to those aspects as well which have a bearing on wage policy.

In the course of further consultation between the Government and the Labor Foundation, a report has been published which points out that job classification is not the only aid to the setting of wages. There must be room for other aspects of functional valuation, such as historic relationships, the economic position of the industry concerned, temporary fluctuations on the labor market, working hours and seniority of the workers, sex. An explanation is given of the term "functional wages" as developed in the practice of setting wage rates and of the principles on which such functional wages are set. Finally, the report emphasizes that job classification is not the final arbiter in wage setting. It is simply a means of determining the most correct grading of the duties of manual workers in industry without considering the manner in which those duties are performed. The possibility must therefore be left open for personal evaluation as well. As job classification is one of the fundaments on which reasonable wage structures are based, the utmost care must be exercised in the manipulation of this aid. It should be applied with consideration for the realities, which in some industries are such that the work cannot be split up into specific jobs. Moreover, there are forms of employment consisting of part jobs for which one may, for instance, adopt a weighted average evaluation.

Furthermore, it is universally acknowledged that it is no easy matter for employees' associations to give the workers the benefit of a piece of scientific research based on practical experience in industry. For the performance of such a task it is often necessary to overcome a certain amount of psychological resistance which is the result of historical factors. Research on job classification is, therefore, regarded as one of the components of wage policy which should be dealt with in joint negotiations between employers and workers. In these negotiations, both parties should have expert information on this technique. In this, great advances have now been made in the associations concerned. Since the wage differential between unskilled and skilled workers is usually too small, the position is now being examined in order to see how far the system of job classification could be used to eliminate this leveling down. Something needs to be done to obtain more competent workers, an objective of great importance for the desired industrialization of the country. Job classification offers the means to this end, since it makes it possible to cause the wage curve to rise more steeply for higher-grade work, and thereby provides a stimulus for competent craftmanship.

Classification According to Wage Zones

Uniformity of classification was established in 1946 by dividing municipalities into five classes for the purpose of wage setting. This problem, which has many economic, social, psychological, cultural, and sociological aspects, is one of great interest because of the tension which this classification tends to set up between town and country. Numerous reports have been issued on this matter, in particular the report of a state committee which has studied this problem very profoundly and whose findings may serve as basis for the Government's future policy, especially in regard to wage policy. As a result of the system of classification adopted in this report, an average difference in pay between town and country of 10 cents per hour is now established in wage regulations.

Incentive Wages

The problem of incentive pay came to the fore shortly after 1945. Before the war piecework and its rates of pay were generally based on "practice." Those who had experience of the way the rates were "chopped" in times of depression regarded piecework with suspicion and aversion which was still more noticeable in cases where it had led to the "sweating system." After the war, however, workers realized that well-studied, impartially determined, measurable, and verifiable rates of pay expressed in time units afforded them a guarantee of income and earning possibilities based on performance, while employers found that such rates tended to lower the cost of the product.

The adoption of measured rates of pay also meant that working performance was regulated in a more responsible manner. In order to see how these rates of pay would develop it was necessary during the first few years to restrict piecework earnings to an excess margin of 20 to 25 percent. In later years this ceiling was abolished, as it automatically became unnecessary under a system of correct rating. In the case of the old rates based on "practice," i.e., not arrived at by time studies, a maximum margin of 10 to 15 percent was adhered to. Measured rates have been more and more widely adopted and very good results have been obtained even in the opinion of those who used to view this procedure with suspicion. Other forms of incentive wages, such as merit rating, extra allowances in respect of rating losses, and the like, have likewise been introduced. It may be considered a unique fact that, after exchanges of opinion among all the associations of industry, within industry, and between industry and government, an absolutely unanimous report has been issued on the subject of incentive wage rating. This report, which deals in a detailed manner with the various possibilities and standards of the rating system, is used as a guide by industry and government.

In a system of incentive rating a distinction is made between individual and collective premiums. There is a certain reluctance, however, to introduce a merit rating system on a large scale. The general opinion is that, in a planned wage policy like that pursued in the Netherlands, the adoption of a system of merit rating entails the danger that the workers will be awarded premiums not varying to any appreciable extent, which would be tantamount to an unwarranted all-round increase in wages.

There is no division of opinion in Holland as to whether and to what extent the workers should be allowed to participate in drafting wage rating systems and in expressing their opinion on them. As incentive rating forms part of the over-all wage policy, it is universally acknowledged that the workers have a right of codetermination also in this matter. Wage rating systems are, therefore, dealt with in collective bargaining. Several unions have engaged the services of wage rating experts. Although workers do not generally possess the special knowledge required for mastering the techniques of wage rating, it is essential that they have confidence in the established rates. This, too, is an argument in favor of making this matter a subject for negotiation with the workers.

Wage rating committees have been formed in most industrial establishments; the membership consists as far as possible of workers' representatives who have some competence in wage rating. Employers' associations and trade unions alike attach great importance to the necessary time studies. In many establishments there are separate time study departments. The task of the wage rating committees is mainly to deal with any objections that might be raised against specific rates or their method of application.

Furthermore, various collective agreements also contain certain special stipulations, relating for instance to diploma premiums, long-service premiums, etc.

The Factor of Need

The calculation of basic hourly wage rates related to the cost of living as mentioned above refers to families of average size—man, wife, and two children—and is applied to able male adult workers. The lower age limit for them is usually set at about 23 to 25 years. With this as starting point, juvenile rates are established which are expressed as percentages of the rates for adults. Up to now different rates of pay for male and female workers have been maintained, particularly on grounds of differences in needs, training costs, and the like. Following the conclusion of the Convention in 1951 in the International Labor Conference at Geneva regarding remuneration for equal work of equal value, the Government in consultation with industry is now investigating whether this Convention can be ratified by the Netherlands and, if such ratification is possible, in which manner the principle of equal pay could be put into effect. A system of children's allowances was also introduced.

The Drafting of Wage Regulations

According to the Special Decree on Labor Relations of 1945, wage regulations and collective agreements have to be approved by the Government Mediation Board. This Board consists of a number of government-appointed experts whose task it is to determine wages and other conditions of employment for entire industries as well as for individual establishments. Before the Board makes a decision it is required under the terms of the decree of 1945 to obtain advice from the Labor Foundation in all cases of considerable importance.

In practice, nearly all collective agreements and wage regulations pass through the hands of the Labor Foundation. The drafting of wage regulations and collective agreements is, however, in the first instance, the business of the relevant employers' and employees' associations. The organizational structure of industry is such that employers' and employees' associations now exist in practically all industries. In many industries there are permanent negotiating bodies (Trade Councils, etc.), constituted on a basis of equal representation, in which the necessary preparatory discussions are held before they submit their final proposals to the Board. These proposals are simultaneously sent to the Labor Foundation, since it is supposed to give its advice to the Board. For this important task the Labor Foundation has appointed a separate Wage Committee to which the central associations of employers and workers have nominated wage experts. The Wage Committee holds its sessions on a set day of the week; it prepares advisory reports which the Labor Foundation transmits to the Government Mediators. The Wage Committee carries on with the parties concerned discussions of the wage proposals submitted. These so-called hearings provide time for the discussion of any objections of the Wage Committee with the parties, and for amendments of some of the proposals if necessary. In addition, the Wage Committee holds discussions at regular intervals with representatives of the Board. Special attention is being paid to individual current difficulties associated with specific proposals or to the situation that has arisen because—as happens in isolated instances—the Board had deviated considerably from the recommendations made in the advisory report of the Labor Foundation.

These advisory duties of the Labor Foundation in connection with wage policy constitute the most important work of the Foundation. This is shown, for instance, in the large number of advisory reports issued by the Foundation to the Government Mediation Board: from May 1945 to November 1955 more than two thousand reports were made. The Wage Committee held roughly five thousand meetings with employers' and employees' associations on wage regulations or collective agreements. Many of these dealt also with the settlement of differences between employers' and employees' associations regarding proposed wages and other conditions of employment; meetings were also held in cases where labor relations were likely to be disturbed. The mediatory function of the Labor Foundation has undoubtedly gone a long way toward achieving the necessary stability of labor relations in the interest of employers and workers alike. For a country like the Netherlands, which in prewar times was so acutely affected by conflicts due to opposing interests, this means that such conflicts have been superseded by intensive cooperation and a system of consultation based on the realization that in the sphere of social policy the workers are partners of their employers on a footing of equality. The controlled wage policy—the most vital part of the over-all social policy—thus established the right of codetermination of the workers in social matters.

Government influence on wage policy and the establishment of standards as criteria for government decisions have of late given rise in some quarters to the question whether wage policy should not be given somewhat more liberty. Deviations of basic hourly rates of pay, both upward and downward, should be made possible, it is said, in view of special difficulties of particular enterprises, on the one hand, and of the possibilities that may be open to them under favorable economic conditions, on the other hand. However, no change of wage policy in this sense is likely to be made in the near future, since only recently the highest organ of industry, the Social-Economic Council, issued a unanimous advisory report to the Government stating that in the near future it will be necessary to continue the wage policy pursued up to now. Pending the development of the new industrial bodies referred to in the closing section of this article, the controlled wage policy will thus be maintained in its entirety.

Further Development of the Social Structure

The development of the machinery of organized negotiations reached its culminating point after the war in the Labor Foundation and its activities. To eliminate any possible misunderstandings it must again be pointed out that, though it cooperates with the Government, the Labor Foundation is a private institution which deals exclusively with social problems.

Immediately after its formation, the Foundation—representing the joint associations of employers and employees—was of the opinion that efforts should soon be made to bring institutions into existence which operate under public law. The manifesto of the Labor Foundation of May 1945 emphasized that the fulfilment of this objective and the question of promoting further cooperation in the economic sphere should at once be studied by government, employers, and workers.

In 1946, on the initiative of the Labor Foundation, the Government set up a committee to investigate the possibilities of an industrial organization under public law.[4] The committee was to ascer-

[4]The idea of an industrial organization began to develop in the Netherlands around 1920, though until 1940 its realization was confined to the formation of advisory committees of the Government in which industry was represented by both employers and employees.

tain in what way industry could be integrated within the Government's own organization and the new industrial bodies be given regulatory powers.

In 1949 an Industrial Organization Act was passed. Some fundamental principles concerning views of life or conceptions of the form of society formed the deeper background of this Act. The main issue throughout was to find ways and means of establishing a new relationship between state and society, with religious and other groups expressing their views. This spiritual background is to a large extent responsible for the social policy that has been pursued in the Netherlands since the last world war; it is characterized by an unwritten law of cooperation in industry and by the principle of close contact and deliberation between government and organized industry. Out of this cooperation emerged the Act Governing Industrial Organization under Public Law, promulgated on February 14, 1949, after having been prepared by a committee on which government and industry were represented. A phase of social development was thus carried to its conclusion.

The Act is a legal framework within which new industrial bodies can be built up. The law creates a two-part structure, comprising a Social-Economic Council and the organized groups of associated industries. The Social-Economic Council (SEC), referred to in the Netherlands as SER, is regarded as the highest organ of industry. The Council consists of 45 members, 15 of whom are nominated and appointed by the Government (these are independent experts, not representatives of the Government), 15 by the central and other representative organizations of employers, and 15 by the central organizations of workers. The outstanding feature of the Council is that it is constituted on the basis of free association of employers and workers. The members vote without receiving instructions or entering into consultation, which means that in a formal sense they cannot be regarded as "representatives" of the associations by which they were appointed. In practice, however, they do act as "exponents" of certain currents of opinion in social problems.

The task of the SER is not only to act in an advisory capacity but also "to put industrial activity at the service of the Dutch people and to promote the interests of industry and of the persons engaged in it." This implies that the Council is meant to form a bridge between community interests and industry, including the employers and workers concerned. The Council has authority to issue decrees, its decisions are of a legal nature, while the Government has the right to annul or suspend these decrees insofar as they are in conflict with law or with the interests of the community. In this way, means are provided for the exercise of repressive control. In some cases, preventive control can also be exercised. Thus the SER has an advisory and an administrative task.

The administrative functions of the Council consist in preparing and supervising the other industrial bodies which represent a vertical or horizontal organization of industry, namely, the commodity alliances and industry alliances. In this field, the Council can exercise control by issuing decrees.

The assignment of advisory tasks to the SER was intended to transfer to the Council various functions of the Labor Foundation in the field of social affairs. This transfer has been proceeding. The advisory functions of the Council deal with implementing the law and with all matters of a social or economic nature.

During the period of about five years that the Council has been in existence it has done work on a very large scale. It has expressed opinions (some of them periodical) on many industrial problems, among them: wages, consumption and investment restrictions, part-pay and unemployment insurance, and the associate problems of wage compensation, a share in ownership for workers, rent, employment, equal pay for equal work for men and women, the sick fund organization, old-age insurance, children's allowances, shift work for women and juvenile persons in industry, the social position of defective persons, a possible ban on the employment of girls of 14 in industry, agricultural labor laws, the system of wage policy in the future.

Of a different nature are the advisory reports issued by the Council on such matters as administrative and penal jurisdiction, insurance brokership, credit control, economic competition, Benelux problems, transport problems, the land rent problem, among others. Advisory reports are prepared by committees appointed by the Council on which the three sections of which the Council is composed are represented.

In addition, the SER has important functions to perform in regard to Works Councils. Along with the Act Governing Industrial Organization under Public Law there is also a Works Councils Act. It designates the SER as the organ that sets the rules regarding the constitution and working procedure of the industrial committees for the Works Councils. The law requires that, in establishments in which there are twenty-five or more workers with the right of vote, aged 20 or over and having been uninterruptedly employed by the establishment for at least one year, Works Councils shall be set up. It is the task of the SER to form industrial committees for different groups of establishments; these committees are to ensure compliance with the provisions laid down in or stipulated by virtue of the Works Councils Act. The SER has formed a permanent Works Councils Committee whose sole task it is to take preparatory steps for the establishment of these industrial committees. For this purpose the Works Councils Committee confers with the representative associations of employers and employees. Here again we find that great importance is attached to the principle of consultation. In this way efforts are made to arrive at appropriate industrial committees for the various branches of industry—on which employers and workers have seats on the basis of equality of status—so that all the establishments concerned shall within the stipulated period have Works Councils of the requisite form. The Works Councils, viewed as instruments of cooperation in the individual establishments, are ideally adapted to promoting a community spirit between the partners in industry.

To many workers, industrialization means totally different conditions of life—which is yet another reason why it is considered so important that, through the medium of Works Councils, the workers should gain a better insight into the details of running a modern industrial establishment and also become familiar with the procedures in the establishment in regard to social and economic matters. In this way the worker will feel that he is no longer a mere extension of a machine or a tool of the "capitalists." Instead, he will realize that he is an essential part of the whole process of production, and that besides having an "internal" responsibility in regard to the closed community represented by the establishment he also has an "external" responsibility in regard to his task on behalf of the community as a whole. The industrial committees shall in due course become merged into the organized groups of associated industries. In this way organizational cooperation will be achieved at different levels: from the establishment, via the industry, to the Social-Economic Council. A high level of training is essential for those who hold office in the labor unions.

The administrative tasks of the SER are closely related to the formation of an industrial organization under public law which finds its expression in commodity alliances and industry alliances. These new industrial bodies might appropriately be referred to as legal communities invested with government authority.

The commodity alliances are conceived of as vertical forms of organization, comprising enterprises which operate at different stages of the process of production and distribution of certain products or groups of commodities. These product groups comprise for instance producers, wholesalers, processing industries, importers, exporters. They are the appropriate organs—administered on the basis of equality—for economic affairs and authoritative functions.

The industry alliances are to be horizontal forms of organization in industry. They consist of enterprises which perform similar functions in economic life, operating either as producers or wholesalers, retailers, etc.

The activity of these groups of associated industries will be limited to social matters such as the regulation of wages and other conditions of employment, hiring and firing of workers, vocational training, employment, social funds, and the like.

The formation of these organized groups of associated industries and groups dealing with specific products gives rise to various problems during the present preparatory period. Among them is the question as to whether it is possible, within the framework of the general policy of controlled wages, to leave the development of the wage structure to the executive committees of the organized groups of associated industries.

The most essential aspect of the new industrial organization under public law is that efforts are being made to bring about a new state of mind in industry (that is, among employers and workers) which, being primarily concerned with the interests of the community, will overcome conflicts that have their roots in history, and finally lead to the integration of state and society.

Obviously, this development will be of particular importance in the new relationship to be established between industry and government. In all these movements it is necessary in the long run to take into account the democratic basis of the Dutch social structure, which means that efforts must be made to bring about a form of society in which the full exercise of democracy is secured. For this further development and for the success of this new social organization, it is of fundamental importance that a new social structure shall be established in which the interests of the community are in the foreground. The new form of society thus involves a new system of cooperation between government, employers and employees, with consequent new possibilities for the welfare of the whole community.

IV

Collective Bargaining in France*

ADOLF STURMTHAL

THE PRESENT French law on collective agreements, adopted by the National Assembly on second and final reading February 9, 1950, represented a decided effort to reduce the State's share in the determination of wages and working conditions. In this respect the law marked a victory for free collective bargaining and a reversion from the rising tide of "statism" in labor relations, the climax of which had been reached in 1946.

This will emerge more clearly from a brief historical review of the principles and legal foundations of collective bargaining in France. Such a review will distinguish five periods, each marked off by the establishment of a new legal basis for collective agreements: the first period lasted from 1919 to 1936; the second, from 1936 to the outbreak of World War II; the third, from 1940 to 1946; the fourth, from 1946 to 1950. The present stage begins with the 1950 legislation.

The Statute of 1919

The freedom to organize unions was recognized in 1884, thirteen years after the revolt of the Paris Commune had profoundly

*This is an enlarged and slightly revised version of an article originally published in the *Industrial and Labor Relations Review,* Vol. 4, No. 2, January 1951. Thanks are due the Fulbright Administration and the Social Science Research Council for assistance in the research of which this chapter is a part-product.

shaken the nascent Third Republic. But it was only in 1919 that the legislature proceeded to establish legal foundations for collective agreements. This delay was due partly to the slow rate of progress of French unions, partly to the ideology of revolutionary syndicalism which opposed collective agreements as a betrayal of the class struggle. During World War I, however, many French Syndicalists, led by Léon Jouhaux, had adopted a patriotic attitude widely at variance with their traditional revolutionary antimilitarism. This opened an era of revision of the syndicalist doctrine. Though torn by intensive internal dissension, the unions emerged better organized and numerically stronger out of the war and ready to adopt new methods, among them collective bargaining. Thus the Congress of the Confédération Générale du Travail (CGT), held in Lyon in 1919, justified the support now given to collective bargaining by stating:

> It would be a profound error to see in collective agreements a form of collaboration (between employers and unions). The collective agreements whether they cover a plant, an area, or a nationwide occupation have transformative values, because they limit the authority of the employers, because they reduce the relations between employers and employees to a bargain which encourages the effort without dulling the energy, since the worker has thus the satisfaction of reducing the employers' absolutism by introducing into the workshop or plant the control of a power not subject to exploitation by the employer, of a force of emancipation: the union.

By establishing the legal basis of collective agreements, the conservative majority of the Chamber elected in 1919 hoped to direct the energies of French syndicalism into new, less political, and less revolutionary channels.

The legal principles of the Act of March 25, 1919 placed collective agreements under the general heading of the law of contracts and combined this with the principle of full freedom of association. It followed that collective agreements were valid only between the contracting parties and had no force with regard to third parties. Any number of unions with overlapping or identical jurisdiction could be formed, each free to conclude agreements for its membership. The hope that a network of collective agreements would be built upon this basis was soon disappointed. In order to function, this legal system would have required strong, well-disciplined, and united labor organizations. None of these conditions was present. Membership in the largest trade union confederation, the CGT, was reported to be 2,400,000 in January 1920 (the official statistics of the Ministry of Labor reported only 1,581,000). By the end of 1920 the CGT admitted having lost 1,100,000 members. A year later the two trade union centers into which the CGT had split had a combined membership of 550,000. The unions were then engaged in a bitter internecine struggle which had led to the establishment of two trade union centers—the CGT and the Communist-led Confédération Générale du Travail Unitaire (CGTU). In addition, there were large numbers of nonaffiliated unions, some of them "company unions" ("yellow syndicates" in French workers' parlance) and the first beginnings of the Catholic Trade Unions, the Confédération Française des Travailleurs Chrétiens (CFTC).

Under the circumstances, the labor organizations were incapable of inducing most of the French employers to conclude collective agreements. The number of unorganized competitors would have been too great; the guarantees for the observance of the agreement which the unions could offer were much too dubious to cause the French employers to come to terms with the unions. Most of the employers were unwilling to abandon their traditional "master-in-our-own-house" attitude, and the rapid decline of the strength of the unions encouraged them in their belief that the unions were too weak to impose collective bargaining.

As far as immediate effects were concerned, therefore, the law of 1919 was of little consequence. It led, however, to interesting discussions about the legal nature of the collective agreements, which helped to prepare the second phase of their history. A number of jurists, led by Professor Duguit, questioned the legal classification of the collective agreements. They were not simple contracts, but of a different legal nature: they were "actes-règles," statutes of the profession having a character similar to that of public statutes. This concept made rapid progress among the labor lawyers and became the predominant legal interpretation in

France. It was officially endorsed by the legislature under the Popular Front régime of 1936 and was made the cornerstone of the new law adopted on June 24, 1936, as a consequence of the famous "Accords Matignon" of June 7, 1936.

The Statute of 1936

This law, enacted when the Popular Front was at the height of its power, made a deliberate effort to adjust the system of collective agreements to the conditions of a country in which trade unions were relatively weak in members, unstable, and divided by philosophical, religious, and other considerations. The law provided, therefore, that collective agreements be concluded by "joint commissions," combining spokesmen of the "most representative organizations" of employers and employees. The Minister of Labor was given power to "extend" these collective agreements, in full or in part, to all enterprises of the same kind within the territory referred to in the agreement. In this way the private contract acquired the power of a public decree, and its observance could be enforced with the methods applicable to any other public decree. In addition to calling forth action of a civil nature, such "extended" agreements had, therefore, the power of penal sanction as far as wages were concerned. The "joint commission" appeared as a quasi-public organ which made laws when the Minister of Labor approved. The fact that the Minister could not change the agreement, but at the most could restrict its "extension" to certain provisions confirmed the "legislative power" of the commission, as did the fact that the "extended agreement" lost its validity when the original agreement expired or was changed.[1] As a result of this system, there were two kinds of collective agreements in France: those valid only for the parties to the contract, and those endowed with general validity. There were some 5,780 agreements of the first kind concluded between 1936 and 1939, and some 680 of the second kind.[2]

[1]It is interesting to compare this system with the American method of "extension" introduced by the system of "exclusive bargaining rights" in combination with the majority principle of the Wagner Act.

[2]Jean Brèthe de la Bressaye, "Le Nouveau Statut des Conventions Collectives du Travail," *Droit Social,* Vol. 10, No. 3, March 1947. Before the National Assembly,

As these figures indicate, the enactment was followed by the conclusion of a large number of agreements. Trade union membership rose to staggering heights. The merger of the CGT and the CGTU in March 1936 enhanced the power and prestige of trade unionism.

A number of important legal problems arose as a consequence of the Act. First of all, it was necessary to define the concept of the "most representative" organizations, particularly on the trade union side. For even after the merger of the CGT and CGTU in 1936, French trade unionism remained split into a number of rival organizations, of which, in addition to the CGT, the Catholic unions of the CFTC and a large number of unaffiliated, so-called "autonomous" unions were the most important. Little legal precedent existed for the solution of this problem. Some references were made to the statute of the International Labor Organization requiring that nongovernmental delegates to the ILO conferences be appointed upon presentation by the most representative organization of employers and workers. However, only one case under this clause had come before the International Court in the Hague, that of the Dutch Workers' Delegate. In its decision the Court had pointed out that, all other elements being equal, the number of members would be decisive in determining the representative character of the organization.

A 1936 circular of the Minister of Labor addressed to his staff, in particular the labor inspectors who had a share in the determination of the "most representative" organization in collective bargaining in areas smaller than the entire nation, enumerated a series of factors to be considered. It stated that the size of membership alone was not decisive. The following should also be taken into consideration: the age of the organization, its share in past negotiations, the amount of its dues and the regularity of their payment, the character of the statutes, and the conditions of affiliations (i.e., whether the workers had joined freely or under the pressure of their employers).

The circular indicated that more than one organization might

P. H. Teitgen, Minister of State, reported that 687 agreements had been extended, among them eleven national agreements. Cf. *Le Monde,* Jan. 5, 1950, p. 5.

be described as "most representative." This contradicted the interpretation given by Prime Minister Léon Blum during the parliamentary debates preceding the adoption of the law, but practice has followed the circular rather that Blum's statement. All later official texts make it clear that more than one organization can be "most representative." For this interpretation—which is in opposition to American ideas—its advocates appealed to the "spirit of French individualism," the great ideological diversity of the French workers, etc. No less important, it may be assumed, was the strategic need of preventing the CGT—although at that time under strong non-Communist leadership—from obtaining a trade union monopoly at the expense, in particular, of the Catholic labor organization and of the Confédération Générale des Cadres de l'Économie Française (CGCE, created in 1937).[3]

It is clear that the designation of a union as "most representative" had reference to the territorial framework of the negotiations. It was not necessarily the same union which was designated to take part in the negotiations of a national or a regional or a local (or possibly plant) agreement. A similar distinction held true for negotiations dealing with particular categories of workers.[4] The designation was made by the Minister of Labor for negotiations on a national agreement; by the labor inspectors for negotiations in small regional units. Against these designations, an appeal was possible to the Higher Arbitration Court (Cour Supérieure d'Arbitrage) and, after its suspension by decree of September 1, 1939, to the Conseil d'État, a High Court specially dealing with the legality of administrative actions. The Minister's circular had no binding legal force for the courts but served as a guide.

In spite of the important changes in the legislation on collective bargaining, the concept of the "most representative" organization survived. It was retained in the emergency legislation enacted at the outbreak of World War II, when the "most representative" labor organizations were empowered to designate the "délé-

[3]Since 1944 this organization has called itself CGC. It organizes semiprofessional and technical employees.

[4]This principle is not clearly stated in the texts but has been upheld in a number of decisions.

gués du personnel," a kind of shop steward. After the war, the same principle was used for the establishment of the lists of candidates for the election of the Comités d'Entreprises (joint committees of labor and management to deal with any question affecting the welfare of the workers and to consult on issues relating to the general functioning of the enterprise). It is, therefore, important to follow its further evolution.

A circular of the Minister of Labor of May 28, 1945 repeated essentially the same characteristics as those referred to in the circular of 1936 but went beyond it in three respects: it added as another factor to be considered the "patriotic attitude" of the organization during the war and the occupation; it emphasized the need for particularly critical examination of organizations restricted to one establishment; and finally it designated some organizations, the CGT and the CFTC,[5] as fulfilling the requirements of the circular. This circular caused a good deal of difficulty. It was used in particular by the CGT to oppose the participation of the Confédération Générale des Cadres (CGC) in the joint commissions. As a consequence, a joint decision of the Prime Minister and the Minister of Labor on March 13, 1947 stated new principles, stressing the membership of the organizations. Accordingly, all eligible organizations could be considered as "most representative" provided they enrolled 10 percent of the total union membership in the branch of industry and 25 percent in one of the occupational groups to be considered. For the discussion of special parts of the agreement, those organizations might also be admitted which had 33 percent of the union membership in the particular professional group. If no organization fulfilled these requirements, the one with the highest proportion for the entire industry and the organization with the highest proportion in the particular professional category would be selected. All other organizations might address written communications to the president of the joint commission and be informed by him about the progress of the negotiations.

This decision required the unions (and employer groups) to

[5]This is, in some respects, the first official document recognizing the representative character of the minority trade union confederation. Cf. Gaston Tessier, "La C.F.T.C.," *Droit Social,* Vol. 8, No. 3, March 1945, p. 107.

submit documents proving their membership claims, their dues, and the regularity of their payment. This proved extremely difficult. Some organizations refused to make known their membership; others made obviously exaggerated claims. Nevertheless, a table of the organizations admitted to the joint commissions was finally drawn up. It indicated that of the twenty-three branches into which, for the purposes of collective bargaining, all economic activities were divided, the CGT was represented in twenty-three, the CFTC in thirteen, the CGC in twelve. In addition, the national Syndicate of Assistant Druggists was represented in one branch. In most branches the employees were subdivided into workers, foremen and white-collar workers, and cadres.

The split between CGT and CGT-FO (Confédération Générale du Travail-Force Ouvrière, a non-Communist trade union confederation) in 1947–1948 made necessary a further revision. It was made, again jointly by the Prime Minister and the Minister of Labor, on April 8, 1948. It stated simply that for all categories of employees the three major organizations were admitted: CGT, CGT-FO, and CFTC; for the discussion of collective agreements relating to the cadres—the CGC; for agreements referring to particular groups alone or of limited though national significance, the Minister of Labor could designate other organizations as "representative." He had the same right for particular cases with regard to other organizations.[6]

The Vichy Statute of 1941

The development of collective agreements which had been given a powerful impetus by the law of 1936 and the rapid growth of the trade unions did not last very long. After the failure of the General Strike on November 30, 1938 and the renewal of the conflict between Communists and non-Communists in the

[6]A group of deputies belonging to the Catholic "MRP" (Mouvement Republicain Populaire) proposed on March 27, 1947 the introduction of a system of proportional representation. According to this proposal, the employees would be divided in each of the twenty industrial branches into four electoral colleges: workers, white-collar people, foremen, semiprofessional and technical staff. In a secret vote they would select their representatives in the joint commission, who would then be appointed according to proportional representation. This proposal found little support.

CGT came the outbreak of the war. A decree of October 27, 1939 stabilized working conditions "for the duration" at the level of September 1. Other decrees, of November 10, 1939 and June 1, 1940, gave the Minister of Labor authority to fix wages. The Vichy régime dissolved the trade union confederations and employers' federations by the "law" of August 16, 1940, which was implemented by a decree of November 19, 1940. This decree ordered dissolution of the CGT and of the CFTC and of a somewhat ephemeral semi-Fascist organization, the Confédération des Syndicats Professionels (CSPF), which had been founded in 1937 in conjunction with the Parti Social Français. Instead, Vichy proclaimed on October 4, 1941 the "Charte du Travail" which abolished free trade unions and, of course, free collective bargaining. The revival of collective bargaining had to wait for the liberation.

This revival was preceded by the reunification of the CGT in an "underground" meeting of Communists and non-Communist labor leaders in Le Perreux on April 17, 1943 and the refusal of the CFTC to join in a united trade union movement as proposed by the CGT. Maintaining the decree of June 1, 1940, the Minister of Labor continued to determine wages, and uniform wage changes were decreed several times by government authority.

The Statute of 1946

On December 23, 1946 a unanimous decision of Parliament, adopted almost without discussion, marked what was intended to be a first step toward a return to collective bargaining. In essence, the new law enabled the joint commissions to meet again and to determine working conditions. Wages, however, continued to remain within the province of the Minister. This, it was argued, was necessary because of the inflationary effects of ill-considered wage increases; because of the necessity of carefully planned occupational wage differentials, so as to direct the labor force into socially important channels; and, finally, as the Minister of Labor Daniel Mayer stated, to give control of the labor market to the State, under the slogan of the "Économie Dirigée," the "controlled economy."

While the law was an advance in the direction of collective bargaining as far as working conditions were concerned, it marked a step in the opposite direction in that it required the Minister's approval for all collective agreements. His approval implied at the same time the "extension" of the agreements. Thus no agreement was valid unless the Minister approved it, and such approval made the agreement automatically a public regulation for the entire occupation or branch of industry within the local limits laid down in the agreement itself. The former division of agreements into two classes—those with limited validity and those "extended" to nonrepresented employers and employees—disappeared. Moreover, the law determined the sequence in which agreements could be concluded: first national, then regional, local, and plant agreements, each based upon the preceding higher level agreement.

The law provided for the establishment of two organs for its implementation: the "joint commission," whose composition on the union side has been briefly referred to above, and a Commission Supérieure des Conventions Collectives, an advisory body for the Minister, which examined the general economic effects of agreements before the Minister approved them.

To prepare the conclusion of national agreements the Commission Supérieure established a classification of twenty branches of activity. As far as wages were concerned, however, the Minister operated with a much larger number of categories. Moreover, differing from the practice between 1936 and 1939, one and the same agreement was to cover the working conditions of all employees—workers, white-collar people, and cadres. Only after the national agreements were approved by the Minister could agreements on a smaller scale be concluded. These—with the exception of individual firm agreements—would also cover entire branches of activity within certain areas. Only at the level of the firm agreement was it possible, therefore, to work out specific conditions appropriate for one or several plants belonging to the same firm, but still within the framework of the higher agreements.

The joint commissions met, at the request of one of the workers' or employers' organizations designated as "most representative," upon invitation of the Minister of Labor or his representative. This set off a series of squabbles about the admission of unions apart from the CGT, which—after two decisions of the Conseil d'État—was settled by the decisions of 1947 and 1948 described above. In fact, the excitement was hardly warranted; exactly one collective agreement of any significance was established under the law, that of the bank clerks.

The reasons for this failure were threefold: first, the determination of wages was excluded from collective bargaining and retained by the Minister of Labor. In a period of inflation, practically the entire attention of the workers was centered on wages. Second, the law of 1946 exempted the nationalized enterprises from collective bargaining altogether. Their wages and working conditions were determined by law. For some of the most active union federations—coal, gas, electricity—collective bargaining in the strict sense was, therefore, meaningless. Third, the conflicts among the trade unions weakened all of them.

The pressure for unrestricted collective bargaining increased in the course of 1948 and 1949, the more so as price controls and rationing were rapidly abandoned. The Government hesitated. It feared that a wave of wage increases would endanger the stability of the currency. The employers were less recalcitrant, but they pointed out that the unions were asking at the same time for "freedom of wages" and the continued maintenance of a minimum wage determined by government authority. Finally, in November 1949, the Government submitted the draft of a new law on collective bargaining. The draft had a highly unfavorable reception among all trade unionists. They objected that the State still retained too large a part in wage determination, and that through compulsory arbitration the right to strike, though guaranteed by the Constitution, was in fact abolished.

The Present Statute

In exchange for concessions on these issues, the Government succeeded in salvaging three main points during the parliamentary discussions:

1. The Minister of Labor is free to decide in the light of circumstances whether to "extend" collective agreements to workers and employers not represented by the partners to the agreement. The law thus returned to the principles of the legislation of 1936. The labor organizations had asked that the "extension" be automatic, once an agreement was concluded. Under the law of 1946, as will be remembered, the Minister was free to approve or disapprove an agreement. His approval carried automatically the "extension."

2. The determination of a national minimum wage for all occupations—called "minimum vital" in French labor parlance—is prepared by a government-appointed Higher Commission of Collective Agreements on the basis of a family budget. But the Government itself makes the final decision. By that method the Government wished to avoid a general wage increase by way of a substantial increase of the minimum. (Minimum wages for the different occupations can of course be set higher than the "minimum vital" in the different collective agreements.)

3. For the nationalized enterprises, the law provides (Article 31 o):

> When the personnel of a public enterprise is not subject as regards the conditions of work which are the object of collective agreements to a legal statute or a particular regulation, collective agreements may be concluded following the clauses of this part of the law.

The list of enterprises with statutes was established by a decree.

In its essentials, the new law returned to the principles of 1919 and 1936. It abandoned the strict hierarchy of the law of 1946 which required that national agreements must precede regional ones, regional agreements those limited to one town, etc. The agreement does not require government approval, and the settlement of wage questions may be included in the agreement. The role of government is thus restricted principally to the calling of meetings of the joint commissions; to a decision on whether to "extend" the agreement, certain parts of it, or none of it at all; to determine the minimum wage; and some activities regarding conciliation and arbitration. In some respects, the law shows a good deal of originality, as, for example, in the requirement that collective agreements must contain a clause providing for equal pay for equal work to men and women; that the minimum wage is to be determined by reference to the elaboration of a typical family budget, but not necessarily on this basis alone; that the labor inspectors have the right to control the application of all parts of an "extended" agreement—not only of the wage clauses as in the past. The fact that agricultural workers are included within the scope of the law is less of a novelty than might seem at first sight. The law of 1936 included them as well, although it did not provide for the "extension" of their collective agreements. A decree of July 7, 1945 organized a mechanism similar to that of the joint commissions for agriculture and gave automatically the force of law to the resulting decisions. Since in the future the collective agreements of the agricultural workers will require "extension" before having the force of law (and being subject to the supervision of the labor inspectors, particularly important in this field), it might be asked whether the law does improve the status of agricultural labor—as probably intended by the lawmakers, who seem to have forgotten the existence of the decree of 1945.

Conciliation and Arbitration

One of the bitterest battles in the parliamentary discussion of the present law concerned the issues of conciliation and arbitration of labor conflicts. The original government draft provided for compulsory conciliation and arbitration; only after the completion of this process was a strike legally permissible. This proposal met with the unanimous disapproval of employers and unions alike. Albert Gazier, Socialist deputy, pointed out that

> to impose compulsory arbitration against the unanimous opinion of the workers' and employers' organizations . . . in a field in which the only effective sanction is that of public opinion, at a time when public opinion rejects the principle, means to do absolutely ineffective and therefore dangerous work.

The employers seem to have been motivated by a fear that the government controls which France had just eliminated would return by a back door if compulsory arbitration with the pyramid of labor courts which the Government provided were to be established. On the workers' side, it is sufficient to recall the tradition of revolutionary syndicalism to understand that the concessions made in 1936—under a socialist-led Government!—to the principle of arbitration were not easily renewed, particularly in the presence of a large labor organization under Communist control. The postwar Constitution contains a statement guaranteeing the right to strike. The workers' organizations pointed out that compulsory arbitration would inevitably abrogate or at least restrict this right.[7] Moreover, the government project, though labeled arbitration, hardly contained any of the features commonly understood by that term. Thus all members of the arbitration board were government-appointed and the parties had no say in their selection.

No explanation has been given as to the reasons which caused the Government to depart from the precedents of 1936–1938, the only precedents of any significance in French social history, apart from the "Charte du Travail" of the Vichy régime (law of Oct. 4, 1941), whose clauses on compulsory arbitration remained a dead letter.

The system of conciliation and arbitration established in 1936–1938 proceeded in a wisely tentative fashion. It was based on two main laws—those of December 31, 1936 and of March 4, 1938

[7]It is true that the Constitution states that the right should be exerted "within the framework of laws which regulate it." The fact is, however, that with one exception no such law has been passed. Thus, after a strike of civil servants, Prime Minister Ramadier announced on February 14, 1947 that a law prohibiting a strike of civil servants, representing the authority of the Government, and those concerned with the security-services ("fonctionnaires d'autorité et de sécurité") would be prepared. But the Minister instructed to do so never did his job. It happened to be Maurice Thorez, leader of the French Communist party, then Vice-Prime Minister. A proposal of a number of deputies, led by Deputy Queuille, providing for certain restrictions of the right to strike of some categories of workers and of the civil servants, did not get beyond the Parliamentary Commission. An emergency law voted in December 1947 expired in 1948. The only permanent law is that proposed by Paul Reynaud and Jules Moch in August 1948, forbidding strikes of police agents while admitting their right of union organization. Finally, Communist resistance to United States arms shipments to France caused the adoption of an additon to Art. 76 of the Penal Code, aiming at sabotage in connection with work for national defense in peacetime.

—together with a number of decrees. Its main outlines were these: If the collective agreement did not provide for procedures of conciliation and arbitration or if it did not apply, or finally, if no such agreements existed between the parties involved in the dispute, the following procedure applied:

1. Conciliation commissions were established by unions and employers' organizations in every department, and on the national level for each industry, and finally, on the confederal level (between CGT and the employers' confederation. Confédération Générale du Patronat Français) which would in successive, but very rapid, stages deal with conflicts, even before an open break occurred.

2. If this procedure remained ineffective, arbitration took place on two levels: first, by two arbitrators, one designated by each side; second, if the latter procedure was fruitless, by a "surarbitre," chosen by the Prime Minister from a list established in advance by employers and unions.

A major addition to this system was the establishment by the law of March 4, 1938 of a higher arbitration committee dealing, as a court of appeal, with alleged violation of the law by the arbitrators, or, at the request of the Minister of Labor, with violations of the public interest.

The draft was thoroughly changed by the parliamentary commissions. The commission of the Lower Chamber provided for compulsory conciliation and voluntary arbitration, with appeal to a new Higher Arbitration Committee. The Upper Chamber, the "Conseil de la République," made an effort to introduce compulsory arbitration, at least for conflicts which "may endanger the functioning of services and activities necessary for the life of the nation," but the commission of the Lower Chamber rejected this proposal, and by now, though the Prime Minister still defended compulsory arbitration, the Minister of Labor showed much less enthusiasm for it. The final text corresponded in all essentials to the proposals of the commission of the Lower Chamber. However, since most deputies felt that in this field all regulation was bound to be tentative and subject to revision, the clauses on conciliation and arbitration were not made part of the "Labor

Law" ("Code du Travail"), while those on collective bargaining were included in it.

"All labor conflicts," says Article 5 of the law, "must compulsorily and immediately be submitted to the conciliation procedure." The parliamentary decision did not make clear whether this obligation exists prior to the outbreak of a strike (or lockout) or following it. Most probably a strike (or lockout) may legally precede conciliation or even occur during it. The procedure may be either determined by the collective agreement or, in the absence of such an agreement or if the agreement does not provide for conciliation machinery, it is that established by the law: national, regional, departmental, or local commissions, each consisting of an equal number of employer and union representatives—designated by the "most representative" organizations—and up to three government representatives.

A similar division of contractual and legal machinery is established with regard to arbitration. However, since arbitration is not obligatory, in the absence of a contractual obligation, the two sides must agree on the use of the legal machinery and the arbitrator (the law uses the singular). Following a classification widely accepted in Anglo-Saxon countries, the labor conflicts coming up before the arbitrator are divided into those dealing with the interpretation and application of existing obligations and "the other conflicts," particularly those that arise over "salaries and working conditions which are not determined by law, rulings, collective agreements or understandings" and those concerning "the negotiations and revision of clauses of collective agreements." The arbitrator decides the first according to law, "the other conflicts" according to equity.

Conciliation agreements and arbitration awards dealing with the interpretation of existing agreements, with salaries and working conditons, have the same force as the agreements themselves. If they concern "extended" collective agreements, they may themselves be "extended" by the same procedure as the original agreement. The force of agreements or awards which do not deal with salaries and working conditions is not covered by the law.

Communism and Collective Bargaining

The new law on collective bargaining represented a step forward toward freely negotiated agreements between employers and unions. But it made this step under highly unfavorable conditions.

French trade unionism is divided into many competitive organizations. At the time of the "Accords Matignon" in 1936, the intention was probably to make eligible for collective bargaining the "most representative" union only. This, as was pointed out above, soon proved politically impossible for, under that system, the CGT would have had a monopoly in almost all branches of industrial activity, while the Catholic unions would have been restricted to a few sections of trade and commerce. To this, the Chamber objected violently. Thus, the principle of multiunion representation in collective bargaining was accepted. It led inevitably to two chains of consequences: greatly increased difficulties in arriving at agreements and an eternal struggle for a change in the method of selection of the "most representative union." Union rivalry at the conference table expressed itself in a process of competitive demands. Every union endeavored to demonstrate that its competitor was "giving in" too readily to the employers, and the union representatives were reluctant to accept reasonable compromises out of fear of their rivals. To demonstrate that no better result could be obtained, the unions "tolerated" strikes with or without official approval—sometimes with the result that even the previously obtained concessions were lost.

The struggle for admission to the "charmed circle" of "most representative union" was essentially waged with political weapons, since it was the Minister who decided in the last resort. Thus French labor relations were (and continue to be) made dependent, to a large extent, upon the political influence of each union.

This was complicated by the fact that the largest of the trade union centers, the CGT was dominated by the Communist party. Labor relations were thereby connected not only with the issues arising between French workers and their employers, but also those existing between the French Communist party and the French Government, or even between the Soviet and the French Governments. Thus the first postwar years, when the Communists were represented in the Government and Franco-Russian relations were fairly harmonious, were extraordinarily quiet in the factories as well. From the summer of 1947 on—the Communists having left the Government and the Marshall Plan beginning to embitter Franco-Russian relations—successive waves of strikes expressed at the same time the social dissatisfaction of the workers, the political struggle in France, and the friction between the Soviet Union and France. In the nature of things collective bargaining requires that both parties be prepared to accept commonsense solutions and ultimate cooperation. It is difficult to see how it can successfully operate when it is called upon to settle issues of foreign policy as well as those of industrial relations.

But the difficulties are by no means all on the workers' side. French employers have accepted collective bargaining only as the lesser evil compared with government determination of wages. The unions have little reason to believe that the employers have really abandoned their old "master-in-my-own-house" ideas.

This is partly the result of the lack of a tradition in collective bargaining. Apart from a brief flare-up after 1919 and the period from 1936 to 1938, France has never known a developed system of collective agreements. Neither employers nor workers have any sustained experience in collective bargaining. The Government is reluctant to abandon its controls, since no one feels certain as to the results of free collective wage determination.

Indeed, it is difficult to see how the system would operate under French conditions if moderately high employment levels were to coincide with strong union organization. The low degree of competition in French industry, the emphasis on national agreements, and the lack of central control over local union activities are factors that might jointly produce irresistible inflationary wage pressures.

The situation at the time of the enactment of the new law had the opposite result. The unions were (and are) weak. The CGT, though still a large organization, had been beaten again and again in the last years, and the political center of gravity of France had shifted to the Center and the Right. In spite of high levels of profit in many branches of industry, French employers are rarely willing to make collective bargaining work. The CGT insisted upon a solution of "fringe issues," which would have been extremely costly, and upon trade union rights in the plants which French employers were unlikely to grant. Under the circumstances collective bargaining developed rather slowly.

Mere agreements on wages which the law allows were more frequent in the first period after the enactment of the law. In the first three months some seventy-five such partial agreements were concluded, among them eleven national agreements. It is significant for the state of French labor relations that the majority of those agreements, forty-four in all, and ten of the eleven national agreements, were concluded after a strike.

Collective Bargaining in Nationalized Industries

A peculiar problem of collective bargaining in France is raised by the existence of a large number of nationalized enterprises. As has been mentioned, nationalized enterprises are divided into two classes: those to which collective agreements are applicable and those in which wages and working conditions are set by law. The first are the enterprises operating as units in a competitive branch of industry, i.e., where nationalization did not apply to the entire industry (e.g., the nationalized banks, insurance, Renault); the others are large monopolistic industries, entirely or almost entirely nationalized (coal, electricity, gas, and, for most practical purposes, the railroads).

Collective bargaining in the second group consists essentially of negotiations between the unions and the Government, since it is the latter which must propose to Parliament whatever changes in the "statute" of the workers seem necessary, or enact them by decree. To ensure unified government policy, it has been provided that the Minister for Finance must sign all decrees dealing with the wages of the employees of nationalized enterprises subject to a statute. But this makes also fairly certain that advantages granted to one group will rapidly become generalized. Clearly, such negotiations are of a vastly different nature from those carried on between unions and private employers. Although strikes in nationalized enterprises have not been at all infrequent, they are difficult strikes from the point of view of the nation as

BK1

well as of the workers, since they easily carry the connotation of an insurrection against the democratically elected Government of the country.

In nationalized enterprises in the competitive sector wages and working conditions are determined by the normal process of collective bargaining. In fact, however, this process is greatly affected by the nature of the enterprise. Nationalized enterprises in France —differently from England—are administered by councils in which various interest groups, among them the personnel itself, are represented. In most cases these councils elect a Director General, with the approval of the Minister under whose jurisdiction the enterprise falls and to whom the Director General is responsible. As a result collective bargaining in this type of industry would mean that the union is dealing with a council a part of which consists of representatives of the union. It is not easy to see how these union representatives could avoid the pitfalls of divided loyalty, nor how a council divided against itself could effectively defend the interests of the establishment. In practice, however, the main burden of the negotiations has fallen on the shoulders of the Director General—the more so as the council members are unpaid officials who devote only their spare time to the business of the enterprise.[8] But the Director General is under the orders of the Minister to whom he is bound to refer matters of great significance. Indeed, during the first series of negotiations which followed the enactment of the new law on collective bargaining, the Ministers clearly told the heads of the nationalized enterprises how far they could go in their concessions to the workers. Although in theory these enterprises are to be run like independent industrial and commercial establishments, they are in fact under close governmental direction.

The representation of interest groups in the direction of French nationalized enterprises was devised to avoid the shortcomings of "étatisation," which French syndicalism branded in the severest terms. In the final resort, however, this elaborate structure leads, nevertheless, exactly to the result which it was supposed to avoid,

[8]See Adolf Sturmthal, "The Structure of Nationalized Enterprises in France," *Political Science Quarterly*, Vol. 57, No. 3, September 1952.

namely, to the Government having the final say on wages and working conditions.

From the union point of view, Government influence on collective bargaining is, however, by no means altogether objectionable. Even though delicate problems may arise in such negotiations, the Government is a far more "understanding" employer than most private enterprise in France. The most forward-looking collective agreement concluded in the first five years under the new law is probably that of the Renault automobile factory which is a nationalized establishment. In signing that agreement Force Ouvrière attributed its merit to "the very great possibilities which negotiators in good faith have, thanks to the system and the particular climate of a nationalized enterprise such as the Régie Renault."[9]

Collective Bargaining and Wages

The postwar years until and including 1948 were years of inflation; whatever the relationship of cause and effect, rapid price increases compelled the Government to decree wage rises; 1949 was the first year of relative price stability and the wage level remained fairly constant with only a slight upward trend. From the middle of 1950 on—the beginning of the Korean crisis—the price level started again its rapid upward movement. Between February 1950—when free collective bargaining was established—and December 1950, the index of 135 wholesale prices rose from 2,057 to 2,140 (base 1938 = 100). This index figure was abandoned early in 1951. Instead, a new index figure of 319 commodities was introduced with 1949 as base year. This index shows for 1950 an average of 108.3 and for December 1951 a level of 151.5. Apart from the summer months of 1951, price inflation continued into 1952. During the following three years, however, the cost of living remained stable. Inflation has thus been the dominant economic fact for about half of the six years since collective bargaining got its new start in 1950. Concern with the

[9]More about this agreement, p. 150. This praise of nationalized industry as an employer is less frequently heard than facts would seem to warrant. In particular, there is little enthusiasm among the rank and file about the nationalized enterprises.

rising cost of living and with the maintenance of living standards was one of the main themes of industrial relations, at least until 1952.

The emphasis of collective bargaining has been placed upon wage contracts rather than full collective agreements. By July 1952 more than a thousand wage agreements were registered, the bulk of which were concluded after September 1950. At about the same time—namely, June 14, 1952—the number of collective agreements was 324 (including a large number of annexes). Of these, 39 were national agreements, 137 if the annexes are counted as well. Three of the national agreements were "extended," two agreements in the textile industry and one applying to freight-handling on the railroads.[10] The remaining agreements were of a regional, local, or plant nature.

Between 1953 and 1955 collective bargaining spread, though wage settlements still hold a lead over full collective contracts. For the latter the law stipulates requirements as to content on which unions and management have rarely been able to agree. Moreover, national agreements are intended to be followed by local or regional settlements which would complement the rather general provisions of the national convention. This, however, has been done only in a rather small number of cases, partly because unions are usually ill equipped for negotiations on the lower levels.[11]

Among the agreements those of the metal industry play an outstanding part, particularly those of the Paris region which sets the wages and working conditions of the largest single group of industrial workers in the country. Yet neither unions nor employers "see in collective agreements the essential element in the mechanism of labor relations."[12]

A survey of the existing agreements shows interesting relation-

[10]Cf. Renée Petit, "Le Contenu des Conventions Collectives du Travail," *Droit Social,* 15e année, No. 7, July–August 1952, p. 454. The "extension" is announced in the *Journal Officiel,* e.g., Dec. 20, 1951. For developments in 1953–1954, see Jane H. Palmer, "Recent Wage Policy in France," *Monthly Labor Review,* Vol. 77, No. 6, June 1954.

[11]See Val R. Lorwin, *The French Labor Movement* (Cambridge, 1954), pp. 194–197.

[12]Pierre Waline in the *Revue Économique,* February 1951, quoted by Lorwin, *op. cit.,* p. 212.

ship between legal and contractual arrangements. The area of trade union freedom—roughly corresponding to the problems covered in the United States by the Taft-Hartley Act—is dealt with in collective agreements, but the law compels the partners to the contract to include certain clauses on the subject in the agreement. Thus the right of the workers to belong (or not to belong) to unions must be stated in the national collective agreements, together with an undertaking on the part of the employer not to discriminate against workers because of their membership (or lack of membership) in unions. Details of the application of these principles, however, are subject to bargaining. Indeed, some of the most controversial issues have arisen in this area; the collection of union dues, the distribution of union publications, the holding of union meetings in the shops have been strongly rejected by French employers. One case of a "check-off" does nevertheless exist[13] not without arousing doubts whether such a clause is compatible with "trade union freedom."

On the other hand, matters which formerly were included in collective agreements have become part of legislation. This applies to the institution of shop stewards (délégués du personnel). The law of 1936 required that clauses on shop stewards be included in collective agreements that were to be eligible for "extension." Since then, this matter has been regulated by law and collective agreements can only provide supplementary details. Similarly, the Joint Factory Committees (Comités d'Entreprise), a postwar institution, are provided for by law. The collective agreements add supplementary details on election, financing, and the like.

Productivity has become the subject of a long Article (67) in the textile agreement (which was concluded without the CGT). It states explicitly that increased productivity must "increase wages and individual or collective advantages," that it should not lead to "excessive efforts" of the wage earners or to dismissals. Redundant labor should be employed in other capacities, if necessary in other plants of the industry; if separation is inevitable, the worker is entitled to a dismissal pay equivalent to three months

[13]It concerns a small professional group engaged in the synchronization of motion pictures. Cf. Petit, *loc. cit.*, p. 458.

wages. For the engineers and "cadres" in the rubber industry, the collective agreement provides that transfers but no dismissals are possible as long as the volume of production in the particular department of the firm remains unchanged. If the firm cannot meet this obligation, the employers' association has to carry it out.

A new approach to the problem of productivity—new at least for France—was made in the Renault agreement of Sept. 16, 1955, patterned after the General Motors-UAW agreement. This contract provided not only for an immediate wage increase and an extension of paid vacations from two to three weeks, but also for an annual improvement factor of 4 percent for the remainder of the life of the contract (two years). In exchange, the contracting unions accepted the obligation not to call a strike before having exhausted legal and contractual conciliation procedures. This contract was signed by FO, CGC, independent unions, and after some delay by the Christian trade union. The CGT refused to sign, but arranged for a referendum among its members and discovered to its shocked surprise that close to four fifths of those who participated in the vote accepted the contract. Other automobile and metal establishments have since followed the pattern of the Renault agreement.[14]

Interesting also are clauses designed to ensure stability of employment. Some are compulsory. They refer to dismissal periods, the length of time between the notice of a dismissal and its actually becoming effective. This is usually different for different grades, with longer periods for engineers and white-collar workers, and one to two weeks for workers. Though not a legal obligation, dismissal pay is often provided for, depending on the length of service. White-collar workers and higher staff receive usually more favorable treatment and, in general, such clauses are found more often in agreements covering these categories of employees than in those dealing with production workers. Thus dismissal pay is

[14]Peugeot and SNECMA signed similar contracts in December 1955. These clauses, as well as the contracts of the Parisian metal industry, express a spirit of understanding for personnel problems connected with productivity increases which is by no means universal in French industry. For an example of a different approach, though couched in diplomatic terms, see the report of the committee on productivity of the National Council of French employers. CNPF, *Bulletin du Conseil National du Patronat Français,* 6e année, No. 84, July 20, 1952, pp. 34–35.

provided for in the agreements covering the banks, social security administration, engineers and "cadres" of the chemical industry, white-collar workers, technicians and foremen in the rubber industry, but also in the textile industry.[15]

The "Minimum Vital"

While inflation was progressing, changes in the cost of living furnished the main impetus for bargaining.

No agreed or even widely respected index figures of the cost of living are available. There is an index of "aggregate prices of family consumption" (indice d'ensemble des prix à la consommation familiale), which deals with five classes of consumption goods and services: food and drink, heat and light, manufactured products, services, and miscellaneous (cigarettes, tobacco, newspapers). Altogether 213 articles and services are included. This index is based upon the expenditures of a family of four persons, including two children of less than sixteen years, living in Paris; the head of the family has an occupation below that of a foreman in industry or of a bookkeeper in commerce.[16] This index (base 1949 = 100) shows for 1950 a rise from 106.9 in June to 117.4 in December. For December 1951, the figure was 142.9. The index disregards important food items (fruit and vegetables), but for the rest gives food a high weight (58 percent). The fluctuations of this index are, as a consequence, largely determined by the variations of food prices.[17]

Whatever influence this index has on wage determination, it exerts mainly by way of a different concept, that of the "minimum vital." This concept, roughly equivalent to a "minimum real income required," plays an important part in French collective bargaining. Its postwar history may be said to have had its beginnings in the work of a joint (government, employers, and union)

[15]Cf. Petit, *loc. cit.,* p. 527.

[16]The research for this index is carried out by the official "Institut de Statistique et d'Études Économiques" (I.N.S.E.E.). Cf. also *Bulletin du Conseil National du Patronat Français,* 5e année, No. 60, Dec. 20, 1950, and No. 61, Jan. 20, 1951.

[17]It is perhaps worth noting that the new index reduces the weight of beef consumption, but introduces an item representing the consumption of horse meat, according to the actual consumption patterns of Parisian workers in 1948–1949.

committee set up in February 1947; it established a "typical budget"—usually referred to as "Budget-Delépine" after the name of the president of the committee—upon which the calculation of the "minimum vital" was to be based. Although the calculations of this budget continue to be made, they have had little influence upon collective bargaining.[18] Instead, the working out of a standard budget has become one of the main subjects of bargaining itself.

The main trade union centers as well as the "Union Nationale des Associations Familiales" (a federation of associations of heads of large families) work out monthly figures for what they regard as the proper budget on which to base the computations for the "minimum vital." These computations are then submitted to the Commission of Collective Agreements (Commission Supérieure des Conventions Collectives) which, under the law of February 1950 has to recommend to the Government a guaranteed minimum wage for all occupations, on the basis of a "typical budget."[19]

Needless to say, agreement is not easily established as to the budget and consequently the minimum wage. The food part of the budget is the relatively simpler aspect of the problem since the work of experts in nutrition can be used as standard. Even so, there were disagreements about the number of calories required (between 2,700 and 2,900 a day) for a bachelor worker living in Paris in his own room and doing his own housework. The Commission has settled on 2,872 calories. The more serious disagreements refer to the non-food parts of the budget. Clearly, almost any decision on this subject is as plausible as any other. In fact, therefore, each meeting of the Commission has been the scene of intense wrangling

> among the representatives of employers, of wage earners, peasant leaders, and representatives of the associations of large families, each with index figures in their hands, established on different foundations and justifying exactly opposite policies.[20]

[18]A special "typical budget" has been established for the civil service.

[19]See "Les Travaux de la Commission Supérieure des Conventions Collectives tendant à l'Établissement d'un Budget-Type," *Revue Française du Travail,* September–October 1950.

[20]J. Lajugie in *Revue d'Économie Politique,* 61 année, September–October 1951, p. 837. Early in 1954 agreement was reached only because the employers' delegates

For, in its practical effects, the setting of the "minimum vital" forms an important part of collective bargaining.

The Role of the Government

While the French unions have insisted upon what they somewhat euphemistically called "the return to free collective bargaining," they did not, in fact, wish to rely exclusively upon their economic strength. This lack of self-confidence was fully justified by early 1950. In two large, but unsuccessful strike movements in 1947 and 1948 the CGT lost a good deal of its prestige and a substantial part of its membership. With the founding of "Force Ouvrière" (FO), the division of the French trade union movement made further progress, though FO has not proven capable of absorbing more than a part of the workers who left the CGT. As a result, there are three major trade union confederations in the field—CGT, CFTC, CGT-FO—the CGC[21] and a number of smaller trade union centers: Confédération des Syndicats Indépendants; CGSI, previously known as CTI, strongly influenced by labor leaders who had taken a part in the Vichy Government, but including also "non-collaborationist" leaders of strong anti-Communist leanings; an insignificant anarchist confederation (CNT); and an autonomist confederation (FNSA). To this must be added a number of non-affiliated organizations. Some unions who broke away from the Communist-dominated CGT, among them the powerful Teachers Union, prefer to remain unaffiliated.

In fact, only the three major Federations and the CGC play significant parts in collective bargaining, but the rivalry among all of them is intense enough to weaken union influence in general. The majority of the French workers belong to no union whatsoever.

Really "free" collective bargaining would under these circumstances hardly have produced any substantial advantages for the French workers. Government intervention was needed. Its most

left the meetings. Raymond Lévy-Bruhl, "L'Évolution des Salaires," *ibid.*, 65 année, July–October 1955, pp. 765–766.

[21]CGT—Confédération Générale du Travail; CFTC—Confédération Française des Travailleurs Chrétiens; CGT-FO—Confédération Générale du Travail—Force Ouvrière, all three with a potential universal jurisdiction; CGC—Confédération Générale des Cadres, an association of unions of foremen and engineers.

direct—though by no means only—form was the setting of the minimum wage for all occupations.

The first decision of this kind was made in August 1950, when the minimum hourly wage for a male worker in industrial plants in Paris was set at 78 francs. Later changes occurred in March 1951 as a consequence of a strike movement, when the minimum was raised to 85 francs (an increase by 11.5 percent although the Commission had found an increase in the cost of living of 12.5 percent); and in September 1951, when the minimum was raised by 14.9 percent to 100 francs, although this time the Commission set the increase of the cost of living at only about 9 percent. The Government felt certain that retail prices would continue to increase, and its decree anticipated these developments. Further increases occurred at later dates bringing the minimum wage in industry for Paris up to 121.50 francs in 1954.

In general, these increases were fairly well reflected in the general wage structure. Contractual wages are so close to the legal minimum that changes in the latter provoke adjustments all along the wage hierarchy.

> One dramatic example: on Wednesday, March 21, 1951, the Paris metal trades association signed a wage agreement with several unions. On Friday the government raised the minimum wage. By Saturday the employer association raised the wage scales in the 3-day-old contract.[22]

A different method of change for the minimum wage has been introduced by a law of July 18, 1952. Under the pressure of rapidly rising prices, the question of automatic wage adjustments to changes in the cost of living was raised by the unions and in Parliament, as early as January 1951. Prolonged deliberations, government crises, and compromises were necessary to produce a law. Communists and Socialists strongly objected to it. Its main provisions may be summarized as follows: the minimum wage is to be adjusted if the cost of living as measured in the Index of 213 articles has risen by at least 5 percent; no two changes can be made within four months; only upward revisions of the minimum wage in the light of changes in the cost of living are possible; the procedure

[22]Lorwin, *op. cit.*, p. 223.

remains essentially the same as before, with the Government acting upon advice from the Commission of Collective Agreements. The starting point was set at an index figure of 142, which the unions criticized as too high.[23]

Needless to say, this procedure falls far short of maintaining real wages. The delays in adjusting wages to cost-of-living increases, the restriction of the adjustment to the minimum wage alone,[24] the limitation of the adjustment to five month periods, and the fact that the procedure becomes operative only after a rise of 5 percent —all tend to make substantial reductions of real wages possible. In fact, however, the law has had no practical application.

Wage Differentials

The setting of the minimum wage involved regional differentials, although the law itself does not speak of several "minima." The minimum wage mentioned so far refers to the Paris region. The rest of the country is divided into various regions with corresponding reductions of the minimum wage. These regional wage differentials are traditional in France, but the unions have long insisted upon their reduction or elimination. As a consequence, the maximum differential of the minimum wage which was set at 20 percent in 1950 was reduced to 13.5 percent in 1951. The actual zone differentials and their development throughout 1954 are shown in Table 1 (page 156).

The regional differentials have thus shown considerable stability. As far as one can judge, they exceed differences in the cost of living and are thus real wage differences.[25]

The most striking fact is the discrepancy between the legal and the actual differentials. Changes of the minimum wage tend to reduce the geographic differentials, but only for a short time. They

[23]Cf. A. Philbert, "Le Problème de l'Échelle Mobile des Salaires," *Droit Social,* 15e année, No. 9, November 1952.

[24]Even though the general wage level seems to move with the minimum wage, it does so only with delays.

[25]A similar, but not identical, system of zone differentials exists for the family allowances and another one for agricultural wages. The same town may be in different zones for each of these payments. Cf. Pierre Fournier, "Le Problème des Zones de Salaires," *Droit Social,* Vol. 19, No. 2, February 1956.

Table 1. AVERAGE WAGE DIFFERENTIALS IN THE PROVINCES COMPARED WITH PARIS.

Legal Differential of Minimum Wage	Average Wage Differentials				
	January 1951	*July 1951*	*January 1952*	*July 1954*	*January 1955*
(%)	(%)	(%)	(%)	(%)	(%)
3.75	10.7	9.8	9.7	13.3	13.1
7.50	17.4	16.7	15.6	18.4	16.8
11.25	22.4	21.2	20.3	22.8	20.6
13.50	25.0	23.9	23.5	25.6	22.3

Source: Lévy-Bruhl, *Revue d'Économie Politique,* several issues.

reappear unchanged or even enlarged, after a few months. As far as earnings are concerned, the differentials seem to be even larger than those of rates.

A striking reduction of wage differentials has taken place—as in many other industrial nations—with regard to the sexes. While female labor was paid about 70 percent of the corresponding male wage in 1938, this differential dropped to 15 percent early in 1946 and to slightly more than 5 percent in January 1951. It was thus considerably lower than in most countries of western Europe.

The interindustry differentials have shown considerable stability. With a few exceptions, the rate of increase of average wage rates in the different industries has varied little around the average. Many deviations from the average tended to even out over time. This will emerge from Table 2.

Printing, for instance, whose average wage rate shows a high rate of increase during the first period considered, had a low rate of increase between 1950 and 1952 and ended up, for the whole period, not far above the national average.[26] Still, market in-

[26]In view of the well-known remarks of Prof. Ross regarding the use of percentages in comparing wage increases (A. M. Ross and W. Goldner, "Forces Affecting the Interindustry Wage Structure," *Quarterly Journal of Economics,* Vol. 54, 1950), it should be pointed out that the similarity of percentage changes does not imply that the absolute wage increases were uniform. During a substantial inflation the predominant influence on wages is the rise of the cost of living and adjustments to the latter, though imperfect, proceed by fairly similar processes in all industries. This would apply particularly to a country like France where government-determined wage changes, centrally decided, were the rule. Differences in the timing of the adjustments are then the main explanation of short-run differences in the behavior of average wage rates. Some of these lags may be related to differences

Table 2. INDICES* OF AVERAGE HOURLY WAGE RATES† ACCORDING TO INDUSTRY, JAN. 1946 = 100

	Jan. 1949	*Jan. 1950*	*Jan. 1952*	*Jan. 1954*	*Jan. 1955*
Metal Prods	295	293	464	478	519
Mechanical Ind	293	306	478	510	544
Glass	287	288	484	511	542
Pottery	270	278	427	450	490
Construction	261	271	430	460	486
Chemical	288	299	487	520	559
Food	286	299	482	520	565
Textiles	309	317	512	532	573
Clothing	296	305	474	501	558
Leather	283	292	445	470	517
Wood	268	274	438	468	516
Paper	290	299	487	520	566
Printing	295	316	467	517	555
Miscell	290	298	474	512	555
Transport	281	293	459	493	529
Commerce (Food)	294	307	491	528	576
Commerce (Non-Food)	289	295	476	507	552
Sanitation	280	286	456	487	535
Average	287	297	470	500	539

*Adapted from Lévy-Bruhl, *Revue d'Économie Politique,* 1952, p. 559; 1955, pp. 764–781.

†The "average hourly wage rates" in this table are calculated on the basis of base wage, cost-of-living allowances, and bonuses for a worker over eighteen, fully able to work. Not included are overtime allowances for night or Sunday work, transportation allowance, etc. This is, therefore, neither an hourly wage rate, nor average hourly earnings, according to United States usage. Cf. "France," Labor Statistics Series, I, Consumer Prices, Consumer Expenditures, Wage Rates and Earnings Series (U. S. Department of Labor, Bureau of Labor Statistics, Division of Foreign Labor Conditions, June 1952), p. I–30 (processed). Also A. Aboughanem, "L'Organisation et le Développement des Statistiques Sociales en France," *Revue Française du Travail,* 6 année, No. 7–8–9, July–August–September 1951.

fluences, expansion and contraction of industries played their parts. Potteries and construction were consistently behind the national average.

These figures do not go back far enough to allow comparisons between the present and the pre-World War II interindustry wage

in the power—primarily, though not exclusively, political power—of the unions or occupational groups. Cf. J. L. Guglielmi and M. Perrot, *Salaires et Revendicationes Sociales en France 1944–1952* (Paris, 1953), pp. 50, 61–62.

structure. As far as such a comparative study can be made, it seems to indicate that the French wage structure has followed, on the whole, the pattern of that of most industrial nations. Mining has moved into first position, while clothing has lagged. Agriculture has gained. On the other hand, the entire wage structure seems to have become somewhat narrower, i.e., average differentials in earnings from industry to industry have dropped.[27] This, too, corresponds to a fairly general trend in western Europe. The "coefficient of variation" for average earnings in selected French industries—the standard deviation for average earnings expressed as a percentage of the unweighted average of these earnings—has dropped from 25 in 1938 to 17 in 1949. The figures for 1954 are not fully comparable to those of 1938 or 1949, but the trend seems to have continued. The bulk of these changes in the interindustry wage structure appears to have occurred during the war and right after it.

Few data are available as to skill differentials. An index of hourly rates for four classes of skills ranging from common laborer to skilled worker (ouvrier qualifié) shows that the skill differentials have decreased about 10 percent between January 1946 and January 1952. From about the middle of 1951 on, however, there was a slight tendency for skill differentials to widen, but this did not last very long. During 1954–1955, a new squeeze on the differential set in.

Policy statements to the effect that skill differentials should be maintained or re-established have been frequent; yet one of the main influences making for changes in the wage structure was the adjustment of the wages to rises in the cost of living by way of flat wage increases. This process had the effect of improving the relative position of low-paid workers.[28] Even in 1954, however,—a year of price stability—skill differentials have shrunk; while the minimum wage was raised twice during the year, the adjustment of the higher wage rates to these increases proceeded too slowly to take full effect before the end of the year.

[27]Cf. "Changes in the Structure of Wages in European Countries," *U. N. Economic Bulletin for Europe,* second quarter, 1950, Vol. 2, No. 2 (Geneva, October 1950). Some of the conclusions in the U. N. study do not apply to developments after 1949, the terminal date of the data.

[28]This is not recorded in those data for the interindustry wage structure, which are unweighted wage averages.

The rates of increase for the lowest and the highest class of skill are compared in the following table.

Table 3. *RATES OF INCREASE OF INDICES OF HOURLY WAGE RATES FOR MEN. (SURVEYS OF THE MINISTRY OF LABOR)

	1949	*1950*	*1951*	*1952*	*1953*	*1954*
Common Laborer..........	4	21	31	3	4	10
Skilled Worker............	3	17	35	3	4	5

*Extracted from Lévy-Bruhl, *loc. cit.* 1952, p. 557; 1955, p. 769.

In addition, there are figures comparing the average wage rates —as defined above (Table 2, n.†)—of five skill classes. These classes are: common laborer, specialized (heavy) laborer, semiskilled worker, skilled worker, and highly skilled worker. The data from which these figures are derived do not include the mines, the railways, and the transport, and place relatively high emphasis on larger establishments.[29] For October 1951 the following proportions are given: if the wage rate of the common laborer is set at 100, the other four classes are paid at the rates of 107, 115, 129, 152. This, however, does not include those parts of earnings that come under the heading of "social wages,"[30] or other allowances, which are independent of the skill of the worker. If these elements are taken into account, skill differentials of earnings are far lower than those stated above.

There may, of course, be offsetting factors such as upgrading or noneconomic rewards, such as prestige, connected with higher ranking jobs. Yet, on the whole, the range of occupational differentials appears very narrow indeed. This may well be one of the fundamental problems of the social and political structure of the country.

Employment throughout the period considered has been almost consistently high, as one would expect in view of the inflationary trend up to 1952 and the persistent boom in the later years. The

[29]Yet the survey on which these figures are based has been described as "the most general and representative" of the surveys dealing with wage rates. Cf. A. Aboughanem, *loc. cit.*, p. 424 (see note to Table 2).

[30]See p. 160 ff.

narrowing of differentials has thus proceeded during a period of high employment and advancing wage rates.[31]

Earnings

In order to pass from hourly wage rates to earnings, the hours of work must be considered. On the whole, effective hours of work have been rather high in the postwar era compared to prewar. From about 39 in 1938, and 43 weekly hours early in 1946, they have risen to around 45 and have stayed close to this figure. This corresponds to an increase of about 18 percent of earnings. Hours between 40 and 48 are to be paid a supplement of 25 percent, those above 48 a supplement of 50 percent. This is a very important fact in comparisons of the standard of living between prewar and postwar earnings.

Hourly rates and number of hours worked determine only one element in the French workers' earnings. "Social" wages are tremendously important. Among them the most substantial are the family allowances. Various other allowances and bonuses and the "transport compensation" introduced late in 1948 for Parisian workers have also to be included.

The family allowances are monthly payments made by publicly organized systems to workers with families. The amount paid out depends only upon the size and composition of the worker's family, not upon his earnings. The money is raised by a pay-roll tax. In essence, the family allowances represent a redistribution of workers' incomes in favor of large families at the expense of bachelor workers and those with small families.

In order to keep up with inflation, a number of increases of the allowances were made. On the other hand, the pay-roll tax was also increased after the war. The importance of the allowances is shown in Table 4.

It is interesting to compare these figures with the varying amounts of the monthly minimum wage. For October 1, 1951, for instance, the minimum wage of 16,800 francs is less than the family

[31]The absence of substantial unemployment, however, went hand in hand with significant, though probably decreasing, concealed unemployment in the form of excessive manpower in a number of industries.

Table 4. MONTHLY AMOUNT OF FAMILY ALLOWANCES IN THE SEINE DEPT. (IN FRANCS)

	1 Child		*Two Children*	*Three Children*	*Five Children*
	Less than 5 Years	*More than 5 Years*			
From April 1, 1939.......	75	75	225	450	900
From April 1, 1940.......	75	75	450	450	1,050
From April 1, 1941.......	300	150	525	900	1,800
From Jan. 1, 1942.......	340	170	595	1,020	2,040
From Jan. 1, 1944.......	450	225	788	1,350	2,700
From Sept. 1, 1944.......	675	338	1,249	2,228	4,050
From Aug. 1, 1945.......	900	450	1,665	2,970	5,670
From July 1, 1946.......	1,130	565	3,390	5,650	9,040
From Feb. 1, 1947.......	1,243	622	3,729	6,215	9,944
From Aug. 1, 1947.......	1,400	700	4,200	7,000	11,200
From Dec. 1, 1947.......	1,700	850	5,100	8,500	13,600
From Jan. 1, 1948.......	2,100	1,050	6,300	10,500	16,800
From Sept. 1, 1948.......	2,400	1,200	7,850	13,650	22,850
From Dec. 1, 1950.......	2,850	1,425	9,400	16,350	27,400
From April 1, 1951.......	3,000	1,500	9,800	17,050	28,550
From Oct. 1, 1951.......	3,450	1,725	11,284	19,622	32,845

Source: Lévy-Bruhl, *loc. cit.,* 1952, p. 564.

allowance for a worker with three children (19,622 francs), and slightly more than half the allowance for a father of five children. Two thirds of the latter's income—if he was working at the minimum wage—would be derived from his family allowance.[32] It follows that earnings vary to a considerable extent according to the size of the worker's family. Wage comparisons must refer, therefore, to this factor. On the other hand, the worker's social security con-

[32]Income tax allowances for children are important for relatively well-paid groups while family allowances are relevant for the income of low-paid workers so that the number of children becomes a key factor in determining net incomes after taxes. As an example, I quote (from Georges Rottier and Jean François Albert, "The Social Services and Income Redistribution in France," in *Income Redistribution and Social Policy,* Alan T. Peacock, ed. (London, 1954), p. 101, footnote 3) the following figures for net annual income according to family size for two employees, one earning 175,000 francs a year, the other 1,000,000 (A and B). It is assumed that the wife does not work and that contributions to social insurance and income tax have been deducted:

	A	*B*
Single	171,500	829,000
Two children	269,250	1,031,250
Four children	394,000	1,175,000
Eight children	614,000	1,439,800

tributions must be deducted from his gross earnings. They amounted to 4 percent of the wage in 1938 and have increased to 6 percent since 1945.[33] Finally, for the workers in the Paris area, a monthly flat transportation allowance must be added which amounted to 500 francs from October 1, 1940, when it was introduced, to February 1, 1950. Since then, it has been set at 800 francs.

Statistics of earnings are highly unsatisfactory. For the brief period since 1949, an index of monthly earnings exists for two wage zones. (Paris and the zone with a deduction of 7.5 percent.) The wage earners selected are bachelors, fathers of two children, and fathers of five children. For Paris, this index shows an increase of money earnings of 66, 60, and 54 percent, respectively, when the average of 1949 and January 1952 are compared. In January 1955, the figures were: 195, 180, 175 (1949=100). For the 7.5 percent zone the figures are 63, 58, and 52 percent for January 1952, with January 1955 at 187, 173, 170, respectively. However, it is doubtful whether the reported earnings of 1949 were correctly stated. Wages, then, were still subject to open government regulation and actual wages probably exceeded in some cases those set by the Government. To this extent, the wage increases since 1949 are overstated. For whatever they are worth, these figures must be read against the background of an increase in the price of family consumption goods of 46 percent during the period up to January 1952. This would indicate a slight rise of real earnings for family heads and a more substantial increase for bachelors. A comparison of real earnings with the prewar situation is even more difficult in the light of changes in earnings structure, family allowances, social security contributions, taxes, and living patterns. Raymond Lévy-Bruhl[34] estimated "that the purchasing power of the wage earner in 1951 is approximately equal to that of the wage earner of 1938. . . ."[35] This

[33]This applies only to those workers who come under the general social security system. For some industries, such as mining and the railroads, special systems have been set up.

[34]Lévy-Bruhl, *loc. cit.*, May–August 1952, p. 567.

[35]The discussion on comparative real wages in France has proceeded for some time as an argument about the base year or years for comparison. If 1938 is used as base, then the real weekly earnings (with family allowances or other supplements, but without overtime) in July 1952 are 124.8 for men and women combined. For men alone, the index figure would be 109.6 (which tends to show the decrease in differentials between the wages of men and women). The index of direct real earn-

an increasing portion of the French worker's income is being received independently of his effort and skill.

Summary

This rapid survey of the state of French industrial relations more than five years after the enactment of the law of February 1950 suggests a number of tentative generalizations:

1. Collective bargaining still plays a secondary role in regulating industrial relations in France. The State, on the one hand, and the more or less unilateral decision of the employer, on the other, play a more significant part than bargaining between employers and unions. This is not altogether undesirable, from the point of view of the workers or of French tradition. Government intervention has probably been more favorable to the workers than bargaining would have been and it is in the mores of the country to regard law and administrative decisions as more permanent settlements than collective agreements. The tendency to transform habitual or contractual arrangements into law has been unmistakable. Even collective agreements, being mostly based on multiemployer and multiunion bargaining, and rarely supplemented by local and regional agreements, have some of the attributes of legal regulation. Only recently has there been some emphasis on plant agreements.

2. A basic fact underlying these developments is union weakness, particularly in what is in the United States the most fundamental area of union activity, namely, collective bargaining. Even under conservative governments, labor has had usually more influence on political decisions than its economic strength gave it on the outcome of collective bargaining. This is the more intriguing as the tradition of the French labor movement is not only "unpolitical" (say, in the sense of early AFL views), but even "antipolitical"—ordinary political methods were altogether rejected.

3. One of the significant aspects of French collective bargaining is that it unites at the bargaining table on one side the representatives of several unions, and on the other side those of united employers' association. The existence of several sharply competitive unions in the same plant is frequently described as an expression of

French national characteristics which emphasize differences in ideology and wish to give expression to them. Yet it seems that on the employers' side the same national characteristics do not prevent uniformity. It should be kept in mind, however, that a principle such as that of exclusive "bargaining rights," American style, would result in most French industries in a monopoly of union representation by the Communist-dominated CGT. That principle would also be difficult to establish and maintain (as the history of the concept of the "most representative" union shows) against the powerful political pressures that surround and permeate labor relations, particularly as regards the determination of wages and working conditions. Most probably, multiunion bargaining will continue to be one of the sources of French union weakness.

4. French employers are far better organized and better equipped with research and other facilities than the unions, particularly at the regional and local levels.

5. More important still is the spirit in which many French employers view unions and collective bargaining. It is hardly an overstatement to say that both were imposed upon French management by political means and against bitter resistance.[41] Although there are employers that have come around to more modern views, a large number still regard unions as "outside interference" and industrial relations as not very much different from a subspecies of semifeudal dependency.[42]

6. Until about 1952, the race between prices and wages was the main issue of wage policy in France. Although it seems unlikely that wages have consistently pressed upon prices and made inflationary developments inevitable, it may well be that the particular form of collective bargaining used in France has made it more likely that price increases will follow wage increases. It is plausible

[41]After capitulating to the pressure of the Popular Front Government in 1936 and accepting the principle of collective bargaining in the "Matignon Agreement," the leader of the French employers found himself disowned by the membership and resigned. Cf. Henry Ehrmann, *French Labor—from Popular Front to Liberation* (New York: Oxford University Press, 1947), p. 53.

[42]On the general economic outlook of French management, see David S. Landes, *French Business and the Businessman: A Social and Cultural Analysis. Modern France, Problems of the Third and Fourth Republics,* ed. E. M. Earle (Princeton: Princeton University Press, 1951), pp. 334–353.

The employer-union agreement at the bargaining table has not, however, been duplicated in the legislative halls. While settling their current differences largely without strikes and also without compulsory government intervention in individual disputes, employers and unions have been engaged in a titanic political battle over their respective positions in society. The unions have demanded an equal share for the workers in the management of industrial life, and the battle over this claim for "codetermination" has been hotly waged.[3] Its ultimate outcome will greatly affect both the fortunes of the contestants and of several of the political parties. This choice of political over industrial warfare is not new in Germany. Bismarck chose legislative answers to the working-class challenge in the 1880's, and labor generally preferred political over industrial approaches to reform in the Weimar Republic.

This chapter is devoted, however, to the associations of employers and workers for collective bargaining purposes and the relationships between their respective organizations, rather than to the efforts of the opposing parties to affect the over-all distribution of power between capital and labor. To an amazing degree the parties have returned to the *status quo ante*. The unions, the employers' associations, the contracts, and the laws are much as they were before Hitler. The twelve-year reign of the National Socialists has left behind it few obvious traces in the realm of labor relations. When the Nazi slate was wiped clean and the parties wrote their new arrangements, two momentous changes, however, were made: (1) the trade union movement became politically independent for the first time, and (2) the Government could no longer impose the compulsory arbitration to which it had resorted increasingly under the Weimar Republic.

Organized Employers

It would be a gross caricature to portray the employers in Germany as organized and the workers as unorganized, but, like many caricatures, it would contain some essential truth. Employers' organizations are more widespread than workers' organizations,

[3]See William H. McPherson, "Codetermination: Germany's Move toward a New Economy," *Industrial and Labor Relations Review*, Oct. 1951.

and they possess stronger economic weapons. The unorganized employer is a rarity, whereas the unorganized worker is not. Employer association discipline is sometimes a harsh fact, whereas disciplinary authority of unions over their members is almost nonexistent. Yet the employers' associations in postwar Germany were invited back into existence by the unions because the alternative was no collective bargaining at all.[4]

Employer organization in Germany runs counter to no established traditions of an individual firm's independence—quite the contrary. The German economy is marked by semi-industrialization in a semimedieval society. Small employers of the "job-shop" variety belong to guild-like "Innungen," which have strict control over apprenticeship as well as trade practices, and to more generalized handicraft associations. Larger employers have their industrial associations which are concerned with price levels, marketing arrangements, and the like. The Chambers of Industry and Trade more broadly represent employers in such matters as taxation and trade reporting. Some of these organizations, despite American and British efforts during the occupation to the contrary,[5] again exercise semigovernmental authority. Employers' associations thus are only one of several close-knit managerial organizations, all of which express the same preference for private law as the governor of inter-employer relations, as against the free market or public agencies. Employers' associations are considered a natural response to unions and not a suspect form of imitation.

Employers in Germany, with rare exceptions, never bargain directly and independently with the unions. Medium-sized and large employers carry on their relations through specialized employers' associations, whereas small employers often bargain through their handicraft associations.

The organization of employers to deal with the unions is by no means a postwar phenomenon. Prior to 1933, relationships

[4]Except perhaps by the works councils, some of which bargained with their employers in the disorganized period following the end of the war, but this possibility was not an attractive one for the unions.

[5]For a presentation of American policy see *Decartelization in the U. S. Zone of Germany* (Office of Military Government for Germany [U. S.], Dec. 1948). See also Vaughn Smartt, "Gewerbefreiheit," *Information Bulletin,* Office of United States High Commissioner for Germany, April 1951.

sion, selective price cutting has been practiced against the non-comformist, or purchasers at the next stage in the productive process have been advised not to deal with him, or exhibition at fairs has been made difficult or impossible. In this close-knit employer community, the banking institutions, with their control over credit availability, can be and have been used as enforcement agencies. Taken altogether, as one employer said, "It can be a question of survival."

Actually this power is not often used for disciplinary purposes. Its adequacy makes its application infrequent. Trade union policy also greatly reduces the need to resort to force. The unions are not equipped to utilize the "whipsaw" tactic of playing one employer against another in contract negotiations or grievance settlements. They have no plant organizations which can push for and obtain separate and more favorable contracts from individual employers. Nor do they have much to do with grievances. These are initially processed by the unaffiliated works councils (shop steward committees locally elected in each plant) and may subsequently be referred to governmental Labor Courts which follow fairly uniform settlement lines. Beyond lack of the weapon, the unions favor uniformity of treatment not only of organized but unorganized employees as well.

In the absence of trade union pressure to break the line, it might appear that no discipline at all might be required, but this is not the case. An employer may fail to belong to the association and to support it financially; or he may cut wages below contract rates and thus constitute "unfair competition"; or he may make too many wage or nonwage concessions to his workers in an effort to "pirate" labor; or he may violate certain trade practices; or he may support the unions politically to a greater extent than deemed wise. In each of these instances, some discipline may be brought to bear upon him. The need to discipline grows more out of inter-employer than out of union-employer relations. This does not mean that all employers' associations use coercive methods, for some have followed the practice of completely voluntary participation and adherence; and discipline, in any event, is directed more at the small than the large employers.

Association Functions

Although all the basic employers' associations negotiate contracts, they administer them to a lesser degree than is sometimes the practice in the United States.[10] Grievance handling is left to the employer and the works council, and to the Labor Courts, and is not policed by the associations. The individual employers, particularly the larger ones, are also given a major measure of freedom in improving on basic contract terms, either unilaterally or in conjunction with their works councils. In the absence of aggressive unions pushing for, and then extending, local improvements, these individual betterments are not universally costly, unless used to "pirate" scarce labor. Such improvements usually affect wages only moderately (a 5 or 10 percent excess over contract rates, with the major exception of North Rhine-Westphalia since about 1953 when a great boom in the Ruhr has raised rates in the metal-working industry particularly to as much as 50 percent over contract levels) but may go quite far along social lines: canteens, kindergartens, vacation homes, medical facilities, and so forth. These latter cannot, in any event, very easily be put into industry-wide contracts.

Discipline is useful not only at the intra-association level, but also at the inter-association level. Here the federations and confederations are effective in keeping individual industry associations from setting too high a pattern for wage increases. Persuasion, in these instances, is the basic tool and sometimes the only one available. The federations and confederations are, nevertheless, effective in preventing undesired patterns from being established.

Each association has its own elected governing board, and often a separate negotiating committee, which can bind the members to a contract it negotiates. Votes and financial contributions are usually based on number of employees or volume of output, which gives preponderant influence to the larger employers. A manager is appointed by the executive board. He assists in negotiations, presents cases to the Labor Courts, and may sit as an employer

[10]See Clark Kerr and Lloyd H. Fisher, "Multiple-Employer Bargaining: The San Francisco Experience," in Richard A. Lester and Joseph Shister (editors), *Insights into Labor Issues* (New York: Macmillan, 1948).

representative on these courts, may act as attorney for the member firms, is in charge of research and publicity. The manager is not customarily an independent force in the association, although his power appears to be growing.[11]

Currently, the single-industry associations at the state level are generally the most active and influential employers' associations. The trend, however, is toward multi-industrial groupings at the federal level, including the National Federation of Employers' Associations as the peak organization. As this trend progresses, the employers' association hierarchy comes more to parallel the union structure. The unions, though less powerful economically, are as yet the more highly centralized in their operations.

Organizational Forms of Employers' Associations

The basic employers' association covers, usually, geographically a state and industrially a single product; for example, the Bavarian meat dealers belong to one association, the Bavarian ice manufacturers to another, and the Bavarian mineral water producers to still another. It is these groups which negotiate with the unions. They are not always organized, however, by state and product; nor are these the only associations. Occasionally an association covers less or more than a single state; for example, the textile employers of Northern Bavaria or the private railroads of all Western Germany; and occasionally also a large group of products, most notably the very strong Metal Employers' Association which encompasses manufacturers of such diverse products as automobiles, steel, machine tools, and electrical appliances.

Beyond these basic associations are a number of federations. There are vertical federations, such as the national metal employers' association, drawing together the local associations in the several states; and horizontal federations, such as the General Federation of Employers of Württemberg-Baden, uniting specialized industry associations in the state; and an over-all confederation of all employers' associations with headquarters at Cologne.[12] More informally organized are joint committees drawing together state

[11]The same individual frequently manages several small associations.

[12]Bundesvereinigung der Deutschen Arbeitgeberverbände. Additionally, there are substate groupings, such as at Nürnberg in Bavaria.

level employers' associations which deal with the same union, as for example the various employers' associations in the food industry which bargain with the Food, Beverage and Restaurant Workers' Union. The small employers have their handicraft associations, which cover individual crafts and operate on a more localized basis, but which in turn are federated over wider economic and geographical areas culminating in a central association at the national level.

Taken altogether, the many associations and layers of federations and committees completely blanket employer interests. Employers whose plants include many, a few, or no union members are included together. They are represented in collective bargaining by their basic associations, and before administrative, judicial, and legislative bodies by these associations, but especially by the various federations and confederations.[13] The employers of Germany can and do speak with few voices. Although no statistics are available, it is generally accepted that they are better organized than the workers. Few belong to no association and many of those who do belong have plants only partially or not at all unionized. Thus the members of the employers' associations have more employees than the unions have members in private employment.

The Trade Unions

Ranged against the primarily industry-by-industry associations of employers are sixteen unions. The largest of these is the Metal Workers' Union, which has nearly a quarter of the more than 5,000,000 members of the Federation of German Trade Unions—Deutscher Gewerkschaftsbund (DGB). The Metal Workers' Union includes workers in iron and steel plants, automobile factories, foundries, machine shops, electrical equipment factories, and many others. It is matched by the widely inclusive Metal Employers' Association. The multi-industrial character of this and the other unions creates special problems of internal cohesion and contract coverage.

Even more all-embracing than the Metal Workers' Union is the

[13]They are concerned with such political questions as legislation on social insurance, works councils, vacation pay, and Labor Courts.

Public Services, Transport and Traffic Union. This includes federal, state, and local civil servants; truck drivers; workers in gas, water, and electric power plants; longshoremen; state foresters; inland-waterway and deep-sea water-transport employees; street railwaymen; and many others. It would be difficult to assemble in one group more diverse types of workers than government office workers and longshoremen, or merchant seamen and state foresters.

The next two large unions are more homogeneous. The Mine Workers' Union includes both coal and hard-rock miners, but the former are by all odds the more important. This is the only union which approximates complete organizational coverage of the workers assigned to it. The Railway Union takes in administrative, operating, and maintenance employees of the railroads. Since the railroads are largely state-owned and engaged in transport and traffic, it might seem more logical to add the railroad workers to the potpourri jurisdiction of the Public Services, Transport and Traffic Union. This, however, would offend the sensibilities of the railroad employees, who in Germany as elsewhere consider themselves somewhat apart.[14]

These four unions of metal, public service and transport, mining, and railroad workers encompass nearly 3,000,000 members, or three fifths of the DGB total. Three more unions, of about equal size, account for an additional million members. The most influential of these is the Construction Workers' Union, which takes in not only all the building crafts but also employees of building suppliers. This union is important beyond the size of its membership because of the pattern-setting influence of its contracts and, strangely enough, the radicalism of some of its leaders. It has not, however, organized so much as half of the workers in its allotted area. The Chemical and Ceramic Workers' Union[15] and the Textile and Clothing Workers' Union are the other two moderate-sized groups. The first has real organizational strength, but the second inadequately covers the employees in its jurisdiction (about one third) and is economically very weak.

[14]For a short period the railroad workers were within the jurisdiction of the Public Services Union but quickly fought their way out.

[15]The jurisdiction of this union includes, among other things, rubber, rayon, and glass.

The remaining million members of the DGB are scattered among the remaining nine unions. Three of these have organized effectively within their jurisdictions (half or more). They are the Printing and Paper Workers' Union, the Post and Telegraph Workers' Union, and the Leather Workers' Union. Two more have respectable memberships (about 200,000 each) but have no greater inclusion of the workers in their fields than the Textile and Clothing Workers' Union: the Woodworking Union and the Food, Beverages and Restaurant Workers' Union.[16] The remaining four unions are important more for the hope their jurisdictions express than for their accomplishments. They afford the DGB little more than paper coverage of the remainder of the German economy. They are the Agricultural Workers' Union, the Commerce, Banking and Insurance Workers' Union, the Education and Science Union, and the Arts and Professions Union.

The DGB thus is composed of four large unions, each of which has brought in half or more of the workers in its jurisdiction; four whose strength is negligible; and eight of intermediate size. None of the sixteen is a craft union, and only two—both in government-dominated fields where the workers insist on separate recognition of their positions in society (railways and postal service)—cover a single product or service. The multi-industrial form of organization is the chosen instrument of unionization.

Multi-industrial Unionism and Disuniting Forces

The multi-industrial character of German unionization is quite remarkable in the face of the segmentation of the society in which it operates. Indeed one might expect to find a greatly fractionalized labor movement. Aside from important political and religious divisions among the workers, skill and status are matters of most serious import in Germany. A man is known as a journeyman or white-collar worker or technical employee or professional man; and his occupational classification is both more meaningful and less subject to change than in the United States. The cherished position of the public officials (the Beamten) is one illustration. Apprenticeship is taken much more seriously, also, and journey-

[16]The latter has jurisdiction over domestic servants.

men are formally licensed by the handicraft associations. It would appear likely then that the organizational lines of the unions might follow and re-enforce the occupational lines which so clearly define status and authority in German society.

Multi-industrial unionism runs counter not only to the occupational consciousness of the German worker but also to his syndicalistic tendencies. The German worker is much less mobile than his American counterpart, not only occupationally but also in his movement from plant to plant and industry to industry. Long-service employees in each company are more in evidence and more honored. The worker tends to identify himself with the problems of his particular industry and especially of the particular plant he serves. Yet the unions, by and large, run across industrial lines.

The historical trend, however, has been in the direction of multi-industrial unionism. Prior to 1933 there were about two hundred national unions in Germany. These fell into three main classes (Social Democratic, Catholic, and Democratic); and within each of these groupings there was clear recognition of the distinctions between manual workers, salaried workers, and civil servants. Each had its separate unions and federations. Salaried workers and manual workers in the same industry belonged to different unions; and in public enterprises manual workers were separated from the higher levels of civil servants. Among the manual workers, organization was partly by craft and partly by industry; but within the industrial unions craft departments were often recognized. The industrial territories covered by each union generally were more narrowly defined. The postwar labor movement dropped occupational group, craft, and many of the industrial dividing lines, and encompassed all workers in sixteen vertical unions; ignoring the formerly recognized distinctions between civil servants and noncivil servants, between manual and white-collar workers, among crafts, and, to a lesser extent, among industries.

The decision to attempt multi-industrial unionism did not come about without antecedents. Although the early unions in Germany were almost universally craft, a movement toward industrial amalgamation began in 1891 with the formation of the Metal

Workers' Union, followed shortly by the Leather Workers and Woodworkers. Spreading mechanization, which changed skill requirements, and the organization of employers along industrial lines were among the factors responsible. In 1925 it became the announced policy of the chief union of manual workers, the Social Democratic Allgemeiner Deutscher Gewerkschaftsbund (ADGB) to favor, but not force, the industrial principle. In 1933, there were about thirty craft and industrial unions of manual workers affiliated with the ADGB.[17]

Trade union leaders, in reviewing experience prior to 1933, reached the consensus that a much smaller number of unions was desirable in the postwar period. The powerful employers' associations had taken advantage both politically and economically of the splits and cross-splits in the labor movement; and the disunity of the labor movement had contributed to the accession to power of the National Socialists. The necessity to rebuild completely the trade union structure, and without the encumbrance of existing jurisdictional lines and hierarchies, made possible the bold stroke of providing universal coverage in sixteen unions. The Socialist ideology of working class unity to which many of the surviving union leaders adhered supported this attempt.[18]

The multi-industrial approach, despite the factors militating against it, has shown considerable survival value, although its purity has not been preserved. Several factors contribute to this. The unions have not ignored status considerations. The Railroad Workers' Union and the Post and Telegraph Workers' Union do not follow the DGB logic of combining all public workers together, and their separate existence acknowledges the prestige desired by these two groups of workers. The unions for Education and Science, Commerce, Banking and Insurance, and Arts and Professions provide compartments for the more highly educated employees distinct from those containing manual workers.

[17]For a history of the gradual consolidation of unions in Germany before 1933 see Richard Seidel, *Die Deutschen Gewerkschaften,* Franz Mittelbach Verlag, Stuttgart, 1948, pp. 43–49.

[18]The union movement after the war did not start out with sixteen organizations. There were variations by locality and zone, but by the time the DGB was formed in 1949 this number had been settled on.

Within the individual industrial unions there are also frequently separate departments.[19] Some of these departments, as in the Public Service, Transport and Traffic Workers' Union, follow industrial lines and, for example, the harbor workers have an organization of their own; others follow occupational lines, as in the case of the Metal Workers' Union where, for example, technical employees have formed their own subgroup. These departments have their own officers and hold their own meetings. Experts chosen from them sit in on negotiations or arbitrations concerning the group. The multi-industrial unions frequently negotiate separate contracts for each industry they cover, and almost always for the white-collar workers distinct from the manual workers. As yet there seems little if any tendency, however, for these departments to separate into independent unions.

Aside from the departments, there are other outlets for craft and syndicalist interests. The handicraft shops with their complement of apprentices, journeymen, and masters, and the Handicraft Associations with their strict control of apprenticeship allow for expression of craft instincts; and the works councils, which perform at the individual plant level many of the functions carried on by the unions in the United States, represent the workers in their plant-by-plant concerns. To the unions are left the more general problems, which can be treated quite broadly, such as negotiation of basic wage rates and determination of social policy for the working class movement. Beyond this, the individual worker is relatively passive about the union structure erected around him and, whatever his preferences might be, is inclined to accept the institutional arrangements made by his leaders.

Members of two groups in particular, however, have resisted inclusion in the multi-industrial approach: white-collar workers and higher ranking civil servants. They have formed the Deutsche Angestelltengewerkschaft (DAG) and the Deutscher Beamtenbund (BB). Both reflect the pre-1933 separation of white-collar workers and civil servants from manual workers and the continuing occupational distinctions, as well as the greater political conservatism of the members of the two groups. The DAG cuts across industrial

[19]Fachgruppen.

lines and is much opposed to the joint inclusion of manual "proletarians" and office workers in the same union; the BB asserts the necessity of preserving the privileged class position of the public officials.[20]

Union Authority

Power in the trade union movement is concentrated at the peak of the organization pyramid. In fact, a more accurate view of the union movement can be obtained if an upside-down pyramid is visualized, resting on a firm apex and rising level by level—with the shifting sands of the membership on a platform at the top. The union movement is often referred to as "Düsseldorf," the city where the national DGB has its headquarters. The allied occupational authorities at the end of the war had hoped to help build a new trade union movement based on strong local organizations, for the pre-Hitler unions had similarly been more effective at the federal than the local level. Consequently, they forbade, at first, organization across state and later across Zone frontiers and encouraged county (Kreis) level activity.[21]

By 1950, however, power had risen, like cream in milk, to the top. This may be illustrated in several ways: (1) All basic social, economic, and political policy is made at "Düsseldorf"; whereas the employers speak with several voices, the trade union movement speaks with one. (2) The national DGB within its own organizational structure and the national office of each industrial union

[20]In addition there are a handful of smaller independent unions of railroad engineers, police officers, sales clerks, and other specialized groups. The DAB (Deutscher Angestellten Bund) which also appeals to white-collar workers is politically to the Right of the DAG, which on occasion is rumored to be on the verge of amalgamating with the DGB.

[21]For a description of the revival of unions in 1945 and early 1946, town by town and industry by industry, see *Die Gewerkschaftsbewegung,* (Deutscher Gewerkschaftsbund [British Zone] 1949), pp. 22–41. See also M. A. Kelly, "Labor Relations in American-occupied Germany" in *Labor in Postwar America* [Colston Warne, editor] (Remsen Press, 1949); M. A. Kelly, "The Reconstruction of the German Trade Union Movement," *Political Science Quarterly,* March 1949; Military Government of Germany (U.S.), *Labor Organizations in the U.S. Zone of Germany,* April 15, 1946; *Industrial Relations in Germany 1945–1949* (London: His Majesty's Stationery Office, 1950); Oscar Weigert, "Labor Relations in the U.S. Zone of Germany," *Monthly Labor Review,* April 1948, and J. F. J. Gillen, *Labor Problems in West Germany,* Office of the United States High Commissioner for Germany, 1952.

in its jurisdiction can remove any elected or appointed trade union official at lower levels or veto his election or appointment. Although this power is circumscribed and is sparingly used, it exists. (3) Financial expenditures are concentrated at the higher levels. For example, the Printing and Paper Workers' Union distributes its income as follows:

Community level	10%
District level	25%
National level	50%
DGB contribution	15%

This distribution of income requires some explanation, for the organizational structure of unionism is not the same as in England or the United States. There are no "locals" at the plant level. Dues are collected either in the plant, if it is large, or by house-to-house canvassing, if the employing units are small; and the collectors normally keep a 5 percent fee, which is not included in the above distribution of expenditures. These monies are turned over to the district office. The district organization then returns 10 percent to the community organization (Ortsverwaltung). The bulk of the money is passed to the national organizations and the DGB.

The centralization of authority in so short a period, despite efforts to diffuse it, is revealing of certain basic characteristics of the German trade union movement. To begin with, the unions are not very active at the plant level. The unaffiliated works councils negotiate plant agreements, which supplement and, to an important degree, supplant union agreements, although they may not contradict them; and they process grievances. Union contracts are concluded exclusively at the district and national levels; and strikes, when they occur at all, are run at the district and national levels. With minimal activity at the bottom levels, it is only to be expected that little organizational vigor should reside there. Beyond this is the basic acceptance of leadership by the German worker. There are no "labor bosses" in the American sense, who use undemocratic methods to keep down membership control, for the membership does not demand control. German union leaders are "bosses" in spite of themselves. Although democratic forms exist, membership apathy makes them less meaningful. Authority is concentrated at the top by default. Finally, the German trade union movement is less concerned with collective bargaining on behalf of the daily needs of its members than with class representation at high political levels. This mild form of class war with the employer group over broad questions of societal organization focuses attention on and concentrates power in the top councils of the union movement.

Structure of the Trade Unions

The DGB was founded in 1949 at a convention in Munich[22] as the federation combining the sixteen constituent industrial unions. Earlier there had been federations only at the state and zone levels.[23] The basic body of the DGB in which original authority is vested is the Federal Congress which is comprised of delegates from the sixteen unions and which meets every two years. It elects a president, two vice-presidents, and six other members of an executive board. This board is in charge of daily operations of the DGB—education, press relations, parliamentary relations, research, and the like. The first president was Hans Boeckler, since deceased, who was a strong proponent of centralization. In addition to the executive board, there is a federal board which includes, besides the members of the executive board, the heads of the sixteen unions and the district leaders of the DGB. The federal board makes DGB policy. It acts as the chief spokesman for the working class and issues pronouncements on a very wide range of public, as well as trade union, issues. The sixteen industrial unions exercise great influence on the DGB through their federal board and have become increasingly jealous of their authority as against that of the DGB. Consequently, the DGB has been moving from being a federation to becoming a confederation of unions, more like the AFL.

The DGB has, in addition, state districts. The district chairman and the other board members are elected by the district conference,

[22]It was preceded by a bi-zonal and later tri-zonal council in Frankfurt. The dominant group of delegates, however, came from the British Zone.

[23]For a discussion of developments during this period see R. Taylor Cole, *Labor Relations in Western Germany,* Manpower Division, Office for Military Government for Germany (U.S.), 1948. (Visiting expert series, No. 2.)

subject to confirmation by the federal board of the DGB.[24] The state districts, prior to the Munich convention, had more autonomy, and this subjugation to Düsseldorf led one delegate, Markus Schleicher, then district chairman for Württemberg-Baden, to remark that this was "democracy with a sledge hammer."[25] The state districts carry on educational programs under the direction of Düsseldorf, speak for the trade union movement before state government agencies, nominate union members of the Labor Courts, and "work in accordance with the directives issued by the federal committee."[26] There are, in addition, community committees (Ortsausschüsse) which cover a city or county. Election of committee members, including the full-time chairman, is by a convention of delegates drawn from the sixteen unions. Convention elections are subject to district board confirmation. These committees carry on educational work, assist the weaker unions in their areas, publicize the DGB point of view, conduct public demonstrations like that in May 1952 in favor of codetermination, and the like.

The structure of the individual industrial unions follows much the same pattern as the DGB. There is a bi-annual congress which elects an executive board. This board has the power of confirmation over all other elected and appointed officials within the union; it makes basic union policy; carries on relations with the DGB and the national employers' associations in its field; and either negotiates or assists in the negotiation of union contracts.

Each union has several districts, often following the state borders. The district chairman is appointed by the national executive board based on the proposal of the district conference. There is, in addition, a district committee. The district office is usually quite active. It negotiates and signs most of the contracts with the employers' associations; it represents workers before the Labor Courts; it conducts strikes; it represents the union in state legislation affecting the industry; it frequently takes an interest in works

[24] *DGB News Letter,* Oct. 18, 1950.

[25] Office of Labor Affairs, Office of the United States High Commissioner for Germany, *Labor Affairs Digest,* Oct. 19, 1949.

[26] *DGB News Letter, loc. cit.*

council elections and conduct; it works with the district DGB office; and it supports the community organizations.

Community organizations (Ortsverwaltungen) are established in each city or county where the union has sufficient members. Community-level officers are elected either directly by the members or by delegates from the plants, and usually are nonpaid. The community groups take an interest in the works councils in the smaller plants, encourage workers to join the union, elect delegates to district and national conventions, discuss issues, and pass resolutions. Community groups may be asked to vote on whether a strike should be called or on the acceptance or rejection of contract terms. They normally hold meetings once a quarter; and may call demonstrations or hold mass meetings on political issues, such as the release of a former Nazi, or economic questions, such as an increase in streetcar fares. They may also carry on special programs for youths and women.[27]

In the larger plants there are shop stewards, appointed by the district or community office, who are mostly in charge of collecting dues, and elected plant committees which, on a volunteer basis, promote union membership and influence works council elections. The works council is, however, the more important plant organization. There are no full-time "organizers" or "business agents" as in American unions, for there are no organizational campaigns and the works councils perform many of the duties of the business agent.

Strikes

Phenomenally few strikes have occurred in Western Germany since the end of World War II. There were good reasons to expect them in substantial numbers. The union organization, in its re-created form, was brand new. Strikes are a normal aspect of a membership drive, and 5,000,000 members were brought into the DGB over a five-year period.[28] Much of this period witnessed a

[27]The full-time secretary of an Ortsverwaltung described his job as follows: "lecturing at meetings, training the workers on ideological and social issues, and, secondly, representing them in any action arising in connection with labor law and labor relations, and also on all social bodies, state public insurance institutions, and group accident insurance associations, particularly in pension matters."

[28]This effort was different from the usual "organizational drive," however, for it

great recovery in German production, and the strike cycle is normally related to changes in the index of industrial production. Productivity per man-hour was going up at a good rate, and workers might have been expected to take such action as is often considered helpful to secure a share of the gain.

The DGB was hardly satisfied with the lot of the worker and the role of the union movement in Western Germany, and it was proposing a mildly revolutionary program to seize power from the employers. It would not have been surprising if some of this reformist spirit had evidenced itself on the pavements. The union movement had at first within it and then increasingly outside it and at its heels a vocal Communist group uninhibited about direct action. Furthermore, at the end of World War I there had been a great wave of strikes. From 1919 through 1924, between 10,000,000 and 30,000,000 man-days were lost each year as a result of strikes, and the average strike duration was one to two weeks.[29] During the first six months of 1950, 25,000 man-days were lost and the average strike duration was one day. While this was an unusually quiet period, the entire five years from the conclusion of World War II were relatively quiet.

This startling contrast between the two postwar periods has many explanations, but four factors are of primary importance. First, the trade union movement after World War II was devoted to a policy of civic responsibility. Its leaders had seen the breakdown of the Weimar Republic, which the unions had been instrumental in creating, when the inflation of the early twenties alienated much of the middle class and the depression of the early thirties disaffected many of the workers. As the leaders of an institution which had behind it an interrupted history of over half a century's growth and ahead of it the prospect of guiding the society of the future, the heads of the unions wanted the postwar German economy soundly built. This required uninterrupted work, steady wage rates, and a minimum of social unrest. Such a policy not only recommended itself for Germany's own reconstruction efforts,

---

involved reorganization after the Nazi interlude and reestablishment of the *status quo ante.*

[29] *Statistisches Jahrbuch für das Deutsche Reich,* 1934, p. 32.

but it also served to encourage aid from other nations, particularly the United States. At the end of World War I, only the German army was destroyed, but at the end of World War II much of Germany's productive capacity and of its housing as well lay in visible ruins.

The unions, secondly, were less interested in current economic gains than in legislative victories, particularly in securing co-determination. In order to attract votes from elsewhere than the Social Democratic party, the unions needed to demonstrate capacity for restraint and devotion to the national welfare. Dependent on the liberal wing of the Catholic party for political success, the unions were encouraged to follow the preference of their own Catholic leaders for social peace. Their great cause was a political issue, and strike moderation stood to forward it more than cessations of work would have advanced their less valued economic claims.

In the third place, the unions were weak organizationally and financially. At the local level, where prolonged strikes must be supported, the unions had little strength. The works councils, not subject to union discipline, took the place of union locals in the United States, and there was no other dependable administrative machinery to run strikes. Some fear also existed that strikes would be taken over by the Communists and exploited for political ends, and to a lesser extent that quasi-Nazi "plant protection clubs" might lead back-to-work movements, or that occupation troops might be used to assure a restoration of production.

Strikes, in addition, are very costly. With bargaining on an industry-wide basis, a strike tends to throw out of work a large proportion of the union membership at one time. The expense of such a widespread strike is made very great because of the practice of union payment of high strike benefits. The German worker expects, from one source or another, to receive income every week, and, if a union calls a strike, it is responsible for keeping the income flowing.[30] The unions have not been able to accumulate substantial strike funds in the short period since their re-establishment.

[30]Unions frequently demand and occasionally get, as the price of calling off a strike, employer compensation of workers for the time lost.

While dues average 2 percent of wages, they are not regularly or fully paid, and the unions have heavy costs for administration, education, and social benefits. Partly to reduce costs, many strikes have taken the form of stopping overtime work or calling a one-day demonstration.

In the absence of these factors, a fourth cause would have made widespread strikes impossible. Added to the fact that most of the unions had less than 50 percent coverage of their territories was the attitude of their members toward strikes. Observations of union leaders on this issue are corroborated by a poll taken of union members on their attitudes toward strikes. Less than one third of union members were found to favor either economic or political strikes, and the report on the poll concludes:

> The support of strikes by union members or union sympathizers rises in no case higher than 38 percent, and indeed for all the groups examined in this report rises nowhere higher than a 41 percent minority...Disapproval of strikes—both economic and political—is widespread sentiment among all major elements of the German population.[31]

This reluctance to strike has historical antecedents. Under the Weimar Republic, the strike movement withered away after 1924. From 1929 through 1932, man-days lost through strikes averaged 2,000,000 a year.[32] Beginning in 1933, for twelve years no strikes were permitted. In addition to this atrophy of the strike arm, economic conditions improved steadily after World War II. No wild inflation occurred, and, particularly after currency reform in the middle of 1948, real wages per hour went up steadily. Furthermore, there was the mute evidence of wartime destruction to testify that miracles in improving the standard of living could not be performed.

The individual worker's desire for security fed his opposition to the strike. A strike would cost him reduction in income which

[31]Opinion Surveys Branch, Information Services Division, Office of Military Government (United States), *German Attitudes toward Economic and Political Strikes,* May 1949. A separate study of a one-day general strike in Bavaria to protest the high cost of living showed only 16 percent of the respondents in active favor. The respondents, however, were not divided into union members and nonunion members. (See Opinion Surveys Branch, *Opinions on the Work Stoppage in Bavaria,* Feb. 1949.)

[32]*Statistisches Jahrbuch für das Deutsche Reich,* 1934, p. 321.

he could ill afford and might well threaten his job if it were successful in putting economic pressure on his plant. Many plants, particularly smaller ones, were in a very precarious condition. The strike was viewed as a form of conspicuous consumption which only the more fortunately situated could afford. Some fear was expressed over employer retaliation in a labor market marked by some substantial unemployment. The workers generally expressed a preference for correction of their grievances by political instead of strike action.

In the absence of membership support, the unions were powerless to strike even if they wanted to do so, since the German unions have no real disciplinary power over their members.[33]

Abstention from strikes in the postwar period certainly enhanced the public position of the unions, both nationally and internationally. It probably cost them, however, some loss of militancy in membership and leadership, while the development of stronger local branches, which would have been necessary to carry out strikes of any significant duration, was impaired. The gains were political; the costs organizational.

Collective Bargaining

The collective bargaining process has been less affected than might be presumed by the paucity of strikes. Negotiations have been somewhat lengthened, since there is less frequently a strike date to speed them along. A duration of six months to a year has not been uncommon. The unions have appealed to public opinion and to government agencies to encourage the conclusion of negotiations and have held mass meetings and stop-work demonstrations as proofs of the seriousness of their intentions.

Although pattern-making settlements have several times resulted from strikes,[34] pattern-following settlements, in part, have substituted for strikes. The great pattern-setting relationship has been between the Metal Workers' Union and the several state employers'

[33]The unions can expel members, although they very seldom do, but cannot get them fired from their jobs.

[34]See, for example, the strike of metal workers in Hesse in August and September 1951, and the strike of metal workers in Bavaria in August 1954. The latter lasted several weeks and was the most important single strike in postwar Germany.

associations with which it deals. Of secondary importance has been the building industry as a pattern-setter. The great influence of the "metal pattern" has flowed from the size of the union and the importance and geographical dispersion of the industries with which it has dealt. The impact of the "building pattern" is explainable not so much by the size of the union as the strategic position of the industry in a heavily destroyed nation and the militancy of the union, which in several localities has been under Communist leadership or influence. The settlements for the miners and the longshoremen, among others, also have had repercussions outside their own bargaining systems, but these have been limited by the industrial and geographical isolation of the industries.

There has been no *rigid* following of the "pattern."[35] Weaker unions, like those in textiles and clothing and in agriculture, have not usually been able to match it; the printing trades, as in the United States, have tended to go their own way; governmental employers have not greatly observed it, and this has affected the contracts of the Railroad, Public Service, and Post and Telegraph Unions. The "pattern" has, however, narrowed the area of controversy and facilitated the peaceful settlement of large numbers of contracts.

Third party intervention, via conciliation and arbitration, has been an important strike substitute, particularly in important controversies. Negotiations have been eased also by the reasonable nature of union demands and the willingness of employers to make moderate concessions. Since bargaining was resumed generally in 1947 and 1948, economic conditions have been improving, and this has given the employers some freedom in agreeing to increases. Often, by the time negotiations have been concluded, the larger employers have already voluntarily made increases above the previously prevailing contract rates. Moreover, the unions have threatened strike action, even if they seldom have taken it, and the employers have feared the damage strikes could do to their businesses and to their efforts to regain their domestic and export markets.

[35]In 1950–1951, for example, the pattern was roughly a 10 percent increase, but the range of increases was from 5 to 15 percent.

Quality of Relationships

The spirit of negotiations is in contrast to that in the United States, where pounding the table and sharing a bottle of whiskey testify to equality of power and status. Negotiations in Germany take place in a class society. They are much more formal. For example, concessions are never lubricated by alcohol. It would appear incongruous and a cause for suspicion for employers and workers to drink together. They come from distinct social levels, and among other things wine is generally preferred by the representatives on one side of the table and beer on the other. The employers not infrequently treat the union negotiators somewhat as inferiors, and the union representatives are often put more in the position of requesting than demanding. The lack of easy resort to work stoppages only adds to the inferiority conferred by class distinctions.

Negotiations on the union side are normally conducted by the paid officials without the assistance of rank-and-file members. Sometimes these officials have the authority to conclude an agreement, but often their recommendation is subject to a referendum of the members. It usually takes a two-thirds or even three-fourths negative vote to upset the recommendation.[36]

Relationships have varied surprisingly little from industry to industry. They have all been on a multiple-employer basis, and there has been no great contrast between those noted for peace and those distinguished by war, for they have all been relatively peaceful. Also there have been no collusive arrangements since collusion runs counter to the socialist ideology of most union leaders, and, in any event, the employers need no assistance along lines in which they have shown adequate proficiency. The big differences in bargaining relationships have been determined by the strength of the unions (the Metal Workers have moved sooner and farther than the Textile Workers) and by the nature of the ownership (adjustments have been more cumbersome in public than in private industries). The great exception to the standard

[36]There have been heavy negative votes on several important recommendations, such as the longshore agreement in the fall of 1951, but not of sufficient proportions to overturn them.

pattern has been in the "white-collar" field where, for those workers affiliated with the Deutsche Angestelltengewerkschaft (DAG),[37] employers have dealt on an occupational instead of an industrial basis, usually through the state-level employers' federation.

The wide variations in employer-employee relations have occurred at the plant level. This has been the point at which employer prerogatives in discipline, discharge, job evaluation, and like matters have come into question; at which the master and wage agreements have been subject to modification; and at which contract administration has taken place. The differences here have depended largely on whether or not the works council has been under Communist control, and whether the employer has been strict or liberal in his employee relations policies. Obviously, the two matters have not always been entirely unrelated. Thus the distinguishing features of bargaining systems have not been found so much in the relations between the unions and the employers' associations as between the individual employers and the plant works councils.

Third party participation in labor disputes in Germany, as compared with the United States, is more intensive and quite different in approach. While no exact figures are available, apparently at least 10 to 20 percent of "pattern" wage settlements and perhaps 5 percent of all wage settlements are by arbitration. Reliance on arbitration to determine wage increases springs partly from reluctance to strike, but reflects also the general German tendency to rely on the Government to solve problems.[38] It antedates the postwar period when special limitations subdued strike action. During the Nazi period, of course, all wages were set by decree, but increasingly during the days of the Weimar Republic resort had

[37]The DAG has about 300,000 members. The other leading independent union, the Deutscher Beamtenbund (BB), has a membership of about 100,000 civil servants.

[38]When polled on whether they favored free collective bargaining or government determination of wage levels, 42 percent of respondents drawn from the population at large favored "government fixing of wages," 34 percent favored collective bargaining, and 23 percent expressed no opinion. Surveys Branch, Information Control Division, Office of Military Government (U.S.), *German Attitudes toward Trade Unions,* June 1946.

The DGB, however, strongly favors free collective bargaining. It has stated, "the determination of wages, salaries, and working conditions must be exclusively reserved for collective bargaining." *Economic Policy Program,* March 12, 1951.

been had to third party solutions. In 1930, for example, over 40 percent of all wage agreements, involving 70 percent of all workers, were concluded by arbitration, and mostly by compulsory government boards.[39] While the proportion of agreements settled by arbitration (all of it voluntary) in the postwar period is still far below these figures, it is steadily increasing. It evidences the same reluctance of the representatives of the parties to assume responsibility for setting industry-wide wage scales and of the parties to bear the costs of a freer mode of bargaining.

Secondary (grievance) disputes are referred to third parties in large numbers, and access to arbitration is easy and virtually cost-free.

Third party participation is lodged almost exclusively in governmental hands. There is virtually no arbitration by private persons. This results partly from the absence of groups of neutral individuals, outside of government service, in German society. The religious conflict rules out the clergy; the professors are identified with class educational institutions, and very few of them are specialists in this area; and few lawyers "work both sides of the street" under a caste system which confines social contacts. Public arbitration also is less costly, traditional, and, in the case of secondary disputes, open to the nonunion worker.

Labor Courts

The agencies called upon to adjudicate most disputes are the Labor Courts. These courts, in approximately their present form, were established in 1926.[40] They are open to all workers and employers, whether or not affiliated with a union or an employers' association. They hear only secondary disputes, as a formal rule;[41] but, as a matter of practice, Labor Court judges are commonly appointed by the Minister of Labor as chairmen of arbitration boards requested by the parties to settle disputes over new agree-

[39]W. Woytinsky, *Internationales Handwörterbuch des Gewerkschaftswesens,* p. 157.

[40]See Frieda Wunderlich, *German Labor Courts* (Chapel Hill: University of North Carolina Press, 1946), p. 56.

[41]They were prohibited from adjudicating primary disputes by Control Council Law No. 35, in an effort of the occupying powers to encourage free collective bargaining as against the tradition of compulsory arbitration.

ments, or these same judges are named directly by the parties. The other board members usually are drawn from the same panels of names which are used in appointing the labor and industry members of the Labor Courts, and the offices of the Labor Courts are often used for the hearings. Even when the parties set up their own machinery for settling grievances, they most frequently call upon Labor Court judges to preside. Thus, in both primary and secondary disputes, either formally or informally, the Labor Courts and Labor Court judges have a virtual monopoly on arbitration.

Aside from the Labor Court system, there are conciliation officers in each state who can be used by the parties in connection with primary disputes. It is an interesting commentary that almost every case which goes to conciliation is subsequently referred to arbitration. There are few conciliators, and one of their main tasks is to forward cases to arbitration. Once in arbitration, nearly all cases are disposed of without dissent. This suggests that referral to arbitration, which is always tripartite, often comes more from a desire to spread responsibility than from true inability of the parties to reach an agreement.

Contrary to frequent practice in the United States, the emphasis is always on compromise between the parties, rather than on judicial determination. This is partly a matter of legal requirement, for Labor Court judges in secondary disputes are directed to seek a settlement mutually acceptable to the parties, and this approach carries over into primary disputes as well. Judges are selected for promotion partly on the basis of the percentage of cases which they settle without a decision. This leads to mild coercion by some judges to get the parties to accept with apparent willingness what they would have to accept in any event.

All the courts are tripartite, and tripartitism of itself fosters, and is designed to foster, compromise. Labor Court judges, also, are subject to reappointment every three years, and since they are full-time employees of the Government making a career in this field, they are not anxious to secure the enmity of either the unions or the employers, both of whom are consulted on continued acceptability. In a society with conflicting class ideologies, compromises are safer than decisions on the basis of principles which may fail to have mutual support. The compromise spreads responsibility over several individuals.

Theory of Compromise

Beyond these factors is the central theory of an approach which finds its roots in the German legal system.[42] The process is not viewed as strictly judicial in the narrow sense of the term: "The judge in the labor court looks on most of the cases which he has to decide as questions to be settled from the point of view of social justice rather than as problems which have to be decided in accordance with statutes and precedents."[43] As one judge has explained, there are many cases which cannot be settled on the basis of contract, law, or precedent, but where "experienced social judgment and human law" must be applied. This orientation favors the compromise settlement.

Of the formal cases before the courts, 40 to 50 percent are settled by agreement of the parties and 10 to 20 percent at the appeal stage. Most of these cases have to do with individual grievances over compensation or disciplinary action. Of the cases not compromised, the tripartite board is unanimous on about half of them; on the other half, dissents, while never shown, are implied.

In disputes over new agreements informally before the courts, the awards are almost always unanimous. If the members are not in sufficient agreement to be willing to appear unanimous, usually no award at all will be issued. There is a special reason for emphasis on unanimity in this type of case, for the parties often do not agree to accept the award in advance but instead provide a period of time to decide whether to accept it or not. Unanimity in the award almost assures acceptance, and in fact most awards are accepted. Instead of arbitration, the process is an advanced form of mediation, with the impartial chairman making specific suggestions for settlement and accepting some public responsibility for the one which his co-members favor.

This system of dispute settlement has some interesting results,

[42]For a discussion of the German legal system, see Ernest Fraenkel, "The Labor Courts in the German Judicial System," in Wunderlich, *German Labor Courts.*
[43]*Ibid.*, p. 15.

aside from reducing strikes. The unions of the Weimar days "looked on the labor court statute as one of the proudest achievements of German democracy."[44] Beyond doubt it does open up judicial protection for the worker, but it also reduces the need for union membership and protection. Any worker can gain access to the court, whether he belongs to the union or not. The unions do have trained representatives to help workers present their cases, and some unions will represent nonmembers; yet apparently only about 25 percent of the workers are so represented. The others walk in by themselves or with a friend or relative to speak for them, except at the appeal stage where representation is required and is usually provided by the unions. The unions also nominate all the judges who sit as labor representatives on the court, just as the employers' associations also make nominations. The union judge in the three-man court, however, apparently never seeks to make a distinction between the union and nonunion member as a device for encouraging union membership.

Contract terms are affected also. With the judges concerned not alone with the law or the contract or precedents, many questions of detail and even entire subjects, instead of being specified in the contract, are left to the "social judgment" of the Labor Court judges. For example, very little, if anything, is said about what constitutes a grievance or about disciplinary penalties. The judges are allowed greater discretion, and the parties take less responsibility.

Private Contracts and Public Law

The universal application of contract terms by law expresses, in the collective bargaining field, a central tendency in the relationship of government to economic life in Germany and, in turn, has a profound effect on the operations of employers' associations and unions and on the content of labor contracts. The law on the extension of contracts grows out of the German preference for legal regulation and enforced uniformity of actions. It demonstrates the low value placed on independence of conduct by individual work-

[44]Fraenkel, *op. cit.*, p. 13.

ers and employers. Further, it conforms to the practice of placing public power in private hands.

The basic provision of the law on the extension of contracts is quite simple. Whenever a contract between an employers' association and a union applies to employers with more than 50 percent of the employees in the industry and area, then it may be extended by government decree to all employers and workers.[45] Extension is not automatic however. It must be requested by one or both of the contracting parties and must be found to be in the "public interest" by officials of the Ministry of Labor. An opportunity is given for noncovered employers or workers to protest, but in most cases the request is granted. Apparently the requests are initiated more frequently by employers' associations than by unions.

Through this law a minority of employers in conjunction with a union representing a minority of the workers can, in effect, legislate for all employers and all workers. It turns employers' associations and unions into private governments, with the enforcing power of public government behind them.

This law gains support from both organized management and organized labor. Once the union in an industry is strong enough to force bargaining on some of the larger employers, they become concerned that contract terms apply also to all of their competitors. The law, from the employer point of view, is a means of equalizing the terms upon which labor may be purchased, by removing nonunion competition. The union point of view is not so evident. It might be reasoned that the unions would wish a distinction to be made between union and nonunion conditions so that unionism would be more appealing to the unprotected and unorganized worker. This, however, is not the case. The unions do not view themselves as organizations selling or forcing the purchase of memberships. They consider themselves, instead, the representatives of all workers, both organized and unorganized. Further, the law helps protect employment opportunities in the plants initially covered by contract, and the union can bring under contract coverage members in plants not party to the original agreement.

[45]For the text of the law and a legal analysis, see Alfred Hueck and H. C. Nipperdey, *Tarifvertragsgesetz* (Munich and Berlin: C. H. Becksche Verlagsbuchhandlung, 1949). The original law was promulgated as an ordinance in Dec. 1918.

Results of Contract Extension

The law on extension of contracts has some far-reaching consequences. Organization of employers is made more important than organization of workers. The law is applicable once employers of 50 percent of the employees are covered by the contract, regardless of the number of workers represented by the union. Consequently, there is more pressure to organize the larger employers and more need to discipline them to keep them in the association than there is to force and keep workers in the union. The unions, if they want universal coverage by contract terms, need to be more interested in having a strong employers' association than a strong union. The unions need have only enough members to encourage employers with 50 percent of the employees to band together, and this may require less than 50 percent union membership. In fact, of the sixteen industrial unions, only six have memberships of 50 percent or more of the employees in their jurisdictions. Such unions as the Textile and Clothing, Food, Woodworking, and Building Unions, which include about one third of the eligible workers in their jurisdictions, have many hundreds of contracts which have been extended by law to cover all workers.

It is quite possible, if the large employers are organized adequately enough, for a union contract to cover by law all workers, although the union does not have a majority in any single plant. For the sake of universal contract coverage, the union strategy need be, not the organization of workers, but encouragement of the organization of employers. Employers can put a legal floor under competition by first bringing together within their industry enough employers to represent 50 percent of the employment and then finding a union with at least paper coverage with which to conclude an agreement. In the absence of unions, the employers might wish to create some, provided they did not become too strong, in order to use this device to limit the range of competitive conditions in the labor market.

In addition to reducing union interest in membership, this law reduces worker interest in unions. All workers can be covered by contract terms, whether they belong to unions or not. While the nonmember worker shares the benefits, the independent employer, who is usually small and more inclined to pay low wages, pays the cost of having to follow more uniform terms in buying labor.

The law also influences bargaining in additional ways. It encourages industrial unionism, as against craft, since it is easier for a contract to be extended by law to all employers who make a certain product than to all workers who follow a certain trade. It puts the emphasis, also, on industry-by-industry contracts, rather than multi-industrial contracts, except where the unions are very strong, since employers can more readily be brought together around their interest in product market competition. In order for the multi-industrial contract to be eligible for extension, the union must be able to force a heterogeneous group of employers together in an effort to protect themselves from the union, while at the industry level the employers tend to pull together to restrict competition. It is not by chance, then, that the most important multi-industrial contract is negotiated by the strongest union, the Metal Workers; and that a relatively weak union, like the Food Workers, negotiates contracts covering single industries.

The terms of the contract likewise are affected.[46] They must be broad enough to cover all employers whether direct parties to the contract or not. This leads to contracts which are quite brief and couched in general terms. More important, however, the terms must be at a minimum level, otherwise the employers' associations may not hold employers with 50 percent of the employees or the nonmembers may successfully prevent extension of the contract. Thus the contracts negotiated by the unions become more minimum wage and hour laws than union contracts. The works councils, particularly in the larger plants, draw up contracts with management which make these basic laws more specific in their application and often improve upon their terms. The union becomes a quasi-legislative agency and the works council a quasi-union.

[46]A minor point, but an interesting variation from American practice, is the opening terminology of each contract. It sets forth not so much who are the parties but instead the geographical and industrial territory it seeks to cover.

wage rates for individual jobs and workers, using the wage or salary agreement as a guide, and over social provision for the injured and sick; its competence to present grievances; its right to secure economic information from the company; and even the conditions under which a union representative can attend works council meetings, among other matters. It also defines the prerogatives of management.

The *plant rules agreement* (Betriebsordnung) is also subject to acceptance by the works council. It covers shift hours, rules on attendance, smoking, loitering, and other disciplinary matters, times of payment of wages, the setting of piece rates, the giving of warning notices, identification cards, hiring provisions, welfare facilities, and many other questions bearing on the relationship of the man to his job. It may improve on the base rates or vacation provisions negotiated by the union on an industry-wide basis. These agreements cover more of the same subjects included in the typical contract in the United States than do any of the other forms of contract.

Both the unions and the employers' associations frequently prepare model works council and plant rules agreements to guide local works councils and plants in their negotiations.

Specialized agreements are also found in two fields: vacations and arbitration—matters which are also covered by law. Each state has a very detailed law on vacations and holidays but the parties sometimes choose to improve upon the law and may specify their changes in a separate contract which is subject to change if the law changes. Similarly, some contracting parties have arbitration machinery supplementing the public Labor Court facilities and, again, because of their relation to the law, these arrangements may be set forth by themselves. This machinery is established to handle interpretations of the contract, not to process grievances which are always arbitrated through the Labor Courts. Certain other matters, which are often treated in contracts in the United States, are left largely or exclusively to legal provision, such as rules on dismissals and on sick leave; or are left to the judicial practices of the Labor Courts, such as seniority, which is not in any event so strongly recognized in either layoffs or promotions.

Handicraft agreements are sometimes separately negotiated with the job shop employers and are concerned most importantly with rules governing apprentices, which are more often, however, developed unilaterally by the handicraft associations. These small shops are frequently blanketed under the provisions of the master and wage agreements by action of governmental authorities.

Wages

Bargaining processes and policies result in the minimization, equalization, and formalization of wages. Two policies, though by no means designed for the purpose, taken together are admirably suited for keeping contractual wage rates at relatively low levels. The first is the policy of universal extension of wage agreements, and the second is the policy of establishing rates which will not embarrass the marginal firm. Were the policy to force each firm or group of firms to set contract levels according to selective ability to pay, or to allow employment to take care of itself, or both together, contractual wage rates on the average would undoubtedly be higher.

The universalization of contract terms has already been explored, but the concern with employment has not. The German worker has had several bad experiences with unemployment, particularly during the Great Depression; and he has been willing to pay high prices, including tolerance of national socialism, to eliminate it. Since the end of World War II, partly because of the large influx of refugees, unemployment has at all times existed and been a constant reminder to the employed worker of his potentially precarious hold on a job.[48] In the period from currency reform in June 1948 to the armament boom in the summer of 1950, unemployment generally varied from about 5 to 12 percent of the wage- and salary-earning labor force.[49] The German worker places great stress on employment security. Various polls document this common observation. They show, for example, that

[48]The absence of strict contractual rules on layoffs in accord with seniority makes layoffs more of a threat to all workers than if seniority rules made certain that layoffs of moderate size would affect only the new hands.

[49]See Office of the United States High Commissioner for Germany, *3rd Quarterly Report on Germany,* June 30, 1950, p. 57.

unemployment is considered the leading problem in postwar Germany and that economic security is more highly prized than political freedom—many would give up the right to vote in return for job security.[50] This concern with job preservation is shared by many trade union leaders; a number of them declared in interviews that in bargaining they did not wish to set rates which would cause any job loss.[51] Were they to do so, in any event, contract extension might then be denied as against the "public interest." No employers or employers' association officials interviewed on the subject considered that the unions in bargaining had insisted on increases which would result in layoffs.

This moderation in wage bargaining in the postwar period has rested on more than concentration on job preservation. The unions have adopted a most "responsible" approach toward the economic problems of Germany.[52] They have not wished to retard reconstruction and have been willing to permit large profits as an encouragement to this reconstruction; they have not wished to interfere, by raising costs unduly, with the revival of the export trade; and they have not wished to assume responsibility for an inflationary spiral, the disastrous consequences of which were vividly illustrated by the debacle after World War I. This DGB policy of wage restraint has not been, during most of the postwar period, in opposition to the desires of the membership, if trade union conventions and meetings are any gauge. It has been more popular to promise restraint than excessive zeal. During the past few years, however, during which there has been a moderate rise in the cost of living, the membership has become more anxious for wage increases and, with a pickup in employment, less concerned over unemployment.

Other reasons for the practice of wage moderation have not been so noble: the employers have been strongly organized and have

[50]See Reaction Analysis Staff, Office of Public Affairs, Office of the United States High Commissioner for Germany, *Trends in German Public Opinion—1946 through 1949,* August 1950; particularly pp. 7 and 8.

[51]In 1950, through arbitration tribunals, in at least two important instances (the largest metal trades company in Berlin and the Danube shipping industry) unions agreed to wage cuts as a job preservation measure.

[52]U.S. Bureau of Labor Statistics, "West German Labor's Wage Policy," *Notes on Labor Abroad,* Jan. 1951.

resisted each pfennig of contractual wage increase; widespread use of the strike weapon has been impossible; and first the military government and later the federal government have taken an unfavorable view of rate advances.[53]

Contract rates are not necessarily indicative of actual wages paid. Rates paid, however, have not departed very widely on the average (although more in skilled than unskilled classifications) from contractual levels except, as noted above, in North Rhine-Westphalia metal-working. Employers have raised wages above contract rates to attract labor, or to favor their plant works council, or for other reasons but usually not by great amounts. There has been available the reserve army of the unemployed, and the employers' united front has been against wage increases. Supplementation of contract terms has often taken a more paternalistic turn, such as provision of special canteens and so forth.

In March 1950, the average hourly wage was 1.25 marks[54]—the equivalent of 30 cents an hour at the official, and 23 cents at the unofficial rate of exchange—in manufacturing, construction, and mining. The average rate for women was 0.85 marks. In the first quarter of 1950 real hourly wages were at the same level as in 1938.[55] For several years after the war and in Berlin into 1950, wage orders dating from the National Socialist regime were still in effect.

Beginning with the summer of 1950, however, a number of contractual wage increases, typically about 10 percent, were put into effect. This DGB-sponsored round of increases was encouraged by the price increases which followed the start of the Korean war[56] and by the spectacular doubling of industrial production over the previous two-year period.[57] These increases served to reduce somewhat the Communist party appeal to the workers that wages were

[53]Wage increases were subject to stabilization controls until November 1948.

[54]*Statistische Berichte,* June 1950.

[55]*3rd Quarterly Report on Germany,* p. 61. According to the best available estimates, which are very poor, wages in 1948 comprised about the same percentage of gross value of production as in 1936.

[56]The DGB in March 1951, as part of a statement on over-all economic policy, formally enunciated its wage policy as follows: "The objective of trade union wage policy is to adjust wages to the price structure." *Economic Policy Program,* March 12, 1951.

[57]*Ibid.,* p. 59.

not keeping pace with war-augmented prices. There have been steady but moderate increases in contractual wage rates in each of the intervening years, including 1956, and usually of the order of 3 to 5 percent.

Wage Structure

The wage structure is by American standards rather compressed. The average spread between semiskilled and skilled male workers for manufacturing, construction, and mining was only 10 percent in March 1950, and between semiskilled and laborers, 15 percent—a total spread of 25 percent.[58] The great exception is women. Their average rate was 40 percent below the male rate; it was somewhat more than 40 percent at the semiskilled and skilled levels and somewhat less at the labor level.[59]

Among the states, leaving out Hamburg and Bremen which are not comparable since they are metropolitan areas, the state with the highest average wage rate (Hesse) had an average of hourly earnings in manufacturing and construction less than 15 percent higher than for the lowest state (Württemberg-Hohenzollern).[60] It would be less than this if the occupations and industries were the same, for the Hesse rate is pulled up by the heavy concentration of metal-working establishments. Among industries, the spread from bottom to top is much greater, about 50 percent.[61] The distribution of industries on the ascending scale of average hourly rates is different in two important instances from that in the United States. The metal-working industries are substantially in advance of all other manufacturing industries. How much this reflects the strength of the Metal Workers' Union and how much the National Socialist policy of expanding employment in those industries and the spectacular revival and expansion of the metal-working industries in Germany since 1950, or other factors, is, of course,

[58] *Statistische Berichte,* June 1950.

[59] The statistics do not show what the differentials would be if the same occupations were taken for men and women. Contract rates in the Bremen area for the same occupations show differentials generally of 10 to 30 percent. Office of Labor Affairs, Office of the United States High Commissioner for Germany, *Sex Differentials in Wages and Salaries* (Bremen Area), Sept. 1950.

[60] *Statistische Berichte,* June 1950.

[61] *Ibid.*

impossible to determine. The construction industry has an average rate rather lower than one might expect.[62] Otherwise the rate relationships are not surprising.[63]

Differentials are rather formalized affairs. The standard industry-wide contract sets up about a half-dozen skill grades, and the relationships among them are fairly standard. It also sets up community classifications (city, town, village, and rural) with quite fixed gaps between them, totaling about 15 percent. Interindustry relationships are, however, not at all formalized, nor are they so static, although a tendency toward pattern-following wage adjustments keeps them in some relationship to each other.

Somewhat the same forces explain the emphasis on both equalization and formalization. At work have been Socialist theories of standardizing pay; government influence, whether National Socialist, military, or democratic, working in somewhat the same direction through edict and arbitration awards; and multiple-employer bargaining with its broad settlements. The free market has given way to institutional control, and flexibility and inequality to formality and equality.

Conclusion

Regardless of what they might have done in the thousand years they gave themselves, the Nazis made little permanent imprint on collective bargaining in Germany during the twelve years they were given by history. Quite quickly after the war the old organizational forms and the old methods were reinstated. The employers were again highly organized, the trade unions highly centralized, and bargaining on an exclusively multiemployer basis. Most of the Weimar labor laws were back in almost their identical earlier forms.

[62]Construction wages were cut by government decree in 1930 in an effort to stimulate employment, and the Nazis did not encourage expansion of the construction industry as they did the armament industry. Construction wages in the United States may be comparatively high, for "job control" by the unions has been particularly effective in the building trades.

[63]Office of Labor Affairs, Office of the United States High Commissioner for Germany, *Average Hourly and Weekly Gross Earnings, Average Hours Worked per Week, Manual Workers in the Manufacturing Industries, Including Building, Bizonal Area of Germany, June 1949, October 1949,* p. 12a.

The two principal postwar differences owe as much to occupation policy as to the experience with the Nazis. The first of these is the unification of the trade union movement. Three main organizations operated during the Weimar period: Socialist, Catholic, and Democratic. This fractionalization of the trade union movement, while it did not aid the employers greatly, did make effective opposition to the rise of the National Socialists less possible. The experience of total defeat by the Nazis and the encouragement given by the occupying powers to the formation of a single federation contributed to unity through the DGB in the postwar period. The second is the prohibition of compulsory arbitration. Increasingly, under the Weimar Republic, compulsory arbitration was utilized to settle industrial disputes. This tended to weaken the unions, strengthen the hand of government, and pave the way for Hitler. Again there was a desire to avoid past mistakes, but again also the hand of the occupying powers was at work. The early control laws permitted only voluntary arbitration of primary disputes with voluntary acceptance of the award and limited the Labor Courts to the hearing of secondary disputes.

These two changes, important as they are in strengthening the union movement and supporting free collective bargaining, can not yet, however, be counted as permanent. The Socialists and Catholics still retain their separate identities within the DGB, and important primary disputes are increasingly being sent by the parties to arbitration. If these innovations disappear and the former organizational patterns and settlement practices return, it will be because some of the same basic forces are still at work: the supremacy of political and religious over economic considerations, and the devotion to order and security.

VI

Collective Bargaining in Italy

LUISA RIVA SANSEVERINO

THE COLLECTIVE agreement developed in Italy, as in other countries, out of experience. Indeed, it developed at the beginning of our century[1] as a manifestation of the tendency of occupational groups to establish their own regulations. These regulations were intended to make separate arrangements for specific groups different from the general regulations issued by the state, which were found to be incomplete and fragmentary, as well as from individual regulations established under the prevailing influence of the employers, i.e., of the economically stronger parties.

At the end of World War I, as a result of the increased practical importance of the collective agreement, it was found more urgent than ever to set up legislative machinery for it. However, the change to a new political régime necessarily delayed matters.

With the agreements at the Palazzo Chigi in 1923 and at the Palazzo Vidoni in 1925, the confederation of fascist corporations (Confederazione Italiana delle Corporazioni Fasciste)—the fascist central organization of workers—and the general confederation of Italian industry (Confederazione Generale dell' Industria Italiana)—the organization of the industrial employers—recognized mutually their exclusive group representation for all categories of

Note: The translation from the Italian was prepared by Professor Oscar Ornati.—Ed.

[1]There are early traces of collective bargaining in the middle of the last century as witnessed by a contractually agreed wage list for the printers of Torino in 1848.

workers and employers in industry. This implied primarily recognition of monopoly status for collective bargaining. This was confirmed by the law of April 3, 1926, No. 563. Later on, some of the dispositions of this law relating to collective agreements were written into the civil code of 1942.

Law No. 563 established a single vocational organization (representation of interests—in the terminology of Italian law) for each category of workers or employers.[2] The organization was recognized as the legal representative of the category as a whole. These conditions were considered as necessary and sufficient for the formulation of collective agreements which were generally binding for the whole category to which they referred. The observance of the collective agreement was guaranteed by a triple system of sanctions: civil, penal, and disciplinary.

After fascist legislation was abolished, the collective agreement came back, at least in theory, to the uncertain position that had existed before fascism. However, collective bargaining had, in the meanwhile, established itself as the most important method of controlling individual work relationships; yet, the implementation of the collective agreement was exclusively dependent upon the politico-economic power of the new unions and employers' organizations and the pressure they could exert upon each other.

The current situation of the vocational organizations can be summarized as follows: employers are organized in confederations (and in national industrial federations and local associations) grouped according to the major sectors of the national economy: industry, agriculture, commerce, transportation, banking, insurance, and the like. Some among them, as the Confindustria and Confagricoltura, had been established prior to the advent of the fascist régime, in the years immediately following World War I.

On the workers' side the vocational organizations also go back to those existing prior to fascism. Among them are: Confederazione Generale Italiana del Lavoro (CGIL), Confederazione Italiana Sindacati dei Lavoratori (CISL), Unione Italiana del Lavoro (UIL), and Confederazione Italiana Sindacati Nazionali dei Lavor-

[2]The term "vocational organization" (trade union) is being used in Italy also to designate employers' associations. The term "category" refers to all workers employed in a given trade or industry or to all employers of a given trade or industry.

atori (CISNAL). The major workers' confederations as well as the respective national federations and local associations, have political alignments.[3] The communist nature of the CGIL is well known; the other two major confederations, CISL and UIL, are opposed to CGIL, as a result of their anticommunist position, which is also shared by CISNAL. Although opposition to communism is common to them, it has not led, up to now, to a unification of CISL with UIL, because of their different political orientation. CISL has drawn the majority of its members from the adherents of the Christian-social or demo-Christian political group, particularly the ACLI Catholic organization, while UIL is connected with the democratic socialist and republican groups. Neither CGIL nor CISL and UIL are ready to cooperate with CISNAL because of its fascist background.

Pending the establishment of a complete trade union law which will also provide for registry of all employers' and workers' associations, the Ministry of Labor has acted and continues to act as the government agency to which are submitted copies of the constitutions and the bylaws of the organizations involved, relying upon the data which are furnished to it voluntarily by the organizations or through the Regional and Provincial Labor Offices.

CGIL claims a membership of five million; CISL, two million; UIL, six hundred thousand. These figures are certainly exaggerated. The total Italian labor force is twenty-two million, of which fourteen million are eligible for union organization.

Present Situation of Collective Agreements

On November 13, 1944, before the end of the war, Article 43 of Law No. 369 regarding collective agreements was passed in liberated Italy. This article maintained in effect the collective agreements which had been established during the fascist period. It intended to guarantee to the parties involved the regulations that had been established through collective agreements up to the

[3]The Italian "confederation" corresponds to the AFL or CIO American style or British TUC; the federation to an American international union; the local association to a city central. [Ed.]

time when the new vocational organizations would replace them, either entirely or partially, by new settlements.

Since 1946 collective agreements which were established during the fascist régime have progressively been replaced by new collective agreements. These have an entirely different legal structure, as they are valid only for the membership of the associations that have entered into the agreement, as well as for unorganized employers and workers willing to abide by the collective agreement. Furthermore, it is now possible for individual workers or employers, while members of their respective unions' and employers' associations, to depart from the collective agreement if they do so by specific agreement. A unilateral departure from the contract leads, however, to sanctions for violation of contractual obligations. As a result the legal force of collective agreements is greatly reduced. In addition the collective agreements are not respected to the extent that would be desirable, even by the members of the organizations—both workers and employers—that have entered into the agreement. This happens principally in those regions of Italy and in those occupations in which the workers' organization is not sufficiently effective and where unionization is not extensive (southern Italy, agricultural laborers). A special committee was established in 1955 to investigate the question and report to Parliament.

The need to re-establish a legislative framework in which the collective agreement would be recognized as generally binding was acknowledged by the constituent assembly which prepared the Constitution of the Democratic Italian Republic. The problem of the Assembly was that of trying to attain such a result in a form compatible with the principles of democracy and freedom of association which are the basis of the new order. The aim was to develop a system within which the collective agreement was to be binding also on third parties, i.e., members of a given trade who are not members of the vocational organizations. At the same time, the autonomy and freedom of the organized groups, and the autonomy and freedom of individual workers and employers, had to be protected. The necessary compromise was reached through

Article 39 of the 1948 Constitution. The last paragraph of this Article states:

> Registered organizations, participating in a joint body with representation proportionate to their membership, may establish collective labor agreements which will be binding on all persons belonging to the category to which the agreement refers.

Motivated by democratic principles and by those of trade union freedom, the Constitution refuses to recognize any single vocational organization as paramount because it has the majority or is, as some foreign laws put it, the most representative organization. Instead, the Constitution empowers all registered employers' and workers' associations (endowed with a legal entity through registration) to participate in the negotiation of the collective agreement with a representation proportional to the number of their members.

The program contained in Article 39 of the Constitution is still waiting for legislative implementation. What is required are laws filling the gaps existing in the Italian legal framework in matters dealing with the collective agreement, employers' and workers' associations, the right to strike, and conciliation and arbitration procedures in labor disputes. Each minister who held the portfolio of labor (Fanfani, Marazza, Rubinacci) elaborated his own proposals. None of these has so far been discussed in Parliament. The General Secretary of CISL, Giulio Pastore, also submitted to the Chamber, on February 14, 1951, a bill according to which a collective agreement can, under special conditions, by presidential decree, be made binding on all parties involved without reference to membership in the signatory organization. As it appears in a bill submitted by the present Labor Minister Ezio Vigorelli, this is the direction in which legislative thinking moves at present.

Yet even when a proposal of this kind will be enacted, the collective agreements agreed upon in the manner indicated in Article 39 of the Constitution or made obligatory through a presidential decree will not be the only forms of collective negotiation possible within the Italian framework. Along with this type of agreement, which may be described as a *normative agreement,* the contractual form existing today will continue to be used. Collective agreements under common law applicable only to the members of the signatory associations, which may be called *contractual agreements,* will continue to be legal.

Normative contracts when established will regulate the activities of all workers and employers that are part of a given category. Contractual agreements, on the other hand, cover the members of the signatory associations, as well as unorganized employers and workers willing to abide by the collective agreement. Since contractual agreements are the only form at present existing in the Italian legal framework, the following pages refer only to them.

Bargaining at the National Level

Following what can be considered a tradition in the Italian labor world, collective bargaining is carried on in the great majority of cases by national employers' and trade union organizations, either general (confederations) or category industry-wide organizations (federations). This corresponds first of all to the structure of Italian employers' and labor organizations, which cover not only a single company or group of companies, but the category (textile, mining, etc.) or the production sector (industry, trade, etc.) as a whole.

In addition, the necessity of collective bargaining at the national level may be explained by two other considerations. First, small and middle-sized companies predominate in Italy, while big companies for which a special agreement could be negotiated are comparatively few. Second, there is a question of competition and of mutual defense for the companies as well as for the workers: big companies could afford to pay higher wages than middle-sized and small ones, and workers employed by big companies usually are well organized and in a position to apply for more satisfactory standards. But if collective agreements were negotiated at the company level, the conditions granted by big companies would put in a difficult spot the middle-sized and small companies, where employers cannot afford to pay comparatively high wages and workers are not strong enough to exert sufficient pressure.

The policy adopted and nearly constantly followed is negotiation at the national level, either by sector or by category, and agreements establishing for every company involved a minimum standard of wage and labor conditions. The companies which can afford it are always free to grant supplementary payments, i.e., the so-called superminimum. Lately, however, a trend toward negotiations at the company level is to be reported. This policy was first sponsored by CISL, but now CGIL officially agrees to it.

Intervention of the Labor Ministry

When a collective agreement includes the whole Italian territory in a given sector or category, or is of particular importance from a general point of view, government intervention to mediate —not arbitrate—is recognized. If an agreement is not reached and the situation results in labor unrest or in a strike, negotiations are resumed and concluded with the intervention of the Ministry of Labor and Social Security. It is usually the Minister himself, or one of the Undersecretaries, that follow the progress of the negotiations. The same happens locally, but much more rarely, with the intervention of the Regional and Provincial Labor Offices and also, when a dispute affects public order, of the local government representative (Prefect).

In its intervention, the Government is motivated by its consideration of the impact upon the national economy of the added burden imposed by the new agreements as well as the inflationary dangers which might arise from an indiscriminate attempt to raise wages. Nevertheless, the Government must also take into account the need of the working masses for the gradual improvement of their standard of living as well as the necessity of giving a certain degree of job security, so as to prevent, if possible, a rise in the number of unemployed.

The Government has also intervened to ensure more general observance of collective agreements, especially by medium-sized and small companies. Pending the promulgation of labor laws, the Government has used many indirect ways to insure a more satisfactory compliance with the collective agreement and to reduce disputes arising out of contract evasions on the part of employers and workers. Thus special requirements have been inserted in public contracts stipulating that the contracting firms must observe the minimum wage and labor conditions established by collective agreements. Withdrawal of contracts is contemplated under certain conditions, as has happened on the initiative of the *Cassa del Mezzogiorno,* a government agency in charge of agricultural and industrial development in southern Italy. Instructions have also been given to government employment offices to insure that, when they refer workers to employers, the conditions of work offered to the workers correspond to those established by collective agreement for the different localities.

The Postwar Period

Table 1 reports the number of collective agreements negotiated in the industrial sector during the period 1946–1952 at the national level by national employers' and workers' organizations. These agreements were on the pattern and within the limits of national agreements covering the whole industrial sector, and represent the agreed wage and labor conditions to be followed by all industrial

Table 1. COLLECTIVE AGREEMENTS IN THE INDUSTRIAL SECTOR STIPULATED IN THE PERIOD 1946–1952.

Industry	*1946*	*1947*	*1948*	*1949*	*1950*	*1951*	*1952*	*Total*
Textile	–	5	1	1	2	8	1	18
Paper and printing	–	6	1	4	2	1	–	14
Chemical	–	8	1	5	–	2	–	16
Food	1	2	7	11	1	1	1	24
Metal-mechanical	–	–	1	–	3	–	–	4
Building	1	1	–	–	1	–	1	4
Building material	–	3	1	2	1	2	2	11
Glass	3	1	1	9	3	6	2	25
Mining	2	9	–	1	2	2	1	17
Wood	–	–	1	1	–	–	1	3
Clothing	–	–	5	1	–	–	–	6
Transportation	–	2	1	6	4	11	1	25
Oil and natural gas	1	–	–	2	–	4	–	7
Turism	1	–	–	–	–	–	–	1
Miscellaneous	–	–	2	9	6	5	1	23
Telecommunications	1	2	3	4	–	2	2	14
Services	2	2	3	3	5	3	2	20
Theater	1	5	8	4	8	6	–	32
Total	13	46	36	63	38	53	15	264

Source: Antonio Toldo, *Il Sindacalismo in Italia,* "Centro di Studi Sociali," Piazza San Fedele, Milano, 2nd ed. 1953, p. 161.

companies, without any discrimination among categories. In addition it happened that an agreement referring to industrial companies was later extended or adopted for transportation, trade, insurance, and similar companies.

Seventeen national agreements covering entire industrial sectors were made between 1945 and 1954 (July). They deal with the chief social and economic problems the Italian labor world has had to face in this postwar period: Internal Commissions, regulation of dismissals, and wage scales. Each of these is briefly discussed below.

Internal Commissions

Article 46 of the new Italian Constitution states:

> In order to promote the social and economic improvement of labor, and in accordance with the requirements of production, the Republic recognizes the right of workers to participate, by the methods and within the limits established by laws, in the management of enterprises.

The general right established by this Article can be realized either through Management Committees (Consigli di Gestione), which are organizations concerned with the entrepreneurial functions of a given firm, or through Internal Commissions (Commissioni Interne),[4] exclusively concerned with the relations of a given enterprise with its personnel.

Immediately after the war, Management Committees appeared to be the organizations through which a new arrangement could be established in employer-worker relations. Later their importance decreased. No legal regulation was enacted and no collective agreement was established dealing with Management Committees. Internal Commissions, on the other hand, have always been regulated by collective agreement.

Immediately after the fall of the fascist régime (July 25, 1943), the Badoglio Government proposed to the workers' and employers'

[4]I believe that the literal translation from the Italian expression is more satisfactory than the proposed translations "shop stewards committees" (the stewards are union representatives, while members of I.C. are elected also by unorganized workers) or "grievance committees" (the settlement of grievances is but one of the functions of I.C.).

organizations (at this period this meant the fascist organizations which had been put under trusteeship) that they create workers' organizations within firms on the pattern of those existing in Italy prior to fascism. An agreement to this effect was concluded on September 2, 1943, known as the Buozzi-Mazzini agreement, from the names of the principal representatives of the signatory organizations. It gave to the Internal Commissions powers considerably greater than those of similar organizations that had existed in the past. It established Commissions with jurisdiction not alone in the area of problems and controversies arising in the field of labor. These Commissions were also directed to survey the technical situation of the enterprise and aim at improvements in the productive capacity of the firm. The agreement was put into effect immediately. Internal Commissions were instituted in a large number of firms, and they continued to operate in many forms although their operation was complicated by the political and military circumstances of the time.

The Buozzi-Mazzini agreement was subsequently replaced by the interconfederal agreement of August 7, 1947, negotiated after the removal (September 30, 1946) of the existing block on layoffs. Some restrictions, however, were imposed on the newly gained independence of the entrepreneur in order to avoid a sharpening of the unemployment crisis; the Internal Commissions were empowered to intervene and take action in this area.

The agreement of August 7, 1947, was denounced at the end of 1948 by the Confederation of Industry but the negotiations for a new agreement, initiated immediately thereafter, came to a conclusion only on May 8, 1953. To some extent this delay resulted from the fact that many of the clauses of the agreement of 1947 had been replaced by more general rules regarding layoffs introduced in the two agreements of 1950.[5]

The organization of Internal Commissions (Article 1 of the 1953 agreement) is patterned after the following general directive:

> Internal Commissions will be established in all industrial enterprises employing more than 40 workers to represent all the workers in their relationship with the direction of the firm.

[5]See pp. 222–224.

When a firm employs less than forty workers but more than five, then a single delegate is elected.

There is a single Internal Commission for all employed personnel, but this Commission must be composed of representatives of the white-collar employees as well as of the industrial workers. The representatives are elected separately by the two groups and in proportional numbers, but at least one seat must always be allocated to white-collar employees. Membership in the different Internal Commissions varies from a minimum of three (for plants having between 41 and 175 workers) to a maximum of fifteen (for enterprises with more than ten thousand workers). All the workers of the enterprise, union and nonunion members alike, participate in the election provided they are over sixteen (the minimum work age in Italy is fourteen). All workers over eighteen are eligible to be elected to the Commission. Exceptions are made for those firms employing a very large number of younger workers. The eligibility of a delegate is further limited by the requirement that he must have been employed by the firm for at least nine months.

The members of the Internal Commission are elected for one year and can be re-elected. Their tenure can be revoked prior to the end of their term, by decision of at least 51 percent of the total employed personnel.

The relationship of the Internal Commissions to the trade unions is clearly established by the 1953 agreement which states that the Internal Commissions are to refer to

> the trade-union organizations involved all matters relating to the collective regulation of the work relationship and to the disputes that may arise under the collective agreement.

The function of Internal Commissions has been later defined even more clearly, from a general point of view, in Article 2 of the 1953 agreement. It is the task of the Internal Commission to

> assist in maintaining normal relationships between the workers and the direction of the firm in a spirit of collaboration and mutual understanding to further the regular development of productive activities.

This general statement of functions is further clarified as follows:

The Internal Commission is to deal with the direction of the firm on questions relating to the correct application of the collective agreement as well as of social legislation and health and safety. Action on the part of the Internal Commission does not prevent the Commission from referring any issue to the Government or other agencies.

The Internal Commission is to attempt to solve, if possible, collective or individual controversies arising within the company.

It is its responsibility to consult with management regarding distribution of work hours, arrangement of shifts, vacations, and the introduction of new payment systems, or any other change in rules that management might intend to introduce.

It is the duty of the Internal Commission to formulate proposals for the improvement of production by forwarding to management, after careful evaluation, any proposal which may have been suggested by the workers.

Furthermore, the Internal Commission shall participate in the formulation of regulations dealing with workers' welfare activities, including cafeterias, to insure the more successful development of these activities.

The members of the Internal Commissions enjoy a special status. This subject has often been regulated by collective agreements, as for instance by the agreement of December 12, 1939, for the regulation of transfers and layoffs of workers with trade union duties. The Buozzi-Mazzini agreement of September 2, 1943 extended this protection to the members of the Internal Commissions. Article 14 of the May 8, 1953 agreement states that

> the members of the Internal Commission and the workers' delegates currently functioning as such, as well as those who have so functioned in the previous year, cannot be laid off or transferred without the approval of the trade union and the employers' association concerned.

If approval is not given, a special conciliation and arbitration procedure is started. When the Arbitration Board does not consider the dismissal fully justified, the worker is entitled to an indemnity (in addition to the normal severance payments) equal to his take-home wage for a period from five to eight months. When the Arbitration Board is of the opinion that the dismissal was exclusively connected with the position of the worker as member of the Internal Commission, the worker is entitled to keep his job. This is the only case in which a compulsory preservation of the job is admitted.

Dismissals

Regulation and restriction of the employers' right to dismiss a worker has always played a very important role in industrial relations in Italy. Collective agreements have dealt extensively with this question.

In general, the Italian development is toward the annulment of "socially unjustifiable" dismissals, i.e., dismissals not justified by the individual performance of the worker or by reasons beyond the control of the individual firm. This seems to be explicitly accepted in several collective agreements which have limited the employers' dismissal powers to cases extensively or precisely described.

In the industrial sector (where dismissals were altogether blocked during and after the war up to September 30, 1946), the August 7, 1947 agreement also gave the Internal Commissions additional powers in the matter of individual or collective layoffs. Indeed it was this extension of the Commissions' powers that led to management's rejection of the 1947 agreement and to the prolonged discussions regarding renewal. The long negotiations, revealing a certain rivalry between the Internal Commissions and the trade unions, eventually led to the agreements of 1950, which transferred jurisdiction in matters connected with layoffs to the trade unions and employers' organizations.

Individual dismissals are controlled by the agreement of October 18, 1950, which established the following procedure.

Except in cases in which dismissals are due to disciplinary reasons for which the regular Courts are finally responsible, a worker who believes that his dismissal is unwarranted may request the conciliatory intervention of the trade union of which he is a member or to which he assigns representation. The union will negotiate with the corresponding employers' organization and the representatives of the parties will proceed with an attempt at conciliation. When such an attempt is unsuccessful the worker may request, through the organization in which he is registered, the intervention of an arbitration council consisting of a representative of the employer and a representative of the employee, appointed by their respective organizations, and a chairman, chosen by lot from a list previously agreed upon. If the arbitration council does not believe that the reasons given by the employer for the dismissal are valid, it may reinstate the worker or, if this seems unwise in a given firm, it may require that the employer pay, in addition to severance pay, a fine of a minimum of five to a maximum of eight months of the worker's wage, the amount to be determined in equity.

The most important issue, however, is that of collective dismissals, the significance of which is easily understood in the light of the unemployment prevailing in Italy. A large number of the strikes taking place in Italy are connected with this problem. The workers are opposed to such dismissals and sometimes occupy the plants in which they are employed, and carry out what is called the "reverse strike." Attempts at preventing collective dismissals are contained in many collective agreements (for instance, Article 15 of the collective agreement of December 1952 for the building industry, Article 11 of the collective agreement of March 1953 for the mining industry) which require, instead, a reduction in the hours of work for the whole work force or for different shifts. Additional payments must be made to workers working a reduced number of hours, through a special national Fund to which all industrial employers contribute 1.5 percent of their pay rolls, this being applied only for the first 900 lire (daily) for men and 750 (daily) for women.

Generally, collective dismissals are regulated by the interconfederal agreement of December 20, 1950, which established the following procedure. If a firm deems it necessary to reduce its work force because of a decrease or change in its activity, it must inform the proper employer organization, stating the reasons for the dismissal, the intended date of dismissal, and the number of workers it intends to dismiss. The employers' association will transmit immediately such information to the provincial workers' organizations concerned. Conciliatory procedures between the employers' and workers' organizations, assisted by the representatives of the firm and by the representatives of the Internal Commission, must be terminated within fifteen days from the date on which notification of the intended dismissal has been made to the workers' organizations. Within this period the firm is not permitted to lay off any of its workers. If the conciliation procedure is unsuccessful, the parties will resume their freedom of action.

Wages

While during the war wages and prices were frozen, in the postwar years collective agreements have tried to adjust salaries and wages to the cost of living. This has been accomplished successfully as is shown by Table 2 in which effective wages and wage indices are compared.

The evolution of wage policy through collective bargaining was as follows. Immediately after the end of the war, the first problem was to adjust wage scales effective in northern Italy (which was liberated only during the spring of 1945 and where wages and prices had continued to be frozen) to those effective in central and southern Italy where freedom had brought a certain degree of inflation. This adjustment was the aim of the interconfederal agreements signed in 1945–1946.

During the following period, for political reasons and under the pressure of left-wing parties, the general trend was in favor of raising as much as possible the wages paid to common laborers, who represent the bulk of the Italian labor force. This is particularly shown by the interconfederal agreements of May 30 and June 23, 1947, dealing with industrial and clerical workers.

While this trend favored common laborers, the wages of skilled and specialized workers appeared less satisfactory. As a result, incentives were weakened for those categories most important for the recovery of Italian industry. The interconfederal agreements of August 5, 1949, and December 8, 1950, were, therefore, concluded with the officially stated intention of "re-establishing in the various wage scales a more satisfactory and fair arrangement among the vocational values of the various categories" (laborers, semiskilled, skilled, specialized).

Table 2. Amount and Indices of Bargained Average Wages Paid to Manual and Clerical Workers in Industry.

Years and Months	Amount of Average Wage (in lire)		Indices (1938=100)					Indices (1948=100)				
	Manual Workers	Clerks	Money: Manual Workers	Money: Clerks	Cost of Living	Real: Manual Workers	Real: Clerks	Money: Manual Workers	Money: Clerks	Cost of Living	Real: Manual Workers	Real: Clerks
1938 (average)	16.84	909.08	100	100	100	100.0	100.0	—	—	—	—	—
1948 (average)	884.61	34,672.00	5,253	3,814	4,844	108.4	78.7	100.0	100.0	100.0	100.0	100.0
1951 (average)	1,010.23	41,936.00	5,999	4,613	5,320	112.8	86.7	114.2	120.9	109.8	104.0	110.1
1952 (average)	1,051.49	43,536.00	6,244	4,789	5,546	112.6	86.4	118.9	125.6	114.5	103.8	109.7
1953 (average)	1,080.79	44,463.00	6,418	4,891	5,654	113.5	86.5	122.2	128.2	116.7	104.7	109.9
1954 (average)	1,120.37	46,181.00	6,653	5,080	5,806	114.6	87.5	126.7	133.2	119.9	105.7	111.1
1955 (average)	1,173.75	49,290.00	6,970	5,422	5,969	116.8	90.8	132.7	142.2	123.2	107.7	115.4
1956 (Jan.)	1,189.58	50,090.00	7,064	5,510	6,099	115.8	90.3	134.5	144.5	125.9	106.9	114.7

Source: *Rassegna di Statistiche del Lavoro*, 1956, n. 1–2, p. 96.

Fixed Item: Basic Pay

The fixed item in wage payments is the base pay. For women and children the fixed elements in wage payments are set as proportions of the rates for adult male workers. The basic wage element is generally set by national collective agreement for a production sector as a whole.

A very important national agreement for industrial workers was signed on June 12, 1954. Its importance is partly political since it was signed by Confindustria with the non-Communist workers' organizations, CISL, UIL, and CISNAL (nevertheless negotiations were carried on separately for CISL and UIL and for CISNAL). For the first time a national agreement was signed without the participation of the Communist-dominated CGIL.

The agreement was intended: (a) to unify the old base pay with the cost-of-living indemnity (the so-called "contingency indemnity") as well as with the cost-of-bread indemnity; (b) to have a more satisfactory wage relationship from province to province (regional differentials).

The collective agreements of 1946 established four zones for the base pay but chiefly as a result of the final adoption of the sliding-scale system (1951) and the calculation of cost-of-living indemnities at the provincial level, 95 wage zones came into existence. Under the new agreement of 1954 the number of zones has been reduced to thirteen; the provinces with similar wage levels have been grouped together. Future rises of the cost-of-living allowance will be calculated and paid separately, and only when they reach an appreciable amount will a new wage unification—as was done under the agreement of June 12, 1954—take place.

Piecework Payments

Piecework payment systems generally consist of a normal payment on a time basis, which is thought of as base pay, and a supplement. The procedure for calculation of this supplement includes two stages: the first at the industry or trade level through collective bargaining, and the second at the individual firm level.

The calculation of piecework has been one of the more controversial issues in Italian industrial relations. In particular, uni-

peatedly taken the position (as for instance in Article 33 of the collective agreement for the building industry) that minimum piecework rates are not to be finally established until after a trial period. Furthermore, in some cases (e.g. for the metal industry) it is agreed that

> when piece work earnings have been falling noticeably, the Internal Commissions are empowered to ascertain jointly with management, the cause of the decrease.

Collective agreements require that a worker on piecework have an exact notion of what portion of his individual pay results from the piecework at the time he begins on a given job and at the time he receives his pay. The interconfederal agreement of May 23, 1946, also establishes how a worker may obtain advances on piecework payment.

Coparticipation

The wage to which a worker is entitled can be increased in several different ways. Italian practice is characterized here by a great variety of forms. Three principal categories can be noted: coparticipation, bonuses, and indemnity.

While workers' participation in net returns of the firm is not very common, participation in gross returns is characteristic of some categories of commercial employees (traveling salesmen, insurance agents, etc.). Another type of premium is frequently considered by collective agreements.

Premiums provided in collective agreements may be connected with performance in a very general sense only. This applies to the premiums given to workers at the tenth or twentieth year of seniority (e.g., Article 21 of the collective agreement of June 21, 1956 for the metal industry) as well as to the regular seniority increases provided in many collective agreements. However, in a large number of cases, the premium is tied directly to performance and guaranteed by collective agreement in many different ways: production premium, premium for increases in work load, premium for maintenance, for reduction of waste, premium for regularity of attendance, etc. To the same category belong also other premiums based on efficiency computations of which the most

lateral establishment of piecework rates at the firm level by management has caused trade unions to object. As a result, there is a general tendency in Italy to give increasing importance to collective bargaining on piecework. This, as well as the possible intervention of the Internal Commission, has led to a limitation of the autonomy of the employer in establishing piecework systems based upon the needs of the firm.

Piecework payment regulations within a given category have gained in importance. This phenomenon can be traced back to the collective agreement put into effect on December 20, 1937, regulating piecework payments throughout industry. The conditions established by this agreement, which was later replaced by the interconfederal agreements of December 6, 1945, and May 23, 1946, are still of great importance. Upon this foundation is based the regulation of piecework payments contained in the Civil Code of 1942 (Articles 2100, 2101). According to this the worker must be paid on an incentive basis whenever he is tied to a given production speed or when his wage depends on the time needed in each operation.

Several collective agreements contain particular clauses regarding the payment of piecework wages (e.g., the collective agreement of June 21, 1956 for the metal industry, the collective agreement of July 8, 1949 for the glass industry, the collective agreement of December 5, 1952 for the building industry). All these aim at guaranteeing the worker a minimum income in addition to his base pay. Thus, Article 8 of the agreement of May 23, 1946, for all industrial workers required that

> the minimum income of all workers within a given department working on piece work, must not be less than 10% more than the minimum wages established by agreement.

It is required also that

> in cases in which a worker, working on a piece work basis, does not succeed in earning the minimum established by collective contract, because of reasons independent of his will and his ability, he is entitled to the above stated contractual minimum.

To make this requirement effective the trade unions, following the rules set forth by Article 2101 of the Civil Code, have re-

Table 2. Amount and Indices of Bargained Average Wages Paid to Manual and Clerical Workers in Industry.

Years and Months	Amount of Average Wage (in lire)		Indices (1938=100)					Indices (1948=100)				
			Money		Cost of Living	Real		Money		Cost of Living	Real	
	Manual Workers	Clerks	Manual Workers	Clerks		Manual Workers	Clerks	Manual Workers	Clerks		Manual Workers	Clerks
1938 (average)	16.84	909.08	100	100	100	100.0	100.0	—	—	—	—	—
1948 (average)	884.61	34,672.00	5,253	3,814	4,844	108.4	78.7	100.0	100.0	100.0	100.0	100.0
1951 (average)	1,010.23	41,936.00	5,999	4,613	5,320	112.8	86.7	114.2	120.9	109.8	104.0	110.1
1952 (average)	1,051.49	43,536.00	6,244	4,789	5,546	112.6	86.4	118.9	125.6	114.5	103.8	109.7
1953 (average)	1,080.79	44,463.00	6,418	4,891	5,654	113.5	86.5	122.2	128.2	116.7	104.7	109.9
1954 (average)	1,120.37	46,181.00	6,653	5,080	5,806	114.6	87.5	126.7	133.2	119.9	105.7	111.1
1955 (average)	1,173.75	49,290.00	6,970	5,422	5,969	116.8	90.8	132.7	142.2	123.2	107.7	115.4
1956 (Jan.)	1,189.58	50,090.00	7,064	5,510	6,099	115.8	90.3	134.5	144.5	125.9	106.9	114.7

Source: Rassegna di Statistiche del Lavoro, 1956, n. 1–2, p. 96.

Fixed Item: Basic Pay

The fixed item in wage payments is the base pay. For women and children the fixed elements in wage payments are set as proportions of the rates for adult male workers. The basic wage element is generally set by national collective agreement for a production sector as a whole.

A very important national agreement for industrial workers was signed on June 12, 1954. Its importance is partly political since it was signed by Confindustria with the non-Communist workers' organizations, CISL, UIL, and CISNAL (nevertheless negotiations were carried on separately for CISL and UIL and for CISNAL). For the first time a national agreement was signed without the participation of the Communist-dominated CGIL.

The agreement was intended: (a) to unify the old base pay with the cost-of-living indemnity (the so-called "contingency indemnity") as well as with the cost-of-bread indemnity; (b) to have a more satisfactory wage relationship from province to province (regional differentials).

The collective agreements of 1946 established four zones for the base pay but chiefly as a result of the final adoption of the sliding-scale system (1951) and the calculation of cost-of-living indemnities at the provincial level, 95 wage zones came into existence. Under the new agreement of 1954 the number of zones has been reduced to thirteen; the provinces with similar wage levels have been grouped together. Future rises of the cost-of-living allowance will be calculated and paid separately, and only when they reach an appreciable amount will a new wage unification—as was done under the agreement of June 12, 1954—take place.

Piecework Payments

Piecework payment systems generally consist of a normal payment on a time basis, which is thought of as base pay, and a supplement. The procedure for calculation of this supplement includes two stages: the first at the industry or trade level through collective bargaining, and the second at the individual firm level.

The calculation of piecework has been one of the more controversial issues in Italian industrial relations. In particular, uni-

important is the Bédaux System though it has not been very successful in Italy. Most of the trade unions attempt on the basis of the above-mentioned Article 2101 of the Civil Code to transform such incentive premiums into payments on a piece basis (where changes in the output affect the total wage).

Bonuses

Unlike coparticipation, which requires the existence of some profit (gross or net) or special rates of output, bonuses represent in general a voluntary contribution of the employer. This type of voluntary bonus, however, tends to disappear; several collective agreements provide for bonuses which are an obligation of the employer. Thus, the collective agreement of March 28, 1953 for the mining industry provides (Article 2) for a "premium to workers faithful to the mine" which is equivalent to from thirty to sixty days of total wages.

The most important is the Christmas bonus known also as the 13th monthly wage. At first the Christmas bonus was thought of as belonging exclusively to salaried employees, but it has since been extended to production workers. The most important instrument of this extension was the interconfederal agreement of October 27, 1946 (Article 17). The bonus paid on Christmas Eve corresponds to one month's salary for salaried employees and to the payment for two hundred hours of work for workers.

Indemnities

The payment of an indemnity as provided in collective agreements is an attempt to compensate for: (a) particular expenditures; (b) work requiring special effort; and (c) particular needs.

Group (a) includes indemnities for transfer paid as a per diem; clothing indemnity; compensation for workers using their own tools; or payments to workers who eat at the plant (the so-called mess indemnity), etc.

In group (b) are indemnities, granted through collective agreements to workers on jobs requiring particular strain and physical stamina or which are carried out under particularly unpleasant conditions. One example of this is the collective agreement of

March 28, 1953 for the mining industry which provides for a special payment for underground work (Article 19). The collective agreement of December 5, 1952 for the building industry lists (in Article 10) jobs which are particularly unpleasant and entitle the worker to a special indemnity.

In the third group (c) we find indemnity payments for working in malaria zones often specifically indicated by listing localities. Article 13 of the collective agreement of May 11, 1950 for agricultural workers sets up an indemnity for work in high altitudes. The most important indemnities which can be listed in this third group are not connected with the work performed, but intended to meet special requirements for giving the worker and his family a satisfactory standard of living. Those indemnities are: cost-of-living indemnity and family allowances.

Cost-of-living Adjustments

Such payments represent one of the most important elements in the Italian wage system which is operating under inflationary trends. They are regulated at present for the industrial sector by the interconfederal agreements of November 28, 1947 and March 21, 1951 which have established a special escalator system of wage payments. Negotiations for the revision of these agreements are now being held.

According to these agreements the cost-of-living payment known as "contingency indemnity" is calculated in every province on the basis of a national cost-of-living index. Pay revisions occur every two months. In the interval, cost-of-living payments are frozen. Every variation in the cost of living, calculated on the basis of points, is translated into a cost-of-living payment in terms of lires and expressed in different ratios for salaried employees and for workers. Decreases in the cost-of-living index do not affect payments unless the index has moved down more than four points. As a result of inflation, cost-of-living indemnities gradually increased and before the agreement of May 12, 1954 they had reached an amount much higher than the base pay. This was one of the chief reasons for wage unification (see above) which included in the base pay also the cost-of-living indemnity paid. In May 1954, additional increases in cost-of-living allowances were again calculated separately.

Family Allowances

In addition to the forms of payment which we have described so far, there exist pay supplements connected with the particular needs or the particular conditions of the worker's life. To this group belong the indemnity for the education of children, paid whenever there are no schools available in the work locality (as provided in Article 28 of the collective agreement of December 6, 1950 for the textile industries), and the indemnity for obligations to dependents paid as family allowances.

Family allowances were initiated in Italy as a part of the demographic policy of the fascist régime. The allowances began with the introduction of the forty-hour week and following the interconfederal agreements of October 11, 1934 and June 23, 1935.

In the postwar period the amount of the allowances and related contributions was chiefly set by the interconfederal agreement of

Table 3. FAMILY ALLOWANCE CONTRIBUTIONS.

	Manual Workers		*Office Workers*	
	Percent of Wage	*Ceiling* Daily Wage*	*Percent of Wage*	*Ceiling* Monthly Wage (lire)*
Industry	31.40	900(men) 750(women)	31.40	22,500(men) 19,500(women)
Craft shops	13	900	13	22,500
Banking	48.20	750	48.20	18,750
Insurance	16.50	750	16.50	18,750
Private tax-collecting agencies	35.50	900	35.50	22,500
Commerce	21	900	21	22,500
Agriculture†	97.60	—	31.25	18,750
Special concessions for cultivation of tobacco	18.65	750	—	—
Journalists and professional workers	—	—	21.00	22,500

*Ceiling: Percentage of Wage is applied only to the first 900 lire per day in industry, etc.

†Flat payment per day of actual work.

June 14, 1952 for industrial workers; allowances were also raised for workers employed in transportation, handicraft, commerce, insurance, and agriculture. These collective agreements were supplemented by special laws in order to make them compulsory not only for members of the signatory organizations, but also for all the companies belonging to the category involved.

Family allowances are paid together with the salary or the wage to the worker as the head of the family, who is responsible for the wife, children, or parents. The employer is reimbursed for the payment of family allowances by a special fund established by the National Institute for Social Security, to which all employers pay a contribution for every worker employed.

Table 4. FAMILY ALLOWANCE BENEFITS (IN LIRE).

	Manual Workers (Daily Figures)			*Office Workers (Daily Figures)*		
	Each Child	*Wife*	*Each Parent*	*Each Child*	*Wife*	*Each Parent*
Industry	960	648	330	4,100	2,808	1,430
Craft shops	720	510	330	3,978	2,600	1,430
Commerce	960	648	330	4,100	2,808	1,430
Agriculture	60*	50*	40*	146†	93†	55†
Credit	5,356	5,356	5,356(monthly)	5,356	5,356	5,356
Insurance	3,120	2,496	1,716(monthly)	3,120	2,496	1,710
Private tax-collecting agencies	4,160	2,808	1,430(monthly)	4,160	2,808	1,430
Special concessions for cultivation of tobacco	918	600	330	3,968	2,600	1,430
Journalists and professional workers	960	648	330	4,100	2,808	1,430

*Flat payment in lire per day of actual work.
†For 26 days a month.

VII

Wage Structure and Cost of Labor in Italy*

CESARE VANNUTELLI

BEFORE analyzing the components of wages and of the cost of labor in Italy, it is necessary to consider some fundamental circumstances regarding the origin of the present structure.

1. The wages received by the employees of industrial concerns are regulated by collective labor contracts drawn up by the competent national associations for each group—the national trade unions and the industry employer associations—and are valid for all the concerns represented; in addition, some parts of these wages are regulated by collective contracts drafted by the general confederations.[1] The earnings resulting from this contract system are, therefore, supposed to represent a standard minimum valid for all concerns in a given industry and in a given territorial zone.

2. Unlike before the war, when wages were represented by a single item, or by a few items, wages now consist of a number of

*Reprinted (in a slightly modified and abbreviated version) from the *Review of the Economic Conditions in Italy* issued by the Banco di Roma, Vol. 6, No. 5 (September 1952). A later article by Professor Vannutelli, "Recent Wage Structure and Cost of Labour Changes in Italy," *ibid.*, Vol. 9, No. 2 (March 1955) contains supplementary information. [Ed.]

[1]In Italy the confederations, i.e., the national associations of trade unions and the national association of employers' organizations—similar say to the AFL and the NAM in the United States—negotiate collective agreements for all the sectors of the economy represented by them. [Ed.] See note (p. 212) to Sanseverino article.

elements having different names and that sometimes vary in nature and also in periodicity. This is the result of the process of adjusting wages to the increase in the cost of living, which in the immediate postwar years was carried out through the adoption of various measures, and in general to the changed conditions caused by postwar inflation. Farther on, details will be given concerning the origin and characteristics of the most important elements forming the wages.

3. The social security contributions, which have to be added to wages when calculating the cost of labor borne by the firms, are also made up of a number of items coming sometimes under the same heading and being sometimes subject to different regulations. This, too, is a consequence of the legislation made necessary by the postwar inflation and if this situation still exists, it is because Italy has not yet felt able to face a general reform of social security. This may be, and is, criticized, but the truth is that the caution shown by the Government with regard to the steps taken in this direction has been inspired mainly by concern regarding the cost of such a reform as well as by lack of unanimity of views on the part of technicians regarding the method and objects of a well-organized reform.

In short, the prime causes of the present situation may be said to be the monetary repercussions of the postwar disorder and the attempt to fight free of the inflationary spiral. This attempt took the form of discrimination with regard to charges and the creation of new headings and items referring to earnings. Italy, which had already been unfortunate enough to pass through an inflation after World War I, had consequently some experience in this connection.

With regard to the structure of wages, experience had shown the advantages of establishing, in addition to the previously fixed wages, a new item known as the "cost-of-living indemnity," which could be adjusted according to circumstances and was considered to be of a temporary nature. It could, that is to say, be cancelled should there be a subsequent deflation and it was therefore, in a certain respect, considered as separate from wages. Obviously it is absurd to think that a deflation large enough to reabsorb completely the effects of a preceding inflation of the dimensions caused by the consequences of war could possibly occur. The creation of a separate item like the cost-of-living indemnity has consequently never been more than a temporary device, while postponing a suitable readjustment until steadier conditions were achieved in the country's economy and finance. After World War I, this occurred as the result of a chain of events which, today, may be recognized as having taken place fairly quickly. Between 1924 and 1927, all or almost all of the cost-of-living indemnities (with the exception of some surviving traces that remained in certain categories also in the following years) were absorbed by wages during the process of trade union reorganization which occurred in those years. After the last war, however, the adjustment of similar indemnities, which today go by the names of "temporary indemnity," "bread indemnity," and the like, has been slower. The reason for this may be that this time the inflation was on a much larger scale and much more rapid, although it is also true that it was restricted and checked swiftly and effectively. Probably, however, it is due to the fact that the reorganization of labor relations through the trade unions has been fast since the war, owing to the centralization of trade union action in national, category, or interprofessional organizations. This slowness in the adjustment of indemnities may, in fact, for the reason set forth in point 1, be said to be one of the unfavorable aspects of this centralization.

According to the classification generally adopted, remuneration of industrial workers consists of the following two basic components: actual wages; complementary (or accessory) elements.

In order to obtain the cost of labor, it is necessary to add to the above two elements social charges, which will be dealt with separately.

The *actual wages* consist in turn of the following principal elements: (a) basic pay; (b) temporary indemnity; (c) bread indemnity; (d) readjustment quotas.

The origin, function, and nature of these elements are as follows:

Basic Pay

The basic pay (basic wages for workers, basic salary for clerks) is established by the collective labor contracts drawn up for the different industries by their respective trade union associations. Ideally, it is connected with the wages or salary specified in the contracts of the preceding period, i.e., before the other payments had been created and when the basic pay alone represented actual wages. Immediately after the war basic pay was regulated by interconfederate agreements—special contracts stipulated by the confederations for all industries and all provinces. In these contracts—the last of which is dated October 27, 1946—in order to make allowance for the differences existing between one branch of industry and another and between one locality and another, special tables were compiled by branches of industry, by localities, and by industrial status, with certain deviations according to sex and age.

The industrial categories were divided into five groups: three groups marked with the letters A, B, and C comprised the manufacturing and mining industries in order of importance and level of wages; a group T was for the textile industries; and a group Zero for public utilities in general (electricity, telephones, etc.). The localities were arranged in four territorial zones comprising the different provinces. With regard to skill, a classification previously adopted only for some of the most important industries was generalized and the workers were divided as follows: skilled workers, trained workers, skilled laborers, ordinary laborers. The previously existing classifications continued to be used for clerks. In addition, a new category was considered for the first time in the contracts—the so-called "intermediate," comprising foremen and "supervisors" of manpower in general, who, although their status was that of workers, received the same pay as clerks.

These provisions regarding the basic pay were a noteworthy success as regards structure, organization, and classification of wages. As compared with the previous wage contracts, which were mainly local, a national and consequently centralized organization was achieved for the first time and a clarity and coordination so far unknown were obtained at the time.

It was, however, foreseen that the reorganized trade unions would re-examine the matter and develop separate labor contracts for each category of workers. This was gradually done between 1947 and 1949, in the years when the most important unions worked out contracts regarding both general labor conditions and wages. With respect to wages, the contracts mostly complied with the principles of classification laid down by the interconfederate agreement: each contract specified the industrial sector to which it applied, sometimes making some adjustment and sometimes providing for supplementary indemnities responding to the characteristics of its line of production; the contracts then specified the distribution by territorial zones according to the development of the industry concerned and sometimes provided for unification of these zones; lastly the contract specified the traditional occupational groups in order to establish, if necessary, special pay for each group and in any case to fit the workers into the four standard groups provided for in the interconfederate agreement, as well as according to sex and age.

The basic pay, as a consequence of the category contracts, i.e., the contracts concluded by individual unions and their corresponding employers' associations, shows greater differences than resulted from the first interconfederate agreement. This item represents the fixed part of the workers' earnings which can only be altered by subsequent labor contracts and is the part on which the extra pay for piecework is calculated. It is only on this part of earnings that extra pay for overtime, night and holiday labor, seniority and dismissal bonuses should be calculated. We shall see farther on how the situation has changed in this connection. It should also be made quite clear that the basic pay is the part of the workers' earnings that is regulated by the category contracts (or in the absence of the latter by the interconfederate agreement). The basic wage is an element not normally subject to variations between one locality and another or one firm and another as it represents a minimum common to all firms; changes in it can only be made if the contract is renewed and, consequently, it is a steady element; lastly, it is the basis of the various indemnities in the form of percentages of increase or of specific amounts that some of the most important industrial sectors have found advisable to grant in view of the nature of the work performed.

Temporary Indemnity

The temporary indemnity was created by general agreement among the confederations and represents an additional element of compensation rendered necessary by the high cost of living. This element of earnings varies according to the level of the cost of living in accordance with a sliding-scale system.[2] This system is regulated by general interconfederate agreements and consequently this element is not subject to the control of the category contracts. It is regulated by the resolutions passed locally by the territorial associations in compliance (sometimes with adjustments) with the general rules of the interconfederate agreement.

The temporary indemnity, from the very beginning, varied in size from province to province in relation to the level of the cost of living. The variations in the cost of living that subsequently occurred, after the contract of October 27, 1946, served as a basis for the variations of the sliding scale. Up to 1949 each province calculated the variation in its own provincial index to determine the variation in its temporary indemnity, but since April 1951 the variations in all provinces are based on the national cost-of-living index.

One feature of the sliding-scale system that deserves to be considered in greater detail here is the following: variations in the cost-of-living index cause proportional variations in the amount not of the temporary indemnity, but of the so-called "global" pay, which includes the basic pay and the temporary indemnity; the resulting supplement is added to the temporary indemnity. It follows that the indemnity has increased out of all proportion, altering the ratios that originally characterized the structure of the "global" pay. To obtain a clear and schematic idea of this phenomenon, it should be borne in mind that originally (1946) the basic pay and the average temporary indemnity were more or less the same size, i.e., 1 and 1 so that the global wages were equal to 2. In 1947 the cost of living nearly doubled and consequently another

[2]For more detailed discussion of the system, see my articles "La Scala Mobile dei Salari" and "Le Nuove Norme per la Rilevazione degli Indici del Costo della Vita ed il Sistema di Scala Mobile dei Salari" published in the *Revista di Politica Economica,* in Nos. 3–4, 1948, and No. 5, 1952, respectively.

2, which was included in the temporary indemnity, had to be added to the original 2 representing the global wages. The global wages before and after this doubling of the cost of living may therefore be expressed by the following schematic values:

	Before	After
Basic pay	1	1
Temporary indemnity	1	3
Total pay	2	4

The amount of the temporary indemnity, within each province, is the same for all branches of industry. It was also the same for all occupational groups, except for sex and age differentials. It was assumed that the increase in the cost of living, as far as essential requirements are concerned, hits all workers equally hard. This, moreover, is the principle usually adopted in connection with increases due to variations in the cost of living (the sliding-scale system of the General Motors in the United States is based on a similar principle), since it enables the firms to keep the consequent increase anchored to a minimum instead of taking into account the scale of remuneration.

So long as the increase does not exceed modest proportions, this system has no serious effects. But in Italy, as a result of the increase in the cost of living between 1946 and the first half of 1948, it led, as has been shown above, to the temporary indemnity forming the main part of the remuneration and, consequently, to a leveling of the differences that the basic pay had previously established between one branch of industry and another, and one skill level and another.

It has in fact created a leveling trend, characterized by a very marked attenuation of the differences in pay formerly graduated according to the importance and responsibility of the job. This problem is dealt with below. It is mentioned here for the purpose of explaining why, from April 1951 on, when the sliding-scale system was based on a national index instead of on the provincial indices as previously, there has also been a change in the principle fixing the amount of the variation in the temporary indemnity. Instead of being the same for all workers and all skill groups as in the past, it now differs according to the skill classification of the worker. If, for instance, there is an increase of 10 for ordinary workers, there will be an increase of 12.50 for skilled workers and of 24 for clerks belonging to the first skill class. Consequently, no further leveling as compared with present positions can occur as a result of new increases in the temporary indemnity.

As already mentioned, the temporary indemnity is structurally conceived not only as a variable but also as a transitory element; it may also be reduced (in fact the sliding-scale system contemplates reductions). Consequently, it was conceived as an element that is only complementary to the actual pay and is not to be considered when calculating extra pay for overtime or piecework, and seniority and dismissal bonuses.

Bread Indemnity

The bread indemnity is also a result of the increase in the cost of living. It differs from the temporary indemnity inasmuch as it is controlled by laws and not by contract regulations. Immediately after the war (1944–1945), in view of the lack of an efficiently reorganized trade union organization, a law was passed creating the bread indemnity as a form of social protection. In the subsequent wage readjustment of 1946, this payment was absorbed by a new indemnity which, in order to stress the difference, was called "temporary." Following this readjustment, however, gradual increases occurred in the "political" price at which staple food such as bread and macaroni, still rationed, were sold. To make up for this increase in cost a law was passed creating a special indemnity equal in amount to the extra expense to each consumer, as a result of the higher price, for the quantity of bread he was entitled to. Since progressively larger quantities of cereal products were distributed to workers engaged in heavy and very heavy work and to miners and woodcutters as compared with workers engaged on ordinary jobs, this indemnity was also progressive: 20 lire a day for workers engaged on ordinary jobs, 30 lire for heavy work, 40 lire for very heavy work, and 60 lire for miners and woodcutters. These amounts are those resulting, after successive increases, from the last provision in this connection, dated August 1, 1948. These sums are paid to workers on the firms' pay rolls and to the members of their families entitled to family allowances as well as to persons receiving pensions, indemnities, or assistance from the respective social security and welfare administrations. This indemnity has been granted the legal character of a "refunding of expenses" and is, therefore, not included in remuneration for the purpose of calculating extra pay, piecework, indemnities, and the like. Rationing has ceased to exist for some time, but the bread indemnity has remained in force as the residue of special postwar legislation, and the problem, therefore, presents itself of absorbing it in wages, with the difficulties which will be discussed later.

Readjustment Quotas

The readjustment quotas are the latest distinct element forming workers' earnings. They are a consequence of the measures taken to try to correct the leveling of wages and restore the dignity of the positions occupied by the higher-skilled categories as well as the incentive for workers to improve their position. When the movement of the inflationary spiral was checked, the decision was taken to replace the earlier social principle of granting all workers a standard minimum cost-of-living increase, by the productive principle of granting wages proportionate to the qualifications of the workers. The problem thus arose of integrating the previous standard minimum benefit through quotas that would proportionately reinstate the previously existing scale of wages.

The prewar period was not taken as point of reference for this operation: inflation, the social process of raising the lower-paid groups to a higher level, and, to a certain extent also, technical progress have appreciably narrowed the extremes of the wage scale in Italy as in many other countries and this is undoubtedly part of the social evolution of our times. The most marked and pathological aspects of this phenomenon have been corrected by means of a series of measures adopted in the industrial sector through general agreements among the confederations, with the result that a situation has been reached—as Table 1 shows—that may be described as an intermediate position between prewar conditions and the immediate postwar conditions. It is not possible to foresee whether this process of re-establishing wage differences is now completed or whether other measures in this connection will be adopted in the future. In any case it is certain that the prewar differentials will never be reinstated.

Table 1. LEVELING OF WAGES IN RELATION TO WORKERS' QUALIFICATIONS. Monthly contractual earnings of workers in the engineering industry in Milan.

	1938 Average	*1947 June*	*1952 June*
	Monthly amount (in lire)		
Clerks:			
1st category	1,500	33,677	68,461
2nd category	1,100	28,277	51,738
3rd category A	750	23,577	38,669
3rd category B	600	21,627	32,853
Workmen:			
skilled workers	732	21,681	36,032
trained workers	584	20,672	32,595
skilled laborers	507	20,153	30,996
ordinary laborers	476	19,466	29,201
	Ratios (ordinary laborer = 100)		
Clerks:			
1st category	315	173	234
2nd category	231	145	177
3rd category A	158	121	132
3rd category B	126	111	112
Workmen:			
skilled workers	154	111	123
trained workers	123	106	112
skilled laborers	107	104	106
ordinary laborers	100	100	100

Since the adjustment of wages to inflation was regulated through general agreements among the confederations, it was not possible to follow the principle of increasing the basic wages which are regulated by category contracts. Nor was this desired since it was held to be advisable to avoid altering all the other contractual clauses connected with the basic wages (extra pay, piecework, etc.) and burdening the firms with the heavy additional weight that would have fallen on them if the readjustment increases had to be applied also in this latter connection. Moreover, it was not possible to base these increases on the temporary indemnities which were standardized within the provinces. It consequently became necessary to create a separate element of remuneration, distinct both from the basic pay and from the temporary indemnity, yet one to which the general regulations in force for the temporary indemnity are applied. In the case of workmen, the readjustment quotas have been fixed at a standard amount for all provinces and all branches of industry. The objective of re-establishing differentials was attained first through the agreement of August 5, 1949 and subsequently through that of December 8, 1950, which provided progressive increases for skilled workers, while granting no increase at all to the common laborers at the bottom of the ladder. For clerks, since the difficulties connected with piecework did not exist in their case, readjustments were effected by means of an increase in basic salaries so that this particular item of remuneration does not exist so far as they are regarded.

"Unification" of Wages

The four elements of remuneration listed above are those of a most general character, but they are not the only ones forming the remuneration of certain categories. In the special contracts of the various branches of industry other items have often been added in connection with the peculiarities of the line of production. In some industries these are additions to the basic pay (e.g., engineering, chemical, cement, and other branches), while in others they are indemnities for dangerous or harmful work (e.g., underground indemnities for work in mines), or indemnities relating to special working conditions (e.g., indemnity for work in shifts), or for special responsibilities (e.g., indemnities relative to certain offices for clerks, cashiers' indemnities, etc.). In some industries such as public utilities (electricity, gas, transport, telephones, etc.), the items of remuneration are particularly numerous. This also applies to municipal and civil service, as a result of the special nature of the services and also because the indemnities influence the calculation of pensions. Such indemnities cannot be said to have any great drawbacks; they are the necessary counterpart of the variety of positions and situations of production and are presumably less marked than in some other countries where wages are mainly regulated by contracts relating to individual firms.

On the other hand, there can be no doubt that there are drawbacks in the number of elements forming general remuneration, and this situation has given rise to the problem of "unifying" wages. The problem exists in general and was recently explicitly raised by one of the workers' organizations (the Italian Workers' Union, UIL, which is a Social-democratic organization).

The elements of this problem and the difficulties encountered in solving it may be easier to understand after what has been said above in connection with the origin and nature of the various elements of remuneration. It has been shown, for instance, that whereas the basic pay is suitably differentiated by categories and skill classification, the temporary indemnity is a standard supplement that greatly attenuates the differences; this is the present situation, but it is no easy matter to sanction this state of affairs in the labor contracts of the categories. Some appreciable differences in pay beween provinces having a similar development cannot be justified, and obviously it would be easier to raise those wages in the lower categories rather than lower those in the upper brackets. Unification of the basic salary and of the temporary indemnity would, therefore, mean running the risk of a fairly rapid upward leveling, and this is a fact that cannot fail to cause concern.

Another delicate problem concerns all the extras that are calculated as percentages of the basic pay and which, as a result of unification, would be calculated also in relation to the temporary indemnity. Postwar labor contracts have generally fixed high percentages for these extras (and in particular for piecework), in view of the fact that these percentages apply to about one third of the remuneration. Piecework percentages, for instance, which before the war fluctuated around 10 percent of the minimum guaranteed by the contract are now as high as 20–30 percent. Should unification consist also in subjecting the amount of the temporary indemnity to the calculation of these percentages the result would be a terrific burden that production does not at present feel in a position to shoulder. The unions realize this and consequently suggest a readjustment of these percentages so that the burden for the firms and the benefits for the workers would remain unaltered. In reality, however, a principle which would reduce the "unification" to a mere bookkeeping process is easier to state than to effect.

Complementary Elements of Remuneration

In addition to the actual wages consisting of the various elements described above, there are also *complementary elements* that contribute to form the aggregate remuneration: remuneration during periods of vacation and for certain holidays on which no work is done; Christmas bonus; dismissal bonus.

Many people, and foreigners in particular, are surprised at the existence of these complementary elements of remuneration. However, with the exception of paid vacations which are common to all industrial countries, pay for all holidays falling during the week, a Christmas and a dismissal bonus are characteristic of the Italian wage system. Certain other countries do grant remuneration for some holidays (Sundays excluded)—Germany and Austria 11 days, Belgium and Holland 10, the United Kingdom 6, France 1—but in Italy remuneration is provided for all of the sixteen days a year which are recognized as national or religious holidays. In this way workers who are normally paid on a day basis or according to the number of work hours (the problem does not arise for clerks or for all those who receive a fixed monthly salary) are assured of regular income in the weeks in which holidays fall.

Originally the Christmas bonus was a custom that applied only to clerks; an extra month's pay at the end of the year, given to them by the firm, of its own free will, was a special premium granted in recognition of diligence and faithfulness. In 1937 this custom was included in the labor contract, and the bonus consequently became compulsory for clerks. In 1938 a contract was drawn up that provided for a special premium also for the workers, amounting to the value of one week's work. After the war the premium was increased to the value of two hundred hours, equivalent to one month's work as in the case of clerks.

The dismissal bonus is also peculiar to the Italian system. It is a special element of compensation that falls due at the end of the labor relationship (instead of together with current remuneration or at the end of the year like the Christmas bonus), provided the relationship comes to an end through no fault of the employee's. The amount of bonus is fixed by the category contracts and increases with the worker's seniority. Furthermore, the amount is based on the last salary received so that it increases, regardless of seniority, as a consequence of increases in pay. For the worker this bonus represents the guarantee of an income during the period in which he may remain without a job; and, in the case of workers having many years of service who retire for reasons of age, it is a sum to add to the pension they are entitled to. An outstanding feature of this bonus is the fact that it is based on the last pay. The worker is consequently guaranteed a constant real value such as does not exist in any other insurance or capitalization contract.

It is difficult to calculate the cost of this indemnity. In most contracts which fix the indemnity at about one week for each year of service for workers having a seniority of ten years, a charge of 2 percent of total wages has to be set aside yearly to meet this bonus; in the case of clerks, to whom not less than one month for each year of employment is granted, 8 percent has to be set aside, but this may be reduced to 6 percent as a result of compound interest and assuming a "normal" career. If, however, a general increase in remunerations occurs then all the reserves that have been provided have to be revised.

Social Security Charges

To the elements of remuneration listed above must be added, as already mentioned, social security charges. It would be out of place here to consider even summarily the circumstances which have led to a high level of social charges in Italy and to a remarkably complicated system of contributions.[3]

Briefly, Law No. 210 of April 4, 1952, which came into force on May 1, introduced appreciable changes in the contribution system

[3]In this connection, see my article, "Social Security in Italy," published in the September 1949 number of the *Review of the Economic Conditions in Italy*. Some of the data contained therein have been brought up to date in the present study.

following the new organization of disability, old-age and survivors' pensions. The social security contributions may be divided into three groups as far as the system of computation provided by the law is concerned:

1. Contributions due on the whole pay: these are the contributions relating to insurance against accidents at work, to sickness and maternity insurance, to INA-Casa (for building of workers' houses), to the adjustment of disability, old-age and survivors' pensions, and to unemployment and tuberculosis insurance.

2. Contributions fixed at so much per head: these are the contributions paid through stamps pasted into special booklets and are in fact the residue of prewar legislation.

3. Contributions due on the maximum, namely on the whole pay, but only up to a specific limit (750 lire a day): these are only due for family allowances and for the earnings' integration fund.

The existence of the system referred to under point 3 causes a good deal of surprise and perplexity, particularly in view of the fact that what is known as "the maximum" is well below the level of the average current wages. Foreigners in particular find it hard to understand why such a low level has been fixed, for they know that in all other countries (with the exception of Soviet Russia), similar "maximums" correspond to a level well above that of average wages. Actually, when this maximum was established shortly after the war, it was thought that gradually it would be adjusted to the amount of wages in compliance with the sliding scale. However, this process of adjustment was prevented by difficulties of many kinds and this maximum, fixed at a level that is not in keeping with its function, has been severely criticized. As a consequence, the "maximum" has been abolished, for the present at least, as far as contributions relating to old-age, unemployment, and tuberculosis insurance are concerned. It has, however, remained in force for contributions relating to family allowances and the earnings' integration fund, though its size has been modified: the amount of 750 lire a day has remained unaltered for women in the labor force, but for men the maximum has been brought up to 900 lire a day. This increase in the maximum, which involves an increase in contributions, has been limited to men to avoid burdening the costs of firms (mostly textile firms) which employ mainly women workers. It is particularly the existence of this maximum, and at present of two maxima (one for men and one for women) that complicates calculating contributions as a percentage of wages. In fact, as the maxima are below the level of current wages, the contributions, though supposed to be on a percentage basis, have in practice a per capita value.

The size of the contributions due by employers and workers in July 1952 is shown in Table 2. They are applied not only to actual wages (bread indemnity excluded) but also to remuneration granted for vacations and holidays; only the contributions in the first group are applied to the Christmas bonus, while the dismissal bonus is generally free from all contributions.

Table 2. Social Charges Paid for Workers.

	Paid by the Employer %	*Paid by the Worker* %
1) Contributions calculated on the whole pay:		
— pension adjustment fund	6.60	2.40
— tuberculosis insurance	2.60	—
— unemployment insurance	2.00	—
— accident insurance (avg. contrib.)	3.00	—
— sickness insurance	6.00	—
— maternity insurance	0.53	—
— INA-Casa administration	1.15	0.57
	21.88	2.97
2) Stamp contributions for social insurances:	The amount is fixed by wage groups (ranging from a minimum of 9 lire a week to a maximum of 56 lire)	
3) Contributions paid on "maximum" (900 lire a day for men and 750 for women):		
— family allowances	22.50	—
— earnings integration fund	1.50	—
	24.00	—
	Equivalent to 216 lire for men and 180 lire for women	

Conclusions

In conclusion and in order to complete this analysis of the origin and nature of the different elements of which wages and the cost of labor are composed, a calculation may be made, from which it will be possible to draw some data indicating the current level of wages. For this purpose Table 3 has been compiled as follows:

(a) The data refer to the engineering sector where wages are most representative of industry; (b) the two provinces of Milan and Naples have been chosen as being representative of the differences in the level of wages existing between northern and southern Italy; (c) the minimum contract wages resulting from the contracts in force in the two above provinces have been considered; (d) the data have been supplied separately for men and for women; (e) the calculation has been based on the laws in force in July 1952.

The data contained in this table make possible a number of calculations with regard to: the incidence of the various elements forming the cost of labor on the total amount of labor cost; the ratios existing between wages and the cost of labor for different skill levels; the ratios existing between wages and the cost of male workers and wages and the cost of female workers; the ratios existing between wages and the cost of labor in the province of Milan and in the province of Naples.

A detailed analysis of these ratios would be outside the scope of this article. Since the data given in the table refer to minimum contract wages and to social charges of a general and compulsory nature, the actual situation may be different from that resulting, as a general minimum, from that presented in the table.

As to the size of the differences between minimum contract wages and actual wages, it is not possible to supply exact information. According to some statistics recently computed by the Italian General Confederation of Industry, actual wages would appear on an average to be about 20–25 percent higher than those fixed by contract; however, this is an average to be interpreted with the following qualifications: this difference is generally more marked in the provinces of northern Italy than in those of south-

Table 3. COST OF LABOR IN THE ENGINEERING INDUSTRY, JULY 1952.

Cost of Labor Elements	*Men*				*Women*		
	Skilled Workers	*Trained Workers*	*Skilled Laborers*	*Common Laborers*	*1st Group*	*2nd Group*	*3rd Group*
MILAN							
Basic wages	394.40	355.60	335.60	309.20	248.92	234.92	216.44
Extra 10% on wages[1]	39.44	35.56	33.56	30.92	24.89	23.49	21.64
Temporary indemnity	776.00	764.50	759.00	753.00	662.50	658.00	653.00
Readjustment quotas	146.00	68.00	34.00	—	48.00	24.00	—
Bread indemnity	30.00	30.00	30.00	30.00	20.00	20.00	20.00
Total remuneration	1,385.84	1,253.66	1,192.16	1,123.12	1,004.31	960.41	911.08
Instalments of complementary elements[2]	263.45	238.32	226.63	213.15	190.92	182.57	173.20
Social charges on wages:							
basic contribution	3.50	3.00	3.00	3.00	2.16	2.16	2.16
on "maxim."—24%[3]	216.00	216.00	216.00	216.00	180.00	180.00	180.00
on entire pay—21.88%[4]	296.66	267.74	254.28	239.17	215.37	205.76	194.97
Social charges on complementary elements[5]	64.31	60.20	58.62	56.19	49.00	47.65	46.13
Total social charges	580.47	546.94	531.60	514.36	446.53	435.57	423.26
Aggregate cost	2,229.76	2,038.92	1,950.39	1,850.98	1,641.76	1,578.55	1,507.57
NAPLES							
Basic wages	394.40	355.60	335.60	309.20	248.92	234.92	216.44
Extra 10% on wages[1]	39.44	35.56	33.56	30.92	24.89	23.49	21.64
Temporary indemnity	616.00	604.50	599.00	593.00	523.50	519.00	514.00
Readjustment quotas	146.00	68.00	34.00	—	48.00	24.00	—
Bread indemnity	30.00	30.00	30.00	30.00	20.00	20.00	20.00
Total remuneration	1,225.84	1,093.66	1,032.16	963.12	865.31	821.41	772.08
Instalments of complementary elements[2]	233.03	207.90	196.21	183.09	164.50	156.15	146.77
Social charges on wages:							
basic contribution	3.00	3.00	2.16	2.16	2.16	2.16	2.16
on "maxim."—24%[3]	216.00	216.00	216.00	216.00	180.00	180.00	180.00
on entire pay—21.88%[4]	261.65	232.72	219.27	204.17	184.95	175.35	164.55
Social charges on complementary elements[5]	59.35	55.28	53.26	51.20	44.74	43.39	41.86
Total social charges	540.00	507.00	490.69	473.53	411.85	400.90	388.57
	1,998.87	1,808.56	1,719.06	1,619.74	1,441.66	1,378.46	1,307.42

ern Italy; it is greater in industries not subject to strong seasonal fluctuations (e.g., the engineering industry) than in those of a more accentuated seasonal nature, (e.g., the building industry); and it is more noticeable for the higher ranks (skilled workmen) than for the lower ranks (laborers), for men than for women, for clerks than for workmen. In some cases, particularly in the south of Italy and in small firms not belonging to any industrial organization, wages may actually be lower than the minimum wages fixed by contract.

In addition to the social charges considered above, which are of a general and compulsory nature, quite a number of firms, particularly the larger ones, have other charges as well to bear in connection with private welfare measures. Sometimes, these measures integrate the compulsory services as in the case of private provident funds or sanitary services. But primarily they are measures regarding workers' lodgings, summer or winter camps for the staff and their families, canteens and recreation in the cultural, tourist, and sports spheres. The individual nature of these provisions renders it impossible to make any generalizations regarding their cost and their incidence on the aggregate cost of labor.

Notes to Table 3:

[1]Extra 10 percent provided by the contract for the engineering industry for workers having no form of incentive premium (workers and clerks).

[2]Equal, as percentage of 2,280 hours of work a year, to 19.10 percent of remuneration: 10.21% of vacation and holiday pay and 8.80% of Christmas bonus.

[3]Family allowances 22.50 and integration fund 1.50% of "maximum" fixed at 900 lire for men and 750 lire for women.

[4]The percentage is the result of the following contributions: pension, tuberculosis and unemployment: 11.20%; sickness and maternity: 6.53%; accidents: 3%; INA-Casa: 1.15% (calculated on entire pay, bread indemnity excluded).

[5]All the contributions (in percentages equal to that resulting from the aggregate remuneration) are calculated on the instalment of the vacation and holiday pay and the contributions for sickness, maternity, and for accidents also on the Christmas bonus.

VIII

Collective Bargaining in the United States

NEIL W. CHAMBERLAIN

AT MID-CENTURY the organized labor movement in the United States numbered about sixteen million members in a labor force totaling about sixty-four million, including farm labor. Thus one of every four workers belonged to one of the approximately two hundred national labor organizations or to one of the uncounted unaffiliated unions, which are generally confined to the employees of a single company. (By 1955 another million members had been added, with the ratio remaining the same.) There is nothing remarkable about these statistics, on the surface. They are remarkable only in comparison with the situation less than two decades earlier, when the labor movement numbered no more than three million in a force of not quite forty-nine million or one out of sixteen workers.

Among the principal industries, unions are now strongest in basic steel and steel fabrication; electrical and other machinery; automobiles, aircraft, and shipbuilding; glass and glass products; clothing; meat packing; rubber products; railroads; trucking; maritime trades and longshoring; construction and coal mining. They are weakest, among major manufacturing industries, in: lumber and its products; cotton textiles; silk and rayon goods; hosiery;

shoes; food processing (except meat packing); tobacco manufactures; and chemicals. In nonmanufacturing groups, they have only a slight hold in the service trades and little more than a start in retail and wholesale trade, finance, agriculture, and government (except for the postal service). Clerical groups in all industries are still largely nonunion.

The tremendous expansion in the labor movement is attributable in a proximate sense to two major developments of the 1930's —the first, legislation. By the National Labor Relations Act of 1935 workers generally were accorded, for the first time, government protection of the right to form unions. The previously conceded right had, before then, been effectively nullified by employer opposition. Under the new law workers were empowered to call for a secret election to determine whether they wished to be represented by a union, and if so, which one. If a majority designated some union as representative, that union was given exclusive bargaining rights, and the employer was required by law to negotiate with it, in a good faith effort to arrive at an agreement—which would be reduced to writing. Employers were forbidden to interfere with worker organization in any manner, and this prohibition was at first rigidly interpreted by the enforcing government agency.

This legislation was itself a product of two forces—first, the increasing recognition that group action was necessary for representation of the individual, particularly in large-scale corporations; and second, the depression-spawned view, widely held in the thirties, that it was the failure of wage earners to share adequately in the prosperity of the preceding period which had been largely responsible for the economic collapse. Section I of the National Labor Relations Act reads:

> The inequality of bargaining power between employees who do not possess full freedom of association or actual liberty of contract, and employers who are organized in the corporate or other forms of ownership association...tends to aggravate recurrent business depressions by depressing wage rates and the purchasing power of wage earners in industry....

The other main impetus to the growth of the labor movement was the organization in 1935 (coinciding with the legislation mentioned above, and profiting from it) of the CIO—the Committee for Industrial Organization, later the Congress of Industrial Organizations. This group was formed by the splitting off of a number of unions from the parent American Federation of Labor, in disagreement over organizing policy. The CIO sought to enroll workers in mass-production industries in new unions set up on industrial lines. The AFL, while not opposed in principle to industrial organization, was adamant against disturbing the jurisdictional rights over occupational groups already granted to existing unions.

In the ensuing conflict, two major labor federations came to flourish where only one had previously existed. The competition between the two intensified the drive for members—competition based not on differing political or economic philosophies but on the promise, which each made, that it could do "more" for the workers in collective bargaining—win higher wages, better pension plans, improved vacation arrangements, a superior grievance procedure, and so on.

The enormous increase in union membership plus governmental encouragement and protection was a formula which could only result in the growth of collective bargaining. Within little more than a decade the United States was transformed from an economy in which collective bargaining had a limited incidence in only a few trades and industries, into one in which, in manufacturing at least, collective bargaining is regarded as a "normal" process and its successful conduct as a major determinant of a firm's prosperity.

Moreover, as the years passed, the original bitterness between the two labor federations began to diminish. The popular conceptions, by each of the other—of the CIO as a radical group infiltrated with Communists and of the AFL as a conservative assembly of labor bosses tinged with racketeering and corruption—were largely dissipated by the former's expulsion of eleven Communist-dominated unions in 1949 and 1950 and by the latter's subsequent expulsion of the International Longshoremen's Association, which had been exposed as criminally dominated. Members and officials came to appreciate that in terms of practices and policies there was little difference between the two organizations. The coincidental deaths of the AFL and CIO presidents within a short time of each other provided an opportunity for the new leadership to effect a merger of the two groups in December of 1955. A united labor movement sought to protect its position, as its period of most rapid growth came to an end, and to pool resources for the increasingly difficult task of organizing the unorganized—principally in the South, in small businesses, and in the service trades.

The Legal Basis for Collective Bargaining

As has been suggested, the firm establishment of collective bargaining in the United States during the 1930's and 1940's followed from legal protection of the right of employees to organize unions and the legal obligation imposed upon employers to bargain in good faith with unions which could be presumed, on the strength of elections or more informal evidence, to represent a majority of employees in the specified bargaining unit. The historical importance of this legislation warrants some elaboration of its provisions.

In addition to providing for representation elections, as the basis for certifying a union as the exclusive bargaining agent for a designated group of employees, the National Labor Relations Act enumerated five categories of employer conduct which were to be outlawed as "unfair labor practices." These were: interference with employees in the exercise of their right to form a union and bargain collectively; attempted domination of a union; discrimination against an employee for membership in a union; reprisals against an employee for testifying before the National Labor Relations Board (the agency charged with administering the Act); and refusal to bargain collectively, in good faith, with a representative union.

The twelve years during which this Act was enforced may be divided into three periods. At the start, there was a widespread belief—particularly among employers—that the Act would not survive a test of constitutionality before the Supreme Court, and many employers were accordingly advised by counsel to ignore its provisions. During this period the Board applied the Act sparingly —only to instances of the most flagrant violations—in the hope of securing a strong case to test before the Court. In 1937 it was upheld as to constitutionality, and its administration then passed into a second stage. In this period the Board interpreted its provisions with increasing rigidity, employer hostility to unions was rigorously circumscribed, and the number of cases accepted by the Board increased phenomenally. The nature of the Board's interpretations soon evoked organized opposition and pressure for amendment. Extensive hearings were held before congressional committees, bills were prepared for submission to Congress to revise the Act, and it is probable that only the war's intervention prevented the success of these moves at that time. Nevertheless, as if recognizing that more sweeping changes could be forestalled only if administrative interpretations were made less onerous on employers, the Board entered a third phase, when it gradually relaxed the rigor of its rulings and sought to meet many of the objections which had been raised before Congress.

Efforts to head off amendment failed, however, at war's end. A wave of postwar strikes in virtually all basic industries, of which more will be said later, aroused a generalized sentiment sufficiently hostile to union "excesses" to facilitate passage of legislation which was largely employer-drafted. Under the circumstances, it is surprising that the result was as favorable to the unions as it actually was. The old Act was incorporated bodily, with only relatively minor changes, into the new Labor-Management Relations Act of 1947. So far as collective bargaining is concerned, the chief changes were to proscribe certain forms of union conduct as "unfair labor practices" and to provide for special procedures in the event of national "emergency" strikes (the latter to be discussed later). As for the condemned union practices, they include: intimidation of employees in the exercise of their right to join or *not* to join a union; restraint or coercion of the employer in his choice of bargaining agent (principally, whether he chooses to bargain through an association or individually); efforts to cause an employer to discriminate against an employee because of his refusal to join the union or because of his membership in a competing union; refusal to bargain in good faith with an employer; engagement in a variety of secondary strikes and boycotts; attempts to coerce an employer into awarding work to one union rather than to another; and certain other more minor practices. The composition and procedure of the enforcement agency, which still retains the name of the National Labor Relations Board, were also changed.

The extent of the NLRB's activities may be suggested by its 1954 record. In that year it closed 5,962 unfair labor practice cases and 7,975 representation cases. In all cases where unfair labor practices are found, the Board is empowered to issue cease-and-desist orders, enforceable by application to the courts, and to award back pay where employees have suffered wage losses because of their membership or nonmembership in a labor organization. The 1954 total of back-pay awards was close to a million dollars.

The nature of the Board's findings as to the commission of unfair labor practices may be briefly suggested. On the part of employers, such conduct as the following has been held to be unlawful: surveillance of union activities; threats that union membership or activity would result in economic detriment, such as the closing or removal of the plant, or the loss of employment, pay, promotion, or other benefits; promising wage increases or other benefits to discourage union membership or activity; attempting—other than by a statement of opinion—to influence employees to vote against union representation or against a particular union; inducing or assisting employees to withdraw from a union; penalizing employees for engaging in strikes; refusing to negotiate on some issue on which the employer seeks to retain unilateral discretion; and a variety of manifestations of insincerity in negotiations.

Examples of unfair labor practices on the part of unions include the following: engaging in acts of violence or intimidation in connection with picketing; causing an employer to discharge a dissident union member as a condition of terminating a strike; forcing an employer to engage in discriminatory hiring practices by threatening strike or slowdown; insisting on illegal hiring clauses in proposed contracts; suspending from the union the employees of a customer of a company with which the union was in dispute, for disregarding the union's instructions to cease work on the company's product; picketing the premises of a firm using a struck company's products; seeking to force a self-employed person to join either a union or an employers' association; engaging in a secondary boycott to force an employer to negotiate with a union which had not been certified by the Board as the bargaining representative of the employees; picketing as a means of inducing employees to refuse to perform certain services, in order to force the assignment of work to its members instead of to another group of employees.

A representative union may, however, negotiate an agreement which obliges employees in the bargaining unit to become members of the union after thirty days of employment. This is known as a "union shop agreement." Under such an agreement, any employee who fails to pay his union dues must be discharged at the instance of the union, but the employer is not required to discharge an employee who loses his union membership for any other reason—as, for example, for breach of union rules, refusal to participate in picket-line activity, or campaigning against the re-election of the union's officers.

Legal supervision of the collective bargaining process thus remains an important aspect of the American scene. It cannot be sufficiently emphasized, however, that (except for emergency wage-control legislation) such supervision has nothing to do with the terms of collective bargaining agreements. The NLRB is designed to facilitate the processes of collective bargaining by enforcing certain rules, as above enumerated, as to the relationship between the parties, but as to the terms of that relationship it has no voice whatever. Contractual terms are a product of negotiations between the union and the employer, and the Government has no power to impose terms on the parties except under emergency wage-control legislation such as existed during World War II and following the Korean outbreak. At such times special boards are appointed for the emergency only, and the functions of the NLRB continue as in peacetime.

The Scope of Collective Bargaining

With collective bargaining there comes inevitably the question of the bargaining unit—the employer and employee units which are covered by the same collective agreement. The bargaining unit may range from a small group of craftsmen in a single shop of one plant on up to all the employees in an entire industry on a nation-wide scale. Although national collective bargaining units existed in the United States even before the turn of the century, it would perhaps be fair to say that the prevailing philosophy has always favored small bargaining units in which local determination of conditions by the employer and employees directly affected is most feasible. Despite any predilection for the small unit, however, there remains the need for standardizing labor rates, if collective bargaining is to be made workable and if competitive pressures are to be removed from workers and employers alike. This need has been met in part by the role of the national union, which is responsible for organizing nonunion employees, and which increasingly has been granted or has assumed the authority for enforcing "minimum conditions."

The preference for the small unit, particularly on the part of employers, has not stopped the evident trend to bargaining units of larger size. In one case all the plants of a company may be brought under the same agreement. In another the local firms in a particular trade or industry will begin to negotiate jointly for common terms. There is strong and understandable pressure on bargaining units to expand until they are coextensive with product markets. In such larger units the national union carries even greater influence. The trends toward expansion of the size of bargaining units and (on the union side) toward concentration of power in the national office have occurred simultaneously and not without interaction.

Nevertheless, it is true that the agreement covering employees of a single *plant* is still the most characteristic agreement in the United States, though, in terms of number of employees covered, multiplant and multiemployer agreements are more representative. A survey of 3,376 agreements in 1950—a small sample to be sure, perhaps no more than half of 1 percent—disclosed that 68 percent covered bargaining units limited to a single plant, though 72 percent of the employees covered by all agreements were to be found in multiplant or multiemployer units.

If we concentrate attention on the division of collective agreements between single employer units (whether or not embracing a number of plants) and multiemployer units, we find that an estimated five sixths of all agreements are negotiated in single employer units, and that these cover approximately two thirds of all workers coming under bargaining contracts. Collective negotiation by employers' association is thus less characteristic of the United States generally than is the negotiation of terms by the individual employer (an employer which may range in size, however, from the small shop to a giant corporation like General Motors or U.S. Steel). It is only in a few industries that multiemployer bargaining is prevalent. It was estimated in 1947 that contracts with employers' associations covered between 80 and 100 percent of all employees under collective agreements in the men's clothing, women's clothing, longshoring, maritime, and coal-mining industries, and between 60 to 79 percent of those under collective agreements in such industries as book and job printing, construction, glass manufacture, brewing, trucking and warehousing.

Most agreements negotiated with employers' associations are confined to a metropolitan area. For example, building contractors in, say, the Pittsburgh area are organized into associations of general contractors, of masonry, electrical, plumbing, painting contractors, and so on. Each of these associations will negotiate an agreement with the corresponding trade union covering all unionized employees in the given trade in the Pittsburgh area. Somewhat less commonly, an employers' association will negotiate terms covering a region. An example is the pulp and paper agreement covering employees in some forty plants of a number of companies located in the Pacific Coast states. Least common of all are agreements negotiated by employers' groups on a national or industry-wide basis. These occur only in coal-mining, elevator manufacturing, wallpaper, stove and pottery industries, and to some extent in railroads, flint glass, and men's clothing.

Despite the lesser frequency of multiemployer bargaining and the very small extent of industry-wide bargaining, the pattern of collective bargaining in the United States often leads to results more or less approximating those which would follow from such multiemployer units.

The Pattern of Bargaining

Let us focus our attention on wage changes, for the moment. There is some tendency for the wage increase or decrease which is negotiated in one of the major bargaining units in an industry to set a pattern which lesser bargaining units follow. The wage change which serves as guide is commonly referred to as the "key bargain." Key bargains are not necessarily followed without deviation, but there is a noticeable tendency for the wage change in a given industry to conform, within imprecise limits, to that which is negotiated by the pattern setter.

This phenomenon of wage leadership is not wholly a product of collective bargaining. In the steel industry, for example, the bargain between the United States Steel Corporation and the United Steelworkers is generally recognized as the key bargain. But United States Steel provided a similar wage leadership in the period preceding unionization of the industry. One study indicates that in the 20-year period, 1913–1932, at a time when the steel industry was virtually nonunion, there was "general agreement in the timing and amount of wage changes throughout the industry," and "the United States Steel Corporation took the lead in eleven of the fourteen general wage changes during this period."[1]

Although wage leadership predates the era of the key bargain, the advent of unionization has greatly strengthened the patterned similarity of wage changes within an industry. The union now provides a vehicle for the transmission of the key wage change to all lesser units within the industry and is the instrument for forcing as close an adherence to the pattern as its bargaining strength permits. There thus emerges a wage policy for an industry not vastly dissimilar to that which might emanate from industry-wide negotiations.

The similarity between industry-wide bargaining and key bargaining should not be exaggerated, however. The only detailed study which has been made of the latter relates to the annual wage increases negotiated in the steel industry in the three-year period,

[1]George Seltzer, "Pattern Bargaining and the United Steelworkers," *Journal of Political Economy,* Vol. 59, August 1951, p. 322. Subsequent conclusions concerning steel wage patterns come from this article.

1946–1948. In basic steel, 98 percent of the union members in integrated steel operations received identical wage increases in each of the three years. In nonintegrated steel firms (those producing finished steel but no pig iron or ingots), the degree of uniformity with the key bargain was 94 percent in 1946, 82 percent in 1947, and 70 percent in 1948. The evidence suggests that the key bargain establishes a kind of prima facie case for a wage change of the indicated magnitude in all units of the industry, and that the burden of proving that such a change is not feasible in a particular unit rests with the employer. It thus can be argued that, while pattern bargaining leaves the individual employer with less discretion than he would have if his bargain could be isolated from the rest of the industry, it nevertheless permits a greater flexibility than would industry-wide bargaining by permitting deviation from the industry standard where it can be demonstrated that deviation is warranted.

Because pattern bargaining has none of the formality of industry-wide bargaining, it is not easy to tell just where the pattern ceases to apply. Where formal industry-wide bargaining exists, the agreement itself or the employers' association defines the scope of coverage. With pattern bargaining the area of applicability of the pattern is left largely to union discretion and bargaining power. As economists have long since found, an industry is an almost indefinable abstraction. At times, then, unions have sought to hold employers to a "pattern" which the latter deny is applicable to them. Steel fabricators, for example, making products ranging from pins to locomotives, were held to the 1946 basic steel pattern by the Steelworkers' union, and the cries of anguish from the affected fabricators—some of whom submitted to strikes of six months' duration sooner than concede terms negotiated by the Steel Corporation—were heard even in the committee rooms of Congress. The difficulty of forcing compliance with a pattern which is not accepted as such is indicated by the extent to which the Steelworkers failed to secure fabricators' adherence to the postwar key bargains in basic steel. In one presumably representative district, 85 percent of the members employed in fabricating shops received the basic steel increase in 1946, but the following year the number fell away to 50 percent, and substantially fewer still in 1948.

If the United States is characterized by a relatively low incidence of multiemployer and particularly industry-wide bargaining, the consequence is not, then, a myriad of isolated and unrelated wage bargains. Pattern bargaining supplements the multiemployer bargain to achieve a substantial consistency of wage movements within an industry. Although the evidence is not conclusive, it appears that key bargains provide a point of departure, with any deviations from that standard depending partly on conditions in the local labor markets and partly on the profit-and-loss position of the individual firm.

The influence of the key bargain is believed to extend beyond its industry limits, however. It is commonly argued that in addition to bargains that are "key" for an industry, there are a few which are peculiarly significant for the economy, which tend to set patterns throughout the nation without respect to industry lines.

> When these strategic wage rates have been determined, for all practical purposes wage rates are determined throughout the rest of the system within narrow limits.... The number of really key bargains may be placed in the neighborhood of twenty-five to fifty.[2]

No systematic effort has been made to test this hypothesis, but it is rather widely given credence nonetheless.

The rationale behind this belief rests upon the existence of what Professor Ross has called "coercive comparisons."[3] Workers tend to judge how satisfactory a wage increase (or decrease) is by reference to the treatment accorded other workers with whom they have some reason to compare themselves. A wage increase given by another company may be compared with what one's own employer has done; the rate of a craft may be compared with that of a related craft, and so on. The union in its general wage negotiations is the means by which groups of workers attempt to obtain wage rates (or increases) which bear a "fair" relationship to other rates which

[2]John T. Dunlop, "American Wage Determination: The Trend and Its Significance," in *Wage Determination and the Economics of Liberalism,* (Washington: U. S. Chamber of Commerce, 1947), p. 42.

[3]Arthur Ross, *Trade Union Wage Policy* (Berkeley: University of California Press, 1948).

they regard as benchmarks. The officers of the union know that they will be judged by their success in winning wage awards comparable to those won by other unions, and superior to those of still other unions. The pressure is thus on the unions' negotiators to make good—or fail of re-election to their union office.

The dominant considerations which determine the wage structure are conceived to center in "orbits" of coercive comparison (again the phrase is Ross's). The principal orbits are wage rates (or increases) granted by other companies in the same occupation, industry, or area, and those won by unions which in some sense must be regarded as rivals. While these orbits of comparison may be regarded as chiefly binding on *union* wage policy, they cannot be neglected by employers. They become important determinants of company wage policy if labor unrest is to be avoided. Examples are available of how employers have bowed to the necessity of granting a wage increase of sufficient magnitude to satisfy their union's "political" needs, thereby avoiding the danger of lowered morale, work stoppages, and the agitation connected with organizational raids by rival unions.

It is these orbits of coercive comparison that provide links between the key bargains (and their associated "satellite" bargains). Such comparisons are, of course, not uniquely determinative. As we have seen, deviation from the key bargain occurs even within an industry, and this is no less true of extraindustry wage settlements. To the extent that management's cost of agreeing with the union on the terms of some key bargain makes its financial position seriously weaker, its cost of agreement rises relative to its cost of disagreement. To concede wage rates that threaten the business's survival becomes a grimmer alternative than accepting a strike. Management's bargaining strength thereby rises relative to the union. As the union bargaining officials come to realize the relative positions of the contending parties, they face a decision as to whether it is desirable to call a strike which would likely be a prolonged one, without any assurance of success, or accept a wage settlement somewhat less favorable than the pattern. Union leaders sometimes are able to win additional nonpecuniary concessions of a minor nature which can be made to appear as adequate compensation for the smaller wage award, but sometimes even this comfort is denied to them.

Even should the union call a strike and even should it thereby win the full amount of the pattern which it is following, there is no assurance that this is somehow determinative of the wage structure unless our attention is limited to the very short run. For if management's objection to paying the pattern is not simply a bargaining tactic, the firm can ultimately escape the rigidity of its ties to a pattern which is economically incompatible with survival by suspending operations, selling out, or moving to a more favorable economic climate.

The consequence of these economic considerations is that if a union is itself to survive it cannot force management's adherence to a pattern which deprives management of a return equal to what it can obtain elsewhere, or of a return adequate to compensate for risk and effort. For the pattern, however coercive on the union, will be broken, either in the short run by direct management resistance or in the long run by management's withdrawal from the relationship. Both of these possible resolutions of the conflict between political and economic influences can be observed at any time. Where unions accept and adapt to the firm's weak business position, they are likely to adopt a new pattern, a new comparison, which will be coercive both on it and to some extent on management. The new pattern may be related to the old (a customary 2-cent differential, for example, or perhaps settlements that are expected to be 25 percent below the key bargain) or an entirely new pattern may be developed. Where unions refuse to concede the "unsoundness" of the comparisons which they consider equitable, forcing firms to uneconomic awards or recurring costly strikes, the relationship is ultimately dissolved. Thus, in either event, some pattern is always followed. Whether the firm experiences no great hardship in meeting the pattern, whether it finds this pattern too costly for long-run survival and persuades the union to adopt some new pattern, whether it is held to the key bargain (or some other orbit of comparison) by a union's strength in the short run but is forced to dissolve the relationship in the long run, some pattern is nearly always present.

If one focuses on the existence of such patterns, he may be led to consider that the wage structure is simply the product of politically induced coercive comparisons. But if one concentrates on the economic influences which condition the comparisons and determine their feasibility, he is led to see economic forces as the final arbiter of the wage structure, as determinative of what patterns become coercive.[4] In fact, both influences are significant. The element of coercive comparisons probably makes the wage structure something different from what it would be if shaped by economic forces alone.

It is evident, however, that whether a union is able to enforce that pattern which most nearly satisfies its sense of equity depends on the bargaining relationship in which the firm stands with respect to its customers. A high degree of competition in the product markets has always been a condition unfavorable to union strength, since it makes more difficult the enforcing of a pattern which requires passing added wage costs along to a buying public. Unions have thus become instruments for obtaining market "control" where the numbers of producers make informal understanding or price leadership impossible. Particularly in the consumers' soft goods and the home construction industries have unions sought (with difficulty) to "police" the industry to insure that price competition did not become the basis for wage competition.

For a time the Department of Justice sought to restrain such union actions as a violation of the Sherman Anti-Trust Act, prohibiting combinations in restraint of trade, but this effort proved abortive when the Supreme Court in a series of rulings established the legal interpretation that the Sherman Act applied to the unions only when they entered into specific trade-restraining, price-fixing agreement with employers. Since unions can accomplish their "policing" function without having to incorporate a description of this function into the collective agreement, there is no present legislation which effectively restrains the unions from seeking to lift the burden of competition from their backs.

Unions have thus come to subscribe to the same views on price

[4]This position has been ably stated by M. W. Reder in "The Theory of Union Wage Policy," *Review of Economics and Statistics,* Vol. 34, February 1952, p. 41.

competition that characterize the employers with whom they deal —such competition is much to be desired in all fields except that in which they operate. To the extent that a firm can be protected from the rigors of competition, this will be beneficial both to the firm's profit position and to the union's place in the structure of wage patterns. To a large extent the union's bargaining power rests on the market position of the firm, since it is this which largely determines the firm's cost of agreeing with the union on the terms of some key bargain.

We can distinguish at least three ways in which unions, purely on the wage question, have been in a position to affect the wage structure in the United States: (1) They have identified (more precisely) the wage comparisons which workers regard as equitable or coercive and have added other coercive comparisons springing from the political nature of the union movement itself; (2) they have developed organizations capable of effectively asserting the equity of the comparisons made, making conformity to the chosen pattern more likely to the extent that economic circumstances are permissive; (3) they have developed organizations capable of affecting, within limits, the permissive character of the economic circumstances. Whether these presumed powers of unions to alter the wage structure have actually been effective is a matter we shall want to examine more fully later.

The Postwar Patterns

In light of the foregoing analysis let us examine the wage movements which developed in the United States following World War II.[5]

In November 1945 the United Automobile Workers struck General Motors in support of its demand for a 30-percent wage increase. President Truman thereupon appointed a fact-finding board to inquire into the merits of the dispute and to recommend a settlement. Despite withdrawal of the company from the hearings

[5]Details of postwar wage movements are to be found in the *Monthly Labor Review:* Sept. 1946, pp. 342–345; Dec. 1946, pp. 876–880; June 1947, pp. 992–995; Feb. 1949, pp. 158–164; Sept. 1949, pp. 238–240; Dec. 1949, p. 649; Feb. 1950, pp. 127–129; Nov. 1950, pp. 557–559; Feb. 1951, pp. 130–131; and June 1951, pp. 638–641.

in protest over the board's consideration of "ability to pay" as relevant to the inquiry, the board proceeded with its investigation and in January 1946 recommended an increase of 19.5 cents (approximately 17.5 percent) per hour. As was expected, the company rejected the recommendation. Within less than two weeks, more than a million workers in other basic industries joined the auto workers in striking for pay increases. Among these were the 750,000 members of the United Steelworkers, who originally sought the amount which the fact-finding board in the General Motors case had recommended (19.5 cents) but who had agreed to accept 18.5 cents, a figure which President Truman himself had proposed. After a stoppage of about three weeks a steel settlement was reached on the latter figure, with the companies simultaneously receiving a $5-per-ton increase in the price of steel, which was still controlled. The steel settlement of 18.5 cents became the pattern on the basis of which most of the other major controversies were ultimately resolved. In popular parlance, this became the "first round" of post-war wage increases.

Although the largest number of wage increases received by workers in manufacturing industries matched this first-round pattern, substantial variation occurred, as is suggested in Table 1. It has been estimated that the average increase was more in the neighborhood of 14.5 cents for manufacturing and 8.5 cents for non-manufacturing employees, where increases were received at all. It was in the large mass-production industries that uniformity was most nearly achieved.

Throughout the latter half of 1946 wage rates continued to rise, in part due to tail-end, first-round adjustments and in part due to the first adjustments of what developed into the second round. In the latter category were advances in cotton manufactures, men's clothing, and meat packing. The April 1947 agreement between General Motors and the United Electrical Workers (the latter undercutting the Automobile Workers by their unexpected settlement, in consequence of interunion rivalry, forcing on the Automobile union lesser terms than it had expected to win) set the second-round pattern at 15 cents. It has been estimated that over

Table 1. Estimated Percentage Distribution of Workers, by Amounts of General Wage-Rate Increases, August 18, 1945 to May 1, 1946.

Hourly Increase (in cents)	*All Manufacturing Industries*	*Selected Nonmanufacturing Industries*
Under 5	2.1	13.1
5 and under 6	5.5	16.4
6 and under 7	2.9	10.5
7 and under 8	2.2	10.4
8 and under 9	4.0	7.7
9 and under 10	2.6	3.7
10 and under 11	10.8	17.1
11 and under 12	1.7	1.8
12 and under 13	3.0	3.5
13 and under 14	2.3	1.8
14 and under 15	2.3	3.1
15 and under 16	11.7	3.5
16 and under 17	4.6	1.2
17 and under 18	3.3	1.9
18 and under 18.5	8.5	0.9
18.5 and under 19	21.6	1.0
19 and under 20	1.2	0.1
20 and under 21	4.0	1.2
21 and under 22	0.9	0.1
22 and under 23	0.8	0.1
23 and under 24	0.2	0.1
24 and under 25	1.0	—
25 and over	2.8	0.8
Total	100.0	100.0
Percent of all workers receiving no general wage increase	21.3	59.2

Source: Monthly Labor Review, September 1946, pp. 344–345.

fifteen million workers received increases approximating this pattern (a range of from 10 to 15 cents) during this period.

The succession of rounds became confused in late 1947 as some unions began negotiations for a third postwar increase before other unions had concluded negotiations for their second. Again consumer goods industries anticipated the movement. Even before any major settlement in the heavy industries had been reached, from one fourth to one third of organized workers had received their third advance. Despite the developing trend, United States Steel took advantage of a no-strike clause in its agreement with the Steelworkers to refuse union demands in April 1948, and this lead was followed by most other major steel companies. This effort to stem the third round collapsed the following month. General Motors granted an 11-cent increase and shortly thereafter Chrysler arrived at terms not markedly different. Within the succeeding three months a great many other companies fell into line. Negotiations were reopened in steel, and increases were granted there despite the earlier refusal. Adherence to the pattern was less marked in this wage movement than in the previous two, but still discernible. The increase in durable goods industries averaged 12 cents and in nondurable goods 10 cents, although there was considerable variation from these averages. Nevertheless, within the former category most increases came within 2 cents of the group average.

The fourth round opened with caution. The consumer goods industries, which had previously moved first—even if they did not define the pattern—negotiated many agreements without any wage increases, in view of the softening of their markets. Other groups waited for the outcome of bargaining in the mass-production industries, extending old agreements or providing for reopening on short notice. In May 1949 the Steelworkers presented demands for a general wage increase and a comprehensive retirement plan, concentrating on the latter. When negotiations were stalemated all issues were presented to a presidential fact-finding board, which in September recommended that the wage demand be dropped but that the parties agree upon a noncontributory pension plan. While public attention was still focused on the issue of whether workers should contribute to the financing of pensions, as the steel companies argued, or should be wholly financed by the companies, as the union contended, the Automobile Workers negotiated a pension plan with Ford calling for payment of $100 monthly (inclusive of federal old-age benefits) to employees retiring with thirty years of company service, with payments to be wholly financed by the company. This constituted the fourth-round pattern, if such it can be called. Similar plans were adopted by many of the major manufacturing companies, including those in steel, but the difficulties of instituting comprehensive pension systems, particularly for the smaller companies, prevented any immediate widespread uniformity. Nevertheless, it can be reasonably maintained that the present prevalence of retirement plans had its origin in the 1949 movement. No wage pattern developed in that year.

Although some wage increases, mostly in the neighborhood of 5 cents an hour, were granted in the first half of 1950, no substantial wage movement took shape until after the Korean outbreak. An initial rush by consumers for goods expected to be in short supply, sharply rising commodity prices, the anticipation of military priorities and eventual wage and price controls all set the stage for a new wage push. If one sought to continue the identification of postwar "rounds," this would presumably constitute the fifth. However, by this time any clear definition of a round was becoming difficult. Many unions and employers could not have answered whether they were adhering to some current pattern or catching up with a previous one. Twice during the year, Chrysler voluntarily renegotiated on wages, and U.S. Steel voluntarily reached a settlement in advance of the contract date. Nevertheless, the major agreements continued to act as benchmarks for large sections of the economy, as evidenced by the fact that, although wage increases in 1950 ranged from 7 to 14 cents, in seventeen of twenty-one broad industry categories average increases were confined to a narrower range of 9 to 13 cents.

One significant development of the year was the negotiation by General Motors and the Automobile Workers of a five-year contract calling for automatic wage adjustments in line with changes in the Government's consumer price index, supplemented by an annual "improvement factor" of 4 cents designed to accord employees some share in rising productivity. This 1950 agreement in fact only extended (improving in minor respects) a similar agreement of 1948. The earlier cost-of-living formula had attracted little interest among other unions, coming at a time when price declines (and hence wage declines, if wages were tied to prices) were as likely as increases. In 1950, however, the Korean action removed the possibility of any immediate recession, and the new General Motors' contract stimulated the negotiation of many agreements patterned after it. Prior to its signing, perhaps no more than several hundred thousand employees had been covered by provisions calling for such automatic adjustments, but within a year it was estimated that this number had been increased to more than three million. Despite the power of the General Motors' precedent, important strongholds (like steel) held out against the cost-of-living formula on principle. One objection was that under its provisions workers were always "catching up" to prices that had previously risen, whereas with a straight reopening-of-negotiations provision a union might anticipate price rises in its wage demands. Perhaps an even stronger objection, however, was that increases which were automatically gained when the price index was moving upward could be automatically lost in a subsequent downturning. (General Motors' employees in fact took wage cuts of 2 cents in March 1949 and March 1950, and lost 1 cent more in June 1949 although on this occasion the coincidence of the "improvement factor" payment obviated any actual wage decline.) In recognition of this danger that the money wage gains of the Korean inflation might be lost in a subsequent recession, the Automobile Workers and other unions operating under similar plans subsequently sought and won the agreement of signatory companies to incorporate at least some portion of the cost-of-living increases into basic wage rates.

With the institution of wage controls following military action in Korea, the period of postwar wage "rounds," freely negotiated under collective bargaining, came to an end. The experience of the period appears to support the reality of the "pattern" concept. The fact that deviations from a pattern occur does not destroy its reality as long as the pattern provides the "norm" to which wage changes are referred and in terms of which they are justified. Nor is it necessary to assume that a single uniform pattern provides such a norm. The pattern may differentiate between durable and non-durable goods industries, as indeed appears to have been the case, or allow for other significant variations. It is enough that a strong element of wage-relatedness is introduced by the power of precedent attending a few key bargains.

Finally, in this section on postwar wage trends, we may briefly note over-all relative wage and price movements. The basic data are presented in Table 2. In October 1942, when the Wage Stabilization Act became effective, hourly earnings in manufacturing had

Table 2. Indexes of Earnings in Manufacturing and Consumer Prices for Selected Periods, 1939–1950.

Period	Average 1939 = 100 Average Weekly Earnings: Actual	Average 1939 = 100 Average Weekly Earnings: Real	Straight-Time Average Hourly Earnings	Average 1935–1939 = 100 Consumer Prices
1939: Average	100.0	100.0	100.0	99.4
1942: October	163.0	136.2	132.5	119.0
1945: January	199.1	155.6	153.2	127.1
1946: October	192.7	128.9	173.5	148.4
1947: October	216.8	131.6	194.6	163.8
1948: October	233.0	133.4	212.8	173.6
1950: October	259.8	148.6	227.8	174.8
1953: January	299.7	157.4	263.3	190.4

Source: Bureau of Labor Statistics.

already increased by a third over 1939. This does not imply an equivalent increase in wage rates, to be sure, since it includes the effects of wartime shifts of workers to higher-paying jobs and industries and the increasing numbers employed on night shifts for which premium pay was received. Nevertheless, it is a close statistical approximation to wage rates. A substantial part of this increase was offset by a concomitant rise in prices. Even so, *real* average *weekly* earnings also rose by a third due to longer hours and premium overtime payments. The wartime peak in earnings was reached in January 1945. Price rises in the intervening period had been successfully restrained, but both hourly earnings (exclusive of overtime) and weekly earnings continued to rise, for the reasons noted above. The postwar relaxation of price and wage curbs and the first round of wage increases in 1946 gave impetus to a sharp upward movement. If we assume that by October 1946 the first-round effects had been substantially registered, we find that price movements largely nullified the money gain in hourly earnings of that round, while weekly earnings dropped sharply as hours of employment were cut back. The succeeding wage rounds, despite continued price rises, brought real gains both in wage rates and in weekly earnings. Real weekly earnings by late 1950 still had not recovered the ground lost since the wartime high in January 1945, however, but by January 1953 this earlier peak had been surpassed, and additional gains continued to be registered. By January 1955 average weekly gross earnings in manufacturing, in money terms, were almost 40 percent above the 1947–1949 level (the new base to which the Bureau of Labor Statistics' wage and price series had been converted in 1953), while average straight-time hourly rates in manufacturing had advanced only slightly less. In the same period prices had risen just under 15 percent, so that real wage gains, both hourly and weekly, of approximately 22 percent had been achieved.

Union Influences on Wages: The Short Run

The postwar years sponsored a considerable controversy over the causes of the inflation of that period. Argument has centered for the most part on the issue of whether it was largely, partially, or not at all attributable to the numerous rounds of wage increases engineered by the unions, and whether this secured them any differential advantage over unorganized workers. Has collective bargaining affected the inflationary movement of prices by affecting the timing and the magnitude of wage increases?

A considerable body of opinion exists supporting the view that unions were ineffective influences on wages during this period. The postwar inflation, it is said, had its genesis in an enormous consumer demand supported by liquid reserves built up in the war years, supplemented by investment demand supported by a low interest rate (held low by the Federal Reserve authorities to facilitate Treasury financing). The demand-induced inflation drew wage rates after it, with rates in nonunion sectors increasing along with union rates. There is no evidence that unions did any more than collect the raises that would have come anyway, even though they themselves in some quarters sought to take credit for such "achievements." Comparisons of the magnitude of wage increases relative to price increases after World War I (when workers in many key industries were still virtually unorganized) with wage-price movements after World War II (when unions were a far more potent factor) suggest that the extent of the wage rise relative to prices was no greater—perhaps less—in the later period than in the earlier. There is thus some statistical support for the view that price movements in the 1945–1949 period cannot be made the responsibility of the unions. Indeed, the argument has sometimes been pressed further, with the claim that collective bargaining may have slowed rather than accelerated the upward price rise by the practice of negotiating term contracts. If wage agreements extend over an agreed time period, this introduces a greater lag than is likely to occur when wages are free to move upward continuously.

From this analysis of the postwar period, the argument is sometimes generalized to the future. It is said that unions are unlikely themselves to be the *cause* of inflationary movements. That cause is simply an excess of money demand over product supply. In times of inflation, however, unions—no less than businessmen, farmers, and unorganized workers—will take such advantage of the situation as it affords.

While the line of argument outlined above is becoming popular, the burden of opinion appears to rest with the contrary view. The basis for believing that unionism was at least a contributing factor to the postwar wage inflation lies in the following considerations.

1. It is difficult to conceive that unorganized individuals would have been as alert and energetic in asserting wage demands as were the paid national union representatives who set the demands in motion throughout an industry, and whose reputation, security, and position depended in some measure on their aggressiveness. The competition among union officials to outdo each other in what they can deliver to their membership is a phenomenon peculiar to collective bargaining, strengthening the influence of coercive comparisons made by individual employees.

> The leader who can win an increase which is larger than the average wage increase throughout the economy has made a real gain for his members. When one adds to this the personal rivalry of union leaders for influence and prestige, it seems clear that an atomistic labor movement such as our own must necessarily generate a rapid rate of wage increase. This could be averted only by getting all union leaders to agree to a "code of fair competition," under which no one would demand more than a specified amount in a particular year. The present structure of our

labor movement makes such a comprehensive agreement impossible.[6]

2. Granting that the gains won by unions were generalized to nonunionized sectors of the economy, there is no basis for believing that such sympathetic responses were always equal in magnitude or coincident in time. At the very least, they followed the union gains with a lag, and seldom do unorganized workers win the advantage of retroactive pay which generally accrues to the organized group. There would appear to be here an indisputable temporary advantage for the unionists, repeated with each round of wage increases. In any event, if union-bargained increases set the pace for the nonunion firms and industries, this clearly implies that collective bargaining was in part responsible for the pace of the wage-price spiral.

3. The effect of term contracts in lagging wages behind prices, whatever its original value, was partly dissipated with an increased resort to automatic adjustments based on changes in the government's consumer price index, during the period of greatest inflationary pressure.

4. As Professor J. M. Clark has suggested,[7] in some circumstances wage pressures may turn a latent inflation into an active one. Demand may be strong enough to tolerate price increases without itself forcing them. In such a situation a union-induced wage rise can lead to the inflationary price rise, without more than passive assistance from the demand side.

Somewhat similarly, it has often been remarked that businesses —and particularly the large corporations—in the postwar period of excess demand did not take full advantage of that demand by raising prices as much as would have been possible. There was a considerable inclination to "hold the price line," probably for a variety of reasons—a regard for long-run consumer favor, a fear of more stringent price controls, a public relations concern for good reputation, and so on, considerations more relevant to large-scale

[6] Lloyd Reynolds, "Collective Bargaining, Price Changes, and Employment," *Proceedings of First Annual Meeting,* Industrial Relations Research Association, 1949, pp. 38–39.

[7] In D. McC. Wright, ed., *The Impact of the Union* (New York: Harcourt, Brace, 1951), p. 5.

institutionalized activity than to small-scale maximizing conduct. In such a situation union wage pressures may force the large firm—more reluctantly than perhaps is often imagined—to raise prices.[8]

On balance, it would appear that unions did exercise some upward pressure on wages and prices in the postwar period, from the cost side, though probably not to the extent that is often attributed to them.

Union Influences on Wages: The Long Run

Any influence of unions on the wage level or structure in the postwar period is, of course, only a short-run effect. There has recently been revived a somewhat parallel interest in whether unions can be charged or credited (depending on one's point of view) with having any long-run effect on wage relationships, specifically, with altering the structure of wage rates to the advantage of their members. This is a matter of considerable importance, since a finding that the structure of rates was impervious to union manipulation would suggest that the presumed economic powers of American unions, previously discussed, are actually of little account and that examination of the significance of collective bargaining should proceed more realistically in sociological and psychological rather than in economic terms. A number of studies have been undertaken to settle the issue. The state of the statistical evidence is summarized below.

1. In 1930 Professor (later Senator) Paul H. Douglas published his monumental treatise on *Real Wages in the United States, 1890–*

[8]It is one thing to say that at such times firms may raise prices by more than the wage increase necessitates, and quite another thing to say that without the wage increase they may not have raised prices at all. Once forced to raise prices, they may use such an occasion to add not only the higher labor cost but something in anticipation of future cost increases (thus forestalling another undesirable price revision) or in recovery of the previous nonwage cost increases for which no earlier compensating price change had been made.

The same public relations concern motivates the union, to be sure, but necessarily to a much lesser extent, since higher wages are one of the most basic objectives of unionism, which it cannot forego without serious risk of internal dissension, while higher prices do not concern the business in quite the same way, since at times lower prices would serve its own interests better and in any event it can more easily afford the "long" view.

1926. In that volume he attempted to measure statistically the impact of unionism on relative wage rates, examining the percentage changes in six unionized and eight nonunionized industries over the period. His conclusion was that unionism was initially a source of wage advantage, but the advantage was not widened over the years.

> Unionism, in other words, very probably does give an appreciable increase in earnings during the early period of effective organization, but during the later and more mature years of union development, the relative rate of further progress seems, to say the least, to be no more rapid on the whole for unionists than for non-unionists. Judging by our indexes, indeed, the non-union trades have made slightly greater relative progress since 1914 than the union trades, although their average absolute earnings are still below those of the unionist. It seems clear, in any case, that the increase in real wages during the period studied has been caused primarily by the increase in productivity rather than by unionization.[9]

2. Little interest in testing Douglas's conclusion was shown until 1948, when Professor Ross undertook calculations for the period 1933–1945. His procedure differed from that of Douglas in one major respect. Whereas Douglas had measured the relative effect of union and nonunion conditions in terms of percentage wage changes, Ross argued that percentage changes are significant only if the industries being compared start from approximately the same level of earnings. Since in the period under review there was a wide dispersion in industry earnings, the indiscriminate use of proportionate changes would be confusing rather than revealing. For example, at the start of the period (1933) there was one industry which fell into the wage bracket of 20–25 cents, at one extreme, and one industry which belonged in the bracket of 80–85 cents, at the other extreme. Wage increases throughout the period totaled 58.7 cents for the first industry and 64.8 cents for the second industry,

[9]Paul H. Douglas, *Real Wages in the United States, 1890–1926* (Boston: Houghton Mifflin, 1930), p. 564. Douglas prefaces the above conclusion with the comment: "This analysis is perfectly consistent with the belief that, were trade unionism to be greatly weakened in those trades and industries where it is strong, an appreciable fall in the earnings of the workers affected would result."

increases which in absolute terms were very nearly equal. The fact that the first industry experienced an increase of more than 263 percent while the latter gained less than 79 percent reflects only that the first industry started from a very low level. The phenomenon observed by many economists, that wage differentials have been narrowing over the years, is attributable simply to the statistical effect of indiscriminate reporting of absolute wage increases, which have tended toward uniformity, in percentage terms, Ross argued.

Ross's procedure in calculating relative wage movements over the period was to divide the industries for which data were available into three groups on the basis of the absolute level of wages at the beginning of the period. Within each of these three wage classes he subdivided industries into five categories on the basis of degree of unionization. Percentage changes in average hourly earnings were then computed for each of these subgroups. He was thus able to secure measures of the proportionate wage changes, for industries with varying degrees of unionization, for a wage class characterized by approximately the same absolute level of hourly earnings at the start of the period. By this procedure he was able to avoid much of the bias which he attributed to the disparate absolute earnings of the industries in the Douglas study.

On the strength of the evidence so presented, Ross concluded that differential wage movements were attributable to the degree of organization. "Real hourly earnings have advanced more sharply in highly unionized industries than in less unionized industries, in periods of stable or declining union membership as well as in periods of rapid unionization."[10]

3. This original study by Ross was subjected to sufficient criticism to induce him to make an extensive re-examination of the issue. The data were improved and supplemented, and a change in methodology was made. Fifty industries were grouped into wage classes of 5-cent intervals, according to level of hourly earnings in 1933. Average absolute wage changes for each group were calculated. In eleven out of thirteen groups the average increase be-

[10]His own summary, as given in a subsequent article, "Forces Affecting the Interindustry Wage Structure," written in collaboration with William Goldner, *Quarterly Journal of Economics,* May 1950, p. 256.

tween 1933 and 1946 was more than 50 cents and less than 70 cents. (Even greater absolute uniformity was disclosed within each of three component time intervals.) Ross was impressed not only with the degree of uniformity in absolute wage increases, but also by the fact that "the magnitude of absolute change in earnings in recent years has not been related in any systematic way to the original level of earnings." "It is fair to say, we think, that wage movements have been much more uniform since 1933 than has generally been appreciated."[11]

In consequence of this finding, it was believed that the division of industries into classes based on initial absolute wage levels, as a basis for calculating percentage wage changes, could be dispensed with as an unnecessarily roundabout technique. "Absolute change is a better measure of wage movements in recent years than percentage change, if comparisons are to be made." Accordingly, industries were grouped only according to degree of organization at the beginning of the period and in each successive period. and the average absolute increase for each group computed.

These conclusions emerged from this re-examination: (1) Of those industries substantially unorganized at the start of the period, greatest wage gains were won by those characterized by increasing unionization. (2) The poorest showing both for each time interval and over the period as a whole is attributable to those industries already effectively organized at the beginning of the period. In consequence of these findings, Ross was forced to revise the conclusion of his earlier study. He now asserted that "new unionism (that is, unionization) has been a source of relative wage advantage during the 1933–1946 period, whereas continuing unionism has not." This conclusion, it will be recalled, is very similar to that reached by Douglas in his pioneer study.

4. A study overlapping the time periods of both the Douglas and the Ross investigations has been made by Harold M. Levinson.[12] Using the procedures followed by Ross in his first study, Levinson made detailed calculations concerning the impact of unionization on the structure of wage rates over the period 1914–1947. His

[11]*Ibid.*, p. 265. Other quotations are from the same article.

[12]Harold M. Levinson, *Unionism, Wage Trends, and Income Distribution, 1914–1947* (Ann Arbor: University of Michigan Press, 1951).

findings show almost no correlation between wage increases and union strength in the period 1914–1920, a consistent correlation for the years 1920–1933, and again no correlation from 1933–1947. Indeed, in the latter period the union gains of the preceding period were wiped out.

To explain these seemingly unpatterned statistical conclusions, Levinson offers the following hypothesis. Whether a union's bargaining power is effective in modifying the wage structure to its advantage depends on two conditioning influences: government labor policy, and the level of employment. When underemployment exists and labor is plentiful, and when the Government's attitude is unsympathetic to worker organizations, then strong unions can gain a relative advantage. Employers will be placed in a position where they can effectively throttle any improvement in conditions by unorganized or weakly organized workers, but are not so favored as to be able to take advantage of the truly strong unions. The period 1920 to 1933 answers this description. In times of full employment or overemployment, and with a government favorable to labor, unions gain no comparative advantage. The demand for labor is so strong that any increases won by unions exert a sympathetic effect in the nonunion sector, with employers there forced to raise wages proportionately to hold their work force. Moreover, with government encouragement of collective bargaining, employers hostile to unionization are forced to concede wage increases equal to those won by the unions if they are to forestall unionization of their own shops. The latter explanation might well apply to the period 1933–1941, while the competition-for-labor argument would serve to explain 1914–1920 and 1941–1947. On the whole, however, Levinson's explanation is one of short-run fluctuations rather than long-run movements. Within the 31-year period examined, he finds no consistent relationship between earnings and unionism, and is forced to fall back on short-period analysis largely reflecting the level of employment.

Two other statistical explanations of the interindustry wage structure may be briefly mentioned. Professor Dunlop finds that "the interindustry pattern of changes in average hourly earnings over substantial periods is to be explained fundamentally in terms of the following factors: Change in productivity, change in output, proportion of labor costs to total outlays, competitive conditions in the product market, and the changing skill and occupational content of the industry." He notes that this explanation gives "no distinctive place to the role of labor organization.[13]

Still another formulation[14] pictures the wage system as a product of three forces: (1) technological changes within the industry, of which productivity can be accepted as the index (this indicates the possible gains to which factors and consumers alike may lay claim); (2) the product market structure of the industry, of which degree of concentration of production is taken as the measure (this indicates the extent to which industry factors may preserve technological gains for themselves in opposition to consumers); and (3) the bargaining power of unions, of which degree of unionization is used as the index (this indicates the ability of labor to win a share in the productivity gains in opposition to the other factor participants). In the statistical evidence for the period 1923–1940, Joseph Garbarino, who constructed the above model, finds (as did Dunlop, on other data) that the wage structure is largely explainable by productivity changes, with the remaining variables explaining any deviations. While his model makes explicit room for degree of union organization, it is notable that the unionization element is virtually unnecessary to the correlations which he finds.

These last two studies have been mentioned for the reason that —although emanating from labor economists—they accord very little if any significance to the impact of unions on the inter-industry wage structure. Laid alongside the conclusions of Douglas and Ross, both of whom see only an initial influence of unionism on relative rates, and Levinson, who sees an uncertain influence, we have here impressive testimony to the relative impotence of unionism to affect long-run wage relationships.

Indeed, the present theoretical fashion in the United States appears to be to deny the unions any significant economic impact. The argument is becoming current that the power of a union to

[13]John T. Dunlop, "Productivity and the Wage Structure," in *Income, Employment and Public Policy* (New York: W. W. Norton, 1948), p. 360.

[14]Joseph Garbarino, "A Theory of Interindustry Wage Structure Variation," *Quarterly Journal of Economics*, May 1950, pp. 282–305.

gain wage increases over and above those that its members would have attained in the absence of unions is largely illusory. It is said that this illusion is fostered by the fact that collective bargaining, rather than the employer's unilateral action, has become the established mechanism for transmitting wage increases, but that in both cases the same underlying economic forces determine the size of the increases. The additional fact that the collective bargaining mechanism with its accompanying panoply of colorful labor leaders, protracted negotiations, occasional strikes, and government intervention is newsworthy, in the manner that unilateral employer action is not, adds to the illusion.

There is no conclusive proof for or against this view. The weight of statistical evidence, it is true, suggests that unions are unlikely to exert significant long-run influences on the wage structure. Nevertheless, there are good grounds for resisting this conclusion and for maintaining a reasonable skepticism concerning it. Several may be mentioned. (1) The statistical techniques and assumptions are open to question. In particular, the use of group averages to explain interindustry wage structure and the premise that unionization in itself may be taken as indicative of union strength are subject to criticism. (2) Even taking the weight of statistical evidence as indicating that on the whole unions are incapable of significantly modifying the interindustry structure of wage rates over the long run, before we can be satisfied with such a conclusion we require some logical explanation for the "observed" result. No really satisfactory explanation has been offered. Levinson's ingenious hypothesis relates to the short run rather than to the long run, in both political and economic terms. (3) There is general agreement that one effect of unions has been "to strengthen the ties binding the firm to its industry and to weaken the influence of the local labor market."[15] As we have seen in connection with the postwar steelworkers' wage movements, the influence of the local labor market is not eliminated but is, nevertheless, significantly modified. It would be surprising if this tendency had no impact on the wage

[15]Lloyd G. Reynolds, "Collective Bargaining, Price Changes, and Employment," p. 36.

structure. (4) The union's bargaining power is, to be sure, largely dependent on the extent to which the firm or industry has control over product prices. Admittedly such control diminishes over time, but we are far from saying that the elasticities of demand curves change equally over time for all firms in an industry, or as between industries. The monopoly advantage of some firms and some industries is more time-impervious than that of others, and where this advantage exists a union can exploit it to its own benefit, even if the firm or industry would not have done so independently, perhaps for fear of public censure.

It is unquestionably true that there has been a considerable tendency to exaggerate the chances of a union's obtaining long-run differential gains for its members, just as there has been some tendency to exaggerate the long-run monopoly power of business. This tendency appears to be having its current reaction in a pendulum swing to the opposite extreme of denying that the union offers any significant long-run economic benefit to its members. As is often the case, the truth probably occupies an intermediate position. At least some unions in the United States have obtained differential wage advantages, but the magnitude of their victories has been overplayed.

One economist, Professor Milton Friedman, has ventured the guess that unions have succeeded in raising wages by some 15 percent for perhaps 10 percent of the labor force. The fact is, however, that we do not know. Statistical inference and logical deduction are here somewhat at variance. The writer's own view is that unions in relatively strong bargaining positions have, to some unknown degree, modified the long-run structure of wage rates to the advantage of their members. Evidence does not necessarily lie solely in comparisons between the movement of union and nonunion rates, in different industries, but also in comparisons between the movement of union and nonunion rates of comparable firms in the same industry, studies of which are still lacking, and in contrasts between what the rates of unionized industries would have been in the absence of unionism and what they in fact are, studies of which are not feasible by the same statistical techniques, if at all.

Public Wage Policy in Peacetime

On the one hand, the postwar inflation in the United States and the ensuing controversy over the degree of union responsibility for it and, on the other hand, the concern with the preservation of full employment in the face of a possible and often predicted downturn in economic activity have led to a variety of proposals for "appropriate" wage policy. For present purposes we can best distinguish between (1) policies advocated in the belief that unions are essentially minor actors in the economic scene, having little effect on wages and (2) policies formulated in the belief that the union's economic impact on wages and prices is crucial. It is to be stressed that in both instances we are talking about a wage policy designed for a peacetime situation (though it is no longer clear that we may speak of "*normal*" peace times). We shall discuss wartime controls later.

1. If unions, as presently constituted in the United States, are largely ineffective in their efforts to control economic forces, then little specific attention need be paid them in calculating appropriate economic policy. Inflation or deflation may be attacked directly without regard to the unions. Stabilization policies may be undertaken by the Government through fiscal and monetary programs. Control over the money supply by the Federal Reserve System is the sine qua non when inflation threatens. When it is governmental spending which raises the threat, as during the armaments build-up following the outbreak of the Korean War, monetary control must be supplemented by an augmented tax program. In times of recession, money rates should be eased to stimulate investment, and government works programs—preferably of a short-run, easily contractable nature—should be instituted. Under such a program wage rates may be left to themselves, both in the organized and unorganized sectors of the economy.

On this approach, full employment raises no special threats due to the pressure of collective bargaining in the economy. A full-employment inflation is due to the excess demand which raises prices everywhere, inducing a rise in wages without pressure from the unions, as businesses compete for more workers to expand output. In the postwar years, for example,

> we find numerous instances in which contractors were hiring building trade workers at rates considerably in excess of union wage scales and finding buyers able and willing to pay for housing at inflated costs.[16]

The solution to the problem lies not in a special wage policy or a union-control program, but in limitations on the demand side.

> We need not worry about the dire forebodings of those who deny the compatibility of trade unionism with the objective of high employment and stable prices. We need not set out to disorganize our social life by a war on organized labor. . . . Under the circumstances, it seems wiser to continue over-all control of effective demand and to leave the rest of the economy free to adjust individual prices and wages to the resulting market. The concept of an unlimited monetary demand is, of course, inconsistent with price stability, it is this concept of which we must rid ourselves, not of trade unionism.[17]

Professor Milton Friedman, following substantially the same line of reasoning, has added a slightly different twist to the conclusion.

> If this analysis is right, it means that we face a dilemma, but one that is, at least for the near future, almost precisely the reverse of that which has been most stressed. The difficulty is not so much that strong unions will produce inflation as that inflation will produce strong unions.[18]

Friedman's reasoning is that during an inflation wages must rise, and under collective bargaining such increases are necessarily channelled through the union. It is not that the union itself effects the wage rise, but that it simply acts as the middleman. Nevertheless, it will receive credit for the results, and greater power will be attributed to it than it actually possesses. This process will accord it more political influence, and the result may well be union-stimulated government intervention in economic affairs, on behalf of the unions, perhaps ultimately justifying *presently* unfounded fears as to the inflationary consequences of unionism.

[16]Walter A. Morton, "Trade Unionism, Full Employment and Inflation," *American Economic Review,* Vol. 40, 1950, p. 23.

[17]*Ibid.,* pp. 37–38.

[18]Milton Friedman, "Some Comments on the Significance of Labor Unions for Economic Policy," in *The Impact of the Union,* pp. 230–231.

2. The above policy recommendations are satisfactory only to those who have concluded that collective bargaining has no appreciable economic significance. For those who cannot agree with this premise, the policy conclusion appears inadequate. If unions are viewed as a source of influence over wages and prices, firmer measures are needed.

The problem to be faced is presumed to arise from union insistence on wage increases exceeding increases in productivity, occasioned by intraunion or interunion rivalry. Higher prices must necessarily result. If producers can sell their output at these higher prices, inflation follows. If output cannot be sold, the consequence is unemployment. Which of these (presumed) union-bred evils—inflation or unemployment—is likely to eventuate depends on the accompanying governmental policy with respect to employment.

Let us consider, first, the likelihood that union wage pressures will induce inflation. Such an expectation follows from the premise that the present climate of public opinion is such that any administration which allowed unemployment to develop and persist would be voted out of office at the next election. The passage of the Full Employment Act of 1946, while embodying no employment guarantees, is generally accepted as a government commitment that unemployment will never again be allowed to become a national disaster, as in the 1930's, even though the mechanisms for eliminating it when it appears are undefined and the wording of the Act itself stresses governmental encouragement of private enterprise. Any administration—Republican or Democratic—can expect to fall if it does not conform to this expectation, so that for all practical political purposes the United States is bound to a standard of at least "reasonably" full employment. Where full employment is thus politically guaranteed, "there is no economic mechanism to insure a finite upper limit to the wage (and price) level."

> The actual wage level is, of course, the net result of the various wage bargains struck by individual employers either with unions or with unorganized employees. However, so long as there is some upper bound to the quantity of money the monetary-fiscal authority will allow to exist, there will also be an upper bound to the wage level that can be attained with full employment. . . .

> If the wage level were pushed sufficiently far beyond this upper bound, unemployment would result. . .and bring about a reduction in the wage level. However, a commitment to maintain continuous full employment precludes the operation of this mechanism.[19]

The money supply will be expanded as needed, preventing corrective unemployment from emerging.

Under these circumstances it can be said that wages determine the money supply, rather than vice versa. In the absence of effective monetary restraint, unions can be expected to engineer an inflation in their competitive efforts to capture a wage advantage for their memberships.[20] If rigid adherence to a full-employment policy is an unavoidable political necessity, then the evil foreseen can be avoided only by increasing the legal limitations on union power.

In distinction to those who expect that union wage influence will eventuate in inflationary tendencies, there are those who believe that the unemployment effect will—alternatingly—be fully as important. As an example of this school of thought, Professor Haberler has concluded that unemployment is the only force fully effective to curb union power and that it will in fact do so. His argument runs as follows:

> 1. There is under any given set of circumstances a certain limit beyond which the money-wage level cannot be pushed without either a rise in prices or the appearance of unemployment.
> 2. Our society will not tolerate an indefinite rise in prices.

[19]Melvin W. Reder, "The General Level of Money Wages," *Proceedings of the Third Annual Meeting,* Industrial Relations Research Association, 1950, p. 7. Reder makes clear that the above argument is valid in a nonunion setting, but it would apply with greater force if unions exercise pressures not available to unorganized workers.

[20]It is to be noted that this "pessimistic" view (that unions are contributors to upward pressures on price) differs from the more "optimistic" conclusion that they are passive agents in time of inflation in two particulars only (1) The optimists believe that the money supply can be effectively controlled by the authorities. The pessimists do not agree, but believe that the public demand for full employment spearheaded by the unions makes monetary controls politically infeasible. (2) The optimists believe that lack of monetary control means excessive demand, leading to a situation in which wage increases follow of necessity, unions or no unions. The pessimists believe that lack of monetary control means price increases from the supply side, due to rising labor costs resulting from union wage bargaining.

Sooner or later, steps will be taken through monetary or fiscal policy, or direct control, to counteract further price rises.

3. Labor unions are not satisfied with wage increases on this side of the critical limit; they tend to push beyond it.

Conclusion: Unemployment is inevitable.[21]

Haberler estimates that the "critical limit" will be reached when prices have risen by 5 to 10 percent a year for only "a year or two." Because he believes that unions have the power to force increases of this magnitude, he sees only one alternative to unemployment. If a full-employment-conscious people will not tolerate unemployment, they must curb the power of unions.

An anomalous situation has thus been developing in the United States, whereby if those friendly to labor unions would aid them in escaping from regulations they must plead the economic impotence of the organizations they would protect. If one admits that the unions fulfill the economic role which they claim and do in fact bring wage advantages to their members, he is faced with the difficult question of whether existing political and economic restraints are adequate to control the organized power which he champions.

The Issue of Peacetime Strikes

In 1950 approximately 2,500,000 American workers participated in a total of almost 5,000 strikes.[22] This was about as many strikes and workers involved as in 1951 and 1953, fewer than in 1952 and more than in 1954. Close to 40,000,000 man-days of work were thereby lost or something less than ½ of 1 percent of all estimated working time during that year. This year may perhaps be considered "typical." The figures on idleness underestimate the actual impact of strikes, however, since they allow only for the time lost by those directly involved in a work stoppage. One of the most telling effects of certain types of strikes—those intimately related to producer goods or services, such as in coal, steel, and rail trans-

[21]Gottfried Haberler, "Wage Policy, Employment, and Economic Stability," in *The Impact of the Union,* p. 39.

[22]The figures are those of the Bureau of Labor Statistics and include all work stoppages known to it involving six or more workers and continuing as long as a day or a shift.

portation—is the secondary unemployment occasioned in customer industries of the struck unit. Making an arbitrary allowance for the indirect employment effects, it is reasonable to assume that, in a normal peacetime strike year, strikes are likely to result in a loss of somewhat more than 1/2 of 1 percent of total working time.

In the first full postwar year of 1946, strike losses were approximately three times as great as in a typical year (if we accept the above figures as measuring such a year). While the number of strikes was not much higher, almost twice as many men were involved, and the duration of the stoppages was greater. It was the 1945–1946 period which indeed highlighted the problem of the "national emergency strike." One walkout followed another until virtually every major industry had been affected. The coal, steel, oil, railroad, shipping and longshoring, telephone, telegraph, automobile, farm equipment, electrical equipment, and meatpacking industries were hit in a wave of strikes that appeared to have no end. Nor were the national strikes the only serious disturbances of the period. Local transportation and utility systems were involved, including a brief strike of the tugboat operators in New York City that led the mayor to declare a state of emergency (since up to 80 percent of the city's fuel supplies were thereby embargoed) and the longest electric power strike on record up to that time (one of twenty-six days) in Pittsburgh.

Public irritation with this outburst of aggressiveness was of course intensified by the fact that the wartime period had prevented the manufacture for consumer use of goods of all types. People had been eagerly anticipating a prompt flow of new automobiles, refrigerators, washing machines, houses and housing equipment, and so on, but at the very moment when deferred wish was about to be gratified, fulfillment was snatched away by strike. Moreover, strike settlement in one industry constituted no guarantee of resumption of production, since strikes in other industries might withhold vital materials. There seems to be no question that this surge of strike action at this time was largely responsible for the inclusion in the Taft-Hartley Act of 1947 of a section designed to cope with the so-called national emergency strike.

The Taft-Hartley provision leaves it to the discretion of the

President to determine whether "a threatened or actual strike or lockout. . . will, if permitted to occur or to continue, imperil the national health or safety." In the event of such determination, he appoints an investigating committee which reports back the "facts" concerning the strike, but which is expressly forbidden by the Act to recommend any basis for settlement. On the strength of such a report, the President may direct the Attorney General to obtain an injunction forestalling the strike. This remains effective for sixty days. If no settlement has occurred within that time, the employees are polled on whether they are willing to accept the employer's last offer. If the vote is negative, the Attorney General has no alternative but to request dissolution of the injunction, and the President washes his hands of the matter by referring the dispute to Congress for further action.

Experience under the emergency-strike provision of the Taft-Hartley Act has been mixed. It must be remembered that it was first administered by a President who was avowedly hostile to the Act, who vetoed it only to have it passed over his veto by the required two-thirds majority in Congress. Nevertheless, the partially unfavorable record of the strike-control section cannot be explained on this ground. At least three weaknesses have been revealed. First, in three instances out of twelve in which the Act's provisions were utilized in the period 1947–1954, the strike which the Government's injunction had forestalled was called after the injunction had been dissolved. In these instances the procedure only postponed the strike. Second, the courts have construed the Act's enforceable provisions to run against the "official" union only. A union (the United Mine Workers) and its officers have been fined large sums for refusing to order their members to return to work after an injunction had been issued, but the same union has been held immune from penalty when its officers have asked the members to recognize the Government's injunction and to go back to their jobs but where the members have refused. If the union cannot be identified with the membership, this opens the way to concerted action under the informal leadership of nonofficial "field generals," thereby avoiding even the postponement of a strike. Third, the provision of the Act that forbids the investigating board to make a recommendation for settlement actually robs the board of all function. The President appoints such a board of inquiry only because he believes the dispute is serious, and he does not need their documentation to bolster that belief.

The provision forbidding the power of recommendation was presumably inserted to prevent such boards being used as de facto commissions of compulsory arbitration. Any recommended settlement is actually a blame-placing device: it does not rely on the public's being particularly conscious of or concerned about the terms of settlement proposed, but it does count on its being hostile to whichever party continues the public-affecting strike by refusing to agree to the recommendation. There is thus a presumption—however much it may be denied—that the parties *ought* to accept any recommendation which is made by a board of inquiry, and it was this presumption which some members of Congress found unpalatable, since it smacked of coercion. But if this coercive quality is sacrificed, then the chances of settlement are to that extent reduced, and the chance is increased that the dispute will be left to the parties to fight out by attrition. Since the Act has provided no substitute for the public recommendation, there is thus good reason for believing that termination of the Government's injunction might be expected, at least in some instances, to result in a resumption of the postponed strike.

The issue of what to do about emergency strikes thus remains unsettled. It was noteworthy that in the presidential campaign of 1952 the candidates of both political parties admitted the need for strengthening the strike-control provisions of existing legislation, but neither candidate had a very clear or convincing proposal on how to do this.

There are some, indeed, who question that the problem is really a serious one. For the most part these are people in the labor movement itself and members of the academic profession who are concerned that the control of strikes may seriously jeopardize personal freedom. One of the most effective spokesmen of the latter group was the late Edgar L. Warren, formerly director of the Federal Conciliation Service. Warren made an investigation of strikes which were serious enough to have commanded front-page newspaper attention on both East and West coasts over the 36-year period from 1914 through 1949. Disputes which failed to receive a total of two columns in the Los Angeles Times and of six columns in the New York Times were considered of insufficient importance to be included in the analysis. This left a total of 104 strikes, of which 46 were classed as "more important" in the sense of having been given a total of at least six columns of space in each of the papers mentioned. Of these 46, some 60 percent occurred in the two post-war periods, 1919–1922 and 1945–1949. There were none at all in the 7-year period from 1923 through 1929. Even among the "more important" strikes there have been few which threaten to "imperil the national health or safety." "Vital services have never been completely curtailed because of strike activity," according to Warren, who suggests that the availability of substitutes, the presence of some stocks of the struck good, the willingness of the striking union to continue "emergency" functions rather effectively manage to remove any "peril" from the situation.

Warren concludes:

> Forty percent of those strikes which have attracted nationwide attention during the past thirty-six years were in industries where "necessary goods and services" were not involved. Another 24 percent did not result in a "dangerous curtailment of supplies" because they were in industries where the product could be stockpiled and stock piles were never entirely exhausted. Of strikes in those industries producing necessary goods and services where a dangerous curtailment of supplies might have been created, there were no more than twenty of extended duration; and it may be assumed that in most of these situations the strikes were not entirely successful and substitute facilities were available. Only in the field of public utilities and transportation do we find instances of strikes which come within the definition of national emergencies, and even these industries produce few real crises.[23]

His recommendation is to provide special machinery to deal with strikes in only two kinds of situations: (1) strikes involving public utilities and transportation, and then only when substitute facilities are not available, and (2) in time of war.

[23]Edgar L. Warren, "Thirty-Six Years of 'National Emergency' Strikes," *Industrial and Labor Relations Review,* Vol. 5, 1951, pp. 14–15.

Despite the persuasiveness of this analysis, there is some question whether it will sway publics which are adversely affected by important strikes even though their health or safety is not imperiled. There is some sentiment to the effect that this is an anachronistic method of effecting agreements. The difficulty is, however, that the only likely alternatives which have so far been seriously proposed involve an imposition of terms on the parties, which is a procedure uncongenial to the American scene. Nevertheless, since the end of World War II compulsory arbitration laws have been enacted in a number of states, applying to industries of the "public utility" category, and suggesting that the opposition to strikes involving substantial public inconvenience is sometimes great enough to support strike control whether or not the public's health or safety is in danger, and whether or not private discretion is thereby curtailed. Although the constitutionality of these laws has been called into question, it is only on grounds of conflict with federal legislation, rather than conflict with the civil rights provisions of the Constitution itself.

Wage Policy and Strike Control in Time of Crisis

In the preceding two sections the policy problems that confront the United States due to union wage action and union strike action in normal times have been noted. Except under unusual circumstances these two issues can be kept separate. Wage policy may be pursued without respect to whether a strike is called in one industry or another, since the peacetime wage policy (based on either "loose" or "tight" monetary and fiscal programs) involves no direct controls which a strike could challenge. However, in time of crisis (mobilization for defense or involvement in war), these two problem areas are inextricably joined. Wage controls must inescapably involve some form of direct wage determination, which may be contested by individual unions to whom applied. The contest usually takes the form of threatened strike if the permissible increase is not liberalized, and in an emergency period the loss of vital production cannot be contemplated. The dilemma is thus squarely encountered: enforce wage stabilization but submit to interruption in the production of vital goods, or assure continued production but submit to a rising wage and price level.

To put the problem of wartime controls in this manner is not to suggest that the labor unions are led by unconscionable banditti who are alert to seize upon national misfortune as the occasion for enriching themselves and their members. The labor movement embraces too large a segment of the population, including too many fathers and mothers of youth in uniform, to give any semblance of validity to such a notion. But in any period in which special controls are required the question of equality of sacrifice unavoidably intrudes, and it is—however the psychologists might explain it—apparently human nature to believe that one is being asked for sacrifices not required of others. Price rises cannot be wholly restrained, and their total impact on consumption always appears greater to the consumer than it actually is. The feeling arises that someone is profiting at the consumer's expense, and the consumer—in his role as worker—wants only to "catch up." "Equality of sacrifice" becomes the slogan (obviously immune from ethical attack), under cover of which all interest groups seek something more than they are allowed by the controls program, and the unions are no exception. An easily developed sense of outraged justice can lead to a threat of strike, and if the nation's military position is thereby affected this is the responsibility of those who withhold what is rightfully due.

In the United States the practice of World Wars I and II and of the Korean period has been to concentrate wage and strike controls in the hands of the same board, while leaving price controls in the hands of a separate agency. In an effort to free the wage board of undue union pressure, an effort has usually been made to arrive at some general policy acceptable to unions and employers alike, and on the basis of which the unions will pledge themselves not to initiate strikes. Such a specific pledge was made during World War II on the basis of the so-called "little steel formula," which allowed a 15-percent increase in wages above the level of January 1941. In the Korean war a 10-percent increase above the level of January 1950 was permitted, later modified to allow further increases matching the rise in the consumer price index, and although the unions made no explicit guarantee that strikes would be waived there was implicit in their representation on the wage board the premise that the strike weapon would be used with restraint during the period of the emergency. Such pledges, whether explicit or implicit, are always conditional, however, and the matter can be reopened at any time on the ground that conditions existing when the pledge was made have since changed.

A further difficulty lies in the effect of political relationships which sometimes intrude into wage stabilization policy. The effectiveness of the Wage Stabilization Board, created following the outbreak of hostilities in Korea and the subsequent expansion in military procurement, was first shaken by union withdrawal from the board in dissatisfaction with the 10-percent policy and then largely shattered by the Steel and Coal settlements of 1952, in both of which the President took a hand. By strengthening the position of the Steelworkers before the board by assurances which were taken to mean that stabilization policies would not be controlling in their case, he contributed to an intransigence which won for them the largest settlement in their 15-year history and led to the strange spectacle of the President and the steel industry leaders arguing the merits of the decision and castigating each other over a television network, though not on the same program. In the coal case he expressly overrode the decision of the wage board, granting the Mine Workers 40 cents an hour more than the board had allowed, in a move that was widely interpreted as paying off the union for its support of the Democratic party in the 1952 elections.

Both these instances have encouraged an already developing cynicism as to how effective wage stabilization might be for anything except a brief period of actual involvement in an all-out war. In this respect the analysis of Professor Clark Kerr, himself an active participant in World War II's Labor Board and later chairman of the postwar Wage Stabilization Board, is instructive.[24] Kerr recognizes the ambivalence in the purpose of an agency which is charged with both resolving labor disputes and stabilizing wages. The first function may sometimes require a wage decision contra-

[24]Clark Kerr, "Governmental Wage Restraints: Their Limits and Uses in a Mobilized Economy," *American Economic Review, Papers and Proceedings,* Vol. 42, May 1952, pp. 369–384.

dictory to the second purpose. The result is, says Kerr, that board policy can be expected to vary depending on the "stage" of the crisis, depending, that is to say, on how far stabilization policy can be pushed without jeopardizing production by inducing strikes. He conceives that a wage board in the United States must pursue a course that fluctuates between a lower wage limit and an upper wage limit, the former representing the boundary of union tolerance and the latter the boundary of public tolerance.

The lower limit—"the tightest formula which could survive more than very temporarily"—is one that gears wage increases to increases in the cost of living. Unions will not be satisfied with less, but even here there is some flexibility allowed to the board by its discretion in naming the base date and determining the length of the lag before successive adjustments can be made. The upper limit is one that permits wage increases in line with what would have been expected under normal peacetime conditions. It would provide offsets to increased cost of living, adjustments in line with rising productivity, correction of intraplant and interplant "inequities," continued improvement of nonwage employee benefits such as pensions and health insurance, the elimination of substandard rates of pay, and continuation of individual merit increases. Kerr recognizes that the question might be raised as to whether wage controls based on the upper-limit policy would in fact be controls. He answers that such a policy "would probably not reduce significantly or at all the key bargains in our economy," but it would "keep the non-key bargains in line with the normal pattern." This, he believes, would be an important contribution, since it is his understanding that during a wartime prosperity wages, if unrestrained, are likely to rise fastest in the nonessential industries, thus wiping out the differentials normally existing in favor of the construction and heavy goods industries, those very industries which must be expanded in time of crisis. If the wage program does no more than maintain the normal differentials which facilitate the recruiting of manpower into war industries, it accomplishes an important purpose. "Wage adjustments for the sake of manpower allocation would be largely unnecessary, for the customary wage structure [which the wage board's upper-limit policy preserves] has already made them."

Given these upper and lower limits, what wage policy the board will actually pursue depends on which of three crisis stages the economy is in. These are the precrisis period, the crisis period, and the period of continuing crisis. The first is "the typical period of preparedness, of the garrison state, of the continuing 'cold war.' The percentage of the nation's capacity devoted to military ends is above the peacetime normal and there is likely to be mild inflationary pressure. But there is no war and no public sense of imminent threat." In this period Kerr believes that the wage board must adhere to the upper-limit policy. The key unions get what they would have won in any event, and the nonkey unions bear the brunt of restraint. Only through such a policy is it likely that strikes will be avoided, since the emergency situation is not so grave as to make a no-strike pledge strictly enforceable, particularly against the important unions. And at this stage such a policy is practicable, since the inflationary threat is sufficiently mild that the public will tolerate wage increases conforming to "normal" expectations. Stabilization is thus sacrificed in favor of industrial peace.

The advent of the crisis period requires an increase in military production sufficient to demand stricter control over the price level. At this point some over-all but probably informal political settlement is necessary involving the unions in a commitment to hold the wage line at some broadly defined level, conditional on effective price control. A no-strike pledge would be part of the settlement. On the strength of such a settlement, the wage board could move precipitously from the upper-limit to the lower-limit policy. Only cost-of-living adjustments would be authorized.

If the period of immediate crisis extends into a third period of a continuing crisis, the lower wage limit will prove untenable. "It would soon wear out under the impact of union challenges, employer violations and growing antagonism to controls." In this third period the board will be forced to retreat from one prepared position to the next, each weakening of controls encouraging some fresh assault upon them. In time the board would have to be satisfied with a return to the upper limit. The cycle of direct controls would have run its course. Strong unions would be granted what they would have won anyway, and the board would have to be content to restrain only the nonkey bargains involving nonmilitary production. Any effective dampening of inflationary pressures would have to be left to the monetary and fiscal authorities.

These "realistic reflections of a battle-scarred policy maker"[25] accord to direct wage controls a relatively minor role in wartime anti-inflation policy, based on a belief that the unions' striking power will make wage stabilization difficult. Except for the brief period of the onset of the crisis, Kerr believes the battle against rising prices must be fought out along monetary and fiscal lines—those very weapons of control which, as we have seen, have been urged as the chief restraint on unions' inflationary pressures in a peacetime full employment economy. It may be doubted, however, if this is a practicable alternative. For, as we have seen, such indirect controls are effective only if unemployment is allowed to develop in consequence of union-bargained, out-of-line wage increases. It is unimagineable, however, that a government in crisis would consent to policies leading to loss of production when production was so vital. Monetary policy would unquestionably be eased as necessary to accommodate the rising price level. And since any wage increases which strong unions demanded would be approved by the wage board as the price of forestalling strikes, the inflationary circle would be complete.

There are other reasons for believing that, if Kerr is right in his analysis, the function of direct wage controls will be largely negated. The lower limit which he believes to be "the tightest formula which could survive more than very temporarily" may prove to be impossibly high, for there is some ground for believing that unions tend to interpret "cost of living" as "standard of living" and ask—as a minimum—a wage policy which preserves the latter. Yet it is evident that in time of war the consumption standards of *all* must decline to permit the syphoning off of perhaps half of national output into the channels of war. If strong unions are to be left free to win what they can—with wage board approval—the

[25]The phrase is Richard Lester's, whose comments follow Kerr's paper in the *American Economic Review; Proceedings,* p. 401.

result may be to weaken the Government's anti-inflationary tax weapon. For taxes which reduce consumption could be made the basis for higher wage demands to maintain consumption levels! It is perhaps too early to tell how significant is the demand of several of the largest and strongest national unions (when after Korea the Wage Stabilization Board felt its way to a cost-of-living formula) that income taxes be included in the price index on which that formula was based. As for the significance of Kerr's upper-limit wage policy, Lester has commented, with good reason: "The contention that wage controls have been and will be necessary especially to prevent wage increases by small and unorganized employers in less essential lines of production, I believe to be incorrect," and, moreover, "strikes can be permitted to occur there" with less disruption to the military program. Yet it is this restraint on the less essential lines that is the only power the wage board would possess except for the brief crisis period, if Kerr's analysis is well founded.

One can only conclude that the unions' power of striking is a threat to any program of direct wage controls, but if stabilization policy must be sacrificed to obtain industrial peace to the extent that Kerr foresees, then the prospects for restraining wartime inflationary pressures are glum indeed. It is undoubtedly true that the length of time for which effective direct controls can be maintained is short, but unless it is longer than Kerr anticipates, and unless the lower limit is based on a frank recognition that, however wages are tied to the cost of living, the standard of living of workers temporarily must suffer, it would appear that the Federal Conciliation Service would be about as effective as an emergency wage board.

The Korean war offers little real evidence on this matter. That war was not interpreted as a national crisis. Rather, it represents the precrisis state, to use Kerr's terminology, and while the effectiveness of controls was rather quickly undermined, the same could be said for price controls. The fact is that many economists believed that the continuation of controls was scarcely necessary after the initial impact of the military build-up.

It may be added that in some quarters the fear has been expressed that the "realism" represented by Kerr's analysis is in effect an unconditional surrender to the unions, that the acceptance of their need for "something to take back to the membership" (the political pressure on wage decisions) has gone too far. Perhaps the most persuasive spokesman for this point of view is Clarence F. Randall, president of the Inland Steel Company, whose *Creed for Free Enterprise* was published after the controversial 1952 Steel decision of the Wage Stabilization Board. Randall argues that most of those who have been designated to represent the public on labor boards (a goodly number over the war and postwar years) have been persuaded by union propagandists that concession is the only path to "political stability" in the labor movement, without which a production drive would be badly crippled. Those of his belief are convinced that a more vigorous control policy is enforceable, if public members can be found who will stand up to the unions.

The Subject Matter of Collective Bargaining

Let us turn from issues of national policy concerning collective bargaining to consider briefly some of the subjects which are covered by collective agreements in the United States. The scope is wide, including a considerable variety of provisions concerning such matters as the following, in addition to wages: apprenticeship, assignment to tasks, job transfers, layoffs, discipline, promotions, job classification and evaluation, incentive systems, merit rating, hours, overtime provisions, equalization of work opportunities, special payments for employees called in but for whom work is not available, employment guarantees ranging from so many hours per day to so many hours in the year, rest periods, holidays, vacations, sick leave, group insurance, severance pay, pensions, safety provisions, job content, numbers of men to be assigned to specific operations, standards and rates of operation, and other matters varying from agreement to agreement. It should be stressed that these are matters covered by the negotiated contract and, for the most part, have no connection with either state or federal legislation. Provisions on the above matters are hammered out between union and management independently, in each bargaining unit. While similarities exist from agreement to agreement, the clause is usually tailored to the specific needs of the unit and conditioned by the relative bargaining strengths of the specific participants.

The wide range of subjects concerning which labor unions have insisted on having something to say has led many management people to raise the question, where will it end? To this question there is no answer. It seems evident that the unions will ask for provisions on any matter which they conceive to affect their members significantly, and depending on their bargaining strength they may be successful in their demands. There is no planned move on foot by union leaders to encroach on management's exercise of authority. Most union leaders deny—undoubtedly in all honesty—any interest in sharing in management. Few unionists in the United States have shown public interest in the German experiment in codetermination and in experiments of a similar nature being tried elsewhere. Yet whenever the interests of the membership seem to dictate union concern with some matter previously left to management discretion, there is no question but that that issue will be brought into the bargaining conference. Union participation in a wider sphere of business management can be confidently expected in the future, not as a result of ideological drive but purely as a response to the immediate needs of the membership.

One indication of the significance to both employees and employers of this scope of coverage of the collective agreement has been the increasing proportion of payroll costs which are accounted for by nonwage labor costs. The United States Chamber of Commerce has made biennial computations of the cost of such items, which include pensions, unemployment compensation, paid rest periods, travel time allowances, educational payments, accident and medical-care insurance, vacations, holidays, lost time for such purposes as voting, jury duty, family illness or death, and special bonuses such as at Christmas or on the occasion of profit-sharing distributions. The Chamber's figures show that such "fringe benefits" have risen from 15.2 percent of payroll in 1947 to 20.2 percent in 1953 (of which only slightly more than 3 percent represents payments which are governmentally required, the remainder being various obligations for the most part incurred under the collective agreement). In money terms, such allowances represent an outlay which has increased from $422 per employee per year in 1947 to $817 in 1953.

The Grievance Procedure

Since no agreement is self-enforcing, collective agreements in the United States almost invariably provide for special interpretation and enforcement machinery which is established and operated by the parties themselves. This machinery is commonly known as the "grievance procedure." Most union and many management leaders agree that the grievance procedure is the "heart" of the agreement.

The procedure involves a series of committees to whom may be taken for decision a complaint that the agreement is being unfairly administered. Such a complaint may be made by any individual or group of individuals. The number of appeal stages varies from perhaps three to seven. A "typical" procedure would call for discussion between the following, as an unsettled grievance progresses through the several appeals stages: (1) the aggrieved individual and his foreman, with the elected shop representative present; (2) the general foreman and a general grievance committee or committeeman; (3) the personnel manager and the local union president; (4) a representative of top management and a representative of the national union. Unsatisfactory disposition of the case at any of these stages can be made the basis for an appeal to the next higher stage.

Within the last decade there has come to be almost universal acceptance of the right of the union to appeal a grievance beyond the final committee stage to an umpire or arbitrator, designated and compensated by union and management jointly, whose decision is accepted as final and binding on both parties. In most instances the arbitrator is chosen as the occasion requires, but in large bargaining units, where the number of grievances is often great, permanent umpires are frequently appointed.

In addition to questions involving the interpretation or application of the agreement, questions concerning discipline are also channeled through the grievance procedure. Typical issues that might be raised are whether an alleged act of insubordination constituted adequate cause for discharge; whether a penalty of a month's suspension was excessive for repeatedly leaving early at the end of the work day; whether the evidence justified a disciplinary penalty which would admittedly be appropriate if guilt was established. Typical nondisciplinary cases arising in the grievance procedure are whether the job assignment warrants reclassifying an individual to a higher-paying classification; whether a senior employee was laid off while one with lesser seniority was retained; whether management had adequately established that an individual had superior ability over another with greater seniority, justifying the promotion of the former instead of the latter; whether employees who reported to work but found no work available should be given the "call-in" pay of four hours, even though management could not have foreseen the "emergency" that made operation impossible, and so on, for an amazing variety of possible situations. As the scope of the subject matter of the collective agreement expands, the possible issues that may be brought up in the grievance procedure necessarily increase too.

The rationale behind the grievance procedure is that the guarantee to employees of full consideration of complaints of injustice (including the possibility of decision by an impartial third party, the umpire) eliminates any justification for direct union action to secure redress of wrongs. As a consequence, the establishment of a grievance procedure culminating in arbitration is almost invariably considered a sufficient basis for the union's committing itself to a no-strike pledge for the life of the agreement. While strikes do sometimes occur in violation of such a pledge ("wildcat" strikes), they are seldom premeditated and constitute that sort of violation of "law" which can be expected in some degree in even the most law-abiding communities.

The grievance procedure constitutes the primary means by which large numbers of workers can directly participate in the official functioning of the union and through which they directly share in the administration of the business. No count of the number of grievance representatives has ever been made or is likely to be made, but a safe estimate would probably be upwards of half a million. For these individuals their function in the grievance procedure gives them an opportunity to serve their fellow workers, to accept responsibility, to acquire greater prestige, to take the first step up the ladder of union advancement. It has often been suggested that vertical mobility has been decreasing in American society, that foremen are increasingly taken from the ranks of college graduates, barring others from advancement, and that in any event promotion for most workers stops at the level of foremen. Even should these instances of diminishing upward mobility be generally true, it seems abundantly evident that through the union and the grievance procedure large numbers of workers have opened up for themselves new ladders to climb, leading for some to high union office and positions of authority and responsibility in the community and the nation.

It is often said that the grievance procedure is the most successful aspect of collective bargaining in the United States.

"Human Relations in Industry"

A few words should be said about the increasing interest which management people are displaying in the research findings of sociologists and psychologists in a field which has come to be known as human relations in industry. Social scientists in the leading universities have been conducting rather extensive investigations into such problems as what makes for effective communication between management and worker, what leads to good or poor morale in a work situation, what causes employees to respond to union organizing drives, which factors lead to conflict and which to cooperation in industrial situations—in short, why do people behave as they do. Not only have businesses supported such research; some have been genuinely interested in the possibilities of testing the tentative conclusions so far advanced.

Unions have not been wholeheartedly enthusiastic about this development. They have believed—with some justification—that the findings of the social scientists have been viewed by at least a segment of management as a possible alternative to the union. It has been true that some—obviously an unknown number—of the leaders of industry have, since Elton Mayo's time at the Harvard Business School, tended to view unions as the punishment management has had to suffer for its own sins of omission and commission. If management will, however, try to understand what is on the worker's mind and learn how to influence worker attitudes through an awareness of the techniques of "communication," then management will be able to satisfy worker desires and the unions will wither away as superfluous.

It is probably fair to say, however, that this particular approach to the study of human relations in industry has been on the wane and that the greatly growing interest in this field stems from a desire to learn how best to get along with the unions. Labor leaders remain skeptical, but there is probably less ground than formerly existed for their skepticism.

Conclusion

One topic which has received attention in the human relations investigations mentioned above has been: Why do workers join unions? A union spokesman once rather heatedly remarked to a gathering of research workers that the more interesting and significant question was why some workers did *not* join unions, since it could be presumed that unionism was more "normal" than nonunionism. There is much to be said for this point of view. In the American political ideology, control by the constituency over its own affairs, through representative institutions, occupies central importance. Collective bargaining, with union representation of workers, represents the fulfillment in industry of this aspect of the American creed.

One fear which is being widely expressed is that the unions are now taking back what they have given to American workers, that the centralization of authority in the hands of national union officers and the growth of pattern bargaining increasingly tend to withdraw from the local collective bargaining unit authority over its own affairs. There is more and more talk of "power centers" and "key bargains," and of "satellites" and "pattern followers."

There is solid ground for such fears, despite the partial rejoinder that some matters can only be controlled at higher levels of authority (as perhaps war, on the international scene) and that delegation of authority to representatives in such matters involves an extension rather than a contraction of control over one's own affairs (since previously such matters were entirely beyond parochial control anyway). The basis for the danger is that centralized authority can extend its aegis over matters which are quite within the competence of local representatives: the industry pattern can be applied with excessive rigidity and in unnecessary detail to local settlements; the multiemployer bargain can determine matters which could well be left to individual employer and the union committee.

Perhaps the greatest strength of the American labor movement, however, lies in the development—largely through the grievance procedure—of effective local worker organization trained to make decisions and effect settlements with their own employer. There is some basis here for believing that if centralization of bargaining authority proceeds too far it will develop—has in fact already developed in some quarters—its own corrective in covert accommodation at the local level and, paradoxically, without necessarily weakening the ties between local and national representatives.

The structure of American industry guarantees that fragmented bargaining units would not be workable, but the ideology of self-control implemented by the training ground of the grievance procedure appears to offer some assurance that centralization of union authority will be contained within limits. It remains to be seen, however, how much this underlying tenacity of local autonomy will control the impersonal price relationship, the wage bargain, as it has the more intimate social relationships of the work environment.

IX

An Essay on Comparative Collective Bargaining

ADOLF STURMTHAL

NO ATTEMPT will be made in the pages that follow to present a systematic all-inclusive comparison of collective bargaining in the countries considered in this volume. A systematic comparison of collective agreements themselves was made, prior to World War II, in a well-known volume of the International Labor Office, entitled *Collective Agreements*.[1] In this volume, the main clauses of collective agreements were compared and the place of collective agreements in the various economic systems was examined for a large number of countries.

The purpose of this essay is far more modest. It deals with a small number of issues which during the decade since World War II appeared particularly significant, mainly because they were widely discussed. An attempt will be made to see whether international experience has anything to contribute to the analysis of these problems. The intention is less to produce answers than to give some hints for the direction of future fruitful research.

The main topics examined are: the importance of collective bar-

[1] I.L.O., *Studies and Reports, Series A* (Industrial Relations) No. 39 (Geneva, 1936). Professor J. M. Richardson, then at the University of Leeds, played a large part in preparing this volume.

gaining as a method of determining wages and working conditions; the "extension" of collective agreements; the wage structure that emerged out of collective bargaining in the postwar period; and, finally, wage policy under full employment conditions. The discussion of these topics proceeds as follows:

I. The issue of the importance of collective bargaining is examined first from a quantitative point of view. When this is seen to be unsatisfactory, considerations on qualitative differences in collective bargaining from country to country are presented. Such qualitative differences come under various headings: (1) there may be limitations of the scope of collective bargaining, e.g., some industries are excluded from collective bargaining; (2) the law may limit the content of the bargain, e.g., by setting a minimum wage or in other ways; (3) the significance of the agreement may vary from country to country by greater or smaller degrees of observance of the agreement; (4) the forms and degrees of government intervention in the process of bargaining may vary (this topic is discussed under three headings: long-run "normal" government intervention, nationalization and bargaining, "social wages," i.e., compensation fixed outside of the bargaining process); (5) long-run trends in the significance of collective bargaining.

No general and precise conclusion with regard to the relative importance of collective bargaining in the different countries is presented. Instead, I shall suggest that the nature of the agreement itself varies by a greater or lesser emphasis on the desirability of "order" in the agreement. This concept is related to that of centralization, to the institution of "extension" of agreements, the significance and methods of grievance handling, and to the principle of "order" in the wage structure of which job evaluation is an instrument. Some of these, particularly the institution of "extension" of agreements, are discussed at some length.

II. The second group of topics discussed is the wage structure. Four main types of differentials are examined: skill, interindustry, sex, and regional wage differentials. In every case attempts are made to discuss and compare not only the current levels of these differentials, but also their changes over time so as to obtain insights into the dynamics of the wage structure.

The over-all problem of a "rational" wage structure is then briefly examined, particularly from the point of view of the influence of full employment. This leads to a study of the next major group of problems, the influence of collective bargaining on wage levels.

III. Unions aim at a higher degree of uniformity in wages. Two ways of achieving this are outlined—a more static and a more dynamic method. Different unions seem to emphasize one or the other, the main reason for their choice being the degree of their concern with the employment effects of their bargain.

This leads to a discussion of the relationship between collective bargaining and changes in wage levels. Under this heading comes the widely discussed issue of union wage policy and full employment, i.e., whether full employment and price stability are incompatible. Within the limits of the nature of the available evidence, our examination shows the relationship between stable relative and stable absolute wages as well as the distinction between short-run and long-run solutions of the problem. Some comments follow on the difficulties of transferring appropriate anti-inflationary policies from one country to another.

The Importance of Collective Bargaining

One of the first questions which presents itself to a student of comparative collective bargaining is that of the relative importance of this particular method of determining wages and working conditions. Significant as it may be, this question is impossible to answer in any precise way.

For some of the countries whose collective bargaining systems are examined in this book, statistics exist that indicate the number of workers whose wages and working conditions are set by collective agreements. It is, of course, possible to establish the proportions between this number and the total labor force; in this way we might proceed to rank the different countries in a sequence that might be described as the order of importance of collective bargaining.

Unfortunately, this method would soon run into insuperable difficulties and its results would conceal rather than reveal some of the most fundamental issues as to the importance of collective bargaining. The most obvious difficulty we would encounter is that of determining the size of the labor force which is to be the denominator of the proportion we are trying to establish. What we have in mind is not a statistical problem, serious as it often is, of correctly computing the number, but rather the conceptual problem of the groups to be included in the term. The simplest issue is that of the agricultural laborer. In some of the countries considered—and in some not included in this study—collective bargaining is finding some application in agricultural activities or related industries; in other countries it does not. This, however, is still a manageable problem. More difficult is the issue raised by the tendency existing in Italy to include sharecroppers and farmers on different lease arrangements (mezzadri) in the trade union organization and in a system of collective bargaining itself. Indeed, the federations of agricultural labor, "Confederazione della terra"—form the largest block within the CGIL, and the tenant farmers' organization which is a subfederation of the "confederterra" claims a membership only slightly less than the CGIL union in heavy industry (FIOM).[2]

Although this is in many ways a very significant development within the Italian labor movement, we shall disregard it in the comparative studies that follow. Even then we shall be confronted with a number of more or less difficult qualitative problems. For it is not always easy to decide where collective bargaining ends and other methods of wage determination begin.

1. In a number of countries, the scope of collective bargaining is restricted by special legislative arrangements for particular industries. Thus in Great Britain special arrangements have been made for the determination of wages and working conditions in "certain trades or industries where machinery for regulating the remuneration either does not exist or is not, and cannot be made, adequate for that purpose."[3] Under this heading come the Wages Councils, the arrangements under the Agricultural Wages Acts (1948, 1949),

[2]Confederazione della terra, however, has been described as "less effective" than the CGIL unions in the metal, textiles, and chemical industries, and on the railways. Cf. John Clarke Adams, "Italy" in *Comparative Labor Movements,* W. Galenson, ed. (New York: Prentice-Hall, 1952), p. 449.

[3]*Industrial Relations Handbook* (London, 1953), p. 144.

under the Road Haulage Wages Act (1938), and the Catering Wages Act of 1943. However, as Allan Flanders points out, the boundary between some of these procedures and collective bargaining is rather fluid. The Wages Councils themselves, for instance, engage in a process that is not fundamentally different from collective bargaining. As a result, Flanders, in estimating the quantitative significance of collective bargaining, lumps together the employees coming under collective agreements and those covered by the determination of Wages Councils and arrives at a total of about four fifths of all employees. In France, some of the nationalized industries are exempt from the collective bargaining law of 1950, in the sense that wages and working conditions are determined by a legislative instrument, a so-called "statute." Yet, a process similar to collective bargaining does occur in these industries, even though it does not follow the pattern or the rules of the general collective bargaining arrangements applicable to all other industries.

2. These regulations limit the scope of collective bargaining by restricting what might be called its geographic area in the industrial landscape. In other countries we find other limitations: legislation sets a floor under which collectively agreed wages and working conditions cannot descend. In particular, limitations of the hours of work by legislation (or legislation derived from an international convention) are widespread. A lower limit of wages is set by the United States Fair Labor Standards Act and the various state acts of the same kind.

3. A further complication is introduced by considerable differences among the countries discussed as to the function of collective agreements. In the United States, the agreement serves, on the whole, to determine the wages actually paid to the worker covered by the agreement and the working conditions that apply to him. This is not the case in Germany where the agreement performs the functions of the American Fair Labor Standards Act rather than those of the American agreement. In other words, the German collective agreement sets minima which may be, and often are, changed in favor of the workers by individual agreements between worker and employer or an individual agreement arrived at with

the assistance of the Works Council or, finally, by a plant agreement between Works Council and management. It is clear that in this case the collective agreement is of a different nature from that of the American agreement.

However, experience has shown that even in the United States or Great Britain in periods of labor shortage individual wage rates are often set above the level determined by the agreement. Similarly, cases of "overclassification" of workers occur, which, in effect, secure to the individual worker higher wage rates than those to which he would be entitled under the agreement. In Sweden, rates above those of the collective bargaining have become so frequent during the last two or three years that they have seriously threatened the wage policy pursued by the unions. In such cases, the agreement tends to function in much the same way as in Germany: it provides a floor below which individual arrangements cannot be made. However, in most countries this is an extraordinary situation, a result of acute labor shortages. The problem thus created is part of the wider issue of economic stability under conditions of full employment which will be discussed below. In Germany, on the other hand, such discrepancies between contractual and actual rates are the result of the normal play of the system of collective bargaining. Although it is possible to indicate for Germany how many workers are "covered" by collective agreements, it is exceedingly difficult to indicate those whose wages are actually set by such agreements.

The opposite problem exists in Italy where, as the reports of Professors Sanseverino and Vannutelli indicate, the rates set in the agreements may be above the effective rates. Direct understandings between management and worker have the legal power of abrogating the collective agreement not only in favor of the worker, as in most countries, but also by establishing less favorable wages and conditions. The collective agreement then serves often only as a starting point for negotiations.

4. A further basic difficulty is created by the qualitatively varying degrees of government intervention in the process of arriving at collective agreements. The postwar period has witnessed widely differing forms of such intervention, some of them inherited from

the period of actual warfare. On the whole, government influence upon the process of wage determination was at a height at the end of the war; it then tended to diminish until a revival set in during the great inflationary developments accompanying the conflict in Korea and the subsequent process of rearmament in the West; it has declined again since the end of the hostilities in the Far East. Some of the issues involved in these developments will be referred to below.[4]

Under the circumstances, it is impossible to make more than highly tentative comparisons of what might be regarded as the more or less long-run trends of the government functions in the making of collective agreements as distinguished from the process of contract administration in the countries considered. It is perhaps useful to group these remarks under three main headings: (A) the over-all functions of the Government in the making of collective agreements; (B) the issues presented by the nationalization of industries; and (C) determination outside bargaining.

A. Under the first heading Holland, France, and Norway might form one extreme on a scale; Great Britain and the United States the opposite pole. In the normal course of collective bargaining in Holland, the agreement arrived at by unions and employers' associations must be approved by a Government Mediation Board consisting "of a number of government-appointed experts who are entrusted with the task of determining wages and other conditions of employment both for entire industries and for individual establishments." This Board is bound to obtain the advice of the Labor Foundation or—in the future—of the Social and Economic Council. Since the Foundation and the Council consist of representatives of the central union and employers' federations—in addition to government representatives—collective agreements require two kinds of approval: those of the central associations of management and labor, and that of the Government. The latter's approval is thus a constitutive requirement of a collective agreement. Agreements are made by a process in which the Government plays a vital part.

The French legislation of 1950 does not require government ap-

[4]See pp. 320–321.

proval for all collective agreements—as prior legislation did—but only for those that are to be "extended."[5] The Government's functions in the case of ordinary collective negotiations are limited to the calling of the "joint commissions" which work out the agreements and to the setting of the "interprofessional minimum wage." Experience so far has, however, indicated that the latter function exerts considerable influence upon the entire process of wage determination; the wage structure, as such, follows the movements of the minimum wage rather closely.[6] A further device by which the Government influences the process of collective bargaining is the authorities' influence upon wages in the nationalized enterprises. This will be discussed below. The institutional arrangements of 1950 have followed in time upon a system of direct government control of wages. Compared with this, the regulations of 1950 represent a step toward reduced government influence upon wage determination; but with or without legal authorization, the Government still retains a large measure of influence. Moreover, legislation tends to influence the content of full collective agreements as distinguished from mere wage contracts.

Norway has chosen an entirely different method to make the public interest felt in the process of arriving at collective agreements. The first postwar regulation provided for all changes in wages and working conditions to be negotiated jointly by the central employers' association and the Federation of Trade Unions, together with the particular organizations involved. In the case of disagreement a Wages Board with preponderant government power made the decision. This was, in effect, an attempt to rely in the first place upon the good will, common sense, and the internal discipline of the two associations, buttressed by governmental power as a last resort. After a short period of a wage stop—thus opening the way to governmental control—Norway returned once again to a system placing main emphasis on the internal discipline of the two federations with compulsory arbitration for those "claims for changes in wages and working conditions not approved, or only partly approved, by the Federation of Trade

[5]Cf. p. 138.
[6]See p. 154.

Unions or the principal employers' association." On two occasions more direct government intervention has proven necessary. As a rule, however, government intervention is only subsidiary and serves principally to strengthen the internal discipline of the main federations.

At the other extreme is Great Britain. In principle the Government does not intervene at all in the collective bargaining process. Indeed, it does not even intervene to the extent to which it does in the United States—in order to establish a duty to bargain collectively or to determine the appropriate bargaining agents, except for the nationalized industries for whose boards the duty to bargain collectively and thereby to select the appropriate bargaining agents is established by law. Even at the height of the balance-of-payments crisis, the Government could only recommend the principles by which the advisability of wage changes should be judged; it could not impose them. The acceptance of the principles by the unions was voluntary and indeed, as Allan Flanders' report shows, never complete. Compulsory arbitration was used during the war and beyond it, as long as the unions and the employers agreed with it. As soon as this approval was withdrawn, compulsion was dropped. Even while it was used, it served as a last resort, rather than as a substitute for the contractually arranged or customary bargaining machinery. As compared with the United States—with its NLRB and the wage controls of the Korean crisis—British collective bargaining represents a still purer form of voluntarism and free contract.

It is difficult to fit German collective bargaining into the scale that we have set up. In principle, when collective bargaining was re-established after World War II, it was to be free bargaining, less subject to government intervention than in the later years of the Weimar Republic. In 1930, as Professor Kerr quotes from Woytinsky,[7] "over 40 percent of all wage agreements, involving 70 percent of all workers, were concluded by arbitration, and mostly by compulsory government boards." Compulsion has been dropped and the German unions state that "the determination of wages, salaries,

[7] See p. 194.

and working conditions must be exclusively reserved for collective bargaining." Yet, though arbitration is now voluntary, it is "steadily increasing in importance" and it is "lodged almost exclusively in governmental hands." This is arbitration to determine change in contracts, not to interpret existing agreements. In fact, this process may be more correctly described as government mediation combined with a good deal of government pressure in favor of acceptance of government-sponsored terms.

The particular issues raised by the process of "extension" of agreements will be discussed below in greater detail. At this point it is sufficient to refer to this process by which contract terms are made universally applicable and are given the (juridical) status of a law. The power to do so is almost everywhere reserved to the Government or some body representing the Government. To the extent to which the participants in collective bargaining regard such "extension" as desirable, the Government, having the power to "extend" or not to "extend," acquires influence upon the content of the agreement. Extension is of significance in Germany, France, and Holland among the countries studied.

B. Has nationalization of industry given the Government additional responsibilities in the determination of wages and working conditions? This question refers mainly to Great Britain and France where the years after World War II have witnessed a considerable expansion of nationalized industry.

Basically the answer is that nationalization has not introduced anything entirely new into the process of wage determination, but has rather strengthened existing underlying trends. Thus, in British nationalized industry collective bargaining proceeds essentially the same way as if industry were privately owned, except, as previously noted, that the obligation to bargain collectively is set for the boards in the nationalization laws. In France, on the other hand, the nationalized enterprises have been divided into two groups: those whose wages and working conditions are determined by law, and those subject to the same collective bargaining procedures as privately owned industry. In fact, government influence has been significant in both groups. Wage determination thus reflects to a considerable extent the difference of attitude in the two countries toward government intervention in industrial relations.[8]

It is probably true, however, that in both countries nationalization has strengthened the role of the Government in industrial relations. Wage changes in nationalized industry tend to set patterns for collective bargaining in general and thus take on a significance beyond the particular wage bargain concerned. It follows that the Government is likely to show greater than normal concern for the outcome of collective bargaining in nationalized enterprises. The fear of the government employees in Great Britain "that they were being singled out for discriminatory treatment"—as Mr. Flanders reports — is evidence at least of expected government efforts to set examples. The progress of nationalization is, therefore, accompanied by increasing public intervention in wage determination. But it is by no means certain that all of this is the result of nationalization; it is at least conceivable that public interest in these wage bargains would have been rendered inevitable in any case by full employment. In the absence of full employment the wage bargains of nationalized enterprises may well lose *some* of their special significance. Yet, in the case of France, government intervention in nationalized industry as far as the result of bargaining is concerned, if not in the bargaining process itself, is required by the system itself. And in Britain, nationalization—in the words of Phelps Brown and Roberts, quoted by Flanders—has "probably made the government figure more explicitly in the public esteem as the final court of appeal for wage claims in the basic industries."

C. A further public influence on wage determination which restricts the importance of collective bargaining is represented by what may be called "social wages" or "indirect earnings." A portion of the worker's earnings is independent of his effort (and often of his skill). This part may be determined by collective bargaining—as in the pension arrangements in American industry—or, more frequently, be paid according to rules determined by legislation. It is this latter case that we are referring to. Some of the reports contain interesting information on this item of the workers' earnings.

[8]Other effects of nationalization on collective bargaining, such as its extension to nonmanual workers, have been noted by Mr. Flanders, p. 17.

"Indirect wages" in France consist primarily of family allowances, but also some lesser supplements, such as the Parisian transport bonus and some fringe benefits. As the report on France points out, "somewhat less than one third of the gross payroll was taken up by social charges in 1950." The distribution of this third among the workers is highly uneven. The main item—family allowances—depends upon the size of the family and the age of the children rather than earnings. The proportion between direct and indirect wages varies accordingly with family status, but not infrequently do indirect wages represent more than half of the workers' gross earnings; in other words, indirect wages may exceed direct wages. Altogether, the social benefits of the nonagricultural worker have been estimated at more than 40 percent of their earnings net of taxes.

For Italy, some indications may be derived from the proportion of total labor cost represented by "social charges" as given in Table 3 of Professor Vannutelli's article on "Wage Structure and Cost of Labor in Italy." In the case of the skilled male worker in the engineering industry in Milan, social charges form some 26 percent of the gross pay roll. This proportion is somewhat higher for women workers and higher in Naples as compared with Milan. The inference is permitted that "indirect wages" must represent a sizeable proportion of total direct earnings in at least some cases.

For the United States, Professor Chamberlain quotes an estimate which sets nonwage payments at some 16 percent of the total pay roll. This figure is not fully comparable with those given for France and Italy. The United States figure consists only to a small part of legally required payments; the remainder includes contractually determined payments and some voluntary payments. The French and Italian figures, however, comprise mainly, if not exclusively, the charges required by law; contractual charges may have to be added. Yet, even without those, it is obvious that in France and Italy the existence of indirect wages greatly reduces the significance of the direct wages set by collective agreements.

5. The reports published in this volume seem to agree that collective bargaining has progressed as compared with the method of wage determination by management or government. This proposi-

tion holds true in the first place with regard to the postwar era itself: the often considerable restrictions on collective bargaining during the war and in the first postwar years have been relaxed or altogether abolished. Government setting of wages has all but disappeared. Holland is the only exception to this widespread trend which is most pronounced in France, Germany, and Italy.

Collective bargaining has, furthermore, made considerable progress as compared with the prewar situation. With the re-establishment of free trade unions in Germany and Italy, collective bargaining has returned to these countries. In France, some progress in collective bargaining seems to have been made as compared with the years immediately preceding the outbreak of World War II when most collective agreements once concluded were simply renewed by legislative action.[9] This tended to give the agreements "the character of state-imposed regulation." Needless to say, the long-run advance of collective bargaining over the last half century in all the countries considered is overwhelming. Moreover, even in industries in which collective bargaining has not been established,[10] the possibility of unionization exerts frequently some influence upon wages and working conditions and "sympathetic pressure" is exerted in some way by wages and working conditions determined in collective agreements.

The advance of collective bargaining has been most pronounced by contrast with wage determination by management. Not quite so clear is the long-run picture with regard to government influence upon wages and working conditions. In the short run, say during the decade 1945–1955, government's role has clearly diminished, even if the Korean crisis brought on a temporary increase of government intervention. In those countries—Germany, Italy—which had been subject to totalitarian dictatorships prior to World War II, the trend toward self-government in industry is of still older date. Yet there seems to exist a long-run trend toward new, and perhaps more subtle, public influence on wages and working conditions.

[9]Cf. Henry W. Ehrmann, *French Labor; from Popular Front to Liberation* (New York: Oxford University Press, 1947), pp. 45–46, and n. 20, p. 291. The following quotation is from p. 46.

[10]One is inclined to say, "not yet been established."

Seen over the last three or four decades public concern with industrial relations has undoubtedly increased, and the main expression of this growing concern has been government influence upon the process of wage determination or its results. A part of this development may be ascribed to full employment, but beyond this perhaps temporary element there remains what appears to be a long-term trend of growing public influence upon the wage bargain.

The progress of collective bargaining itself may occasionally be the vehicle by which governmental influence enters into wage determination. Such is the case in Norway or in Holland where the Government appears as a third party in the negotiations. More often government pressure has paved the way for collective bargaining, as in Germany after 1918, in England as Mr. Flanders' reports, or in the United States under the "New Deal." One is tempted to think of a four-phase history of wage determination, beginning with a mercantilistic stage of government wage setting, passing on to a phase of wage setting by employers, then to another phase of relatively "free"—i.e., free of governmental influence—collective bargaining, usually limited to a small number of trades, followed by a stage in which the Government participates as a third partner at the bargaining table. This is, of course, a tremendous oversimplification of a process in which all kinds of crosscurrents, "setbacks," and overlaps have occurred. Yet some elements of truth and insight might be found in this presentation, provided one does not expect more from it than from most historical sequences, namely, general themes with many important variations.

This suggested sequence does not confirm the prediction made by the Webbs: "The Trade Unionists, having obtained the vote, now wish to make use of it to enforce, by Legal Enactment, such of their Common Rules as they see a chance of getting public opinion to support."[11] As Allan Flanders points out, the development in England did not simply lead from collective bargaining to law; indeed, in his words "as the trade unions became strong enough to regulate wages and working conditions by direct

[11]Sidney and Beatrice Webb, *Industrial Democracy* (London: Longmans, Green, 1920), p. 538.

negotiation, they preferred to dispense with government assistance." However, Mr. Flanders then continues: "The part played by legislation and government action in bringing about the extension of trade unionism and collective bargaining to those workers who were unable to establish permanent organizations on their own account throughout the nineteenth century is not always appreciated."[12] In other words, evolution does not seem to lead from collective bargaining to law, but what seems to be evolving at present in the countries considered is a system in which three partners— employer, union, government—operate, with changing relationships of strength among them.

The traditional opposition of "collective bargaining versus legal enactment" thus loses most of its significance. Instead of an either-or, the countries discussed in this volume appear to be evolving various combinations of the two elements. The mixtures differ not only from country to country, but also among different industries of the same country and, of course, among different times as well. And in many cases, the mixture is a synthesis, such as to make difficult, if not impossible, a quantitative statement about the elements that went into the making of the final product. An example of this is the French combination of collective bargaining with government-determined minimum wages—whose changes have tended to alter the entire wage structure according to principles set down in collective agreements—plus family allowances and other supplements determined by law and the influence of government-set wages in nationalized industry which are subject to some forms of what amounts to collective bargaining. To assign numerical expressions of relative influence to each of these elements that make up this highly simplified picture of French determination of wages and working conditions is, I submit, a task beyond our present means of analysis. Even for Britain, we learn that while "the difference in law between voluntary and statutory bodies is clear enough . . . there are no industrial demarcation lines separating the voluntary and statutory parts of the system."[13] In the same industry we find different mixtures of the basic elements.

[12]This was not simply negative assistance that removed hindrances to collective bargaining, but active promotion.

[13]See p. 24. This idea is further elaborated in that report.

In the light of the above, the traditional opposition between law and contract may not be the most significant way of analyzing the processes by which wages and working conditions are determined. Instead of being opposites, these two methods are capable of forming combinations in various ways and have done so in the countries considered. In other words, law and collective bargaining are no longer "pure"—they have had their impact upon each other. A more fundamental classification would distinguish between group and individual decision-making, in a number of different frameworks and compulsions. According to our own experience, we tend to analyze the various forms of group decision-making in terms of either the bargain or the law, but this view carries with it the danger of overemphasizing a secondary distinction to the neglect of more fundamental issues.

"Order" in Collective Bargaining

If the issue of law versus bargain appears to be of secondary importance, it does not follow that there is no interesting distinction to be made among the countries studied in this volume, with regard to the process of wage determination.

The grouping mentioned above—Great Britain and the United States, on the one hand, the remainder on the other—seems to reflect some real differences. Even though both groups represent mixtures of collective bargaining with other elements in proportions that are impossible to analyze, there are some fairly distinct differences between the two groups. The decisive characteristic, however, is not the role of government, but the degree of "order" in the collective bargaining process and even more in its results. Government intervention may be significant in this respect, but mainly because it serves to bring about "order." It is the latter concept which requires analysis.

a. "Order" tends to go hand in hand with centralization, absence of "order" with decentralization. The more centralized the collective bargaining process is, the clearer and simpler are the procedure and the results. Highly centralized collective bargaining almost inevitably calls forth some form of public intervention. In the extreme case, a fully centralized wage bargain in a full employment economy committed to maintain full employment at all times, collective bargaining sets not only wages, but also prices and foreign exchange rates. Public intervention thus becomes the more likely, the larger the segment of the economy is for which a uniform bargain is arranged. But in some ways this is just a by-product of a drive for centralized bargains.

In Norway, Holland, Italy, in Germany—as a result of simple union structure, internal discipline of unions and management organizations, and of area-wide bargaining—in France—partly because local agreements are rare—the emphasis is on the general rule and on the central agencies, both on the union and on the management side. The collective agreement has some of the characteristics of the law in its uniformity and in the reliance on central authority for its administration. Quite different is the spirit of sectional bargaining in Great Britain and the United States. True, there is undoubtedly a tendency toward "the centralization of authority in the hands of national union officers" and the fear has been expressed that "the growth of pattern bargaining increasingly tends to withdraw from the local collective bargain unit authority over its own affairs."[14] Similarly, a trend toward centralization is discernible in Britain. Yet, in both countries there are strong elements that tend to maintain diversity and with it a measure of decentralization quite different from the relative simplicity of the carefully planned structure of, say, Holland. In the words of Allan Flanders, the British system

> has grown into a fairly complete system for regulating the wages and working conditions of the vast majority of employees, upheld by an intricate combination of economic, social, and legal sanctions. To anyone with a passion for uniformity it is a system which must appear most unsystematic. Nevertheless, it has the qualities of its defects. . . .[15]

More clearly still, this idea is expressed in Professor Chamberlain's report on the United States:

> Perhaps the greatest strength of the American labor movement . . . lies in the development . . . of effective local worker organiza-

[14]See p. 306.
[15]See p. 37.

tion trained to make decisions and effect settlements with their own employer. There is some basis here for believing that if centralization of bargaining authority proceeds too far, it will develop—has in fact already developed in some quarters—its own corrective in covert accommodation at the local level and, paradoxically, without necessarily weakening the ties between local and national representatives.[16]

b. In a number of countries one of the most significant expressions of this trend toward uniformity and of the desire to give the character of law to the settlement of wages and working conditions is the "extension" of collective agreements discussed in more detail below.

c. As Neil Chamberlain points out, it is "largely through the grievance procedure" that the local labor organization is kept at a high level of vitality. Grievance handling is in a very important sense a part of collective bargaining, but one that requires a good deal of decentralization to be effective. In the United States it is regarded as the "heart of the agreement" and the most successful aspect of collective bargaining. The British unions, by refusing to accept arbitration for the settlement of issues arising out of the interpretation of contracts, place a good deal of weight upon local understandings. The fact that most of these are informal and that local practice rather than formal agreement is frequently appealed to strengthens rather than weakens the decentralized nature of this process. It is perhaps fair to say, however, that the direct involvement of the union in these processes is considerably less than in the United States.

The tendency to leave this part of collective bargaining to some kind of semijudicial procedure is quite pronounced in many countries of the Continent. Thus the Labor Courts in Germany and similar institutions elsewhere exist apart from the union itself. Indeed, in most Continental countries the union has no organization which could deal effectively with plant problems. The organizations actively concerned with such problems have an independent existence. In this way collective bargaining retains its full uniformity and the character of a law.

[16]See p. 307.

d. The desire for a clear and simple order in industrial relations as settled by collective agreements finds its expression in the character of the wage structure as well. In a number of reports references occur to the "orderly" or "formalized" character of the wage structure. This applies to the Dutch, the German, the Italian wage structures. British wage differentials, on the other hand, as well as the prewar Dutch wage structure have been described as "chaotic." Attempts to make it more rational have been made in England, but without too much success, except—significantly—for the nationalized coal industry.

The outstanding role ascribed to job evaluation in Dutch collective bargaining as a means of bringing order into the "chaotic" wage structure is indicative of the desire for order. In other countries a good deal of doubt exists whether it is possible scientifically to determine the relative standing of jobs with regard to the wage rates to which they are "entitled" according to any objective classification; doubt is also expressed as to whether assuming this were possible, it would be desirable, and whether a system of wage setting can effectively function, if it is based upon job evaluation alone. As to the scientific nature of job evaluation, critics refer to the large part played in it of necessity by the judgment of the "evaluator" as well as to the—at most—ordinal nature of any numerical ranking (i.e., it might be possible to rank jobs according to difficulty, responsibility, danger, and the like, but is it possible to say that one job is twice as difficult as another, or 1.75 times as difficult, etc.?). Is it not inevitable that market pricing of jobs supplements job evaluation, and that in the case of serious conflict between the two, job evaluation will have to take second place?

Assuming that all these problems could be solved, is there not an authoritarian element in job evaluation, the critics ask, even if the union participates in the process? Would it not be more democratic to let the workers themselves decide, by their readiness to accept jobs under the conditions offered, whether wage relationships are fair, considering all the circumstances? This is closely connected with the third point, namely, the need for relative wages to express changes in relative supply and demand conditions and to serve thereby as guides for the adjustment of the labor supply in a dynamic, nonauthoritarian economy.

This implies that a certain degree of "disorder" may very well be essential for smoother adjustments in a changing economy. Some further comments on this point will be made below.

Centralization, "extension" by way of administrative decision, third party-grievance procedures without the full participation of the union, an "orderly" wage structure—all tend to give the collective agreement the character of a law, uniform and static. Decentralization, "extension" by way of unionization and separate contract, grievance procedures involving continued but local bargaining processes, a "chaotic" wage structure—tend to emphasize the contractual, passing, dynamic nature of the arrangements. Yet, this contrast, significant as it is, should not be overstated. True, the "static" approach of the first type of bargaining may do violence to the dynamic nature of the economic process. But any contractual arrangement must interfere with the continually altered market requirements of a growing and changing economy. It is of the essence of a union that it holds up considerations of fairness, health, security, etc., as against the requirements of the market, of efficiency and of profit maximization. The two types of collective agreements with their many subgroups and their shifting characteristics represent fundamentally only different kinds of compromises between these contradictory drives. It would lead far beyond the limits of this essay in comparative collective bargaining to attempt to suggest the possible causes of these different mixtures of similar elements.

The "Extension" of Collective Agreements

The term "extension" of collective agreements refers to the process by which a collective agreement is made applicable to employers and workers outside the ranks of the organizations that have signed the agreement. The "extension" procedure is, therefore, essentially a device to protect employers and unions which have signed an agreement against the competition of nonorganized firms and workers. Strictly speaking the "extension" of agreements is a substitute for—and conceivably a prelude to—the extension of the organization of employers and workers but it may also delay the growth of the organizations. The main argument for this procedure has been precisely the difficulty of making either organization 100 percent effective or even to approximate this stage of organization.

In principle a collective agreement is valid in the relations between the members of the contracting organizations. This implies that in a plant without perfectly complete unionization workers might be subject to two different kinds of wages and working conditions: those that were determined by the collective agreement and those individually arrived at. Since such a situation might threaten the employment of the organized workers and thus endanger the collective agreement, a number of devices have been used to "extend" the agreement to all workers of the plant or at least all those to whom the agreement could be reasonably made to apply. Among these devices are the closed shop or the union shop in which the problem cannot arise because all eligible workers are union members.[17] Another solution was represented by the Netherlands Collective Agreements Act of 1927 (Sec. 14) which provided that employers may undertake in the agreement to observe the agreement even for nonunion workers. A third solution is that of the United States where the bargaining agent selected by the majority of the workers acts in behalf of all the workers in the bargaining unit. In a sense this represents a form of "extension" of the agreement. This "extension," however, is limited to the plants of those employers with whom an agreement is concluded. No protection is given to the contracting partners against the competition of firms not subject to the agreement. It is this kind of protection which the "extension"—European style—is intended to provide. "Extension" in this sense means to make a collective agreement applicable to an entire industry or occupation within the territorial limits applicable to the agreement itself.

Though extension has been sometimes called a European device, its origin is outside of Europe. It can be traced back to New

[17]Attempts to introduce compulsory unionization, which is not precisely the same as a "closed shop," have been made in Great Britain, but so far have been rejected by labor itself. Cf. Allan Flanders, "Great Britain," in *Comparative Labor Movements,* p. 99.

Zealand where in the nineties the awards of the Court of Arbitration could be made applicable to all firms named in the award. It was, therefore, the custom of unions applying for an award to prepare long lists of firms in their application. This need to enumerate the firms was removed by a law of 1936. Long before, in 1908, the principle of extension had been made applicable to collective agreements as well.[18] Extension is used quite frequently.

From New Zealand the idea passed on to Australia. In Europe, a proposal for extension of agreements was made in Switzerland in 1911 but was defeated. The first practical application came as a result of the Central-European revolutions: in Germany, by decree of December 23, 1918; in Austria, in December 1919. The next major advance of the principle occurred during the great depression of the 1930's, when the danger that sharpened competition and mass unemployment might combine to destroy the system of collective agreements itself was at its height. The British cotton manufacturing act of 1934, the French legislation on collective agreements of 1936, the Netherlands law of 1937, and the codes under NRA in the United States contained the principle of "extension." Characteristically, the Scandinavian countries have not made use of this device; it is hardly necessary in countries in which the degree of organization, both on the side of the employers and that of labor, approaches 100 percent and collective agreements thus cover almost the entire labor force.

The post-World War II revival of the "extension" system has brought with it a number of interesting developments. One of the most significant is pointed out by Clark Kerr in his study of Germany. The extension of an agreement requires that the original contract be signed by representatives of at least a significant portion of employers and workers. Multifirm bargaining is, therefore, a necessity. To make sure of this, employers' associations are called for. Hence the otherwise surprising fact, reported by Kerr, that "the unions requested the occupying powers to permit the reestablishment of employers' associations."

Extension of agreements has been reintroduced in Germany at

[18]Cf. L. Hamburger, "The Extension of Collective Agreements to Cover Trades and Industries," *International Labour Review,* Vol. 40, No. 2 (August 1939).

the request of both employers and unions. It is not automatic, but rather in the free decision of the Minister of Labor. However, in most cases extension is granted. The only requirement is that the contract apply to employers who together employ more than 50 percent of the employees in the industry and area.

French postwar legislation has returned to the system of extension as it existed under the legislation of 1936. An attempt was made in 1946, when the first steps toward a resumption of collective bargaining were taken, to make all agreements subject to the Minister's approval which implied at the same time the extension of the agreement. This was dropped in 1950; agreements do not require government approval. The Minister is free to extend certain agreements or not, and he may restrict the extension to parts of an agreement. Extension gives the labor inspectors—officials of the Government—the right to control the application of all "extended" parts of the agreement. Under the legislation of 1936 this control had been limited to the wage clauses of the extended agreement.

1927

Reference has been made above to the Netherland's law of 1937 which introduced "extension" into Dutch collective bargaining. With one change this legislation is still valid; the right to "extend" an agreement has been transferred from the Minister of Labor to the Government Mediation Board. The Dutch legislation—quoted in Dr. Pels' report on Holland—requires that the collective agreement "hold good for an important majority of the persons employed in the industry throughout the country or in a part of the country." The law also enumerates certain provisions of agreements which shall not be included in an extension.

The British law for the cotton manufacturing industry represents the peculiar phenomenon of the extension of an agreement in a country in which the collective agreement itself has no legal validity, though as Allan Flanders points out, it is universally respected. The purpose of extension, at the time it was introduced, was to protect the parts of the industry in which the standards set by the agreement were observed against the competition, sharpened by the depression, of firms with lower wages and worsened working conditions. A further measure comparable to extension has been introduced in Britain by the wartime Order 1305 whose Part III implied, in the words of Allan Flanders,

> that non-federated, as well as federated employers were compelled to comply with the terms of collective agreements. If they failed to do so, they could be reported by a trade union or employers' association operating in the industry to the Ministry of Labour, who could then refer the case to the National Arbitration Tribunal for an award, which was enforceable in a court of law by each worker and against each employer to whom it applied.

Since enforcement in practice was handled by the unions, this arrangement assisted them in organizing drives. When Order 1305 was repealed and replaced in August 1951 by the Industrial Disputes Order (No. 1376), the employers' obligation to observe recognized "terms and conditions of employment" was made less general and absolute. Still, such an "issue"—as the Order calls this kind of a dispute—can be referred to the new Industrial Disputes Tribunal which may by an award require the employer to observe the recognized terms and conditions. Thus, the "trade unions have retained the substance of this support to their voluntary efforts."

No extension exists at present under Italian laws, though Fascist legislation provided that "collective agreements"—if this term could be used to refer to the regulations under the Fascist system —were "generally binding for the whole category to which they referred."[19] The collective agreements established since 1946 are valid only for the membership of the associations that have entered into the agreement. Moreover, individual agreements may depart from the terms of the collective agreements, in either sense, i.e., not only in favor of the workers, but also by worsening the conditions for the workers. However, proposals for new legislation submitted to Parliament provide for the extension of agreements. As is reported in Professor Sanseverino's article on Italy the law proposed by Rubinacci establishes two major requirements for the extension of collective agreements, namely, the registration of the unions and employers' associations which have negotiated the agreement and, second, "that the organizations making up the bar-

[19] See p. 211.

gaining agency be representative of at least 51 percent of the membership and that one more than half of all the organizations involved be represented."

The possibility of extension and the conditions for the extension of collective agreements have an obvious influence upon union strategy. In the case of Germany, extension requires a contract valid for the employers of 50 percent of the employees. The number of workers represented by the union is not specified. It follows that if the union is concerned with universal coverage by contract terms, it must press for the organization of employers to a greater extent than of the workers; of the latter only enough must be organized to induce the employers of half the workers in the industry to sign a contract. The union proceeds most efficiently if it concentrates its efforts on the largest employers, disregarding small plants. In France, no requirements in terms of numbers or percentages of employers or union membership exist for the extension. Any collective agreement signed by the "most representative" organizations of workers and employers is eligible for extension, if the Minister of Labor so wishes. Since the term "most representative" has no longer any definite meaning—all major unions have been described as such—the incentive for unionization is limited to that measure which is necessary to induce the employers' association—on whose side no issue of representativeness is likely to arise—to sign a contract. The legislation in the Netherlands is similar to that of Germany except that in order to be eligible for extension the agreement must apply "to a large majority of the persons employed in the industry concerned, taking into account the particular conditions ruling in that industry." Once again, the emphasis is on the representativeness of the employers signing the agreement.

Extension thus tends to strengthen the interest in the organization of employers rather than of the workers.

> Employers can put a legal floor under competition by first bringing together within their industry enough employers to represent 50 percent of the employment and then finding a union with at least paper coverage with which to conclude an agreement. In the absence of unions, the employers might wish to create some, pro-

vided they did not become too strong, in order to use this device to limit the range of competitive conditions in the labor market.[20]

There are further interesting implications in the extension of collective agreements. The nonunionized worker benefits from the work of the union in establishing the contract as much as does the union member. This does happen also under the American system of extension for the workers of the plant and the category for which the union signs a contract. However, this is likely to be of rather limited importance, compared with the relative proportions of "free riders" to union membership that may exist, under extended agreements, in Germany, France, or the Netherlands. Moreover, various kinds of union security clauses in American agreements are specifically designed to meet this problem. No equivalent clauses exist in the agreements of the European countries to which we are referring. Indeed, the French agreements cannot contain such clauses if they are to be valid; in Holland, if agreements contain such clauses, these are not eligible for extension. French collective agreements must contain a clause on "trade union freedom" which means the right to belong or not to belong to a union; the Netherlands law specifically exempts from extension provisions of a collective agreement

> which aim at...coercing employers or workers into joining an employers' or workers' association as the case may be; bringing about discrimination in treatment between organized and unorganized parties or persons....

Thus, no coercion to bring about union affiliation is supposed to follow from the nonunion workers' enjoyment of the benefits of the collective agreement obtained by the union, although propaganda and persuasion may be used. But where extension of collective agreements is the rule, the drive to enroll new members in

[20]See Clark Kerr, this volume, p. 199. Such employers' strategy, however, requires a sophistication in dealing with labor relations which, until recently at least, not too many employers on the Continent were likely to have. The wish not to have to deal with any union is frequently still stronger than the urge to eliminate competition in the labor market. Moreover, administrative devices such as restrictions of the mobility of labor, may help to reduce the significance of competitive advantages in labor conditions. Cf. M. Gardner Clark's study of Italy, "Governmental Restrictions on Labor Mobility in Italy," *Industrial and Labor Relations Review,* Vol. 8, No. 1 (October 1954).

the union is weakened and the nonunion worker has a lessened material incentive to join the union.

Extension tends to favor industrial unionism since it is competition in the product market that offers the main inducement for the employers to come to terms with the union and see these terms extended to all possible competitors.

Perhaps the most important consequence of extension is in the area of wages and conditions. It is obvious that the contract must be sufficiently general so that it can be applied to an entire industry, including the plants not belonging to members of the employers' association. Thus what is called in Germany the "Manteltarif" (cover agreement) is, as Clark Kerr points out, usually "quite brief and couched in general terms." This is somewhat less true for France or the Netherlands, partly because there are standard clauses that belong in every agreement and are, therefore, best placed into the national agreement which is the one most likely to be extended. More consequential, however, is the influence which extension is likely to have upon the level at which wages are set relatively to the cost structure of the different firms to which the contract is to apply. If the partners at the bargaining table could be certain of the "extension" of their agreement as well as of the cohesion and discipline of their organizations, they could set wages (and prices) fairly arbitrarily. Extension would protect them against the emergence of nonunion employers, since the latter would be subject to the terms of the agreement. As against this stands the danger of breakaways from the employers' association and of a refusal by the authority to extend the agreement. On the whole, it would seem that so far the latter considerations have usually outweighed the inflationary possibilities of extension, though, theoretically at least, the outcome might have been the opposite. At this point, extension meets and sharpens the trends determining the general wage policy of collective bargaining in most of the European countries considered.

Wage Structure

The term "wage structure" is used to designate a number of wage relationships, primarily the differentials in wage rates connected with different skills, regions, sex, firms, and industries, but also the differentials in earnings. There are of course other differentials between the wages of workers doing "the same job" in different industries in the same country, in different firms of the same industry, in different plants of the same firm, and between workers doing "the same job" in a given plant. Skill, sex, occupations, industry, and region, however, seem to be the factors with which the most important wage differentials are associated. On some of these—skill, industry, region, and sex—the reports in the volume contain interesting data.

Skill Differentials

For all five countries of the European Continent discussed in this volume—France, Germany, Italy, the Netherlands, Norway—the reports indicate that skill differentials are rather narrow, compared, say, with United States averages. The picture is clearest in the case of Germany and the Netherlands where available data require little explanation. Dr. Pels' essay seems to indicate that skill differentials in Holland were set at 20 percent of the base wage after the war and remained at about this level since, although criticism has been voiced describing the relationship as excessively low. There are reports that effective differentials have tended to be greater than those provided for in the contracts. For Germany, Professor Kerr points out the compression of the wage structure with skill differentials limited to some 25 percent of the wage of common labor.

A similar figure seems to hold for the remaining European countries examined in this volume as well. The order of magnitude of their skill differentials seems to approximate 20 to 25 percent fairly consistently. In Norway, the situation in different industries is not uniform, with skill differentials all but disappearing for some time in the construction industry. On the whole, in spite of considerable variations among industries, it would appear that skill differentials were rather low.

In the case of Italy and France, there are a number of complications. The average skill differential for Italy is reported to be 23 percent for June 1952 for the contractual earnings of workers in the engineering industry in Milan; if family allowances and other elements of "indirect wages" are taken into account, the skill differential would be lower (see below). These are, however, contractual wages. Actual wages, as Professor Vannutelli points out, are likely to be higher than those set in the contracts. Moreover, this discrepancy between actual and contract wages is more noticeable for the higher ranks (skilled workers) than for the lower ranks (laborers), for men than for women, for clerks than for workmen. To this extent—for which no quantitative measures are available—the skill differentials are larger than our previous indications would lead us to believe.

A five or seven grade classification is used in France.[21] The range of wage rates is given as 152 to 100. This is the ratio of wage rates, not of earnings. Moreover, the "direct wage"—which is dependent on skill—amounts to only about 70 percent of total labor cost in France and—until 1952—even much less in Italy. The "indirect wage" is independent of skill with family allowances forming the largest single item. As a result of this factor, as well as of the importance of family exemptions in the income tax, skill differentials in earnings are on the average greatly reduced, while the size of the family becomes a key factor in determining net income after taxes.

In England, skill differentials have narrowed to a level where the skilled wage exceeds the unskilled by about 20 percent. According to Knowles and Robertson,[22] there "has been a general tendency towards uniformity of skill differentials in different industries—around a level of 80 percent." As far as skill differentials are concerned, Great Britain belongs with the countries of the Continent discussed in this volume.[23]

[21]Cf. the essay on France, p. 159. Details as to the classification of skills for a number of occupations in France are given in Annexe III to Information 221, Oct. 22, 1946, of G.I.M.M.C.R.P., Paris. This operates with seven classes ranging from manoeuvre (common laborer) to P. 3 (professional class 3). These seven classes can be fairly easily transformed into the five classes of the statistics of the French Ministry of Labor referred to above.

[22]K. G. J. C. Knowles and D. J. Robertson, "Differences between the Wages of Skilled and Unskilled Workers, 1880–1950," *Bulletin of the Oxford University Institute of Statistics,* Vol. 13, No. 4 (April 1951). Most of the evidence is quoted in Lloyd G. Reynolds and Cynthia H. Taft, *The Evolution of Wage Structure* (New Haven: Yale University Press, 1956).

[23]John T. Dunlop and Melvin Rothbaum, "International Comparison of Wage Structures," *International Labour Review,* No. 4 (April 1955), classify the British

By contrast skill differentials in the United States seem rather high. For the latter we have certain estimates relating to earnings.[24] If the average earnings for janitors and handtruckers—who stand for the lowest-paid category of unskilled work Group II—are set at 100, then the medians of the earnings of four other categories of workers stood during 1945–1947 at the following index rates:

Unskilled	Group I	115
Semiskilled	Group II	115
Semiskilled	Group I	135
Skilled		155

The much smaller admixture of indirect earnings in the United States indicates that these differentials are greater than those in France or in Europe in general. In the absence of figures on the frequency distribution over the range of the differentials in Europe, these data are, however, merely suggestive.

In all of the countries examined there has been a downward trend of skill differentials during the postwar decade. In France and Italy, this has been followed by some widening of the differentials since the end of the Korean crisis, but this trend has not gone very far and seems to have been arrested. In Norway, as we shall see, some attempts have been made to spread the differentials.

This general downward trend has not been limited to the Continental countries where differentials had been narrow to begin with. The same phenomenon was observed in England and elsewhere. For England, Mr. Flanders indicates that there was a leveling shift in the wage structure;[25] during the postwar years "the

wage rate differentials in a category between the United States on one hand, France and Italy on the other. The figures available to us do not support this classification.

[24]Cf. Harry Ober, "Occupational Wage Differences, 1907–1947," *Monthly Labor Review* (August 1948). "More recent surveys indicate...a somewhat greater tendency to maintain percentage differentials among occupations," "Area Wage Trends for Selected Occupational Groups, 1952–1955," *Monthly Labor Review*, Vol. 78, No. 11 (November 1955), p. 1250.

[25]His explanation for the process which relates it to full employment is hardly plausible. Full employment may make the wage structure more reasonable in the sense that the monetary rewards of a particular job compensate for the degree of dissatisfaction connected with it. There are indications that this process—whose operation was prevented during the days of mass unemployment—has been taking place in the postwar period of full employment. However, there is no reason to assume that a wage structure in which remuneration is proportionate to the dissatisfaction connected with the job, is a more egalitarian wage structure than any other.

wage rates of unskilled workers have risen more than those of skilled workers...the earnings of women have risen more than those of men, and of juveniles more than adults,...salaries have risen less than wages, and least of all in higher ranges."

For the United States, a similar trend has been observed during the postwar years, at least in percentage terms, if not in cents per hour.[26]

There are thus two phenomena to be recorded: an apparently universal or at least widespread trend in the Western world for skill differentials to shrink, and the peculiarly narrow range of such differentials in several countries of the Continent.

As to the first, the conventional explanation looks for the main cause in "the practice of granting flat-rate increases to meet the rising cost of living."[27] While it is obvious that inflation creates conditions that are favorable to changes of wage differentials, it is not quite so obvious why it should have been consistently possible to take advantage of the opportunities for narrowing the differentials. In other words, inflation is a dynamic force that overcomes inertia and custom as regards wage differentials; it thus offers opportunities to revise and modify differentials that no longer correspond to the requirements of the current situation. This, however, does not explain why the revision should have been so consistently aiming at narrower differentials. What is it about inflation that invites the use of flat-rate increases? The answer may be partly in the element of social justice: the increase of the cost of living justifies flat-rate compensation. Inflation may also tend to raise time preference reducing the advantages of time-consuming processes such as that of acquiring higher skills.[28]

[26]Cf. Harry Ober, *loc. cit.* Benjamin H. Higgins, "Wage Fixing by Compulsory Arbitration; The Lesson of Australia," *Social Research,* Vol. 18, p. 334, points out that compulsory arbitration has had similar effects upon the wage structure. "The higher basic wage has been achieved largely at the expense of wages and salaries in the upper brackets." The Australian system, he says, "has improved the position of workers in the lower half of the wage scale at the expense of those in the upper half...."

[27]Knowles and Robertson, *loc. cit.,* p. 121.

[28]This may help explain the peculiar deformations of the occupational wage structure during hyperinflation such as the phenomenon of the cleaning woman having a higher income than the university assistant—a subject well-used in editorials in the German and Austrian press after World War I.

If inflation, however, were the only force at work, we would expect differentials to return to their preinflation level (or at least close to it) once prices begin to stabilize. Some evidence for such a reversal exists in France and Italy where differentials had shrunk rather rapidly. But in neither of the two countries did the differentials return to anywhere near their former level. Long-run forces thus seem to operate as well in the reduction of the differentials. Among them may be rising educational levels and possibly technological changes. Together they seem to have changed the relative supply and demand schedules of skilled and common labor in favor of the latter.

Traditionally, shrinking wage differentials arouse concern about the future supply of skilled labor. Such concern has indeed been expressed during the decade 1945–1955. Thus, the Norwegian Federation of Labor recommended in 1952 that skill differentials be widened, after a prolonged process of narrowing.[29] This was the more remarkable as the Norwegian labor organization among others had been pursuing for a number of years a deliberate policy of "wages solidarity," aiming at a reduction of all wage differentials. To some extent this egalitarian policy had been counteracted by rates above contract paid to higher-skilled workers. Individual bargains thus partly superseded the collective arrangements. Apparently this was not regarded as sufficient or as an acceptable way of maintaining a satisfactory level of skill differentials. Hence the appeal of the Norwegian federation which seems to have had some effect. English reports indicate that the narrow skill differentials have so far not reduced the supply of labor for the skilled trades below the desirable level. "In most of the crafts. . . there are still more boys wanting to start apprenticeships than can be accepted."[30] Yet, just as in Norway, there has been a rebellion in the unions against the narrowing of the differentials. This may just be a protest of custom against the trend of the times, but it is also conceiv-

[29]Benjamin H. Higgins, *loc. cit.*, in referring to the reduced skill differentials in Australia adds a warning that "this result may have been accompanied by a diminished incentive to acquire special skills." A similar concern was expressed at the Swedish Trade Union Congress of 1952.

[30]Reynolds and Taft, *op. cit.*, p. 274.

able that the response of the labor supply to the narrowed differentials has been merely delayed.[31] Some evidence for this may be found in observations regarding the trend of French and Italian workers to move out of industry into small commerce or artisan trades.[32] This may indicate that the more ambitious elements among the workers regard the narrow differentials in these countries as unsatisfactory. If this explanation holds true, it would indicate that adjustments of the supply of skilled labor to narrower differentials could proceed not merely by a smaller number of youngsters entering the necessary training, but also by the transfer of skilled workers to different occupations within industry or outside of industry altogether. Finally, the response may consist of a lowering of the quality of skilled labor rather than, or in addition to, lowered quantity.

The function of skill differentials is primarily to provide incentives to embark upon careers requiring longer and more arduous training. The size of the differential required to bring about this result may be expected to vary not only from time to time, but also from country to country. Variations over time are the result of changing supply and demand ratios, changes in the facilities for education and training, alterations in noneconomic compensation for higher skill, etc., while custom and tradition will tend to pre-

[31] J. R. Hicks, "Economic Foundations of Wage Policy," *The Economic Journal*, Vol. 55, No. 259 (September 1955), maintains that it could be impossible "if differentials are too narrow to maintain full employment without creating a scarcity of skilled labor." For then the intensity of demand required to employ the less skilled will cause a shortage of labor among the skilled. In this way, if effective rates for the skilled do not exceed the collectively fixed low rates, excessively narrow skill differentials become an inflationary force. This will hold true only in the fairly long run when supply (and possibly demand) of skilled labor are adjusted to the narrower differential and provided that narrow differentials do not acquire the force of custom. There is, in principle, no obvious reason why a smaller financial reward, once it has become traditional, should not be regarded as a satisfactory incentive as long as it covers the costs of additional training. Time seems to be the most important requirement for a policy designed to reduce differentials—in two contradictory senses: the effects of reduced differentials need time to materialize and the acceptance of narrower differentials progresses with time. But the degree of acceptance will also depend upon the entire income structure of society and the general expectations regarding income differentials. Ultimately, we are dealing with the entire value system of societies and with changes of this system. See, however, the remarks in the text on France and Italy.

[32] For the French, see the report on France, p. 167. On Italy, see Dunlop and Rothbaum, *loc. cit.*, p. 13, n. 1.

serve differentials once established. Changes in demand or supply ratios will in turn be related to changing technology, changes in the rates of economic growth of different sectors of the economy, and other factors. More important still may be the variations from country to country: incentives that are necessary in one country to produce a certain supply of highly skilled labor may be excessive in another country or vice versa. This may be the result of different noneconomic compensations offered to higher skills—status and prestige—or simply of different "styles of life" in which lesser financial rewards are sufficient to bring about the desired result. Nothing would seem to entitle us, therefore, to judge the absolute size of skill differentials in one country by the experience of another country.

Yet, the order of magnitude of differentials and their behavior vary—with one exception discussed below—very little among the countries studied in this volume. There is no need, apparently, for a French theory of wages as distinguished from an English theory even though some departures from the generalizations of one country may occur and require that even more general propositions be formulated. None of these revisions, however, seems to invalidate the fundamentals of conventional theory. Fragmentary evidence from other cultures does seem to reveal, on the other hand, that differentials vary greatly from culture to culture.

The shrinking of skill differentials in particular, even though there may be an occasional reversal of the trend, seems general in the countries examined. Mature industry, accompanied by rising educational levels, and possibly the declining social disqualifications of manual labor would seem to explain this phenomenon with egalitarian ideologies supporting rather than creating the trend.[33]

The fact that American skill differentials exceed those common to the European countries is, at first sight, puzzling. The inflationary developments of the last decade offered sufficient opportunities for a revision of traditional differentials. As we have seen, they have shrunk but are still far above the European level. The long-

[33]See Reynolds and Taft, *op. cit.*, p. 366. Egalitarian ideas may, however, play an important role in raising educational levels, spreading educational opportunities and eliminating the social disqualifications of manual labor.

run force of universal education has been even longer at work in most parts of the United States than in Europe where, with few exceptions, free universal education arrived later than in this country. The higher degree of unionization of workers in low-paying industries in Europe, more centralized wage bargaining, and perhaps a greater concern of governments with the political consequences of excessively low pay have been suggested as causes. But it is difficult to believe that these points—few of which seem applicable to all European countries or even to all the countries studied in this volume—are a full explanation of what appears to be a consistent phenomenon.

Conceivably, with higher real wages, larger differentials—not only absolutely, but also relatively larger—are necessary to produce the same psychological effect. This would be a logical consequence of a law of diminishing utility of income, and some evidence can be found that it might apply. Larger and larger supplements would thus be required to act as incentives of constant strength when real incomes increase. This logic would then lead us to expect an upward trend in wage differentials in Europe when real incomes have been rising. This does not correspond to our findings, unless we assume that the counterforce of rising educational standards has more than compensated for the effects of increasing income on differentials.

A suggestion of a possible answer is contained in a recent comparative study of "Steel Management on Two Continents."[34] This would indicate that a German plant uses a far greater number proportionately of trained craftsmen and skilled workers than a comparable American plant, while the latter employs many more general foremen and foremen than its German counterpart. Overall, the American plant has a much larger proportion of its labor force in higher skill classes: three times as many in middle management, and more than three times as many general foremen and foremen. If these are representative figures, demand for higher skill would be far more intense in the United States than in Germany, with the exception of the lowest level of the upper skill

[34] F. H. Harbison, Ernst Köchling, Frank H. Cassell, and Heinrich C. Ruebmann, "Steel Management on Two Continents," *Management Science*, Vol. 2, No. 1, (October 1955).

groups. This, if verified on a larger scale, would provide an important element for an answer to our puzzle.

Undoubtedly also the notions of what are proper differentials—i.e., customary acceptance—vary a good deal on both sides of the Atlantic. The absence of feudal concepts of the place in society to which a worker may properly aspire may have played a part in allowing the larger wage differentials to arise in the United States, just as the heritage of the feudal concepts may have helped maintain the highly compressed wage structure in Europe. Restriction of the numbers of working-class children who can complete high school combined with high educational requirements for managerial and professional jobs in Europe may explain the relatively larger supply of skilled manual workers in Europe. In this way a large supply of skilled workers may go hand in hand with a smaller supply of talent for major and minor executive positions. This reasoning would lead us to expect that the progressive democratization of European societies would open up the fan of occupational wage differentials, at least within the range of working-class occupations. The actual trend has been the opposite—possibly as a result of the long-run factors mentioned before, such as rising educational levels and the egalitarian philosophies of the unions in Europe.

The rapidity of economic growth in the United States and—for a considerable length of time—the relative lack of highly skilled personnel among the immigrants would also serve to explain the higher skill premium in this country.

Interindustry Differentials

All reports agree that during the war and the postwar decade profound changes in the interindustry wage structure occurred. The reason for these changes is usually found in full employment, with inflation providing conditions that facilitated the wage adjustments. These changes are remarkably similar from country to country. Mining and agriculture move up the scale; mining often takes the first place as far as average wage is concerned. This corresponds to the market situation after the war when coal was in exceedingly short supply and represents also a rationalization of the wage structure in the sense that one of the most disagreeable, dangerous, and unhealthy occupations achieved the monetary rewards which theory leads us to expect.

In several of the European countries a strong tendency toward a narrowing of interindustry differentials was at work. In Norway, it went under the term of "solidaristic wages policy," but similar policies were pursued elsewhere. This policy aims at reducing wage differentials in general and at raising the level of low-paying industries in particular. Agricultural labor was one of the groups which was to benefit from this trend. Collective bargaining policy in this case, however, worked to effect the same kind of changes which the market tended to produce. With full employment in industry, agricultural wages were bound to rise in order to prevent an excessive loss of manpower to industry. It is thus impossible to ascertain to what extent wage policy contributed to the narrowing of the interindustry wage structure.

The technique of offering flat wage increases to make up for the inflationary rise of the cost of living also contributed to the narrowing of the interindustry differentials measured in percentages. When they are measured in absolute terms, this technique would tend to leave them constant.

Sex Differentials

In most countries this differential tended to drop just like most other differentials. This applies particularly to France and to Norway, while in the case of Germany the unusually large differential against women persisted. Once again, it is not possible to decide whether or to what extent deliberate policy or full employment are responsible. Germany, during a part of the period reported on, had substantial unemployment. In the United States, agreements do not usually allow for any sex differential for the same type of work, although of course not all jobs are equally accessible to men and women.

Regional Wage Differentials

A classification of the countries according to the size of their regional differentials of wage rates would tend to put France and

Italy in one group, England and Germany in another, the United States, Norway, and Holland in between. The first group has the highest differentials, the second relatively low differentials, the United States, Norway, and Holland moderate differentials. This classification does not necessarily apply to earnings.

The average rate differentials for France and Italy are 22.3 percent (January 1955) and 33 percent (1953), respectively. For the United States, where the North-South differential is the outstanding example of regional differentials, we are given an estimate of 16 percent in 1945–1946.[35] British differentials seem to be considerably lower. For Germany, we are told that regional differentials amount to very little, while the Norwegian report speaks of "marked" and "unchanged" differentials. Dutch wage zones provide for a maximum differential of about 10 percent.

No more than suggestive significance can be attached to these figures, for the differentials vary "widely and irrationally from industry to industry."[36] To the extent, however, to which these large averages indicate consistent wage behavior, they would tend to reveal also substantial variations in the productivity of labor. Such diversity presents interesting and important problems for trade unions and collective bargaining. These, however, are outside the scope of this study.

On the whole, regional differentials have shown little consistent change during the postwar decade. But the available measures, being large aggregates, do not allow us to be very definite about this conclusion. In the case of France, information of a more precise nature is available as to the persistence of the differentials. The legal regulation of rate differentials for minimum wages has had only passing influence on the effective regional differentials while changes of the minimum wage have a profound and long-run influence on the other aspects of the wage structure.

Among the reasons for this persistence of the regional differentials are the following: (1) Unionism is stronger in the high wage zones (which are the great industrial centers). (2) The labor market

[35]Dunlop and Rothbaum, *loc cit.*, quoting Joseph W. Bloch, "Regional Wage Differentials, 1907–46," *Monthly Labor Review* (April 1948). See also the following note.

[36]Richard A. Lester, "Southern Wage Differentials: Developments, Analysis and Implications," *Southern Economic Journal*, Vol. 13 (April 1947).

is "more competitive" (it would be better to say "less monopsonistic"). (3) The labor force has higher skills because of the prevalence of manufacturing plants requiring higher skills in the larger towns. (4) Piece rates are more frequent. (5) Living costs are higher in the larger cities.[37]

Fundamentally, real regional wage differentials are thus related to differences in the industrial structure. A similar explanation seems to be implied in Professor Vannutelli's discussion on Italian regional differentials. The salient fact is the spontaneous re-establishment of regional differentials in spite of contractual or governmental attempts to simplify and reduce them. Thus although the contract in the engineering industry does not provide for a substantial North-South differential in Italy, it has been established by way of departures of effective from contractual rates—upward departures in the case of the North, downward or at least less far upward in the Southern areas.

A "Rational" Wage Structure?

In several of the reports, particularly those on Holland and Great Britain, occur references to the concept of a "rational" or "orderly" wage structure. The Dutch report complains about the lack of such a wage structure prior to the war; Mr. Flanders explains that not even in the nationalized industries—except possibly the coal mines—has there been real progress in the direction of establishing a rational wage structure.

It is fairly easy to understand the meaning of the term "chaotic" wage structure which has been used to designate the prewar system. It refers to wage differentials owing their existence either to accident or to situations which no longer exist, i.e., to custom alone, the whole being examined with critical eyes. To some extent, therefore, the "orderly" wage structure of one period becomes the "chaotic" system of the next.

An "orderly" wage structure would then be one displaying three main characteristics: it would express few and rather simple principles of setting wage relationships, preferably expressly stated

[37]See Pierre Fournier, *Droit Social,* Vol. 19, No. 2, p. 79.

and ranked, widely accepted and consistently applied; it would maintain order by fairly frequent adaptations to changing circumstances; it would, however, be stable, i.e., such adaptations would not be so frequent as to create uncertainty.

An orderly wage structure would, therefore, require a judicious mixture of elements of stability with those of conscious and deliberate adaptation—in other words, of custom and arrangement. And the latter would have to be highly centralized in order to ensure the consistent application of the same principles. Collective bargaining, even if we assume it to be free of accidental, opportunistic, and "political" factors, would not be sufficient to ensure an orderly wage structure, unless we postulate perfect centralization of bargaining on both sides.

No room would be left in a perfectly "orderly" wage structure for short-run market considerations. For, even if they were admitted as one of the "principles" for determining relative wages, continual adaptation of relative wages to changing market situations would contradict the requirement of stability.

Among the functions which the labor market performs is that of enabling expanding industries, firms, and regions to obtain the necessary increased labor force. In the absence of direct controls of labor, wage differentials act as incentives for such transfers. In the last resort, a perfectly "orderly" wage structure is compatible only with a highly stable economic situation. It follows that wage structures will be the less orderly the more decentralized the collective bargaining process is, the more changing the principles of wage relationships are that are being popularly accepted, and the more dynamic the economic system is to which the wage structure applies. Attempts to establish rigid principles of wage relationships in that kind of a situation have so far merely led to considerable departures of actual from contractual rates.

Full employment and even more inflation have tended to weaken the force of custom in wage relationships during and particularly after the war and thus opened up an era of fundamental revision of the wage structure. This has made it possible to introduce more order into the wage structure, but where this process went too far, powerful forces seem to have delayed its progress or even reversed it.

Collective bargaining itself is a system making for a higher degree of order, but it does so only to some extent and by methods which affect not only the wage structure but also the wage level.

Collective Bargaining and Wage Levels

For obvious reasons, collective bargaining, to the extent to which it is effective, carries within itself a tendency toward more uniform wage rates and working conditions. By substituting the terms of the contract for individual "contracts" or wage scales unilaterally set by employers, the agreement produces greater uniformity. This applies not only to time rates (and their supplements) but also to piece rates and earnings.

The drive of labor unions toward uniform wage rates throughout a market, the "whole area of the trade" as the Webbs put it, is fundamental to the effectiveness of collective bargaining, although other types of wage equalization have been developed. This drive has been pointed out by students of organized labor since the classic *Industrial Democracy*.[38] The scope of the trend depends upon the size of the market area. Since the latter has shown a significant tendency toward expansion, collective agreements have demonstrated a long-run inclination to extend their area of validity. Nationwide collective agreements seem to have been progressing at the expense of area-wide bargains, and the latter have made progress compared with bargaining on a smaller scale, while plant-wide agreements have lost in significance. Moreover, the area of "sympathetic" influence which the agreement exerts is also likely to have been extended over the long run.

[38]The Webbs' study of *Industrial Democracy* refers to the Standard Rate and adds: "This conception of a consistent standard of measurement the trade union seeks to extend from establishments to districts, and from districts to the whole area of the trade within the Kingdom," *op. cit.*, p. 281. Maxime Leroy in his *La Coutume Ouvrière,* (Paris, 1913), Vol. 1, p. 228, reports that "the respect for the tariff (set by the union) is the great practical obligation of the union members;...he has also the additional duty to report the firms which work under the tariff or the workers who personally accept a lower wage....The member should even report the workers who accept a wage above the tariff." It should be kept in mind, however, that equal wage rates do not mean equal earnings or equal labor costs.

Yet, while this trend toward uniform wage rates is progressing, powerful forces operate to delay its progress or make it somewhat illusionary. In a number of countries, as we have seen above, contractual wage rates have been frequently exceeded by effective rates during the last decade; in other countries contract rates are not intended to be much more than guideposts for effective rates. Among the latter is Germany where the wage rates set in basic agreements form a floor upon which a whole structure of higher rates is established, partly by supplementary agreements between works council and management, by individual arrangements between the workers and management, and by voluntary unilateral action on the part of management. In France, supplementary regional, local, and even plant agreements may change the uniformity of the wage rates set in the basic contracts, but in practice relatively few such agreements have been concluded. Regional wage zones, on the other hand, provide for considerable differentials in wage rates for different areas. Italian contract rates are not only often violated in fact without change in the agreement, but the law itself permits individual contracts to differ from collective agreements in both directions, upward and downward.

In many countries—among them England, Holland, Sweden—contract rates are usually intended to be the effective rates. Still, the pressure of full employment has produced competition among employers for the scarce labor supply with the result that wage rates have often exceeded contract stipulations. The Swedish trade unions have been particularly concerned with this phenomenon, to which they have given the names "wage slide" or "wage drift."[39] Yet, as the Webbs pointed out: "But although the Standard Rate is a minimum, not a maximum, the establishment of this minimum

[39]During 1948–1950, for instance, no wage increases were made in collective agreements in Sweden. Yet in the first of these two years the percentage increase in average hourly earnings of male workers in Swedish industry amounted to 3.5 percent; for the second year it was estimated at 4 percent. Cf. Myers, *Industrial Relations in Sweden* (Cambridge: Technology Press, 1951), p. 29. Part of this "wage slide" was the result of higher productivity under constant piece rates, but the remainder occurred, "because individual workers...got more favorable piece rates or increases in their hourly rates." See also L.O., The Swedish Confederation of Trade Unions, *Trade Unions and Full Employment* (Stockholm, 1953).

necessarily results in a nearer approximation to equality of rates than would otherwise prevail."[40]

For the United States, a similar trend toward more central wage bargains and wider uniformity of rates has been pointed out. In particular, the system of "pattern" or "key" bargains in the United States may be regarded as a symptom of this trend. Yet, there is a significant difference between this type of bargaining and others, not so much in the objective of wage equalization, but rather in the process by which this objective is to be attained. It may perhaps be meaningful to describe the American method as a dynamic, the European system as a more static method of achieving uniformity.

The key bargain is being used by American unions to attain from a favorably situated firm an optimum settlement. This becomes then the standard to which aspire successive bargains in the same industry or in other industries in the area or finally other industries in other areas of the country. The resultant agreements are rarely fully uniform. The Standard Rate is far from being universally established. All kinds of combinations of advantages (packages) occur in practice and often the rate of increase of wage costs represented by these packages is more important than the wage levels themselves. Yet, a tendency toward wage equalization over wider areas manifests itself through the process.

In effect, this approach makes an attempt to use the wage levels[41] obtained under the most favorable conditions as the rate at which ultimately the bargains in the remainder of the industry shall arrive. This objective will rarely be fully achieved.

> Most plants will cluster closely around a single wage level, but one will usually find that the union has left a few plants at lower levels because these plants are unable to pay the standard rate, and yet it seems expedient to keep them in operation. One may also find that in some of the most efficient plants the union has yielded to the temptation to extract a little more than the prevailing scale.

[40]Sidney & Beatrice Webb, *op. cit.*, p. 280.

[41]This term is used here to denote the entire "package" obtained, including non-wage concessions which are simply evaluated at their wage equivalent. This is ordinarily the practice at bargaining sessions themselves when the wage costs of the "package" are discussed separately from the way they are allocated to different purposes.

> In general, however, unions hew closer to the principle of "the standard rate" than to the principle of "ability to pay."[42]

Implied in this process is a certain amount of pressure upon firms unable to pay the rate of the "key bargain," to improve their efficiency and thereby their ability to pay; this pressure is made effective by the readiness of the union, at least under proper conditions, to destroy marginal firms and to permit more efficient firms to expand, at the expense of less favored competitors. It is the extreme form of this process, the elimination successively of more and more firms unable to pay rising standard wage rates, which has been under attack by opponents of nationwide or area-wide collective bargaining in the United States.

Is there a correspondence between nationwide or area-wide collective bargaining and the level at which the Standard Rate is set? In many countries, under this process, contract rates are said to be set so as to meet the ability to pay of the average firm. Thus, the industry-wide agreements in Sweden are reported to result "in a level of wages which the average firm can pay."[43] Indeed, most European unions describe their wage policy in these terms, but it is unlikely that they correctly describe the procedure. For, if they did, they would imply, even with the most elastic definition of the term "average," that a sizeable number of firms in the industry signing the agreement would be unable, at least at the moment of subscribing to the agreement, to pay the contractual rates. In fact, however, contract rates are set at levels acceptable to marginal firms. This is particularly so in the case of Germany where, in the words of Clark Kerr, "the contracts negotiated by the unions become more minimum wage and hour laws than union contracts. . . . Bargaining processes and policies result in the minimization, equalization, and formalization . . . of wages." Among the reasons for this is "the policy of establishing rates which will not embarrass the marginal firm." In varying degrees, this seems to apply to other European countries as well.

What are the reasons for this union wage policy? Contrary to a

[42] Lloyd G, Reynolds, *Labor Economics and Labor Relations* (New York: Prentice-Hall, 1949), pp. 417–418.

[43] Cf. Myers, *op. cit.*, p. 17.

widespread opinion, it is not the fact of area-wide, or industry-wide bargaining per se that inevitably leads to wage rates being set at a level "which will not embarrass the marginal firm." As we have seen above, this type of agreement lends itself to "whipsawing," almost as well as to "wage minimization." The ambivalence of industry-wide collective bargaining emerges particularly clearly from the fact that, while it is opposed by at least some management groups in the United States as causing wages to rise too rapidly and as strengthening monopolistic tendencies, management on the Continent is rather hostile to bargaining by firms or groups of firms. For, as the report on Germany states "were the policy to force each firm or group of firms to set contract levels according to selective ability to pay... contractual wage rates on the average would undoubtedly be higher."

What matters, therefore, is not the instrument itself so much as the use to which it is put and the motivation behind it. Where "extension" of the agreement by administrative action is a major consideration, it is unlikely that wage rates can be set considerably above the level compatible with the ability to pay of the marginal firm. Otherwise, the resistance of firms whose survival would be threatened by the agreement would be such as to strengthen opposition to the agreement within the employers' association, or lead to the withdrawal of employers from the organization so that the latter may no longer represent the required percentage of the industry to make the contract eligible for extension. Even apart from this, the Minister or the agency competent to extend the agreement will find itself exposed to considerable political pressure. Thus, where the unions depend on the action of public authority rather than their own strength to bring competitive firms under the terms of the agreement, the latter is likely to have some of the characteristics of a minimum wage law setting rates that rarely exceed the capacity to pay of marginal firms.

More important, perhaps, are employment considerations. To set wages above the levels compatible with the survival of marginal firms has meant in the experience of many European unions to run the risk of causing what may prove to be long-term unemployment.

Arthur Ross,[44] it is true, has pointed out that, in general, unions do not concern themselves with the quantity of labor sold and that even if they wished to consider the effect of a particular wage bargain upon employment, they could not do so, because the employment effect is not predictable, except under certain circumstances.

Professor Ross states that

> there is no assurance that labor costs will decline even if wage rates are cut; that total costs will fall even if labor costs decline; that selling prices will be reduced even if total costs fall; or that sales and employment will increase even if selling costs are reduced. Therefore, "the real employment effect of the wage bargain is lost in a sea of external forces. The volume of employment associated with a given wage rate is unpredictable before the fact, and the effect of a given rate upon employment is undecipherable after the fact. . . . The typical wage bargain is necessarily made without consideration of its employment effect."[45]

This may overstate the case even for the United States. Almost all forecasts in economic life are probability statements with varying degrees of probability attached to them. We act normally upon such probability estimates and only seldom upon information involving "clear and predictable . . . relationships." The fact, therefore, that no such definite relationship can reasonably be said to exist between changes of wage rates and changes in the volume of employment is hardly plausible reason for the assertion that unions cannot reasonably be expected to act upon the belief that some wage-employment connection exists. Under certain conditions, the probability of an employment effect of changes in wage rates is higher; under others, it is lower. Four situations of the first kind are listed by Professor Ross himself.[46] As such he describes the following: "(1) Compensation is based on piece rates rather than hourly rates (piece rates are more closely linked with unit

[44] *Trade Union Wage Policy* (Berkeley: University of California Press, 1948), esp. Ch. IV. Kirk R. Petshek and Arthur M. Ross, "The Tie between Wages and Employment," *Industrial and Labor Relations Review,* Vol. 4, No. 1 (October 1950). See also G. P. Shultz and C. A. Myers, "Union Wage Decisions and Employment," *American Economic Review,* Vol. 40, No. 3 (June 1950).

[45] Petshek and Ross, *loc. cit.*. p. 100.

[46] *Ibid.*

labor cost). (2) Labor cost is a fairly substantial proportion of total cost. (3) The product market is highly competitive. (4) Part of the industry is nonunion and, therefore, wages cannot be standardized throughout the market." He clearly indicates that bargaining for "a major segment" of the economy could involve more distinct employment effects, but excludes this from practical consideration for the United States as "there is no bargaining mechanism of this kind in existence."[47]

European area-wide or nationwide collective bargaining is typically such a mechanism. It provides for substantially uniform changes of wage rates, reasonably similar movements of costs and of supply schedules and, therefore, of prices in an entire industry within a given area. Even the fact that the change of the wage rates may in some extreme cases be fully reflected in almost proportionate adjustments of the demand schedule does not necessarily eliminate the employment effect. It is conceivable that in a case of this kind real wage rates do not change at all, or if they do rise at first, because prices do not move as rapidly as wage rates, they return to their prior level after a period of adjustment. Yet the employment effect may still appear in the form of balance-of-payment difficulties which ultimately may impose a reduction of the volume of employment.

Thus either changes of relative prices (and) or balance-of-payment difficulties under a system of large-scale bargaining units are likely to bring home the employment effects of wage bargains. As Arthur Ross states, however, theoretical considerations cannot settle this issue of actual union behavior. It can only be decided by observation. In this respect the evidence seems impressive.

Awareness of the "wage-price spiral" goes through the entire post-World War II history of European labor from British and Swedish union self-restraint to the French "cartel de la baisse," a price reduction bloc, formed by the non-Communist trade union centers in 1948.[48] Many observers of European labor since the end of World War II have also pointed out that fear of unemployment

[47]Ross, *op. cit.,* p. 88.

[48]See Val R. Lorwin, *The French Labor Movement* (Cambridge: Harvard University Press, 1954), pp. 128–129.

has been a powerful brake upon trade union action. Clark Kerr's study of German collective bargaining states in particular:

> The German worker has had several bad experiences with unemployment, particularly during the Great Depression; and he has been willing to pay high prices, including tolerance of national socialism, to eliminate it. Since the end of World War II, partly because of the large influx of refugees, unemployment has at all times existed and been a constant reminder to the employed worker of his potentially precarious hold on a job. . . . This concern with job preservation is shared by many trade union leaders; a number of them declared in interviews that in bargaining they did not wish to set rates which would cause any job loss. Were they to do so, in any event, contract extension might then be denied as against the "public interest." No employers or employers' association officials interviewed on the subject considered that the unions in bargaining had insisted on increases which would result in layoffs.[49]

The decision of the Norwegian Trade Union Federation in January 1953 to recommend that agreements not be terminated was based upon the reason—among others—that "Norway's international competitive position would be worsened and full employment endangered by a further rise in wages."

It is thus not simply the collective bargaining technique which matters but the spirit in which it is being used. It is true, however, that the large-size bargaining unit not only facilitates the translation of wage increases into price increases but also contributes to the general trend toward weakened competition in the European economy.

Trade union organization may be more important than the size of the bargaining unit. For in most countries of the Continent—and even to some extent in England—unions have no plant organizations which can push for and obtain separate and more favorable contracts from individual employers and thus engage in whipsawing. Works Councils which, as in Germany, can and do conclude such separate agreements are not union organizations[50] and

[49]See this volume, pp. 204–205.

[50]In some cases public opinion and the workers regard Works Councils as emanations of the union. For Austria between the wars, Charles A. Gulick reports that "the development of the works councils...was...largely determined by the fact of

frequently show syndicalistic tendencies that would prevent the union from using the Councils as instruments of a trade union wage policy, if the unions ever attempted to do so. The absence of the policy and of the tool thus coincide in most, though perhaps not all, cases.[51]

Collective Bargaining and Inflation

The issue as to the way by which wage policy can make full employment compatible with price stability has been widely debated, in the United States as well as abroad. During the first postwar years, the discussion was carried on rather generally on the assumption that whenever full employment exists

> the danger of inflation is acute. Writers on fiscal policy often suggest that the task of avoiding both inflation and deflation is one of extreme delicacy and precariousness, in which a small miscalculation may lead to failure. Reference is made to knife-edges, tight-ropes, the narrow and treacherous straits between Scylla and Charybdis, etc.[52]

This attitude corresponded somewhat to the powerful inflationary trends of the first postwar years while experience since 1953 points toward greater compatibility of high employment levels and price stability.

Four of the countries examined in this volume present sustained experience with the problem of full employment and inflation throughout the entire postwar decade: the United States, Great Britain, Holland, and Norway. France and Germany joined this group at a late stage. The four countries of the first group show the following evolution of their cost-of-living index.

As is to be expected, none of the countries succeeded in escaping inflation altogether. If 1945 or 1946 are used as base years, the United States, Great Britain, and Holland show in 1952 almost

their domination by the trade unions." The problem of the relations between the Works Councils and the trade unions was "completely liquidated" by the end of 1922. "Labor's Workshop of Democracy," Vol. I in *Austria from Hapsburg to Hitler,* (Berkeley and Los Angeles: University of California Press, 1948), p. 209.

[51]See, however, the remarks made above on the relationship between "extension" of contracts and wage levels.

[52]P. H. Henderson, "Retrospect and Prospect: The Economic Survey, 1954," *Bulletin of the Oxford University Institute of Statistics,* Vol. 16, Nos. 5 and 6 (May–June 1954), p. 165.

Table. CONSUMER PRICE INDICES FOR U.S., U.K., HOLLAND, AND NORWAY. 1938 TO 1952

Year	*U.S. Consumer's Price Index*[a]		*Great Britain Improved Index*[b]		*Holland Consumer's Price Index*[c]		*Norway*[d]	
1938.			100		100		100	
1939.	100				100			
1945.	129.4	100	148	100	176	100		100
1950.	172.2		185		240		168	
1952.	191.6	148	221	149	263	149	212	137

Sources:
[a]*Monthly Labor Review.*
[b]Flanders article, p. 54.
[c]Computed on basis of new index; 1949 = 100.
[d]Computed from data in Walter Galenson, *The Danish System of Labor Relations* (Cambridge: Harvard University Press, 1952), pp. 287–288.

exactly the same rate of increase of the cost of living (48,49,49 percent, respectively) with Norway some 12 percent lower (37 percent). The picture would be entirely different if we were to use 1938 or 1939 as the base year. Since, however, Holland and Norway were not free to administer themselves under enemy occupation, the first comparison is more meaningful.

The appearance of a parallel development vanishes upon closer examination. For within the time span considered, the sequence of the price change has been quite different among the four countries. The pre-Korean inflation was strongest in Holland where the cost of living rose by 36 percent between 1945 and 1950, and in the United States where the rate of increase was 33 percent. In Great Britain, the corresponding figure is 25 percent and in Norway 8 percent. The Korean crisis 1950–1952, on the other hand, was accompanied by the highest rate of increase of the cost of living in Norway (26 percent), by the lowest in Holland (9 percent), while in the United States the rate of increase was 11 percent and in Great Britain 19 percent.

What inference upon the behavior of different bargaining systems under full employment can we draw from the available figures?

To anticipate somewhat our conclusions: collective bargaining is a device for raising wages and improving working conditions. It may well be that in situations of long-run full employment, collective bargaining for a time slows down rather than speeds up the rate of money wage increases. Yet, when deliberately used to retard the advance of money wage rates over the long run, collective bargaining fails, and the attempt may endanger unions and the system of collective bargaining altogether. But it would seem that—in the absence of effective totalitarian controls—the other devices employed in the four countries examined did not fare any better over the long run. The problem is in the underlying forces that make for full employment and in the highly exacting definition of full employment rather than in surface symptoms.

Analysis in terms of collective bargaining systems and controls would deal with surface and short-run phenomena rather than the fundamentals. Such an investigation would reveal that competitive collective bargaining and absence of controls combined in the United States to help produce a remarkably high rate of price increase prior to Korea; between 1950 and 1952 the rate slowed down considerably compared with the rest of the world.[53] At the same time, the control system of Holland did not prevent a substantial rise in the cost of living prior to Korea, but it did succeed in limiting the Korean price inflation to the lowest level among the four countries. The temporary policy of union self-restraint in Great Britain did prevent the rise of the British cost of living prior to Korea from out-stripping that of unrestrained and uncontrolled collective bargaining in the United States, but when self-restraint was dropped, the British cost of living did rise faster than the American where wage increases by that time were subject to controls. Centralized collective bargaining in Norway was highly successful in helping stabilize the cost of living up to Korea, from then on inflation on the world markets and the reduction of price subsidies combined to produce a considerable increase of the cost of living.

[53]The extent to which controls restrained wage increases during that period has been questioned a good deal. Market forces are said to have played a far greater part in slowing down inflation. Cf. Clark Kerr, "Governmental Wage Restraints: Their Limits and Uses in a Mobilized Economy"; William Haber, "Some Problems of Manpower Allocation"; "Comments" by Richard A. Lester and Dale Yoder, Papers and Proceedings of the Sixty-fourth Annual Meeting of the American Economic Association, *American Economic Review,* Vol. 42, No. 2 (May 1952).

The picture is thus confusing. Moreover, the data do not bear directly upon the problem. For the problem itself is of an ex-ante nature; the evidence consists of ex-post data. In order to judge the effectiveness of any system or device used to combat the inflationary trends involved in full employment we would need some measure of the strength of the inflationary pressures encountered prior to the enactment of the measures taken to counteract them. It would be obviously misleading to compare simply the changes of the cost-of-living index from country to country and then to infer that the system or device employed in the country with the lowest increase was the most effective in restraining inflation. For the recorded rate of increase of the cost-of-living index is the result of both, the strength of the inflationary pressures and the effectiveness of the measures taken to combat them. The observable facts are that e.g., between 1945 and 1950 the cost-of-living index increased by 36 percent in Holland, 33 percent in the United States, 25 percent in Great Britain, and 8 percent in Norway. To infer from these figures that the Norwegian system of collective bargaining lends itself most readily, and the Dutch least, to effective anti-inflationary policies would be a rash conclusion indeed. As is well known, for instance, the Indonesian conflict put stresses on the Dutch economy which may lead one to the conclusion that Dutch economic policy acquitted itself well, given the circumstances. As if to confirm this, the Dutch cost-of-living index during the subsequent Korean crisis (1950–1952) showed the lowest increase of the four countries considered—9 percent—while Norway had the highest, 26 percent. International price movements, moreover, have probably had a greater effect in Norway than in the United States. Reconstruction put a greater strain on resources in England than in the United States, but required possibly a lesser effort in Holland than in Norway and so forth.[54] Changes in the terms of trade, currency devaluations, elements affecting the balance of payments all relate to the degree of inflationary pressure and all are likely to be experienced in different degrees in different countries.

[54]It is also by no means self-evident that price stability is the highest objective of economic policy. Rapid reconstruction after a war may appear more urgent and, in the judgment of some, be worth a moderate degree of price inflation.

In order to obtain an objective yardstick for the relative efficiency of the various bargaining-control compounds employed, we would thus need some measure of the inflationary pressure to which the price system in the different countries was exposed. Unemployment expressed as a percentage of the labor force could be such a yardstick. Unfortunately, this is again an ex-post fact recording not simply the problem which economic policy in the four countries had to face, but the solution given to that problem. The efficacy of different medical treatments cannot be tested in an experiment in which these treatments are given indiscriminately to a number of people of whom we do not know how sick they were when the experiment began.

Moreover, the use of the unemployment percentage as sole yardstick would imply that wage movements are regarded as the only source of inflationary pressure, that the rate at which wages increase is a function of changes of employment levels only, and that—by possibly contradictory reasoning—unions (or collective bargaining systems) are in full and exclusive control of changes of wage rates. None of these implications seems acceptable.

Yet while the empirical data do not permit us to draw any positive inferences regarding the efficiency of any system of wage determination as a stabilizing device, they may assist us in rejecting certain theoretical propositions.

The cost-of-living index in the four countries indicated increases between 1945 and 1952 which varied between 37 and 49 percent. For the period between 1953 and the second of 1955 (with April-September 1953=100), however, the cost of living shows only relatively minor changes: for the United States, July 1955, no change (1953=100); for Great Britain, a rise of 5 percent; for Holland, a rise of 6 percent; and, for Norway, an increase of 4 percent.[55] In the first period—between 1945 and 1952—the cost of living rose by some 6 to 7 percent annually; in the last two years, by about 2 percent per year. Since employment levels—with one exception, to be discussed later—remained very high throughout the second period as well, it would seem that a good deal more

[55]Source, for Great Britain, Holland, and Norway, U.N., *Economic Bulletin for Europe,* Vol. 7, No. 3 (November 1955), p. 11; for United States, *Monthly Labor Review,* Vol. 78, No. 10 (October 1955).

price stability is possible under full employment than experience between 1945 and 1952 led many observers to expect. Moreover, closer examination shows that in Great Britain, for instance, prices of manufactured goods remained almost perfectly stable throughout the second period, while the other components of the cost-of-living index (food, heating and lighting, services) were responsible for the upward pressure on the index. It is thus not surprising that the discussion of the problem has lost some of its sense of urgency.

We have thus a double task: to suggest possible reasons for the difference in wage and price behavior between the two periods and to examine whether, in the light of the relative stability of the later period, the problem may be regarded as settled.

To begin with the second question—in spite of the apparent stability, some of the disturbing elements remain. In the first place, not everyone would regard the employment level of the United States between 1953 and 1955 as fitting an exacting definition of full employment. Second, price stability in manufacturing was probably related to the rapid increase of productivity in that branch of industry, while the price rises in food, heating and lighting, and in the service industries indicate a relative lag in the progress of their productivity. This is encouraging in the sense that it indicates where the problem resides and that it may be susceptible of a solution. There is no assurance, on the other hand, that a high rate of progress in manufacturing can be maintained at all times. Third, a *consistent* rate of increase of the cost of living by 2 percent per year would be quite disturbing, although irregular moves of the index averaging the same increase over a number of years may have less upsetting results.

In any case, it is a warning against premature complacency that neither Britain nor Sweden feel that the problem has been solved, and that a Swedish government committee has been set up recently to examine the issue primarily in relation to the stability of the foreign exchange rate.

What explanation can one suggest for the differences in wage and price behavior between the early and the later postwar years? There is in the first place a good deal of vagueness in the term "full employment" itself: the supply curve of labor does not turn abruptly to perfect inelasticity; small reserves of labor may exist at prevailing wages or develop at slightly higher supply prices. Next, the critical limit is moved further back, the more rapidly productivity can be increased. As long as there are unused capital reserves, substitution of capital for labor is possible, which tends to counteract to some extent upward pressure on wages and prices. A more liberal import policy or changes of inventories can offset inflationary trends as can appropriate measures of fiscal policy. Measures to facilitate labor mobility without substantial changes in relative wages may help to postpone the emergence of bottlenecks. A number of these factors seem to have cooperated in producing greater price stability during the period 1953–1955.

The fact that full employment during and after the war followed upon a prolonged period of depression may well have greatly added at first to the inflationary forces in full employment. As was pointed out above in our discussion of wage structures, substantial changes in relative wages are frequently a source of movements of the general wage level. The modification of a traditional wage relationship, say in response to a fundamental alteration of the market situation of a particular industry or of a particular kind of labor, will frequently be followed by attempts to re-establish the customary relations. Since in practice money wages can rarely be reduced, such a two-step process will raise the wage level.

Full employment during the war and continued high employment levels afterward when controls were relaxed brought about substantial changes of wage differentials, particularly of the interindustry wage structure. It is plausible to infer that during that time attempts to re-establish traditional relationships occurred frequently and that, as a result, competitive wage increases and price rises took place. It would also follow that, if the new market situation persisted, the altered wage structure would be maintained in spite of the resistance of tradition and would itself, in due course, become customary. Once this stage is reached, the struggle for the re-establishment of the old wage structure ceases. It is not unreasonable to assume that this stage was reached about eight years after the end of the war.

There may thus be a greater degree of compatibility between

high employment levels and price stability than the first postwar years led observers to expect. There is, moreover, little reason to throw the responsibility for inflationary wage rises upon the unions alone or even perhaps primarily upon the unions. A good deal of evidence exists indicating that in the absence of unions, wage rates might move up more rapidly under conditions of full employment than they do when wages are set at discrete intervals by collective agreements. This is pointed out as a distinct possibility in the report on the United States, and is implied in several others. The "wage drift" or "wage slide" in Sweden—effective wage rates exceeding those set in collective agreements—has its counterpart in several other countries. The reports on Holland and England refer to this phenomenon, the latter speaking of "veiled increases," while the essay on Norway refers to "unofficial increases," as well as to the problem created by the wage increases granted to building workers by unorganized employers. Dutch and German sources indicate union and public concern with what the German Minister of Economic Affairs described, in September 1955, as the "theft of labor," i.e., the competitive bidding for workers by employers offering ever higher wage rates (and other inducements).

Even without changes of wage rates, employers can raise earnings with the same effect upon prices by shifting workers to higher-paying jobs, or simply upgrading jobs, or by increasing the number of workers employed on night shifts or overtime with premium pay. Nor is this all. Without any action on the part of unions or any deliberate "labor-pirating" on the part of employers, the same effects may be obtained by workers taking advantage of full employment to shift from lower-paying to higher-paying industries. The problem is thus not the aggressiveness of unions, but rather "full" employment itself. In other words, with free labor markets and in the absence of unions, the upward trend of money wages under full employment might be more pronounced.

The rapid survey made above may indicate that we must make a number of distinctions: between short-run and long-run measures, and between domestically generated and "imported" inflationary pressures. Measures taken during an emergency, and effective as long as it lasts, may prove untenable once the crisis has passed. A small country deeply involved in world trade and highly dependent upon it will be confronted by different problems in its efforts to maintain price stability than large countries with a higher degree of independence from world markets.

It is perhaps not too difficult to devise fairly effective short-run methods to slow down wage and price increases under full employment in a union setting. Even though, for the reasons stated, our evidence is far from conclusive it would appear that union self-restraint, preferably combined with centralized collective bargaining, offers reasonable prospects that the wage line will be held. The presence of a Labor government with which the unions are closely associated greatly enhances the probability that this policy will be effective, and prolongs its life span.

Thus we are told that trade unions and the Labor party in Norway are "two facets of a homogeneous movement. The two are more closely united than is true in Great Britain, for example."[56] Restraint upon the use of union power to obtain money wage increases was rendered easier by the desire to facilitate the functioning of the Labor government and to keep it in power. In exchange, the Labor government provided for the workers a guarantee that a "redistribution of income unfavorable to workers" would be prevented "through price control, taxation and fiscal policy generally."[57] The achievements of the Labor party through its government were thus accepted by the workers as a substitute for trade union action. Union membership continues at a high level, as the Norwegian example indicates, because the benefits obtained through the Labor government are credited to the unions as much or almost as much as to the party.

Action through the political party is thus substitutable for union action, though probably not perfectly. The availability and efficiency of alternative means of action appear to be a prerequisite to a moratorium of union wage struggle. It is thus probably not merely the existence of a labor party that is required, but of a

[56]Walter Galenson, "Scandinavia," *Comparative Labor Movements,* Walter Galenson, ed., p. 155. See also Oliver A. Peterson, "Industrial Conflict—Sweden," *Industrial Conflict,* Arthur Kornhauser, *et al.,* ed. (New York: McGraw-Hill, 1954).

[57]Galenson, *op. cit.,* p. 161.

labor party with which the bulk of the unions is so closely associated that in the view of the union members no clear distinction exists between what they owe to the unions and what is the result of the party's efforts. Since a party in opposition is not likely to produce major practical achievements, party action will be acceptable as a substitute for union activity more readily when the party is represented in the Government.

British experience, however, indicates that though the existence of a Labor government is probably a necessary condition for union self-restraint in peacetime, it is not a sufficient condition. It would appear that a high degree of centralization of the collective bargaining process is equally indispensable.

It is quite true that the larger the bargaining unit, the less is the elasticity of demand for labor and the greater, therefore, the possibility for the unions of obtaining money wage increases. At the same time, the more the bargaining unit coincides with an industry, the easier it is to shift higher wages on to prices. If the wage bargain affects all industries, management resistance to wage demands is likely to dwindle close to zero. Thus, highly centralized collective bargaining makes wage increases easy to obtain. It is then up to the Central Bank and the Government to defend the interests of fixed income recipients and to protect the balance of payments.

As against this, fully centralized global bargaining presents the union leaders with decisions on the distribution of real national income. While any small group of wage earners may believe that it can increase its own share of the real national income by changes in money wage rates and without a change in real total national income, and may in fact do so, a bargaining agent dealing with the total wage bill of the nation will more readily understand that he is discussing real income distribution. This does not necessarily mean that such a bargaining agent would not make an attempt to increase the real income of his constituency by squeezing the shares of other factors of production. A rise of money wages can be a device by which the real incomes of rent and interest recipients are reduced for the benefit of wage earners. Such a redistribution of real national income has, however, its limits in the threatened withdrawal of these factors from the market, unless drastic insti-

tutional changes are carried out. Even so, bargaining will be carried on essentially in real terms. This will make it plain that the sum total of all claims upon the real national income cannot be greater than the national income itself.

This, unfortunately, sounds perhaps more convincing than it is: thus, it is possible for claims to the real national income to exceed the national income (but not gross national product), provided capital is not fully maintained. Even gross home-produced national product can be exceeded if the nation incurs foreign debts.[58]

In any case, this combination of methods and circumstances is neither universally applicable, nor likely to be maintained successfully over the long run. Not only is it highly unlikely that a political labor movement, European style, will be created in the United States in the near future, but centralized collective bargaining can hardly be regarded as universally applicable. We have seen above that collective bargaining proceeds in a different climate in most of the continental countries, as compared with both Britain and the United States. As far as one can judge at this stage, it is exceedingly unlikely that the unions in either of these countries will accept a unified wage policy in the near future. Proposals in this direction have been rejected outright by the British unions. Even a modest proposal for a review of "existing machinery for wage fixing and negotiations" to find out "whether greater co-ordination is desirable with a view to providing greater equity and fairer relativities in the rewards for labor. . ." was overwhelmingly defeated at the Trades Union Congress of 1952. The speaker for the General Council of the TUC pointed out: "The real intention of this resolution is to put Congress into a preliminary canter directed towards the vague and academic proposal expounded during the last few years for a national wages policy."[59] This was, apparently, a sufficient refutation! The reception given to such a proposal at an AFL convention in the United States could not have been any more hostile.

[58]A fuller presentation of the difficulties of a unified wages policy is given in H. W. Singer, "Wage Policy in Full Employment," *The Economic Journal,* Vol. 57, No. 228 (December 1947).

[59]*Report of the 84th Annual Congress,* 1952, pp. 505–509.

Sectional and competitive collective bargaining in Great Britain and the United States as well as the considerable possibilities of unified bargaining in several of the countries of the Continent are the results of historical developments which have produced a sense of class consciousness and class solidarity in one group of countries but very little of these in the other. The relative ease with which a "solidaristic" wage policy could be applied by the Swedish or Norwegian unions, as against the competitive attitude of union leaders in the two Anglo-Saxon countries considered, are symptoms of deep-seated differences in the attitudes of the workers themselves and of the expectations with which they confront their labor organizations and leaders.

While differing views may be held by different observers as to the long-run future evolution of these attitudes, little disagreement is likely to exist as to the persistence of these differences and to the limits which they set to the easy transfer of methods and institutions in the field of industrial relations from one country to another.

Even in the short run, union self-restraint cannot be expected to prove bearable for the unions except where a number of conditions are fulfilled: profits must not be very high, wage differentials should be acceptable to the workers as fair rewards for skill, risk, and the like, and temporary adjustments on the labor markets of different industries and areas should not require more than temporary rearrangements of wage differentials, e.g., in the form of mobility premiums.[60]

The longer the wage stop lasts, the greater of course the difficulties for the union. Where the union plays a large part in contract administration, this may help in making union membership meaningful and provide local union activity of a large enough volume and intensity to prevent paralysis of union life. Yet, the danger is bound to grow of transforming the unions into a huge bureaucratic machinery directed from the top, with little or no life at the grass roots. Trade union theoreticians have been alert

[60]See Gösta Rehn and Rudolf Meidner in *Wages Policy under Full Employment,* Ralph Turvey, ed. (London, 1952). Mr. Inman emphasizes the role of price controls in the Norwegian system.

to this threat.[61] On the other hand, there seems to be some evidence that the danger is not as great in the short run as one might easily assume. Thus, we are informed that

> the local unions have not withered away under industry-wide bargaining and negotiations between national federations. Piece rate negotiations, handling grievances, and other activities keep local union officers busy. The locals also appear to be well informed about the policies and objectives of the central organizations.[62]

Some inference may perhaps also be drawn from the fact that in Norway as in all Scandinavian countries, communist influence within the trade unions has declined under this policy.[63]

The decisive issue, however, is that of the long run. Unions and wage policy alone cannot be relied upon to prevent inflationary developments. Even in Norway, as Mr. Inman reports, legal controls had to come to the rescue.[64] Yet, as the experience of the period from 1953 to 1955 tends to show, the problem is not entirely unmanageable.

In theory, answers have been suggested along two main lines. Melvin Reder relies upon political changes to bring about alternating periods of full employment and less than full employment.[65] When inflation has proceeded at a rate exceeding the limit of tolerance of the independent voter, he turns from the party friendly to organized labor and supports the party associated with business. The latter is thus put into power and is supposed to reduce employment below the inflationary level. This ingenious theory is based upon a number of assumptions of varying degrees

[61]Cf. Rudolf Meidner and Gösta Rehn, *op. cit.* See also the remark of Anatol Renning: "Members begin to look upon the trade union movement as an automaton which delivers a certain living standard in return for a specified payment." (Lonepolitiken under debate, quoted in Galenson, *Comparative Labor Movements, op. cit.,* p. 164.)

[62]Myers, *op. cit.,* p. 18.

[63]But, perhaps, in spite of this policy.

[64]"The trade unions—especially, in the building trades—objected to the attempts of the Employers' Association to prevent unorganized employers granting terms more favorable to the workers than those in the recognized agreements. The Federation tried to persuade unions not to conclude such agreements, but with only limited success: in September 1947 a wages stop law was introduced...."

[65]M. W. Reder, "The General Level of Money Wages," *Proceedings of the Third Annual Meeting, Industrial Relations Research Association* (Chicago, 1951).

of plausibility: that inflationary pressures originate essentially in the labor market; that organized labor is more responsible for inflationary wage pressures than unorganized workers; that inflation is the only major issue in politics; and, finally, that the party associated with business is hostile to inflation. Some of these assumptions have been examined above. The experience of a number of countries—say Britain or Australia—under Conservative governments does not seem to justify placing great reliance in the last mentioned of these assumptions. Business governments are not always hostile to inflation or capable of stopping it. Nevertheless, to the extent to which political change prevents the expectation of price increases from being firmly established, mere uncertainty about the future course of prices could interfere with the process of discounting coming price movements and thus slow down the inflationary trends.

An alternative is that of maintaining the employment level below the critical zone separating price stability from price increases.[66] The objective would be to find the highest employment level at which prices would remain roughly stable, discounting international influences.[67] This would give the unions again freedom to pursue wage improvements without which their continued existence would be in jeopardy. In effect, this means that the level of effective demand would be maintained at as high a level as is compatible with price stability.

What this level is, will depend, among other factors, on the mobility of labor, the aggressiveness of unions and management,

[66]It is important to realize that the two procedures do not amount to the same thing, although over a period the aggregate volume of unemployment may be the same under both policies. The first system would let a rising price trend be followed by a period of stable prices; a drop in prices would, in most cases, require a degree and permanency of unemployment which can hardly be engineered without severe social conflicts. The first system may be described as "hiccoughing inflation," producing over the long run a more moderate price increase. The second line of thought aims at a stable price level.

[67]This is, in effect, the main idea of Gösta Rehn's proposals; in *Wages Policy under Full Employment*. The specific measures proposed to deal with local unemployment pools would have, however, multiplier effects which must be taken into account in setting the general floor under employment. The more ambitious the local measures are and the higher the multiplier the lower must be the employment level at which the general measures aim. Cf. also: L.O.—The Swedish Confederation of Trade Unions, *Trade Unions and Full Employment* (Stockholm, 1953).

the growth of productivity, political considerations.[68] For this reason it seems unlikely that a universally valid "lower limit of unemployment" can be found at which price increases become inevitable. For Sweden and the United States, estimates are nevertheless remarkably close, at 3 or 4 percent.[69] American experience during 1953–1955 seems to confirm this estimate. It seems probable that in most cases the loss of national income involved in a full employment level compatible with price stability, as compared with a higher employment output, would not be serious.[70]

Experience between 1953 and 1955 would thus throw some light upon the long-run problem. Movements of the general money wage level would seem to be dependent upon a number of factors. The volume of employment remains cardinal, but two other elements play a very significant part. One is changes of historic wage relationships combined with differential rates of the growth of productivity; the other is the average rate of growth of productivity. The latter requires little explanation.

Attempts to maintain traditional wage relationships, while the relative marginal productivity of labor has changed substantially in different industries, occupations, and areas, seem to play a key part in wage pressures, second only to general wage movements resulting from full employment. According to the observer's inclination, this problem may be labeled an attempt of people in privileged industries to retain for themselves the advantages of rising

[68]This amounts to the statement that changes in wage levels are functions not merely of employment, but also of a number of other factors. Wages are administered prices into whose setting enter elements of strategy that are not simply and uniquely related to the given situation on the labor market. See Lloyd G. Reynolds, "Wage Bargaining, Price Changes and Employment," *IRRA Proceedings, First Annual Meeting, 1948,* pp. 35–50.

[69]For the United States Sumner Slichter estimated that with unemployment at about 3 or 4 percent "hourly earnings plus other labor costs are likely to rise faster than output per manhour, unless the increase in output per manhour can be materially speeded up or unless employers do a better job of bargaining than they have done up to now." ("The Outlook in Labor Relations," quoted by Jules Backman, Reply, in *Industrial and Labor Relations Review,* Vol. 8, No. 4, (July 1955), pp. 587–588.) Swedish experience seems to indicate that unemployment of less than 3 percent calls forth a "wage drift" of significant proportions. See *Trade Unions and Full Employment,* p. 49.

[70]Cf. the considerations of Professor Svennilsson referred to in Bertil Ohlin, *The Problem of Employment Stabilization* (London, 1950), pp. 18–20.

productivity or the failure of some parts of the economy to progress in step with the more rapidly advancing sectors.

Efforts to bring the lagging sections of the economy up to the speed with which the most progressive parts improve their productivity—a new concept of "balanced growth"—will affect the average rate at which productivity increases in the economy. This becomes, therefore, one of the fundamental factors in attempts at solving the long-run problem of price stability under full employment. Yet, it is unlikely that uniform rates of advance of productivity can ever be obtained throughout a dynamic economy. The problem of customary as against warranted wage relationships does remain. In a sense this illuminates the fundamentals of the issue: tradition versus progress. And since these differ in strength from country to country, no one long-run solution is likely to be equally applicable and effective everywhere.

Note on the Contributors

ALLAN FLANDERS. M.A., Senior Lecturer in Industrial Relations, University of Oxford. Previously served as Research Assistant to the Trades Union Congress from 1943 to 1946 and as head of the German Political Branch in the British Control Commission in Germany from 1946 to 1948. Has studied labor relations in the United States, Germany, Yugoslavia, and West Africa. Author of *Trade Unions* (1952) and the section on Great Britain in *Comparative Labor Movements* (1952). Editor and part-author of *The System of Industrial Relations in Great Britain* (1954). A member of the Labor party, he is Chairman of the Socialist Union and of the Editorial Board of the monthly, *Socialist Commentary*. Joint author of *Twentieth Century Socialism* (1956).

JOHN INMAN. B.A., Cambridge University. Economist in Colonial Office since 1950. Member of the staff of the British Embassy in Oslo, dealing with labor questions, 1945–1949. Member of the Scandinavian Section, Political Intelligence Department, British Foreign Office, 1942–1945. Author of various pamphlets and articles in the field of economics.

P. S. PELS. Former student of Professor Tinbergen. Has done research on the chemical industries in the Netherlands. In 1946 he was appointed Secretary of the Foundation of Labor. Since 1950 he has been serving as Secretary of the Social Economic Council. His main interest is in the field of wage policy on which he published a book in 1950. He has also contributed to several scientific journals.

ADOLF STURMTHAL. Visiting Professor, New York State School of Industrial and Labor Relations, Cornell University, 1952–1954. Now Philip Murray Professor at Roosevelt University, Chicago, Ill. Author of *The Tragedy of European Labor, 1918–1939* (two editions, 1943, 1951; translations in five languages), *Unity and Diversity in European Labor* (1953). Regular contributor to many professional journals in the United States and abroad.

CLARK KERR. Chancellor of the University of California, Berkeley. Past President of the Industrial Relations Research Association. Public member and Vice-Chairman of the National Wage Stabilization Board, 1950–1951. Former Director of the Institute of Industrial Relations and Professor of Industrial Relations at the University of California. Co-author (with E. Wight Bakke) of *Unions, Management and the Public* (1948). Author of various studies of cooperatives and industrial relations, frequent contributor to professional journals.

LUISA RIVA SANSEVERINO. Professor of Labor Legislation since 1934 (University of Sassari, 1935–1936, University of Modena, 1937–1940, University of Pisa since 1941). Member of the Italian delegation to the ILO, 1945, 1946. Among her publications are: *Il Diritto di Privativa nel Contratto di Lavoro* (Patent Rights in Labor Relations, 1932); *Diritto del Lavoro,* (Labor Laws, eight editions, 1934–1955); *Contratto di Lavoro* (Contracts of Service, three editions, 1937–1956); *Il Rapporto Individuale di Lavoro nella Legislazione Camparata* (Individual Labor Relations in Foreign Legislations, 1946); *Il Movimento Sindacale Cristiano* (Christian Trade Unionism, 1951); *Diritto Sindacale* (Trade Union Law, two editions, 1952–1954).

CESARE VANNUTELLI. Professor of Economic Statistics at the University of Rome. Until 1954 he was Chief of the Department of Economics and of Labor Statistics at the Confederation of Italian Industry (Confederazione dell'Industria Italiana) and Director of the publication *Rassegna di Statistica del Lavoro.* Since 1956 he has been Vice-Director of the Labor Service at the Istituto per la Ricostruzione Industriale (IRI). Author of numerous articles in learned journals dealing with wages, the sliding scale, labor statistics, and social security.

NEIL CHAMBERLAIN. Professor of Economics, Graduate School of Business, Columbia University. Occasional arbitrator, but his principal activity (other than teaching) is research in the general area of economics and industrial relations. Among his publications are: *The Union Challenge to Management Control* (1948), *Collective Bargaining* (1951), *Social Responsibility and Strikes* (1953), and *A General Theory of Economic Process* (1955). Prior to his appointment at Columbia, he served as Assistant Director of the Yale University Labor and Management Center.

Index

INDEX

INDEX

INDEX

INDEX